P. F. M. FONTAINE

THE LIGHT
AND
THE DARK

A CULTURAL HISTORY OF DUALISM

VOLUME XI

J.C. GIEBEN, PUBLISHER
AMSTERDAM

THE LIGHT AND THE DARK

P.F.M. FONTAINE

THE LIGHT AND THE DARK
A CULTURAL HISTORY OF DUALISM

VOLUME XI

DUALISM IN ROMAN HISTORY II

DUALISM IN INTERIOR POLITICS
AND SOCIAL LIFE

J.C. GIEBEN, PUBLISHER
AMSTERDAM 1996

To my friend Dr. Willem Otterspeer,
historian, museum director,
author of important and successful books,
and his charming wife Dorrit van Dalen,
anthropologist, development expert

No part of this book may be translated or reproduced in any form, by print, photoprint, microfilm, or any other means, without written permission from the publisher.

© by P.F.M. Fontaine / ISBN 90 5063 247 5 / Printed in The Netherlands

"For all things are called
light and darkness"

Parmenides

CONTENTS

Preface		xvii
I	INTERNAL DISCORD	1
1.	A rift in the solid power base	1
2.	What are patricians, what are plebeians?	1
3.	The boundary	2
4.	The effect of the fall of the monarchy	3
5.	Advantages the plebs had	3
6.	The installation of the tribunes of the people	4
7.	The codification of the laws	6
8.	The road upwards	7
9.	The distinction abolished?	7
10.	The social balance disturbed	9
11.	The crisis of the Republic	11
	a. The preponderance of the senatorial class	11
	b. Revolution as an alternative	11
12.	Tiberius Gracchus	12
	a. Youth and education of the Gracchi	12
	b. Tiberius' entry into political life	12
	c. The Lex Sempronia agraria	13
	d. Roman society split	14
	e. Internal dualism	15
	f. The wealthy and the poor opposed	16
	g. The bill debated in the popular assembly	17
	h. The bill passed	18
	j. The implementation of the Lex agraria	19
	k. A senatorial coup	20
	l. The aftermath	21
13.	A doubtful truce	21
14.	Gaius Gracchus	23
	a. His leading idea	23
	b. Feverish legislative activity	24
	c. Gaius loses ground	25
	d. The Senate hits back	27
	e. The revenge	28
15.	No sulution	29

16.	Marius		30
	a. His ascent to the top		30
	b. Animosity between Marius and Sulla		31
	c. Marius' reform of the army		32
	d. Marius and his political helpers		33
	e. Marius and Metellus		33
	f. Marius' political incompetence		35
	g. Saturninus' party defeated		36
17.	The Social War		37
	a. The question of citizenship again		37
	b. A clash inevitable		37
	c. The war with the allies		38
18.	The Senate under fire		39
19.	The citizenship extended		40
Notes to Chapter I			42

II	CIVIL WAR		51
1.	The contest between Sulla and Marius		51
	a. Sulla appears on the political scene		51
	b. Sulpicius, Marius' 'organon'		52
	c. On the road to civil war		53
	d. Sulla marches on Rome		54
	e. Sulla in power		55
2.	The struggle of Octavius and Cinna		56
	a. Cinna aspiring to power		56
	b. Rome captured by Cinna		57
3.	Sulla undisputed master of Rome		58
	a. Sulla brooding on revenge		58
	b. Cinna's death		59
	c. Sulla's return to Italy		59
	d. Sulla marches on Rome		60
	e. Sulla dictator		61
	f. Sulla's revenge on Latins and Italians		62
	g. Reign of terror		63
	h. The results		66
	j. Sulla's legislation		66
	k. Sulla steps back		67
	l. Who was Sulla?		68
4.	The anti-Sullan reaction		69
5.	Pompey appears on the political scene		71
6.	The Sertorian War		72

	a.	Sertorius the rising man	72
	b.	Recruiting in Spain	73
	c.	Sertorius' Odyssey	73
	d.	The Sertorian War	74
	e.	The 'counter-Rome'	75
	f.	Sertorius defeated	75
7.	Pompey an ineffectual consul		76
8.	Pompey's great victories		78
9.	Pompeius Magnus		79
10.	Pompey frustrated		80
11.	The rising star of Julius Caesar		80
12.	The First Triumvirate		81
13.	The strategy of the Triumvirate		82
14.	Pompey sole consul		82
15.	Caesar marches on Rome		84
16.	Pompey evacuates Rome		86
17.	Caesar fails to catch Pompey		87
18.	Caesar in Rome		88
19.	The Second Civil War		89
	a.	The conquest of Spain	89
	b.	Caesar's quasi-legal authority	90
	c.	Pompey's government in Thessalonica	90
	d.	Caesar's predicament	91
	e.	Pompey defeated in Greece	92
	f.	The fugitive	93
	g.	Death on the Nile	94
	h.	Caesar's situation at the end of the year 48 B.C.	95
	j.	Victories in Asia Minor and North Africa	95
	k.	Triumphs and honours	96
	l.	The defeat of the Pompeians in Spain	97
20.	The road to the end		97
	a.	Still more honours	97
	b.	A royal magistrate	98
	c.	Sings of deification	99
	d.	Caesar and Roman dualism	100
	e.	Caesar's undoing	101
	f.	The Ides of March	103
21.	The aftermath		104
	a.	Antony's emergency measures	104
	b.	Octavian appears on the scene	104
	c.	The funeral speech	105
22.	Postumous deification		106

23.	Octavian and Antony	106
24.	Preparations for war	107
25.	The Third Civil War: the first Italian phase	108
	a. Antony's defeats	108
	b. Rewards and triumphs	109
	c. Octavian master of Rome	110
26.	The Second Triumvirate	111
27.	Terror in Rome	112
28.	The Third Civil War continued	113
	a. The Greek phase	113
	b. Antony under the spell of Cleopatra	113
	c. The Perusine War	114
29.	Antony and Parthia	115
	a. The rise of Parthian power	115
	b. The first clashes between Rome and Parthia	116
	c. The Roman world divided	116
30.	Pompey's son in action	117
31.	Lepidus disposed of	118
32.	The sinking star of Antony	119
	a. The Duumvirate	119
	b. Antony campaigning against de Parthians	119
	c. The dream of Empire	120
	d. Preparations for the showdown	121
	e. Antony's end	121
Notes to Chapter II		121
III	THE EMPIRE OF THE EMPERORS AND ITS END	140
1.	A new era	140
	a. Honours for Octavian	140
	b. Augustus	141
	c. The end of the Republic	141
	d. From Principate to Dominate	142
2.	The Roman dualisms overcome?	144
	a. The external dualism	145
	b. The internal dualism	146
	c. Another abortive Empire of the East	148
3.	The co-regency	148
	a. During the Principate	148
	b. During the Dominate	149
4.	A new capital	151
5.	Two Empires	151

6.		Rome's problems in the East	152
	a.	A dualistic struggle	152
	b.	The problem of Armenia	153
	c.	Warfare because of Armenia	154
	d.	The Romans humiliated	155
	e.	The agreement of 66	156
	f.	The agreement broken	157
	g.	Trajan annexes Armenia	158
	h.	Trajan's invasion of Parthia	159
	j.	The tables are turned	160
	k.	A new Great King	161
	l.	'King of Kings or Iran and non-Iran'	162
	m.	An unexpected intervention	163
	n.	A look at the general situation	164
	o.	Diocletian's offensive	165
	p.	The struggle of Constantius II and Shapur II	166
	q.	The offensive of Julian the Apostate	168
	r.	The regulation of the Armenian problem	171
7.		Rome's problems in the West	171
	a.	Pressure on the frontier	172
	b.	Osmosis	172
	c.	The gathering storm	173
	d.	The Alleman storm	174
	e.	Dacia abandoned	174
	f.	Continuous pressure	175
	g.	The 'Great Migration of Peoples'	175
	h.	The end	177
Notes to Chapter III			178
IV	UNDERPRIVILEGED GROUPS		185
	PART I SUBJECTED NATIONS		185
1.	The protectorate of the world		185
2.	Roman opinion of 'the others'		186
3.	The absorption of 'barbarians'		187
4.	'Materia victoriae'		187
5.	Discontent always smouldering		189
6.	Violent outbreaks of discontent		189
7.	The great Batavian insurrection		191
	a.	The Batavians	191
	b.	The outbreak of the revolt	192
	c.	The first hostilities	194

	d.	Civilis' heyday	194
	e.	The turning of the tide	195
	f.	The end of the revolt	196
8.	Conclusion		196

PART II   THE SLAVES 197

1.	Slavery not a part of the original human condition	197
2.	What is a slave?	198
3.	The better-off and the worse-off slaves	198
4.	A source of tension in Roman society	200
5.	The sources of slavery	201
6.	Slavery as a dualistic institution	202
7.	Early slave-risings	203
8.	The First Sicilian Slave-War	205
	a. The beginning of the revolt	205
	b. King Eunus	206
	c. The revolt beaten down	207
9.	The Second Sicilian Slave-War	208
	a. The cause of the revolt	208
	b. The oubreak of the revolt	208
	c. King Salvius	209
	d. The Roman reaction	210
10.	The rising of Spartacus	210
	a. Who was Spartacus?	210
	b. The origin of the revolt	211
	c. The first successes	212
	d. Between north and south	212
	e. The Roman counter-offensive	213
	f. The end	214
11.	The easing of the dualistic tension	215

PART III   THE WOMEN 216

1.	Which women?	216
2.	Female slaves	216
3.	Companions worthy of respect	217
4.	Love and divorce	218
5.	The 'Roman model'	218
6.	A paradox?	219
Notes to Chapter IV		220

V	THE JEWS IN THE HELLENISTIC WORLD	228
	PART I THE JEWS IN THE HELLENISTIC WORLD	228
1.	The numerical range	228
2.	The dispersion of the Jews	229
3.	Concentrations of Jews	230

PART II   THE SITUATION OF THE JEWS IN THE EASTERN
DIASPORA BEFORE THE ROMANS CAME 231

1. On thelevel of the state 231
2. The story of Esther 232
3. The problems posed by this book 233
4. Relations on the polis-level 236
5. Jewish citizenship 237

PART III   THE OFFICIAL ROMAN POLICY 238

1. The policy of the Roman government with regard to the Diaspora Jews 238
   a. How Rome dealt with foreign religions 238
   b. The Jews as a special problem 239
   c. The official regulations 240
   d. Collusion between Romans and Jews 241
   e. Toleration and irritation 242
   f. The Jews of Rome in difficulties 242
   g. Caligula and the Jews 244
2. The Jewish homeland 244
   a. The first contacts between Rome and Judaea 244
   b. Hasmonaean conquests 245
   c. The Hasmonaean High Priest a Roman vassal 246
   d. Rome and the Herodeans 247
   e. Judaea made into a province 248
3. Messianic expectations 249
   a. Herod's fear of a Messiah 249
   b. Mutual distrust in Palestine 249
   c. A dualistic distinction 250
4. Rebellious movements in the Jewish land 251
   a. Rebellions throughout Galilee, Peraea and Judaea 251
   b. Uproar in Jerusalem 251
   c. No mortal masters 252
   d. Bad incidents 253
   e. Felix after the Zealots 253

		f.	The Sicarii in action	254
		g.	Growing anarchy	254
		h.	The outbreak of the revolt	255
	5.	The First Jewish War, A.D. 66-70	256
		a.	Fighting in Jerusalem	256
		b.	Zealot and Roman ferocity	257
		c.	A failed Roman attack on Jerusalem	258
		d.	Palestine liberated	258
		e.	Vespasian in command	259
		f.	The reduction of Galilee	259
		g.	The reduction of Agrippa's townships	261
		h.	John of Gischala	262
		j.	Civil war in Jerusalem	262
		k.	Vespasian leaves the scene	264
		l.	Jerusalem besieged	265
		m.	The end of everything	266
		n.	The last stand	268
	6.	Why was the Temple destroyed?	268
	7.	Between the two wars	271
		a.	The heavy hand of Rome	271
		b.	New Jewish rebellions	272
	8.	The Second Jewish War, A.D. 132-135	273
		a.	The causes of the rebellion	273
		b.	The revolt of Bar Kochba	274
		c.	The aftermath	275
	9.	The later phases	276
		a.	Judaism turned in upon itself?	276
		b.	The situation of the Jews from Cyrenaica to Asia Minor	278
		c.	Should we speak of dualism?	279
		d.	Conclusion	281

PART IV GREEK AND ROMAN AUTHORS ON JEWS AND JUDAISM   282

1.	Greek authors	282
	a. Theophrastus	282
	b. Hecataeus	282
	c. The Jews as 'philosophers'	283
	d. A harsh word	284
	e. The tone changes	284
	f. Posidonius	285
	g. Apollonius Molon	286
	h. Alexander Polyhistor	286
	j. Diodorus Siculus	286

		k.	Nicolaus of Damascus	287
		l.	Pompeius Trogus	287
		m.	Strabo	288
		n.	Lysimachus	288
		o.	Apion	289
		p.	'On the sublime'	290
		q.	Plutarch	291
		r.	Conclusion	291
	2.	Roman authors		292
		a.	Cicero	292
		b.	Varro	292
		c.	Other authors	293
		d.	Tacitus	293
		e.	Juvenal	294

	PART V PUBLIC OPINION	295
1.	Sympathy for Judaism	295
2.	Friction between Jews and Gentiles	296
3.	The causes of anti-Jewish attitudes	297
4.	Jewish apartheid	298
Notes to Chapter V		301

VI	ROMANS AND GREEKS, GREEKS AND ROMANS	318
1.	The non-Greek origin of Rome	318
2.	The first contacts	319
3.	The Greeks brought under Roman control	320
4.	The Romans as barbarians	321
5.	The Romans unbeloved	323
6.	Some positive views	323
7.	The Romans and the Greek language	324
8.	Characteristics of the Greeks according to the Romans	326
9.	A dualistic relationship	328
Notes to Chapter VI		331

PREFACE

I feel it would not be a bad idea to preface this volume - the eleventh in a series - with a summary of what is to be found in the ten foregoing volumes. After all, I cannot expect that many readers will be prepared to read through all of them. Of course, I hope that some will do so, and I am bold enough to suppose one could profit by it. For what I wrote so far, with the addition of this volume and the next one or two, may be read as a history of Antiquity. So many aspects are touched upon in it that I feel that this claim is justified. It is true, of course, that by no means all events and phenomena are dealt with, but no other work of this nature can hope to be completely comprehensive. A good reason to read my volumes might be that my work is fundamentally different from all other histories of Antiquity. It can give the reader an unprecedented view of the ancient world, India and China included, since it is looking at history, so to speak, from the reverse side; it considers what does not fit, what did not come together, what remained apart and separate, and why. These aspects are usually neglected by historians because they, like all other people, love wholeness and harmony.

I join to this Preface a Manual. On the premise that not everyone will feel inclined to read the work in toto, at least I can guide scholars and other interested readers to their fields of study and interest. In the Manual these fields are tabulated, with reference to the corresponding volumes, chapters, and sections.

The concept of 'dualism' is surrounded by quite a number of misunderstandings. The most popular of these is that dualism has its origin in ancient Iran, particularly in the Zoroastrian religion. To quote only one author, "Iran

XVIII

is the classical country of dualism", so runs the very first sentence of Duchesne-Guillemin's little book on Iranian religion [1]. This surely is the honest conviction of many people, scholars and others; in their opinion the religion of Iran is the historical cradle of all dualisms. They feel that a phenomenon like dualism must have an origin in time and in a certain area. But I do not believe at all that dualism has such a well-defined historical and local origin. The phenomenon as such is far too wide-spread to connect its origin with some point on the time-chart or to look for it in a specific area of the world.

Furthermore, it is a widely held notion, especially among scholars, that dualism is a philosophical concept not occurring outside the field of philosophy, with the exception, perhaps, of the history of religions. Describing the Zoroastrian religion in a book published in 1700, and mentioning the Persian Magi, Thomas Hyde, a professor of Hebrew in Oxford University, spoke of them as 'dualists'; the term, therefore, began its career in the context of Iranian religion [2]. But in 1734, in his 'Psychologia rationalis', Christian Wolff not only spoke of 'dualists' but also of 'dualism'. And Wolff broadened the notion beyond the meaning given to it by Hyde. He transferred it to the field of philosophy by stating that the spiritual and the corporeal, the immaterial and the material, are substantially different [3]. From then on the study of dualism followed two lines, one in the history of religions, the other in philosophy, sometimes separately, and sometimes in one context.

There is, however, not the slightest reason for confining the study of dualism to the field of philosophy and/or that of the history of religions. If dualism means 'unsolvable oppositions', it will, indeed, occur in these fields. But I cannot see why similar oppositions should not occur also in other sectors of human life, for instance, in politics or in political ideology. If people ask me for an example of what I mean by 'dualism', I always mention Hitler's idea that Jews were vermin that had to be destroyed; this was the theory that he turned into a horrifying practice.

Not rarely I hear people dub every opposition, of whichever kind, as 'dualistic'. As soon as two things are opposed, there obviously is dualism. But if the term is used in this very broad sense, it becomes so vague that it loses all significance; it would then be utterly impossible to write a work on it. For there are endlessly more oppositions that are connected by intermediate terms than irreducible ones. Oppositions of the first kind are extremely frequent; everyone of us uses them hundreds of times a day : warm and cold, old and young, strong and weak, and so on. Most of them have shifting meanings. A young man may find some person old whereas this person does not consider himself old at all.

There is, however, yet a far more serious misunderstanding. I can best present it in the words of Mr. R.W. Jordan who reviewed volumes II and III of this work in the 'Classical Review' (1989, X, pp. 268-269). Mr. Jordan, while admitting that there are dualistic tendencies in Greek thought, reproached me that I do not try to place dualistic thought in the context of non-dualistic or anti-dualistic thinking. My main failure seems to be that I do not present dualism as a coherent system (or anti-system). In my reviewer's own words, I do not make out my case that 'dualism' is a key-concept for historians of culture. But I never attempted to make out such a case.

Varying a famous dictum by Karl Marx, I must state that, in my opinion, the history of mankind is not the history of dualism. Dualism is neither a concept nor an ideology. The prevaling mania of our time is to turn everything into an ideology. We are fond of -isms. By coining the term 'dualism', we are putting it on a par with liberalism, Marxism, nominalism, historicism, and other ideologies and intellectual systems ending in -ism. But it cannot be stressed often enough that dualism is nothing of this kind. It is not an intellectual system, not a philosophy, not a concept, not a religion. It is something quite different. Therefore, it cannot be set against non-dualistic systems, for then we would be comparing things of a different order.

What I am doing is looking at the back of a tapestry. People gaze admiringly at the beautiful picture presented to them on the front. They do not bother to look at the other side. For there they would see nothing but a confused mass of threads. Now human history, although not a tapestry but a mobile process (like a movie), has its own loose threads. Seen from the back, history displays disconnectedness. Historiography is "especially well suited to the notions of continuity, wholeness, closure, and individuality that every 'civilized' society wishes to see itself as incarnating against a merely 'natural' way of life", writes Hayden White [4]. But studying the political, social, mental, and intellectual implications of the rougher, more fragmented, more disunified side of world history may yield unexpected results.

In my work I am not presenting an harmonious picture of continuity and wholeness, quite the contrary! I consciously take the risk that my work will, to some extent, hit on the blind spot of many scholars. True enough, "it is part of our human condition to long for hard lines and clear concepts. When we have them, we have to either face the fact that some realities elude them (i.e. the concepts) or else blind ourselves to the inadequacy of the concept" [5].

There is a last argument that should be refuted. It is a constantly recurring theme of western thought that dualism is the exact opposite of monism. The term 'monism' was created by the Christian Wolff whom I mentioned already; he was highly instrumental in inventing new terms. He divided philosophers into 'scepticists' and 'dogmatists', and then the dogmatists into 'monists' and 'dualists'. In this way he popularized the notion (which has itself become a dogmatism) that monism and dualism are opposed ideologies. But in fact monism and dualism are chips of the same block, generated by the idea that all that exists can be grouped under one unified concept, either monism or dualism.

The only philosopher who understood that they are not opposed but, on the contrary, belong together, is Ludwig Stein. He expressed this in the following terms. "Monism and dualism are two types of thought that both have their foundation in man. But, in the antithesis 'monism-dualism', the issue is not that they are contradictorily opposed but rather that they are a contrasted pair of concepts connected with each other in the manner of correlation" [6]. Monism can very easily give rise to dualism, since, because of its exclusiveness tending to one-sidedness, it always leaves a residuum that finds no place in the prime concept and cannot be explained by it. This residuum sometimes reasserts itself by opposing itself to the monistic concept, even to such a degree that a dualistic opposition originates; in such a case the opposition monism-dualism becomes dualistic itself. Many dualistic

XXI

systems have a monistic starting-point; dualism then sets in one stage lower. This is particularly the case in Gnostic systems, for instance in Simonianism with its monistic prime concept of the Boundless Power (Vol. VII, Ch. III.1f), and in Valentinianism where it is the Depth that is the primal cause of Being (Vol. VIII, Ch. VIII.5a).

I hope the field has been sufficiently cleared now to present a description of what dualism really is. In all the Prefaces of 'The Light and the Dark' I have given the same definition. There is dualism when we are confronted with two utterly opposed conceptions, systems, principles, groups or kinds of people, or even worlds, without any intermediate terms between them. They cannot be reduced to each other; in some cases the one is not even dependent on the other. The opposites are considered to be of a different quality - so much so that one of them is always seen as distinctly inferior and hence must be neglected or destroyed.

The final statement by the Congress of Messina on Gnosticism in 1966 spoke of "two principles that are the foundation of everything that exists in the world" [7]. The main influence on the composition of this declaration was that of Ugo Bianchi. Elsewhere this scholar expressed himself as follows. "Dualistic are religions and views of life according to which two principles - both of them having been there, it seems, from all eternity - are the foundation, really or apparently so, of everything that exists or presents itself in the world" [8]. The reader will understand that I find the application of the term 'dualism' to principles, religions, and views of life only, too restrictive. My own scope is considerably larger. However, in another essay Bianchi enlarged his definition so much that it approaches mine. Dualistic is "every system in which the creation of the world and its legitimate control are the work of two forces which are thought to be in contradiction to each other, sometimes, however, in a complementary way" [9].

There is some sort of a typology of dualism possible, although one should use its terms only sparingly; there are so many variations mentioned that the wood might easily be lost in the trees. But one important variation is entirely relevant, namely that of absolute and relative dualism. In absolute (or radical) dualism the two principles are coeval; they are from eternity and their origin defies every explanation. This is the case, for instance, in Orphism where there is an unbridgeable opposition in man who belongs to two worlds (Vol. I, Ch. IV.10), in the philosophy of Empedocles with its two eternal principles of Love and Hate (Vol. I, Ch. II.9), in Iranian Zervanism with its opposed coeval gods Ormuzd and Ahriman (Vol. V, Ch. I.5), and in Manichaeism with its primeval and coeval principles of Light and Darkness (Vol. IX, Ch. IV.10).

Cases of radical dualism are, however, rare. This brand of dualism requires thinking in terms of two utterly distinct and separated worlds of which only people with a very special turn of mind are capable. And then, it will be justified to ask whether this mode of thought is a real possibility, for, when all is said and done, the two worlds somewhere connect, namely in the brain of the dualist.

The most common type of dualism is the 'relative' or 'moderate' form which occurs when the second principle, the lower, inferior one is deduced from the first and is dependent on it. This term can be applied to the Pythagorean ideology, since this starts from a concept of unity (Vol. I, Ch. I.11,12), to the philosophy of Heraclitus in whose doctrine the Logos-Fire is primary to anything else (Vol. I, Ch. II.6), and to that of Parmenides for whom Being precedes Seeming (Vol. I, Ch. II.8).

Dualistic ways of thought can also be referred to in terms of their attitude regarding the difference in quality of the two principles. Dualisms built on the opposition between good and evil may be dubbed 'ethical' which is the case in most Gnostic systems; if in the end the good principle triumphs over the bad one, we may call this 'eschatological' dualism. The dualism of the Essenes, which is essentially ethical, is also eschatological (Vol. VII, Ch. V.9). But if the two systems continue to exist alongside each other, then 'dialectical' dualism would be the better term. To quote an example, in Parmenidian philosophy Being and Seeming go on existing together, as 'frères ennemis'.

Finally, one can draw a distinction between procosmical and anticosmical tendencies. In a procosmical system evil enters the cosmos from outside; in an anticosmical one it is an integral part of the cosmos itself.

Gnostic systems are invariably anticosmical; during the gestation of the cosmos something goes wrong, with the result that the world, mankind included, must be described in negative terms. Perhaps it may sound disquieting to classical scholars, but I do not believe that Greek systems were procosmic. Mostly they tend to be anticosmical; this is at least decidedly the case in Orphism [10].

Dualism may occur everywhere and at any time, but dualistic trends always appear in dispersed order. Large segments of society may be 'holistic' but here and there some cracks, some deep fissures may be detected. However, neither do these hang together nor do they offer a coherent picture of a dualistic counter-society. I believe that the expression 'dualistic society' would be a contradictio in adiecto, since its application would implie that there were two societies. All the same, dualistic ideologies have sometimes attempted to combine opposite elements into some sort of system. This remains a very rare occurence. I found only a few dualistic systems : the Pythagorean fraternity (Vol. I, Ch. I.15), the Orphic religion (Vol. I, Ch. IV.10), the doctrines of Er pedocles, Heraclitus, and in particular, Parmenides (Vol. I, Ch. II.6,8 and 9), those elements in Plato's teaching that show a strong tendency towards dualism (Vol. III, Ch. III.20-22), the Gnostic systems (Vols. VII, VIII and IX), Zoroastrianism (Vol. IV, Ch. IV.8,9) and still more Iranian Zervanism (Vol. V, Ch. I.4), Indian Yoga (Vol. V, Ch. II.22) and finally Chinese Daoism (Vol. V, Ch. III.25). This seems a lot but it is in fact a rather meagre harvest for all the long periods and many civilizations I have studied. Furthermore, the impact of these systems was not great. Pythagoreans and Orphics remained small, élitist groups, like Yogis and Daoists. Most dualistic philosophies did not become popular or widespread; of these Platonism had the widest dispersion. The greatest success was for Zervanism and Manichaeism.

Where do we find the origin of dualism? I have already expressed my disagreement with the popular notion that it is Iranian dualism. There was already dualism before anyone had ever heard of Zoroaster; there always was and there still is dualism that is in no way connected with the Iranian prophet. Nor should we think of Manichaeism, although this is for many people the dualism par excellence. Mani the dualist was preceded by many older dualists. No, the real fountain-head of dualism is human nature; it is something in man himself. In other words, it is an anthropological phenomenon. If this is correct, it will not surprise us that it keeps occurring everywhere and always.

This does not imply, however, that everyone is a dualist, secretly or openly, consciously or unconsciously. Quite the contrary! Most people, almost all people, love harmony, connectedness, some sort of 'holism'; it is only a minority that thrives on oppositions, a minority that can be vociferous, influential and powerful. I am thinking here of Hitler as an outspoken dualist [11]. In my opinion dualism, like beauty, exists in the beholder's eye; dualists prefer to view reality in terms of opposites. This does not mean that it is only conceptual or mental; it has a secure footing in theory and practice. Hitler's destruction of the Jews was only too real.

We should not think of dualistically minded people as psychiatric cases. They are, more often than not, quite normal. There may be personal circumstances that turn people into dualists. But perhaps they also feed on less personal and more general experiences. I am not thinking here of abstract philosophical reasonings or the impact of certain religious doctrines. It could rather be that the acceptance of peculiar creed, a Gnostic one, for instance, is the result, first of circumstances in the personal sphere, and secondly, of a confrontation with 'existential' issues, I mean such as concern humanity in general. The question is whether there is something in the construction of the world, something really present, that might give rise to dualism, something that does not wholly fit, I am thinking here of loose ends, gaps in fundamental explanations, unsolved contradictions, anomalies.

There are, for instance, paradoxes. A paradox, according to R.M. Sainsbury, is an "apparently unacceptable conclusion derived by apparently acceptable reasoning from apparently acceptable premises" [12]. A paradox, therefore, is a logical derailment. Many paradoxes, like that of Achilles and the tortoise, are not really paradoxical, but some are unsolvably so, like the paradoxes of Grelling and Russell. Still more disquieting is Gödel's theorem, the so-called 'incompleteness theorem', which implies that no logico-mathematical system carries in itself the means to solve its anomalies; for this one should refer to the one-higher system which, however, copes with the same problem. And so on. Which means that mankind will always remain saddled with contradictions, inconsistencies, and anomalies.

A combination of more general and more personal causes of a dualistic mentality can be found in the male-female opposition. If man's philosophy of life begins with man himself - "the proper study of mankind is man", wrote the English poet Pope -, then his basic starting-point would inevitably be the fact that human beings are anatomically different and that this distinction leads to very different functions in life. Hence an observer can draw the conclusion that the whole order of the world must, in consequence, be twofold, and furthermore, that there are higher and lower orders of existence which are hard to reconcile with each other. A case in point would be, again, Adolf Hitler, a dualistic thinker and politician if there ever was one. I sincerely believe that the difficult relationship between his parents encouraged and stimulated his innate tendency towards dualism. If this is correct, then Hitlerite dualism had its origin in the man-woman structure.

In the physical sphere we see that the human body is not symmetrical; its two halves are not identical. The right hand has a definite prevalence over the left which is not a harmless difference. In the less personal, historical sphere we find that world-history is punctuated with wars, even in our century which has hardly seen a year without war. There seems to be a curious tendency at work in humanity to turn order into chaos, as though chaos were the easier and more self-evident thing by far. With this anomaly we have to live. Louis Menand calls this 'the incommensurability of the world' which, according to him, is the basis of dualism [13]. But the greatest and most painful anomaly is the fact of death. This eats into the very core of our existence. Death is a non-concept; the idea of life is incompatible with that of death. The opposition of life and death which we all experience is a dualistic one.

Ours is a world full of fissures, contradictions, and oppositions. We are fundamentally incapable of coping with this world, with our existence, with ourselves, unable as we are to manage the affairs of this world as they should be managed by homo sapiens. We have neither the brains not the practical ability for it. However, by far the greater part of humanity succeeds in getting along reasonably well in an imperfect world. But some people, everywhere, in all times, in every culture, are viscerally unable to follow this example. I am not suggesting that they have, for instance, carefully studied Gödel's theorem, or that they have deeply pondered on war and peace, life and death. But they are vaguely but at the same time strongly and painfully uneasy about the state of the world and the human condition [14].

To return now to the more personal sphere. When trying to comprehend the world, we interpret it and we summarize it. Summarizing is necessary since the world presents itself to us as a confused welter of phenomena and events. We have two ways of creating order in this bewildering chaos : we group and we separate. We bring phenomena, persons, and events together under headings and general concepts, like world, universe, history, mankind, nation, town - the list is endless. We use such concepts many times every day. The other way of ordering is opposing phenomena, events, persons, which we do just as frequently : day and night, summer and winter, love and hate, young and old, man and woman. Mostly such oppositions are only relative. A man coming out of the polar cold of a winter night and entering an unheated room may find it comfortable. In our own period the frontiers between old and young are shifting.

It may happen, however, that opposites such as these grow more virulent; then they become harsh, bitter, and irreconcilable. The man-woman relation may serve as an example. In the Jewish, Christian, and humanistic traditions the sexes are seen as equal but different. This difference can be stressed to such a degree that women are considered distinctly inferior and not fit to play a part in public life. This was the case in the Athens of the classical period (Vol. II, Ch. IV.4) and in ancient India (Vol. V, Ch. II.14, 16, and 20).

The gap between opposites may become so wide that it is finally unbridgeable. Then we are in the presence of dualism. The most rampant dualistic oppositions are those between life and death, good and evil, the One and the Many, male and female, and being and seeming. We are all of us confronted with such oppositions, but there are people who feel attracted by them, who thrive on them. We can say that they have an innate tendency to dualism. In Antiquity we are poorly served with detailed biographies; only very rarely do we get a glimpse of personal developments. I have described the apostle John as somebody with a penchant to dualism (Vol. VII. Ch. IV.5b). He and his brother James were called 'the sons of the thunder' by Jesus [15]. When the inhabitants of a Samaritan village refused hospitality to Jesus and his company, these two fiery young men wanted Jesus to bid fire come down from heaven and destroy them [16]. The apostle John was probably influenced by his ambitious mother Salome, the driving force behind him [17]. The Dutch professor Chorus characterizes John as a man of passion, living in a strong tension between reality and ideality [18].

We may also cite Plato as a person with a distinct proclivity towards dualism. Decisive stages in his development were that he, wanting to become a tragic poet, realized that all had been said already, and still more, his disillusionment with Athenian democracy which had condemned his venerated master Socrates to death (vol. II, Ch. III.1a and c, 22). In the case of Mani, we can detect the starting-point of his dualism in the breaking up of his parents' household. When living in Ctesiphon, his father Patek was converted to Mughtasilism. This sect did not approve of relations with women, not even in marriage; in consequence, Patek left his wife and went south in order to join a Mughtasila community, taking young Mani with him. The relationship of his parents is of decisive importance for a child. If this is harmonious, it teaches him that all is well with the world. But if there is discord, or even a divorce, the result may easily be catastrophic; it can totally disrupt the child's view of life. This may apply to Mani who saw his father reject his mother (Vol. IX, Ch. IV.9b). Born radicalists, stimulated by experiences in the personal sphere, can become aware of the adverse elements in the fabric of the world; when they come into contact with a dualistic group, such as a Gnostic sect, its doctrine may then give body and substance to their perhaps still vague perceptions.

XXVIII

The notion that there are people with an innate tendency for intensifying normal oppositions into unbridgeable ones, not only in philosophical thought or in religious conceptions but also in daily life and in the most common relationships, is also valid for nations and civilizations. Let us focus our attention on ancient Iran, seen by many as the cradle of all dualism, in the shape of the Zoroastrian religion. Religious dualism, however, occurred in Iran long before the great prophet. Several older and more recent authorities are of the opinion that this dualism originated in the physical nature of the country. Arriving from the steppes of Central Asia, the invading tribes found a land marked by strong oppositions. In Iran there are forbidding mountain ranges but also fertile plains, and such habitable stretches alternate with burning waterless deserts. Whereas the summers are usually stifingly hot, the winters bring severe cold. We may, therefore, agree with Mary Boyce that "these sharp contrasts tended ... to foster a dualistic way of thought, a tendency to see the opposition in things which was to find such profound and sharply defined expression in Zoroastrianism itself" [19].

In an overview of the ancient world it might be possible to draw up a hierarchy or a scale on which we place the civilizations of that world according to the degree of dualism and the number of dualistic oppositions found in them. It must be remarked, however, that no civilization, no nation is ever free of dualism. At least one or two forms of it are present even in the most 'holistic' of them; there are 'loose ends', anomalies, contradictions in everyone of them.

The least dualistic of all ancient societies was ancient Israel. Jewish religion which dominated and governed the life of the Jewish nation collectively and individually, took an essentially optimistic and harmonious view of human existence. This was based on an intimate relationship between the Creator and his creation, between God and his people. The Bible presents a 'whole' in which God, world, nature, man, belong together, what the German philosopher Wilhelm Schapp would call an 'All-Geschichte'.

None the less, even this monotheistic and religious society had its 'loose ends'. There was, for instance, the 'nomadic ideal', the idea that the desert was the purer country where Israel 'in her youth' had been alone with Jahve. By contrast, the Canaanite soil, the home of so many idols, was seen as somewhat polluted. Deeply religious persons like the Essenes, John the Baptist, and Jesus, returned to the desert in order to be alone with God. There existed in Israel an at times rather sharp dualism between what Fohrer calls (in German) a 'restaurative' attitude to existence and the general historical acceptance of 'Canaan' [20].

The communal and daily life of Israel was dependent on the unity of creed and cult, secured by the stipulations of Mosaic Law. The priest, the servant of the community, acted as the objective executor of the communal rites; he did not owe his function to himself. There was, however, a certain residual fear that certain forces of creation could turn themselves, not against God, but against mankind. There existed a strong tendency to lay such dangerous forces by magic. Now magic is the exact opposite of cult. The magician is serving his own interests or those of his principal; he is gratifying his own egotistic impulses. The theological problem is that magic denies the omnipotence of God; man is trying to exploit the powers of nature regardless of God's rule of the world. The Old Testament quotes numerous instances of the use of magic by Israelites. The Law and the prophets constantly fought this tendency; the victorious attitude was finally the cultic one (Vol. IV, Ch. II.10b).

The religion of Israel was monotheistic. The stand it took regarding other gods was uncompromisingly dualistic. It denied any form of contact, even any form of compatibility, between Jahve and the gods of other peoples; consequently, religious commerce of his people with the creeds and cults of other nations was strictly forbidden. Foreign gods are idols; they are constantly derided and vilified. Nevertheless, Israel always felt the lure of idolatry. The prophets conducted a running fight against idols. In fact, the castigation of idols is one of their great preoccupations. One is sometimes tempted to suspect that this ferocity betrays a certain fear that such gods might really exist after all, and that they might even succeed in taking Jahve's place in the hearts of his people (Vol. IV, Ch. II.9).

XXX

On the non-theological level we see the opposition of the two kingdoms, Juda and Israel, that were so often locked in bloody, internecine warfare, and that of the Jews and the Samaritans (Vol. IV, Ch. II.14).

Egyptian society too was, on the whole, non-dualistic. But here also we find dualistic elements. There was the difference of the Two Lands, north and south, the Delta and the Valley of the Nile. Although they became united under a common Pharaoh, they always remained different, even in their manner of expressing themselves in language. There was even a difference of quality for the Valley seems to have had a kind of precedence over the Delta; the populations never forgot that they were different. Of course, they were connected by the one Pharaoh. But Pharaoh was in fact two kings in one person, the king of Upper and the king of Lower Egypt; he wore two crowns and was crowned twice (Vol. I, Ch. I.2e).

We also detect a sharp opposition between the desert and the habitable country along the Nile, the Red Land and the Black; in Egyptian consciousness the contrast between these two areas meant the contrast between death and life. Corpses were buried in the desert sand, the 'eternal habitat of the dead'. The distinction was carried over into mythology, with the terrible enmity between Seth, the doglike guardian of the desert, the Red Fiend, and Osiris, the protector of the black, fruitful soil, the benevolent Master (Vol. IV, Ch. I.1).

We should also mention the opposition of the 'true men' as the Egyptians saw themselves, and the lesser breeds, including all non-Egyptians. The Egyptian people, highly content with themselves and living in splendid isolation, looked down in deep contempt on all others, whom they considered less than human (Vol. I, Ch. I.3). But the fiercest form of dualism was that of life and death. The Egyptians took incredible pains in order to survive in the afterlife. Death as an existential fact was simply denied by them. Who does not know of the rites to secure a place in the hereafter, of mummification, for instance (Vol. I, Ch. I.7)?

Ancient China has its place among non-dualistic societies. The basic Chinese world-view does not imply a fundamental dualism. We should, however, not overlook an important element of dualism. To be civilised, to be human, to live in harmony with Heaven, means to be Chinese. China is congruent with the Universe. This implied that non-Chinese do not possess a fully human existence (Vol. V, Ch. IV.15d).

Almost everybody seems to think that the famous pair Yin and Yang is dualistic. This is a misunderstanding. Yin and Yang are not ideas but matter, albeit of the most ethereal sort. Yang is Left, and Yin is Right; Yang is the stuff of which light and the sun are made; Yin is to be found in the moon and in darkness. As such they are complementary, together making a whole (Vol. V., Ch. IV.15e).

The two most dualistic societies in all Antiquity were those of Greece and India. Both were riddled with unsolvable oppositions. This will not please the lovers of all that is Hellenic. We all prefer to consider existence, if not as perfectly harmonious, yet in any case as a congruent whole. Classical scholars, in my opinion, seem to have preserved something of what I might call the 'Hölderlin-vision', the favourite notion of nineteenth-century neo-humanism. I mean the idea that the Greeks were a luminous people, the forerunners of a new, creative, and highly intelligent human race, of an harmonious world. It is still somewhat hazardous to suggest that even the Greeks knew tragedy and failure in their social and political life. Of course, present-day scholars are quite ready to admit that the Greeks were coping with fierce oppositions but these were obviously all for the best. A Dutch professor of ancient history wrote to me that she did not combat the idea that the Greeks knew polary, even unbridgeable oppositions. In her opinion, however, these are no indications of an (existential) crisis nor did they obstruct the human fulfilment of the Greeks. On the contrary, they are indispensable in the course of historical development. But unbridgeable, that is, dualistic oppositions are not wholesome at all. They have a negative influence on society and people, they retard developments and may even be destructive. There is no good in dualism.

First of all, there is the dualistic opposition of Greeks and barbarians. In the opinion of the Greeks the polis was the exact image of the cosmos, the fundamental ordering of existence, and this was what the barbarians lacked. The polis meant freedom, self-determination, political

XXXII

participation; the barbarians only knew subjection, subservience, servitude. The greatest, the most essential difference, however, was that the Greeks had the 'paideia', the proper way of being human. This again was utterly denied to barbarians. The basic contrast is particularly reflected in language. There is Greek and there is gibberish (every other language) (Vol. II, Ch. III.3).

This opposition became historically exemplified in the struggle between Persia and Hellas. All great historical empires have known a strong, even an overpowering structure, Persia still more than all its predecessors. The traditional structure of domination and control was perfected by the Persian kings in an incredible way. Here we are confronted with a basic antagonism between the Greek world as such and that of the Middle East that may be thought of in dualistic terms. The Hellenes never cherished the idea of becoming linked together in this way. They acknowledged a moral authority (viz. of rules of conduct) but not an all-embracing political structure. This is the backdrop of their resistance to the Persian onslaught (Vol. II, Ch. I).

That the Greek world possessed no overall structure had very evil consequences. The Greek states, although sharing the same language, religion, customs, and the same basic attitude regarding the 'barbarian' outer world, nevertheless lacked every form of cohesion or federation or confederation. Their relations with the other poleis display the clearest possible picture of an 'anti-structure' which is the exact and dualistic opposite of structure. The Greek space was an anarchistic vacuum in which the poleis, or at best their alliances, moved about like atoms and collided with each other. But their atomic weights were different, and this is the deepest cause of the internecine, the dualistic Greek wars of the fifth and fourth centuries B.C. (Vol. II, Ch. II).

In Greek opinion the work of the free man was to govern the city, to cultivate art and science, to teach, to administer justice, and last but not least, to wage war. For the rest there were slaves. Slaves were property, part of the possessions of their master; he might dispose of them, just as he might dispose of anything he owned. Slaves were not human, they were objects, things, 'automata'. Hellas was a slave-holding society; the Greeks of the classical period simply could not have managed without slavery. So there

XXXIII

existed a dualistic bipartition of human beings in their world (Vol. II, Ch. IV.4i,j).

This world knew the oldest élitist fraternity ever, the Pythagorean one. It was an élitist company with a special way of life, vegetarian, of course, and keeping carefully apart from the common run. Its basic ideology was profoundly dualistic. Although the Pythagoreans venerated the One as a god or as something divine, they believed in two opposite principles. These were the 'apeiron', the unlimited, and the 'Peras', the Limit (the cosmos and the surrounding void). This basic pair is followed by several others (they handle a list of ten), like the One and the Many, Right and Left, Even and Odd, Male and Female (Vol. I, Ch. I).

Dualism is also found in many Presocratics (Vol. I, Ch. II), especially in Parmenides with his two utterly opposed worlds, that of Being and that of Seeming (Vol. I, Ch. II.8). The first Greek philosopher whose work we possess in its totality is Plato. Him we may safely characterize as a dualistic thinker. A great many dualistic oppositions occur in his works. In the microcosmos we meet that of body and soul, and next that of man and society in which the individual person is almost non-existent, to say nothing of the opposition between philosophers and non-philosophers.

This last opposition leads us to the macrocosmos. The primary oppositions carry many names, the One and the Many, Peras and Apeiron, Same and Other, Monad and Dyad, all of them dualistic. From the viewpoint of the theory of knowledge there is constant talk of the intelligible and the non-intelligible, of knowledge and opinion, of Being and Seeming. Finally, there is the preeminent opposition of the Forms and concrete things. Now this last opposition was not meant by Plato to be one. Quite the contrary! But according to Aristotle, there is an unbridgeable distance between Forms and concrete things - and this is the aporia into which Plato had landed himself (Vol. III, Ch. III). In the Hellenistic philosophers, especially in the Middle Academy, many of these dualistic elements are once again to be found (Vol. VI, Ch. III).

India too is a country that is brimful of dualistic oppositions. The origin of all Indian dualism is probably the subjugation of the autochthonous

XXXIV

population by the invading Aryans around 1500 or 1400 B.C.; in the eyes of the conquerors the indigenous inhabitants were simply subhuman (Vol. V, Ch. II.9). It is not impossible that the slaves were, partly at least, descendants of the subjected race, the Dasyus; in India too slaves were no more than a marketable commodity (Vol. V, Ch. II.13).

The deep divisions of Indian society are mirrored in the caste system; all castes saw each other as mutually exclusive. No greater catastrophe than to be without a caste, to be casteless, an 'outcaste'. It was indeed possible to be expelled from one's caste, in case of grave and repeated misdemeanour. Nobody would help such a person, nobody would stay with him; unless his wife followed him he remained utterly alone. To be an outcaste is, however, not identical with being a 'pariah', an 'untouchable'; pariahs belonged to a caste, although a very low one. They were subjected to a system of 'apartheid' that was downright dualistic. The ordinary Hindu shunned every contact with them for fear of becoming defiled himself (Vol. V, Ch. II.15).

The invasion of the Aryans meant the arrival of a 'macho' race of warriors and conquerors; this had dire consequences for the situation of women who now became decidedly the lesser sort. Sons became all-important, whereas daughters were not welcome. Polygamy was widespread, that is, for men, since women had to be content with one husband. The distance between husband and wife grew dualistically wide; a man was incapable of seeing in his wife a person of the same worth and value as himself. Women were not very much helped by Buddhism. The Buddha himself did not think highly of women; on the whole, his religion saw women as inferior to men (Vol. V. Ch. II.14).

There are strong dualistic tendencies in Indian mythology. There are powers from above and powers from beneath which are dualistically opposed. The high gods, the devas, are almost with exception benevolent; the lower divinities are demonic and malicious (Vol. V, Ch. II.17). These oppositions spill over into Indian philosophy where we find Unity and Diversity (the One and the Many), Male and Female, and above all Matter and

XXXV

Spirit, as dualities which can easily assume a dualistic character (Vol. V, Ch. II.16).

In the Brahmanic religion the Brahmans were in the possession of the truth; this secured them a privileged position, the more so since this knowledge was not directly open to everyone. The Brahmans considered themselves and were considered a highly superior class. The true Brahman renounces the world; he sets himself apart from human society and even over against it. His position vis-à-vis ordinary existence was (and is) dualistic (Vol. V, Ch. II.18-19).

In the Hindu religion we are struck by the uneasy relationship between the male and the female. Hindu mythology knew a 'Great Goddess', the Maha-Devi, the wife of Shiva. Women, especially mothers, are seen as the images of Maha-Devi, and, in consequence, must be respected. Gradually she became the dominant female divinity in the Hindu pantheon. But "the dominant woman is dangerous in Hindu mythology" [21]. Maha-Devi is a goddess with a dual, not to say a dualistic character since she is mild and fierce at the same time. This difference is mirrored in the attitude of Hindu men towards their wives whom they venerate as mothers and whom they fear as erotic seducers (Vol. V, Ch. II.20).

I can only mention in passing the profound dualism of Yoga with its radical rejection of the world (Vol. V, Ch. II.21). Buddhism, just like all other Indian religions, is basically built on a dualism between personal existence, fundamentally selfish and thoughtless as it is, and the state of unworldy contemplation that leads on to the final loss of all that is self (Vol. V, Ch. II.23).

Returning westward now, we come to ancient Iran, in the eyes of many scholars the cradle of all dualisms. Religious dualism in this part of the world developed in two stages, that of Zoroastrianism and that of Zervanism; when people speak of 'Iranian dualism', they are unwittingly referring to Zervanism instead of to Zoroastrianism. The core of Zoroaster's message is that there is only one god to be venerated, Ahura Mazda, the Wise Lord. On the face of it we may seem to be in the presence of monotheism, perhaps even monism. Ahura Mazda is 'spenta', that is, 'working' : he is causing effects. His

XXXVI

spenta is realized in a number of spirits, the principal of whom is Spenta Mainyu, the Holy Spirit. But here the dualistic split begins. Spenta Mainyu has a twin, Anya (or Ahra) Mainyu, the Evil Spirit. This is not a creature of Ahura Mazda; the latter, as being all-good, cannot be the father of Ahra Mainyu who, therefore, must be thought of as uncreated (Vol. IV, Ch. IV.8). Ahura Mazda takes precedence over Ahra Mainyu, simply because the Good is superior to Evil. Therefore, Zoroastrian dualism is not radical but relative. Good and Evil, the good and the wicked, will fight each other as long as the world lasts. But at the end of time, Ahura Mazda will establish on earth the so-called 'second existence' over which he himself will reign. There the faithful will enjoy the eternal bliss of Paradise (Vol. IV, Ch. IV.9).

The Zervanite variant, in fact an heretical variant of Zoroastrianism, is much more radical than the doctrine of the great prophet. True enough, Zervanism too starts from a monistic principle, called 'Zervan' which means 'Time'. But this apparently monistic principle remains so vague and abstract that it does not really play a role. Furthermore, the uniqueness of Zervan is impaired by the fact that there is an unexplained woman about. Zervan and this anonymous woman become the parents of Ormizd (Ormuzd) and Ahriman. They share the power over the earth and mankind between them. The real source of all evil is Zervan, but Ahriman is just as bad as he. Ormizd, the good one, is a secondary divinity. The good and the bad are presented as equals; both account for one half of the universe in which, therefore, good and evil are present in equal parts. They will always fight one another inexorably (Vo. V, Ch. I.5).

I often had the occasion to observe that classical scholars and historians know next to nothing of that remarkable phenomenon, the Gnosis (Vols. VII, VIII, IX). The Gnosis originated in the same period and in the same region as Christianity. They resemble each other in the respect that both are religions of redemption. But whereas in Christianity redemption is contingent on the cross of Jesus Christ, in the Gnosis it is effectuated by Knowledge, that is, by a specific and esoteric kind of Knowledge which is given to a minority of people only. In contrast to the orthodox Christian Church, the Gnosis existed in numerous, even hundreds, of sects, mostly only small groups. But some of them had a large following, the Basilidians (Vol. VIII, Ch. VII), the Valentinians (Vol. VIII, Ch. VIII), the Marcionites (Vol. IX, Ch. II), and above all, the Manichaeans (Vol. X, Ch. IV). To many people 'Manichaean' has become synonymous with dualistic. Only one of the Gnostic sects is still in existence, the Mandaeans in southern Iraq (Vol. IX, Ch. III).

There has been much discussion on what 'Gnostic' means and what not. Even experts do not agree on what is the main characteristic of the Gnosis. Is it the redeeming Knowledge? The Fall? The Saviour? The elect? The rejection of the world? The eschaton? The problem is that not all systems dubbed 'Gnostic' (by no means all of them call themselves 'Gnostic') display all these features simultaneously, and/or emphasize them in different ways. There is, however, one Gnostic element on which all scholars agree : its dualism. This does not mean that these scholars all consider dualism the distinguishing feature of the Gnosis. But to quote Karl Prümm : "One should always insist on a metaphysical foundation of dualism as the true characteristic of what Gnosis is" [22].

Prümm is speaking of 'metaphysical' dualism. This is correct but it is not enough. Gnostic systems are always poised on two types of dualism. First, there is metaphysical dualism : the upper world, the Pleroma, is essentially different from and opposed to the nether, material world, the cosmos with mankind. This is horizontal dualism. Next there is anthropological dualism, between the elect, the chosen, the saved, the Gnostic pneumatics (a minority), and the hylics, the matter-people, who will not be saved. This is vertical dualism; it is only present in the nether world (Vol. VIII, Preface p.15). Gnostics prosper on radical oppositions; with them it is always either-or, with nothing in between. Metaphysically, there is the opposition of the good God who, however, remains a 'deus absconditus', and the bad Demiurge with his helpers who created this world - a world that has been evil since its inception. Then there is the ethical dualism of Good and Evil. This leads to the anthropological opposition of the few elect, of those who 'know', and the 'massa damnata', the great mass of people who unwittingly go to their doom.

XXXVIII

Finally, a few paragraphs must be devoted to a special brand of dualism, imperialistic dualism. The most simple meaning of 'imperialism' is that of building an empire; by 'empire' I mean a state in which more than one or several nations that formerly led an independent existence are now united under one rule. Toynbee uses to call such political entities 'universal states'. In his opinion, "a universal state is ex hypothesi alone within its own world"[23].

Empires attribute to themselves qualities that are lacking in other, more simple states. Not only do they believe themselves to be immortal - which means possessing a godlike nature -, but they are first and foremost 'universal', that is all-embracing. In fact, all empires tend to be world-empires encompassing the whole world; no empire is ever content with its own frontiers. The uniqueness of an empire implies that it does not acknowledge other states whose ratio existendi is to be engulfed by it. Empires virtually deny the right of existence to other states; they consider them non-existing. In consequence, there runs a sharp dividing line between fully authentic states and the non-existent ones. This constitutes a form of dualism with far-reaching political and historical consequences (Vol. IV, Ch. III.1).

It is a highly intriguing historical fact that the region stretching from central Anatolia to the Delta of the Euphrates and the Tigris, along an axis running from the north-west to the south-east, saw the birth of the first real empires. The oldest of these is that of Sumer in southern Mesopotamia (Vol. IV, Ch. II.2). Its king around 2435 B.C., Luzalzaggisi, stated that the god Enlil "threw down the lands under his (the kings's) feet; he conquered from where the sun rises to where it sets". North of Sumer lay Akkad (vol. IV, Ch. III.3). Its king Sargon conquered far and wide. The first lord of all Mesopotamia was Hammurabi (1793-1750), the founder of the Babylonian Empire (Vol. IV, Ch. III.5). Next came the two Hittite Empires, the old (17th century B.C.) and the new ones (14th-13th cent. B.C.) (Vol. IV, Ch. III.6). Assyria, one of the greatest aggressor-nations of the ancient world, reached its apex between 900 and 612 (Vol. IV, Ch. III.7) in which year it was thrown down by Babylonia; the New Babylonian Empire, made famous by its king Nebuchadnessar II (Vol. IV, Ch. III.8), was overrun by the Persians in 539 B.C.

XXXIX

The Persian Empire (Vol. IV, Ch. IV.3) was the inheritor of all the imperialisms of the past; at its greatest extent it stretched from the Indus to the Aegean and from the Nile to the Caspian. Its kings styled themselves 'King of Kings'. Its claims were taken over by Alexander the Great when he conquered the whole Middle East (Vol. IV, Ch. IV.3e).

The greatest imperialistic power of all Antiquity was, of course, Rome. The Roman Empire (the subject of Vol. X) was the largest ever; its rulers never paid the slightest regard to the right of independent existence of any other state or nation whatsoever. In its later later days, however, this truly 'universal state', found on its path a truly 'universal church', the Christian Church, and with this encounter a new and long struggle began.

With this volume too business was as usual. Dr. J.R. Dove, a native English speaker and an emeritus professor of English and American literature in the University of Oulu in Finland, corrected the English of this book, from time to time pointing out an inconsistency, a contradiction or an omission. My daughter, Dr. Resianne Smidt van Gelder-Fontaine, a philosopher, although having a full-time job and a full-time family, found the time to read through the whole volume and present me with a number of useful and sensible remarks. My dear wife Anneke corrected the one-but-last version on typing errors. As always, I stress that the responsibility for all that the book contains is my sole responsibility, scholarly contents, English, typography, and lay-out. Mr. J.C. Gieben, my friendly publisher, steered the thing through the press as quickly and efficiently as ever. I am grateful to all of them.

Volume XII will describe the conflicts Christianity had with the Roman Empire and Judaism.

P.F.M. Fontaine
Amsterdam NL

XL

NOTES

1. Jacques Duchesne-Guillemin, Ormuzd et Ahriman. L'aventure dualiste dans l'Antiquité. Paris, 1953. P. 1.

2. Thomas Hyde, Historia religionis veterum Persarum, eorumque Magorum. Oxoniae, MDCC. Pp. 163/164.

3. Christian Wolff. Psychologia rationalis. Sect. I, Cap. I, par. 39 and 43; Sect. III, Cap. I, par. 555; Sect. IV, Cap. I, par. 665. 1734.

4. Hayden White. Droysen's Historik. Historical writing as a bourgeois science. in : The Content of Form. Narrative Discourse and Historical Interpretation. The John Hopkins University Press. Baltimore and London (1987). P. 87.

5. Mary Douglas, Purity and Danger. An Analysis of the Concept of Pollution and Taboo. London, 1984 (1966 1). P. 162.

6. Ludwig Stein, Dualismus and Monismus. Eine Untersuchung über die doppelte Wahrheit. Berlin, 1909. P. 14.

7. Studies in the History of Religions (Supplements to Numen), XII. L'origini dello Gnosticismo. Colloquio di Messina, 19-18 Aprile 1966. Leiden, 1970. Pp. XX-XXXII.

8. Ugo Bianchi, Il dualismo come categoria storico-religiosa (1973). Selected Essays on Gnosticism, Dualism and Mysteriosophy. Studies in the History of Religions (Supplements to Numen), XXVIII. Leiden, 1978. P. 8.

9. Ugo Bianchi, Le dualisme en histoire des religions (1961). Essays on Gnosticism (see preceding note).

10. The reader will recognize here the typology of Bianchi, Dualismo, in Essays, 58-62. My description, however, is somewhat different of that of B., because my scope is considerably wider.

11. See for Hitler's dualism Vol. VI, Preface pp. XXVIII-XXIX, and Vol. VIII, Preface pp. XXV-XXXII.

12. R.M. Sainsbury, Paradoxes. Cambridge, 1988. P. 1.

13. Louis Menand, New York Review of Books, 25.VI.1992.

14. For a more extensive treatment of these matters I refer the reader to the Preface of Vol. IX.

15. Mk.3:17.

16. Lk.9:52-55.

17. Mt.20:20-24; Mk.10:35-41.

18. A. Chorus, Een pyschologische kijk op de vier evangelisten. Haarlem, second impression (w.d.), Pp. 82/83.

XLI

19. Mary Boyce, A History of Zoroastrianism I, 18/19. Leiden, 1975. Handbuch der Orientalistik. Erste Abteilung. 8. Bd. 1. Abschnitt. Lieferung 2. Heft 2A; see further my Vol. IV, Ch. IV.5.

20. Georg Fohrer, Theologische Grundstrukturen des Alten Testaments. Berlin/New York, 1972, 61. See Vol. IV, Ch. II.10c.

21. Wendy O'Flaherty, Women, Androgynes, and other mythical Beasts. Chicago/London (1980). P. 77.

22. Karl Prümm, Gnosis an der Wurzel des Christentums? Grundlagenkritik der Entmythologisierung. Salzburg (1961). P. 12, note 2. This is also the opinion of Ioan Couliano, Les Gnoses dualistes de l'Occident. Histoire et mythes. Paris, 1989. Pp. 167/168.

23. Arnold Toynbee, A Study of History. Vol. III, p. 57. London, 1955 2 (1954 1).

MANUAL

This manual is designed for those readers who do not want to read the whole work, but, instead, want to see what is said in it about the subject(s) they are interested in.

I   ON DUALISM AS SUCH

          Prefaces of Vols. I, VI, IX,
          Vol. IV, Ch. IV.4

II   PERIODS AND CIVILIZATIONS

          1. Greece
             Vol. I Archaic and early classical periods
             Vol. II and III Fifth and fourth centuries B.C.
             Vol. VI The Hellenistic world
          2. Egypt
             Vol. IV, Ch. I
          3. Mesopotamia and Anatolia
             Vol. IV, Ch. III
          4. Israel
             Vol. IV, Ch. II
          5. Iran
             Vol. IV, Ch. IV, Vol. V, Ch. I
          6. India
             Vol. V, Ch. II
          7. China
             Vol. V, Ch. III
          8. Roman history
             Vol. X

III   POLITICAL HISTORY

          1. Greece
             Vol. II
             Vol. VI, Chs. I and II
          2. Rome
             Vol. X

3. Egypt
   Vol. IV, Ch. I.1-4
4. Mesopotamia and Anatolia
   Vol. IV, Ch. III.1-9.
5. Israel
   Vol. IV, Ch. II.14
   Vol. VI, Ch. II.11
6. Iran
   Vol. IV, Ch. IV.1-3
   Vol. V, Ch. I.1-3
7. India
   Vol. V, Ch. II.1-11
8. China
   Vol. V, Ch. III.1-5

IV SOCIAL HISTORY

1. Greece
   Vol. II, Ch. III.3
   Vol. II, Ch. IV.4
2. India
   Vol. V, Ch. II.13-15

Since esoteric religious movements are socially distinct from the rest of the population, we may subsume these too under this heading :

3. The Pythagoreans
   Vol. I, Ch. I
4. Eleusinian mysteries and Orphics
   Vol. I, Ch. IV
5. Yoga
   Vol. V, Ch. II.21
6. Jainism
   Vol. V, Ch. II.22
7. Dao
   Vol. V, Ch. III.25
8. The Essenes
   Vol. VIII, Ch. V
9. Almost all Gnostic movements
   Vol. VII, Ch. III, Vols. VIII and IX

V HISTORY OF RELIGIONS

1. Pythagoreanism
   Vol. I, Ch. I
2. The Olympian religion
   Vol. I, Ch. IV.1-8
3. The Eleusinian mysteries
   Vol. I, Ch. IV.8
4. The cult of Dionysus
   Vol. I, Ch. IV.9

5. Orphism
   Vol. I, Ch. IV.10
6. Greek shamanism
   Vol. I, Ch. IV.11
7. Egyptian religion
   Vol. IV, Ch. I.5-7
8. The religion of Israel
   Vol. IV, Ch. II
   Vol. VII, Ch. VI
9. Religions of the Middle East
   Vol. IV, Ch. III.10
10. Iranian religion
    Vol. IV, Ch. IV.4-12
    Vol. V, Ch. I.4-5
11. Mazdakism
    Vol. V, Ch. I, Appendix
12. The New Testament
    Vol. VII, Ch. IV
13. The Essenes
    Vol. VII, Ch. V
14. Hermetism
    Vol. VIII, Ch. II
15. The Veda
    Vol. V, Ch. II.17
16. Brahmanism
    Vol. V, Ch. II.18-19
17. Hinduism
    Vol. V, Ch. II.20
18. Yoga
    Vol. V. Ch. II.21
19. Jainism
    Vol. V, Ch. II.22
20. Buddhism
    Vol. V. Ch. II.23
21. Confucianism
    Vol. V, CH. III.16-21, 23-24
22. Mohism
    Vol. V, Ch. III.22
23. Daoism
    Vol. V, Ch. III.25
24. The Gnosis
    Vol. VI, Ch.IV
    Vol. VII, Chs. I-III
    Vol. VIII, Chs. III-IX
    Vol. IX

XLVI

VI PHILOSOPHY

   1. Pythagoreanism
      Vol. I, Ch. I
   2. Ionic and Eleatic philosophy
      Vol. I, Ch. II
   3. Sophists and Socrates
      Vol. III, Ch. II
   4. Plato and Aristotle
      Vol. III, Ch. III
   5. Hellenistic philosophy
      Vol. VI, Ch. III
   6. Indian philosophy
      Vol. V, Ch. II.16
   7. Chinese philosophy
      Vol. V, Ch. III.15
   8. The philosophy of Philo
      Vol. VIII, Ch. I

VII LITERATURE
   1. Greek epics and lyrics
      Vol. I, Ch. III
   2. Greek tragedy and comedy
      Vol. III, Ch. I

VIII HISTORIOGRAPHY
   1. Greek historiography
      Vol. III, Ch. III.1
   2. Old Testament
      Vol. IV, Ch. II.1-6
   3. New Testament
      Vol. VII, Ch. IV.1-2.

CHAPTER I

INTERNAL DISCORD

1. A rift in the solid power base

The term 'solid power-base', that I have used to refer to Rome's territory such as it was around 390 B.C. [1], does not imply that it was manned by a united people. This was far from being the case. During the centuries following the fall of the monarchy Rome was torn apart by a social conflict so fierce that we must dub it dualistic. It was the long-drawn out conflict between patricians and plebeians.

2. What are patricians, what are plebeians?

I mentioned the patricians earlier. This word is derived from 'patres', the fathers; it does not indicate the natural fathers of Rome but an institution. Livy traced the origin of this institution to Romulus himself, the legendary founder of the city, who nominated a hundred senators to serve him and his successors as councillors; "because of this honour they were called 'patres', and their descendants 'patricians' [2]. These last words imply that not every patrician was a member of the Senate. Patricians were also priests, magistrates, and judges [3]; in fact, they shared all the public offices between them. They were wealthy, had long pedigrees, and saw themselves as the guardians of public life and morals. We may think of them as the nobility of Rome.

The rest of the population was referred to as the 'plebs', and its members as the 'plebeians'. Until these days both words have kept their negative connotations : 'the masses, the great unwashed, the city rabble, the proletarii' [4]. It was certainly regarded as a non-people, the mass of those who were not patricians. They were the artisans, shopkeepers, and day-labourers, originally mostly poor. The regulation that they were forbidden to marry a patrician (the reverse was also true) kept them at their proper distance. None of the public functions was open to them, except one : they were allowed to fight and die for the sake of Rome on the battle-field.

3. The boundary

"Plebeians most frequently are cast opposite the Senate." Romulus "drew a boundary between those who were eminent for their birth, approved for their virtue and wealthy for those times ..., and the obscure, the lowly and the poor" [5]. The dualism in this relationship, however, was not absolute since plebeians were clients of patricians, that is, they were economically dependent on specific noble families. Romulus had meant the connection to be "a bond of kindness befitting fellow citizens" [6]. The patricians were patrons of their plebeian clients, for instance, they had "to explain (to them) the laws of which they were ignorant", and, in general, "to secure for them both in private and public affairs all that tranquillity of which they particularly stood in need".

However, this patronage cost the clients money, for, among other things, they were obliged to ransom patrician children who were taken prisoner, and "to share with their patrons the costs incurred in the magistracies and dignities" [7]. We may conclude with Mitchell that "a fundamental economic distinction remained a constant presumption : the struggle was between haves and have-nots" [8]. It is possible that this description of the social situation in ancient Rome, based as it is on the reports of ancient authors, is somewhat anachronistic. It could be that the class distinctions in the time of the monarchy were not yet so sharp as they became later [9]. It seems, for example, that the prohibition of intermarriage dates only from 465 B.C.

4. The effect of the fall of the monarchy

Some of the kings favoured the plebs in order to play them off against the nobility [10]; the last king, Tarquinius Superbus, is reported to have treated patricians and plebeians in the same denigrating way [11]; the plebeians thought that this served the patricians right [12]. When the monarchy was abolished, the political power that the king had held fell into the hands of the patricians. The end of the monarchy, therefore, did not ring in a new and better era for the plebs, quite the contrary! The plebeians were now deprived of the little protection they had received from the kings. At first, when the nobility still feared that the plebs would welcome a return of the kings, they cajoled them with tax concessions and by supplying an abundance of food [13]. But as soon as the senators were convinced that there was no chance of the reinstitution of the monarchy, "the plebs was exposed to the injustice of the great" [14].

5. Advantages the plebs had

I have described in Chapter II of Volume X how every Roman citizen was assigned a place in society by means of the classification of the comitia centuriata, the army assembly. The place each one had was determined by the 'census', that is, by his fortune or the lack of it. As I explained there, the comitia were organized in 'classes', in this way the wealthier ones could outvote the poor. In the beginning this meant that the nobility was able to dominate the assembly. But nobody could prevent plebeians from becoming rich, and some of them did, even becoming very wealthy. On account of their growing capital such plebeians automatically became members of a higher classis. This made it harder for the patricians to vote against the interests of the plebeians. This was the first advantage the plebs had.

The second, still more important, was that the nobility could not fight the wars of Rome alone; riding out themselves on horseback, they also needed infantry which was supplied by the plebeians, the origin of the famous Roman legions. In other words, the aristocratic Senate could achieve nothing without the help of plebeian soldiers. These soldiers, if they had not fallen on the battle-field, returned home ill and covered with scars; at home their debts stared them in the face. And they were without any influence on the conduct of public affairs.

6. The installation of the tribunes of the people

When in 494 B.C. the Senate refused to discuss the problem of the debts [15], it heard the people grumble and feared a revolt; to have the plebs out of the way and to bring them under military discipline, they ordered mobilization. This immediately unleashed a downright rebellion. Livy says the plebs wanted to murder the consuls who had called them to arms, but one of their leaders persuaded them not to use violence. Instead, they left the town and made camp on the Mons Sacer, the Holy Mountain (probably the Aventine); anyhow, they were at an hour's distance from the Forum. They fortified their camp with a stockade. This event is called the 'secessio plebis ad Montem Sacrum', which signifies "their (the plebs) 'retirement' from the rest of the Roman community, in the sense of a literal physical departure" [16]. It was a dualistic separation : we here - they there [17].

The Senators in Rome panicked! They even considered fleeing the town; the patricians and such plebeians who had remained naturally were mutually afraid of each other. Finally, a parliamentary was sent to the Mons Sacer who succeeded in calming down the plebs and inducing them to return [18]. Of course, this did not go without concessions. The plebeians were granted officials of their own, the 'tribuni plebis', the tribunes of the people [19]. Originally, there seem to have been no more than two of them but in the following decades more were added until there were ten in 449 B.C. [20]. These tribunes served as a rampart for the plebeians; they acted as the defenders of the plebs against oppression by the nobles.

It is a very curious and painful commentary on the attitude of the patrician senators and magistrates who were the natural and constitutional defenders of all the people, that they did not prove able to protect the plebeian majority of the population. As we saw above, most plebeians were clients of patricians, but obviously their patrons failed to offer the guaranteed protection, especially when they considered their own interests threatened, when, for instance, their clients were also their debtors (as very often was the case).

To understand the task of the tribunes, we must realize that they were functionaries but not magistrates; their position was not based on law. We should not think of the tribunate as a democratic institution; democracy was something that remained foreign to ancient Rome throughout the whole of her long history. The tribunes did not function as part of the constitutional machinery but rather had to clog it if necessary. Mommsen even called this institution "a permanent revolution, incompatible with the uniform ordering of the body politic" [21]. There existed strong dualistic elements in Roman social and political life. Livy stated, probably disapprovingly, that the effect of the plebeian agitation was that "two bodies politic (civitates) were made out of one, each with its own magistrates and laws" [22]. We might well ask when there had been only one body politic.

The tribunes could safeguard plebeians from arrest and execution or being thrown into prison by their creditors. They could also call the plebs together to take decisions, the so-called 'plebiscita', a word that has found a place in European languages. They were held to be inviolable so that they could not be taken to task either by the Senate or by the magistrates on account of their official acts; infringement of their rights could lead to a process conducted by the popular assembly which might result in a death sentence. This last stipulation was made in 449 B.C., when the tribunes were declared 'sacrosancti', a word that denotes that the safety of these functionaries essentially was an affair of the gods. Whoever maltreated them, his head would be 'devoted to Jupiter' [23] which means that the guilty magistrate would become an outlaw.

7. The codification of the laws

In an important respect the plebeians were severely handicapped : Roman law was not codified. Judges made use only of an oral interpretation. Since those judges were all patricians, they administered justice as it suited their own interests; accused plebeians were absolutely helpless in the dock. This led to such glaring injustice and caused such violent tension between the two classes of society that in 449 B.C. the plebs again 'seceded' to the Aventine. Although some historians doubt that this second 'secessio' really took place, the fact is that the laws did become codified (a commission to do this had been installed already in 451 B.C.). The result of this codification is called 'the Twelve Tables', since the laws were written on twelve bronze or wooden plates and set up in the Forum, to be consulted by everybody [24].

The importance of the codification can hardly be overrated; Livy says that it was 'the fountain-head of all public and private law' [25]. It is the first great expression of the Roman genius for legislation, of the Romans' "unparallelled talent for precise legal definition which is one of Rome's greatest gifts to humanity". These are the words of Grant who characterizes those who drafted this legislation as 'hard, practical thinkers' [26]. The original Twelve Tables were destroyed during the Celtic invasion of 387 B.C., but after that event "they were meticulously reconstructed and remained legally valid ... For century after century they retained a dominant position in the education of every Roman citizen" [27]. A young Roman, aspiring to become a magistrate, first of all needed a thorough grounding in Roman law.

The improvement for the plebeians resulting from codification consisted in the fact that they now could know on which articles of law they were sentenced. But since those articles remained as harsh as before, there was no real amelioration of their lot. In consequence, the plebeians were not contented at all. It seems that the prohibition of intermarriage between members of both classes remained in force, although the number of patrician families was constantly declining and fresh blood was urgently needed. But, in spite of this problem, the patricians "carried their persistent distaste for intermarrying to the lenghts of suicide" [28]. The ban was lifted later, when is not exactly known [29]. This does not mean, however, that there was suddenly a flood of patrician-plebeian weddings.

8. The road upwards

Individual plebeians, mostly wealthy men, some more wealthy than some patricians, made their way upwards. In the long run the public offices could not remain closed to them (officials did not receive a salary so that one had to be well-to-do to become one). One after the other the offices were opened to the plebeians. The first was that of quaestor, in 421 B.C., but it was only twelve years later that the first plebeian was appointed to this office. It was only in 367 B.C. that plebeians became eligible for the consulate; the next year already saw the first plebeian ever as consul. The censorship followed in 351 B.C., and in 337 the office of praetor.

The religious offices were defended by the aristocrats with the utmost tenacity, as though religion would be degraded when plebeians officiated. However, from 300 B.C. on members of the plebs could become pontifices and augurs. The consequence of the fact that plebeians could hold office was that they too became senators, since ex-officials were automatically admitted to the Senate. It was, at least in theory, a blow to the power of this body that after 287 B.C. plebiscites were also operative without senatorial approval [30].

9. The distinction abolished?

Does all this mean that the distinction between the social classes had been abolished? By no means! It subsisted, although not so sharply as previously. First of all, the vast majority of officials were, as ever, patricians; during the last centuries of the Republic not many plebeians became consuls, quaestors, or whatever. "No plebeian family acquired the prestige and influence that was enjoyed by some old patrician clans" [31]. Secondly, those plebeians who became members of the Senate, were not entitled to the name of 'patres'; they were only considered 'conscripti' = added, so that the senators were addressed as 'patres (et) conscripti'.

An event, highly revealing for the relationship between the two classes, occurred in 287 B.C. Since the plebeians had won equality before the law and were now eligible for all offices, the tribunes of the people were no longer necessary - that is, in pure constitutional logic. The old aristocratic clans saw it thus and wanted to abolish the tribunate, but probably not for reasons of constitutional logic. Once again tension ran high; for the last time the plebs 'seceded' to the Holy Mountain. The result was that the tribunate was recognized as constitutional. This incident proves that the mistrust of the patricians for the pebleians remained inveterate.

As long as the Republic lasted, plebeians could not be elevated to the patriciate, although under certain conditions a plebeian woman could become a patrician by marrying one [32]. The reverse was not true. Were the (very special) conditions not fulfilled, then the patrician was deprived of his status, similarly in the case of a patrician youth who was adopted by a plebeian [33].

Since, however, in the last days of the Republic the number of patrician clans had greatly diminished, Caesar, Augustus, and other emperors conferred patrician status on whole plebeian families. But even so the social distinctions remained discernible since there were now 'gentes maiores' = the old patrician clans, and 'gentes minores' = the new ones. The chairman of the Senate as well as the Emperor, at least in the first period, had to come from the old stock.

What had, slowly but certainly, come into being was what Endre Ferenczy calls 'the patricio-plebeian state' [34]. Of course, the realization of this process took a long time, since the patrician clans defended their positions inch by inch. Yet even when the process was realized, we have to remind ourselves that it was only a minor segment of the population that reached the level of their aristocratic counterparts.

It will be clear that the old dualistic distinction gradually wore away. It finally lost all meaning when Constantine the Great around A.D.

325 introduced the title of 'patricius' which did not denote a member of the patrician class but was given to deserving persons as a personal title. Even barbarian kings, like Odoacer and Theodoric, became 'patricii' [35].

Concluding, we might say that from the third century B.C. patricians and plebeians no longer fought each other; although it had taken a long time, the plebeians had finally got what they wanted. The leading plebeian clans had virtually become the equals of their counterparts.

10. The social balance disturbed

The Romans of the second century B.C. looked back on an history of their town and society that stretched back for more than five centuries. The Republic, the constitutional form they had given their political existence, was by then already three centuries old. During these centuries the small and insignificant city of the sixth century had become the capital of a great empire. But the political organization had remained unaltered. Rome's "constitution and her social structure were those of a city-state; but the city-state of Rome now found herself mistress of an empire which included the whole peninsula of Italy and provinces so remote as Spain, Africa, and Macedonia" [36]. This implied that the political and social balance of the Republic would be endangered by unexpected upheavals. And such upheavals did not fail to occur.

In the third century B.C. Rome enjoyed a period of social rest. But this did not last long. Wealth in these centuries mainly meant landed property; rich plebeians were rich because they were great landowners. In this way a new class came into being, that of the 'nobiles', composed of patrician and plebeian landowners, a kind of new aristocracy, the 'nobilitas', with its own vested interests. These nobles saw themselves as lawfully entitled to occupy all the important offices in the state, to the exclusion of everybody else. It should be noted that the conquest of Italy was not the work of the old aristocratic power-élite but of the nobility, that is of the leading patrician and plebeian clans together [37].

The nobles not only looked down upon but even tried to shut out upstarts, the 'homines novi', who did not belong to their circle but who nevertheless had the cheek to aspire to an office. However, they did not always succeed in keeping the door shut on such undesirable persons, as the example of such famous men like Cato and Cicero, both 'homines novi', proves. So the old dualistic distinction between patricians and plebeians was replaced by that of nobles and non-nobles, especially the ambitious 'homines novi', a distinction that was based on capital. Later this distinction too disappeared since the emperors did not favour the nobles [38].

After the Second Punic War the balance got disturbed even more. Italy had always been a land of small farmers. But the great landowners I mentioned above had become rich by buying the small plots of the farmers and combining them into large domains, the so-called 'latifundia'. Since this usually implied a change from crop growing to pasturage, the traditional farmer became superfluous. They flocked to Rome (and other Italian cities) hoping to find work there. But there was no work. There was, materially, no equivalent to the industries of Manchester and Chicago that absorbed the agrarian masses of the nineteenth century. These unemployed presented an acute problem.

The place of these farmers in the countryside was taken by slaves, mostly prisoners of war. They had to work the land and tend the herds for the absentee landlords. Badly housed, badly fed, and badly treated by the overseers, they had a far from enviable fate. The social fabric of Rome was, therefore, threatened from two sides : by the unemployed in Rome and other towns, and by the discontented masses of slaves in the countryside (there were enough slaves to form a large army, if someone were to take the lead). The discontent of the unemployed in Rome aggravated the already existing tension between nobles and non-nobles which now became, to a large extent, a new tension between haves and have-nots.

11. The crisis of the Republic

a. The preponderance of the senatorial class

The politics of the Roman Empire were almost exclusively in the hands of the senatorial class, in particular of those of the nobility. The opposition between this class and the other sections of Roman society grew steadily sharper. The senators were the experts on imperial affairs, while the commercial middle class and still more the artisans, shopkeepers, and small farmers felt ill at ease with the affairs of Spain and Macedonia, with the result that the comitia were steadily losing influence. There was as yet no one-man rule but there was certainly one-class rule. The senatorial families provided the members of the Senate and filled almost all the posts of the magistracy. It became increasingly difficult and almost impossible for a 'homo novus', however wealthy and influential he might be, to become, for instance, a consul. This meant that all the important state functions were the apanage of senatorial families. In a political respect Rome was an oligarchy.

The dividing line with the knights, the equestrian class, became evermore well-defined. The equites, being virtually excluded from political leadership, turned to commercial affairs and in this way became a class of capitalists. They traded with all parts of the Empire, they were the possessors of mines and industries, they were also great landowners. Rome never became an industrial city, but, instead, the financial and commercial centre par excellence.

b. Revolution as the alternative

"The crisis which obtained in the state and society of the Romans since the Second Punic War, was not recognized in its significance by the Roman politicians for a long time" [39]. They were blinded by external successes and driven by their imperial ambitions, they had no time to spare for internal reform. After all, the organization of the Republic functioned tolerably well. All the same, in view of the growing social tensions, a reform was urgently necessary. But, as Joseph Vogt maintains, since the aristocratic form of government was still firmly entrenched in Roman life, this reform could only come from the nobility. The alternative was revolution [40].

12. Tiberius Gracchus

a. Youth and education of the Gracchi

The first attempt to reform Roman society came, indeed, from members of the nobility; it was initiated by two brothers, Tiberius and Gaius Gracchus, who belonged to the noble family of the Sempronii [41]. The two Gracchi were related to the outstanding families of Rome; their mother Cornelia was a daughter of Scipio Africanus, and a niece of Aemilius Paullus, the victor of Pydna. Of all the twelve children of Cornelia and her husband Tiberius Gracchus [42], only three survived, our two brothers and their sister Sempronia. Having become a widow when still young, Cornelia devoted her time to the upbringing of her sons. She became the paragon of Roman education [43]. She raised her boys with such meticulous care that Plutarch could say that they owed their virtues more to education than to nature [44]. Her system of education seems to have been a blend of Hellenic paideia and a training in the traditional Roman virtues [45]. We cannot say how great Cornelia's influence on her sons was exactly, but that she influenced them is certain. Cicero who had read her now lost letters, said that "it appeared that they were reared rather on their mother's discourse than on their mother's milk" [46].

b. Tiberius' entry into political life

Tiberius, who was ten years older than Gaius, had his first experience of Roman life in 146 B.C., when his brother-in-law Scipio Aemilianus took him to the siege of Carthage. There, barely fifteen years old, he distinguished himself by his courage; according to Plutarch, he was the first on the wall during the storming of the Megara quarter [47]. His first public assignment came in 137 B.C., when he became quaestor; he accompanied the consul to Spain where the Numantines had to be combated. On his voyage thither, when travelling through Etruria, he saw the deserted farmsteads. Once in Spain, he did not acquire a particularly flattering idea of the Roman legionaries [48]. He realized that reforms were necessary. In the Senate of which he was a member, he belonged to the reform party under the leadership of Appius Claudius [49].

What greatly upset Tiberius Gracchus was the decline in Rome's fighting power and, in consequence, of her political might. Speaking of the Italian race, he lamented that "a people so valiant in war, and related in blood to the Romans, were declining little by little into pauperism and paucity of numbers without any hope of remedy" [50]. It must be understood that Italy had always been the great reservoir of recruits for the Roman armies. But now the disinherited peasants had gone to Rome and other cities to live idle lives there. It was no use, said Tiberius, to replace them by the slaves who were now working the land; these were "useless in war and never faithful to their masters" [51].

c. The Lex Sempronia agraria

Tiberius' great chance came in 133 B.C., when he was elected tribune of the people [52]; the right to introduce laws was connected with this function. He immediately took the offensive by proposing a law forbidding everybody to hold more than 125 hectares (= ca 290 acres) of the public domain; two sons of a landowner could possess another 125 hectares each, but no family was entitled to more than 1000 hectares (= 2470 acres) [53]. This implied that the great landowning families had to cede a lot of land. An additional clause forbade owners to sell their land. The land that would be at the state's disposal again, was to be allotted in small parcels to Roman paupers whom Tiberius hoped to make into free peasants in this way, and probably in the first place into reliable soldiers. "What Gracchus had in mind in propagating the measure was not money, but men", stated Appian succinctly, and he added quotations from Tiberius' introductory speech to the same effect. He asked "whether a citizen was not worthy of more consideration at all times than a slave; whether a man who served in the army was not more useful than one who did not; and whether one who had a share in the country was not more likely to be devoted to the public interest" [54]. This is the so-called Lex Sempronia agraria [55]. A state commission of three members was to be appointed to control the redivision of the public domain [56].

d. Roman society split

The rousing speech with which the tribune introduced his law proved how deeply the Roman citizens were divided against one another. "The wild beasts roaming over Italy have at least their layers, their nests, and their holes to which they can retire. But the men who fought and died for her (Italy) have nothing whatsoever, no more than light and air; they are constrained to wander about with their wives and children, without shelter and without homes where they can find lodgings. Their commanders", Tiberius continued, "lie when they, to encourage the legionaries, admonish them to fight valiantly for the tombs, the temples, and the altars of themselves and their forefathers. For there is not one out of so many poor Roman citizens who could show a home altar or a sepulchral monument of his ancestors. Instead, those poor people go to the war to fight for the pleasures, the riches, and the superfluity of others. And they are falsely called lords and possessors of the inhabited world, although they have not an inch of ground to call their own" [57].

Tiberius' Lex agraria split Roman society from top to bottom, between those who possessed land and those who were landless. It should not surprise us that this happened so suddenly. In fact, it was not so sudden. Roman society was fundamentally unstable. The first paragraphs of this chapter have described the long and acrimonious struggle between patricians and plebeians. This struggle ended with conferring full political rights on the plebeians. The fragile equilibrium that had been attained in this way was not long afterwards disturbed, because another social opposition appeared on the scene, that between capitalists, mainly the great landowners, as described above, and the have-nots, the 'proletarians', the people who possessed nothing but their 'proles', their offspring. The difference with the inital situation of the plebeians is that, whereas these had no political rights, the proletarians were full Roman citizens who, in consequence, could vote for Gracchus' proposal. Which they did.

e. Internal dualism

In Volume X we have studied Rome's imperialistic policy throughout the ages; we have seen how the Roman Empire came into being. In Chapter I of that volume I have characterized this policy as dualistic. Rome denied the right of independent existence, and not rarely, the right of existence tout court, to all other peoples. It was always 'them or us' and 'all or nothing' ('winner takes all'), which led to great cruelty, callousness, and utter ruthlessness in the execution in this policy. May we expect that these hard and tough power politicians would handle the social problems of Rome in a spirit of harmony? That they would carefully strive after balance and equilibrium? It does not seem probable, and it did not happen. The turmoil roused by the introduction of the Lex agraria marked the beginning of a long century of bloody civil strife which led to the end of the Republic and the introduction of one-man rule.

What was to come is described by Appian in the following terms which I shall quote in full. "The sword was never carried into the assembly, and there was no civil butchery, until Tiberius Gracchus, while serving as tribune and bringing forward new laws, was the first to fall a victim to internal commotion; and with him many others, who were crowded together at the Capitol round the temple, were also slain. Sedition did not end with this abominable deed. Repeatedly the parties came into open conflict, often carrying daggers; and from time to time in the temples, or the assemblies, or the Forum, some tribune, or praetor, or consul, or candidate for these offices, or some person otherwise distinguished, would be slain. Unseemly violence prevailed almost constantly, together with shameful contempt for law and justice.

As the evil gained in magnitude, open insurrections and large warlike expeditions against their country were undertaken by exiles, or criminals, or persons contending against each other for some office or military command. There arose chiefs of factions quite frequently, aspiring to supreme power, some of them refusing to disband the troops entrusted to them by the people, others even hiring forces against each other on their own account without public authority. Whenever either side got first possession of the city, the opposition party made war nominally against their own adversaries, but actually against their country. They assailed it like an enemy's capital, and ruthless and indiscriminate massacres of citizens were perpetrated. Some were proscribed, others banished, property was confiscated, and prisoners were even subjected to excruciating tortures. No unseemly deed was left undone" [58].

This is the history of the civil wars in a nutshell. We can summarize it in a few words : Rome's internal policy assumed the same dualistic character its imperialistic policy had. The methods of imperial warfare were transferred to the scene of the interior. This is strongly accentuated by Appian's words that the opposing party treated Rome as 'the enemy's capital'.

f. The wealthy and the poor opposed

To return now to 133 B.C. and the proposed Lex agraria. In his speech Tiberius sharply delineated the social situation as it was then : on the one side the privileged class of wealthy and politically powerful landlords, on the other the disinherited class of powerless proletarians. Tiberius' proposal was extremely radical, and he himself was perhaps not tactful enough to steer it along the cliffs. "Believing that nothing more advantageous or admirable could happen to Italy, he took no account of the difficulties surrounding it" [59]. The proposal was "extremely disturbing to the rich", states Appian laconically. "They collected together in groups, and made lamentation, and accused the poor of appropriating the results of their tillage, their vineyards, and their dwellings ... All kinds of wailings and expressions of indignation were heard at once. On the other side were heard the lamentations of the poor - that they were being reduced from competence to extreme penury, and from that to childlessness, because they were unable to rear their offspring. They recounted the military services they had rendered, by which this very land had been acquired, and were angry they should be robbed of their share of the common property" [60]. Thus we see the two groups in Roman society bitterly and inimically opposing each other.

g. The bill debated in the popular assembly

Tiberius did not have his bill debated in the Senate for the obvious reason that he felt his colleagues would not pass it. He went straight to the concilium plebis, the popular assembly, with it. If he had hoped to have a walk-over there, he was wrong. The senators, who were also the big 'possessores', had, scheming behind the scenes, won over one of the tribunes to their side, a young man of twenty, Marcus Octavius. They hoped he was ready to veto the bill (which was the right of a tribune). Tiberius, 'an illustrious man, eager for glory', introduced his bill to the assembly and defended it warmly [61].

The good news spread all over the country-side, with the result that the second meeting was packed. From near and far people came flocking in [62]. "The crowds poured into Rome from the country like rivers into the all receptive sea", writes Diodorus, "buoyed with the hope of effecting their own salvation, since the law (the Lex agraria) was their leader and ally, and their champion a man subject neither to favour nor to fear" [63]. But not all of those present were partisans of Tiberius. By no means! Landowners came who felt their possessions threatened. "The newcomers took sides with their respective factions ... and exasperated against each other kindled considerable disturbances ..., some intending to prevent its (the law's) enactment by all means, and others to enact it at all costs" [64]. Diodorus, who writes that the parties clashed violently, describes the commotion in the assembly as 'billowing forms and patterns like waves of the sea' [65].

When Tiberius had delivered that rousing speech to which I have alluded, Octavius rose to veto the bill; he did so reluctantly, because he was a personal friend of Tiberius, but he stood under great pressure by the Senate [66]. This was a very threatening move, since a veto by only one tribune blocked a proposal. By every means Tiberius tried to persuade his friend to witdraw his veto, but when he did not succeed in this, he declared that he was ready to suspend all public business and prevent all public expenditure [67], which was within the power of a tribune. With his own seal he sealed the doors of the temple of Saturnus where the public treasury was kept, to prevent the quaestors from touching the money [68]. The senators showed how deeply they felt injured by going about in mourning-attire. Tiberius on his part prepared himself for the worst by carrying a short sword under his toga [69]. Enough to show how high tension ran already.

h. The bill passed

When an attempt at mediation by two senators had failed [70], the decision was left to the concilium plebis. On the voting day Tiberius began by proposing to depose Octavius as tribune on the ground that he had acted against the popular interest. All thirty-five tribes voted in favour of this proposal. After this nothing could prevent the passing of the Lex Sempronia agraria [71]. Appian says that Octavius slipped away unobserved [72], but Plutarch has it that Tiberius ordered one of his freedmen to drag him from the tribunal. Then a furious mob rushed upon the young man trying to molest him. Some rich people rescued him by linking their arms around him and spirited him away. The mob cooled its fury on one of his servants who was blinded - all much to the distress of Tiberius [73]. These were the first blows in the civil wars.

j. The implementation of the Lex agraria

The next step was the appointment (by the concilium plebis) of a commission of three men who would redivide the ager publicus; they were Tiberius himself, his brother Gaius (who was serving in Spain under Scipio Aemilianus at that time), and his father-in-law Appius Claudius [74]. "The election of Claudius", says Stockton, "is significant, in that it shows that the princeps senatus himself in effect publicly set his imprimatur on the law, and hence too by implication on the bypassing of the body whose doyen he was and on the deposition of Octavius" [75]. Appian says that the people feared that nothing would come of the reparcelling of the land if the family of the Gracchi did not take the execution of the law into their own hands. "Tiberius became immensely popular by reason of the law and was escorted home by the multitude as though he were the founder, not of a single city or race, but of all the nations of Italy ... The defeated ones ... talked the matter over, feeling aggrieved, and saying that as soon as Gracchus should become a private citizen, he would be sorry that he had done injury to the sacred and inviolable office of tribune (i.e. by the deposition of Octavius - F.) and had sown in Italy so many seeds of civil strife" [76]. It is a moot point, indeed, whether or not the deposition of a tribune was legally defensible [77].

The Senate tried to sabotage the work of the commission by refusing to pay for its expenses [78]. This irritated the people; the temperaature rose still higher when all of a sudden a client of Tiberius died. Immediately rumours were rife that he had been poisoned by the rich. Tiberius clad himself in mourning-garb and recommended his wife and children to the people as though he already despaired of his life [79]. Just at this juncture it became known in Rome that the deceased king of Pergamum, Attalus III, had bequeathed his kingdom and his treasures to the populus romanus [80]. Tiberius at once saw his chance. On his proposal the assembly decided to divide the Attalid money among the poor citizens so that they would have a small capital to buy the necessary implements for their work on their newly acquired land. What was, however, really revolutionary is that Tiberius was of the opinion that the people should decide on the fate of the Greek cities which were under the sway of Pergamum [81]. This meant nothing less than that Tiberius wanted to transfer the political leadership of the Empire from the Senate to the concilium plebis. We can understand how much the senators hated him for all this [82].

k. A senatorial coup

In the summer of 133 B.C. the moment arrived for the election of new tribunes. Tiberius who desired very much to stay in office, lobbied right and left, but in order to thwart him it was contended that the same man could not hold the office twice in succession [83]. His enemies took recourse to the very effective expedient of accusing him of aspiring after kingship [84]. Hadn't the Pergamene sent him a royal diadem of King Attalus and a purple mantle [85]? Some observers must have felt a vague premonition that the Republic was heading towards one-man rule.

The voting day on the Capitoline hill went by in such incredible confusion that it is impossible to present an exact account of what happened. "Tiberius had beforehand communicated to them (his partisans) a signal to be displayed if there were need for fighting" [86]. When Tiberius appeared in the assembly, a great shout of enthusiasm arose from his adherents who thronged around him in order to protect him if need be [87]. Voting began but had soon to be stopped enough as opponents of Tiberius tried to make their way through the multitude to the centre where the voting took place [88].

While this disturbance went on, the Senate was in session. Nasica, the pontifex maximus, urged the consul to save the state by killing the tyrant, Tiberius, that is. The consul refused, saying that if the tribune was wrong, he should first have a trial. Nasica flew into a rage, wound the borders of his toga around his head, made many senators do the same, and departed with them to the Capitoline hill, surrounded by their armed clients. They dealt out blows left and right, so that people fled before them, tumbling over one another in their panic [89].

When the senatorial band entered the assembly, Tiberius' adherents did not fight them, overawed as they were by the sight of these august persons [90]. The assailants made short work of the assembly. They broke up all the furniture, and what was worse, killed more than three hundred citizens. One of these was Tiberius. His body, together with those of all the others, was thrown into the Tiber [91]. "This was the first rebellion among the citizens of Rome", concludes Plutarch, "that ended in murder and bloodshed, since the kings had been chased away" [92]. And blood would continue to flow for a century.

1. The aftermath

Some of the supporters of Tiberius were executed on the orders of the Senate, among them his teacher Diophanes, and also a certain Caius Billius who was enclosed in barrel filled with serpents and vipers. The Senate also resorted to a device that would become extremely popular in the next decades. Adherents of the unlucky tribune were banished from Rome without form of process [93]. When Scipio Aemilianus, who was in Spain beleaguering Numantia, heard what had happened to his brother-in-law Tiberius, he coined this epitaph for him : "So perish all others who do such things!" [94]. The conclusion of Bernstein is that "the sentiment on Scipio's lips must also have been in the hearts of the great majority of those who controlled politics in Rome" [95].

13. A 'doubtful truce'

Although the land-owning class had now dualistically and successfully disposed of the Tiberian faction - for the landlords it obviously was a question of 'either them or us' -, the process of the redistribution of the ager publicus went on. So it might seem that Tiberius was postumously victorious. However, it was a 'doubtful truce' [96]. The agrarian commission had no easy task. "A great number of embarassing law-suits sprang up", writes Appian who describes at length the litigation that was the result of the reparcelling of the land [97]. An additional problem was that land had to be reclaimed from the Italian allies who, of course, protested loudly; they chose Scipio Aemilianus, who now, in 129 B.C. was back from Spain and who was elected consul, to be their advocate [98].

We know already that he was no great admirer of the Lex Sempronia, but he dared not attack it openly; instead, he insisted on the great difficulties in its execution [99]. When he was imprudent enough to tell the concilium plebis that Tiberius "had been justly slain if his purpose had been to seize the government", he was booed by the whole assembly. He then made a revealing retort. "How can I, who have so many times heard the battle shout of the enemy without feeling fear, be disturbed by the shouts of men like you, to whom Italy is only a stepmother?" [100].

The great internal problem of the Republic was that it always comprised dualistically opposed classes of the population : in the first half of its existence the patricians and the plebeians, in the second half the optimates (the best!) and the proletarians. For the ruling class the second one hardly counted. Scipio doubtless expressed the sentiment of his social group : that Mother Rome had children and stepchildren, that inside her walls there lived authentic Romans and rabble. The once so popular Scipio, the destroyer of Carthage and Numantia, became the object of popular hatred; he was accused of being "determined to abolish the law of Gracchus utterly and for that end was about to inaugurate armed strife and bloodshed" [101]. When, shortly afterwards (we are in 129 B.C.), Scipio was found dead in his bed one morning, it was instantly rumoured that he had been murdered by his enemies [102].

The process of the redivision of the ager publicus had now virtually come to a stop so that "the populace, who had been so long in the hope of acquiring land, became disheartened" [103]. How the optimates thought of the presence of so many 'stepchildren' in Rome was demonstrated in 126 B.C. by a proposal of the tribune M. Junius Pennus that all non-Romans should be expelled from the imperial city. 'Rome for the Romans!', seems to have been his motto. Since he died soon afterwards, nothing came of his bill. Cicero found it inhuman : "to debar foreigners (these foreigners were mostly Italian allies - F.) from enjoying the advantages of the city is contrary to the laws of humanity" [104].

14. Gaius Gracchus

a. His leading idea

In 124 B.C. Gaius Gracchus, ten years younger than his brother Tiberius, came to the fore. Although he was not yet thirty, he had already seen fourteen years of service outside the capital, twelve as a soldier in Spain and two as quaestor in Sardinia [105]. Once back in Rome, he soon showed how great an orator he was, so powerful that, according to Cicero, he would not have found his equal, had he lived long enough [106]. When he entered the city after his return from Sardinia, "the populace thronged around him ... and greeted him with acclamations and applause : such was his extreme popularity with the common people" [107]. They saw in him Tiberius redivivus.

    As Heinz Bellen wrote : "Gaius Gracchus was, even more deeply than his brother, convinced that the power of the Senate had to be broken, should the state regain its balance" [108]. In his opinion the preponderance of the Senate made the political fabric lop-sided. The idea alone was sufficient to make the senators panick. Cicero makes one of them, C. Laelius Sapiens, who had been a close friend of Scipio Aemilianus, say that it would mean the absolute separation of the people from the Senate, if questions of the highest political order were to decided by the people [109]. The reader should keep in mind that, constitutionally, all political decisions had to be taken by the senatus populusque romanus, that is, not alone by the Senate. Gaius himself took his distance from the senatorial class by saying that "very wicked men had killed his brother Tiberius" [110]. There is no doubt that he hated the senatorial class most heartily.

b. Feverish legislative activity

When Gaius became tribune of the people in 124 B.C., two years of legislative activity began, so frantic as the Republic had never seen before [111]. The first of his measures was probably the Lex frumentaria, the grain law. Its purpose was to make a regular supply of grain available for Roman citizens at fixed prices [112]. We are not very well informed about this law, but it seems that the grain price was not only fixed but also kept low, since Appian says that the distribution was made at the public expense. Tiberius enemies did not see it as the social measure it was meant to be but as a ruse to cajole the people and as a means of playing a trick on the Senate (the great landowners were interested in high grain prices).

Cicero saw a massive hand-out of public money in it [113]. An indignant senator protested that he did not want to have his goods divided among the rank and file [114]. Cicero also wrote that the law greatly pleased the people since they had to eat without having to work for it; right-minded persons (the 'boni', the 'good') were against the law because it would make the plebs lazy; he complains that there will always be an opposition between the popular appetite and the political wisdom of the rulers [115]. All this goes to show how deep the cleavages ran in Roman society. But Gaius retorted that "what for us (the nobles) is a demonstration of wealth is for them (the people) a necessity" [116]. The Lex frumentaria was placed on the statute-book indeed, and although Gaius was certainly genuine in his care for the plebs, there can be no doubt that he won much popular support by it.

We cannot enumerate all the legal measures introduced by the indefatigable Gaius, but one of the most important must be mentioned, the Lex iudiciaria, the law for the judicature. It was an attempt to break the monopoly of the Senate in juridical matters. Last calls this 'the most famous achievement of Gracchus' [117]. What it did was to exclude members of the Senate from the juries and to replace them with 'equites', the knights, who were wealthy men but, as not belonging to the senatorial class, politically powerless. Up to that moment senators had sat in judgment over their peers which had led to scandalous acquittals. But from now on their crimes - above all the extortions in the provinces - would be judged by others, by men who were not friendly disposed towards senators and who were not their secret complices [118].

This law entailed a real shift of power. Appian (no admirer of Gaius Gracchus) epitomized the new situation in these words. "Having bought the plebeians as it were (i.e. by the Lex frumentaria), he began, by another like political manoeuvre, to court the equestrian order, who holds the middle place between the Senate and the plebeians ... It is said that soon after the passage of this law Gracchus remarked that he had broken the power of the Senate once and for all ... For this (law) ... exalted the knights to be rulers over them (the senators) and put senators on the level of subjects" [119]. Florus (no admirer either) stated that the Lex iudiciaria had changed the homogeneous Roman state into a two-headed one [120]. But it is only possible to speak of a unified state if one, were to identify the interests of the state with those of the governing class. This, of course, was precisely the attitude of the senatorial class. In reality the social and political situation had always been utterly dualistic with the division of Roman society into the powerful and the powerless.

c. Gaius loses ground

In 122 B.C., during his second term as tribune, Gaius proposed the so-called 'Lex de sociis et nomine latino', the law on the allies and the Latin name. Appian's report on this law is probably the most accurate. Gaius proposed to give the Latin allies full Roman citizenship; up to this time the Latins had only the right of suffrage (the ius Latii), the right to vote, if only they happened to be in Rome on a voting day. To the other Italian allies Gaius would not grant full citizenschip but, instead, the right of suffrage. Appian suggests that this extension of the voting rights would help him "in the enactment of laws which he had in contemplation" [121].

Once again the senators became greatly alarmed; they feared to be confronted with a solid block of opposition to their might, consisting of the knights and the people. They issued a decree that "nobody who does not possess the right of suffrage shall stay in the city or approach within five miles of it while voting is going on concerning these laws" [122]. Plutarch remarks that it was a very strange thing that all non-Romans, even allies and confederates, had to leave Rome for some days [123]. The senators also persuaded one of the tribunes, M. Livius Drusus, to interpose his veto to these laws without giving his reasons for this.

Gaius Gracchus was now losing ground. There seems to have existed no great enthusiasm among the plebs for this extension of voting rights, while yet another measure of his bred bad blood. His idea was to establish a colony where Carthage had once stood, to be called Junonia. This project was impopular, first because Scipio had cursed the site and forever devoted it to sheep-pasturage, and secondly because the proposed six thousand colonists were to come from all over Italy instead of from Rome only. Gaius went to Africa himself, together with his friend Fulvius Flaccus, another tribune, in order to lay out the site, but it was soon rumoured in Rome that all kinds of evil omens were observed there [124]. So when Livius Drusus proposed to found twelve new colonies on Italian soil, the Roman people turned away from Gaius [125].

Caius Fannius, one of the consuls of that year, incited the concilium plebis against Gaius by asking them how much room would be left for their games and festivals, when the Latins were given full Roman citizenship [126]. The result of all this agitation was that Gaius Gracchus was not reelected tribune for the year 121; he had fallen from the favour of the plebs and was now a private citizen [127]. His enemies laughed but he said, ominously and mysteriously, that they did not know how deeply his actions had enveloped them in darkness [128].

The confused and overheated political situation would in former times have induced the Senate to appoint a dictator, but this august body had no wish now to be overruled by an autocrat; such an appointment would have signified that it was unable to cope with the situation. Therefore, it "preferred to meet special dangers by giving special instructions to ordinary magistrates" [129]. Such makeshift measures show that the constitutional fabric of the Roman Republic was tottering.

d. The Senate hits back

Opimius was now consul, and under his leadership part of Gaius' legislation was effectively demolished. Plutarch expressly states that his opponents tried to provoke him into violent action so that they would have a reason to kill him [130]. Gaius was imprudent enough to provide himself with an armed body-guard and to appear with his partisans on the Capitoline hill [131]. In this feverish atmosphere a nasty incident was almost inevitable. A sergeant of the consul, a plebeian named Antyllius (or Antyllus), tried to make his way through the throng of Gaius' adherents, using, so it seems, insulting words. In the ensuing brawl he was killed. The next day friends of Opimius placed the naked corpse just in front of the Senate House; passers-by could witness the extra-ordinary spectacle of the haughty senators streaming out of the building and mourning the death of a simple plebeian. But this did not help them at all, for the plebs, sensing what was coming, now veered back to Gaius, 'the only remaining protector and defender of the people' [132].

When the Senate ordered Gaius and Flaccus to appear and justify themselves, they did not appear but, instead, resorted to violence. Or rather, Flaccus did, with Gaius following his lead only reluctantly. Plutarch says that, after a night of carousing, Flaccus, still intoxicated with wine, went to the Aventine hill with his armed band and occupied it [133]. Now the Aventine was the hill to which the plebeians had resorted repeatedly during their long conflict with the patricians; perhaps this explains why this site was chosen by Flaccus. The temple of Diana on the top became his fortified stronghold. What he and his party hoped to achieve was that the Senate would begin negotiations with them [134]. They were wrong! The Senate meant business.

Whether the 'senatusconsultum ultimum', the so-called 'ultimate decree' [135], was issued before the occupation of the Aventine or immediately after is not known, but issued it was. With this decree the Senate ordered the consul L. Opimius to defend the state from harm [136]. The Senate, said Cicero, defended the state with words, Opimius with arms [137]. It was left to the consul to act as he saw fit [138].

Opimius told the senators to arm themselves and ordered the knights (who, for once, were acting in unison with the Senate) to assemble the next morning at the temple of Castor and Pollux at the Capitol, each with two armed servants [139]. Flaccus attempted to negotiate by sending the youngest of his sons to the Senate, but Opimius demanded the surrender of the rebels [140]. Once again it was 'either them or us'; the Senate dubbed Gaius' party 'tyrants' [141]. When Flaccus sent his son a second time to the Senate House, Opimius had the boy arrested and ordered his men to attack [142]. It became an attack in due tactical form. Under the command of an experienced officer the men scaled the northern slope of the Aventine hill; Cretan archers created such havoc among the occupants on the top that they soon took to flight.

Flaccus tried to save himself in a bath-house but was killed there, together with his other son [143]. Gaius offered no resistance at all but fled to the temple of Minerva; there friends prevented him from taking his own life. He then descended the steep proclivity of the hill and reached the wooden Pons Sublicius on the Tiber. While two of his friends defended the entrance to the bridge, he safely got to the other side, accompanied by one of his slaves. Somewhat further he was either overtaken and killed or the slave killed his master at his request and afterwards himself [144].

e. The revenge

Plutarch wrote that Opimius, a very hard man [145], even although he was only a consul, usurped the power of a dictator [146]; it was yet another step on the road to one-man rule. When the severed head of Gaius Gracchus was brought to him, carried on the point of a javelin, he paid out its weight in gold to the bearer [147]. The younger son of Flaccus who was arrested before the fighting began and, therefore, had not taken part in it, was nevertheless killed too. The corpses of Flaccus and Gaius were thrown into the Tiber [148]; their houses were given over to the populace to be plundered [149]. Their goods were confiscated. The widows were forbidden to wear mourning, while the wife of Gaius was robbed of her income. The victors raged furiously among the adherents of Gaius (not all of them had defected from him) three thousand of whom were killed; all the corpses were thrown into the Tiber. The Senate, obviously believing that it had restored unity in the state, had a temple built on the Forum and dedicated it to Concordia [150]. All this happened in 121 B.C.

15. No solution

Although years of relative quiet followed the victory of the Senate, it was less complete than it thought. Opponents might have been killed, but the great social and constitutional problems remained. These were the problems of the unemployed, the unsatisfactory position of the Italian allies, and, most serious of all, the question whether the Senate was henceforward to dominate public life as it had done for centuries [151].

What was really at stake in the Roman Republic was this. The old opposition between patricians and plebeians, since long defunct, was gradually becoming replaced by that between optimates and populares, the nobility and the people. The first instalment of the fight between these two classes had been the conflict over the Gracchian reforms. We should not think of the leaders of the populares as democrats; the Gracchi, Caesar, and Augustus belonged to the nobility themselves, while Marius came from the equestrian class, although he voluntarily paraded as a man of the people [152].

"It was the doctrine of the Optimates that nobles alone should be regarded as eligible for the consulship : any man born outside this ring who essayed to rise on his merits to the highest magistracy was a homo novus, exposed to all the obstruction and petty resentment which are the inevitable lot of the social upstart. This was the issue over which the fight grew hottest." The opinion of the populares was that "candidates for office should be sought from the citizen-body as a whole, and magistracies should be conferred on the ablest men that could be found" [153].

16. Marius

a. His ascent to the top

In Volume X I have already written extensively about Marius [154]. Let me, therefore, shortly summarize the first part of his career. Caius Marius was a 'homo novus', born around 157 B.C. in a village near Arpinum (Arpino) in the valley of the Liri into an equestrian family. He was not connected with or related to the great noble families. He made his way upwards through serving as a professional soldier and officer. Capable as he was, he was elected to public offices, such as praetor and quaestor; later he was proconsul in Spain. He became important enough to marry a woman of high standing, Julia, an aunt of Julius Caesar. That he was reelected so often was the political effect of the fact that he was so successful as a general. "Marius' way to to the top started with the war against Jugurtha", which began in 111 B.C. The first phase of this war (11-109 B.C.) "went off without success and certainly without honour for Rome, because of the incompetence of the generals and soldiers" [155]. In 109 B.C. the far more able Metellus went to Africa as commander-in-chief, taking Marius with him as his legatus (second-in-command). Between them they restored discipline in the army and began to drive back Jugurtha.

This does not signify that the haughty nobleman Metellus and the homo novus Marius saw eye to eye. Quite the contrary! When Marius in 107 B.C. had gone to Rome and had been elected consul for the first time, he got also the command in Africa, and the embittered Metellus went home. Marius acquired the consulate on an anti-nobility ticket; he made most of the fact that he was a homo novus. He proved to be an excellent orator with a solid grip on the people. "The commons were so excited that all the artisans and farmers, whose prosperity and credit depended upon the labour of their own hands, left their work and attended Marius, regarding their own necessities as less important than his success. The result was the nobles were worsted and after the lapse of many years (to be exact, thirty-five years - F.) the consulship was given to a homo novus" [156].

It was by his own merits, Marius proclaimed, that the consulate had fallen to him; he had won it in the face of the cowardice and the luxury of the rich, who knew nothing of the art of war. What recommended him to the people were the bodily wounds he had received in the public service which he regarded with pride [157]. We see Marius here, consciously or unconsciously, accentuating the widening distance between the nobles and the people. This is proved by words of Sallust who wrote that "he attacked the aristocracy persistently and boldly, assailing now individuals and now the whole party" [158]. "Compare me, a homo novus, fellow-citizens, with those haughty nobles. What they know from hearsay and reading, I have either seen with my own eyes or done with my own hands. What they have learned from books, I have learned by service in the field ... They scorn my humble birth, I their worthlessness; I am taunted with my lot in life, they with their infamies", and so he went for a long time vilifying the nobles as much as he could [159]. No wonder that the nobles hated him [160]!

b. Animosity between Marius and Sulla

Marius went back to Africa and brought the Jugurthine War to a successful end (107-105 B.C.); on January 1, 104 B.C. he led the captive Numidian king triumphantly through the streets of Rome. However, it was not to Marius, but to Sulla, his quaestor, to whom Jugurtha was treacherously delivered by his African enemies. Sulla was imprudent enough to boast of this achievement as though it was he who had decided the African War [161]; he was fortified in this opinion by the opponents of Marius [162]. This, said Plutarch, "was the first cause of the pestilent and mortal enmity that there always existed between Marius and Sulla since then, an enmity that arose to destroy and ruin the city of Rome" [163]. It was also the first sign that the friction between parties or social groups was slowly but surely turning into a struggle between powerful individuals.

c. Marius' reform of the army

Marius' victory over Jugurtha was his first great military achievement. The second was the reform of the army. As I wrote in Vol. X [164], strange as it may sound, republican Rome had no army in the proper sense of the word; instead, it had a citizen-militia. Roman citizens were called up for military service as often as the need arose. And it arose very often! The militia-men stayed away from home for months, even for years, which they resented; they got no pay which made them so keen on plundering. Rome had neither professional officers nor a military academy; the art of war was learned by everybody in the field.

In view of the very broad assignments of the armies of the late Republic, it was urgently necessary that they should become professionalized. This was what Marius did. The militia-men of yore who, when all is said and done, were no more than amateurs, were replaced by professional soldiers recruited from the poor of Rome and Italy. The soldiers were paid, fed, and equipped by the state. Strictly speaking, the 'new model army' was not a standing army either, because the idea was that the legions were to be disbanded once a campaign was over. In practice, however, victorious generals preferred to keep their army together and house the troops in barracks in order to have them ready at hand.

As a consequence, a deep mutation took place in the Roman state. Luciano Perelli states that "the professionals were not deeply attached to the ancient constitutional order; they exchanged fidelity to the state for devotion to their commander ... with the result that the army became an autonomous political force in the period of the civil wars" [165]. It will be evident that ambitious generals who envisaged a political career now had a powerful instrument at their disposal. This was another milestone on the road to autocracy.

Marius proved his own worth and that of his new legions by successfully repulsing the attempts to invade Italy by the Germanic tribes of the Cimbri and Teutons in the years 102/101 B.C. [166]. In view of this imminent danger he was elected consul in 105 B.C. for the second time and was, contrary to the rules, reelected five times on end. We are coming ever closer to one-man rule.

d. Marius and his political helpers

After his final victory over the Germanic tribes in 101 B.C. Marius had become so powerful that he could do what he liked. In 100 B.C. he became consul for the sixth time. "But of statesmanship to match his generalship he showed not a spark" [167]. He left the struggle against the optimates largely in the hands of a real popularis, the ambitious, unscrupulous, and often dangerous demagogue L. Apuleius Saturninus who was tribune in 103 B.C. and again in 100 B.C. [168]. A second leader of the popular party was Cn. Servilius Glaucia who was fiercely anti-senatorial. Saturninus was a powerful orator; this earned him many adherents. He used his influence with the people to help Marius to the consulate in 102 B.C. [169]; he also sponsored measures for endowing Marius' veterans with land in North-Africa (to ingratiate himself with the soldiers, it is suggested) [170].

In 101 B.C. envoys of King Mithridates of Pontus arrived with their pockets full of money with which to bribe the senators. Although ambassadors were considered inviolable, Saturninus insulted them. In consequence, he was committed for trial before a court consisting of members of the senatorial class. It almost cost him his head. But he persuaded the public that "he was being made a victim of the Senate's partisanship in violation of justice, and pointed out that it was because of his concern for the common people that he was being treated in this way". On hearing this, the populace, present at the trial, assumed such a threatening attitude that the court hastened to acquit the accused. And once again the culprit was elected tribune [171].

e. Marius and Metellus

The reader will remember that not much love was lost between Marius and his former commander in Numidia, Metellus, whom he had replaced.

Metellus' colleagues, the optimates, saw in him the real victor of Jugurtha which coincided with his own idea of the events [172]. He had celebrated his triumph in 106 B.C. and had received the cognomen of 'Numidicus'. He knew that Saturninus was the man behind Marius; Metellus being censor in 102 B.C. [173], tried to evict him and Glaucia from the Senate 'on account of their disgraceful mode of life', but the other censor would not have it [174].

The year 100 B.C. saw a curious triumvirate with Marius as consul, Saturninus as tribune, and Glaucia as praetor. There was yet another candidate for the tribunate, a certain Nonnius, a nobleman who was an outspoken opponent of Saturninus and Glaucia. On leaving the comitia he was set upon by the worthy couple, who, together with a band of ruffians, chased him into an inn, and stabbed him there. Nobody dared call Saturninus to account since he was a tribune [175]. This shows that the quality of Roman public life was sinking to a very low level.

However, Metellus was a far more formidable enemy than this Nonnius. Working closely together [176], the three conspired against Metellus who was the figure-head of the optimates [177]. They set him a carefully prepared trap. In the concilium plebis, Saturninus brought forward a bill, yet another Lex agraria, stipulating that lands of the ager publicus should be redistributed; this was a move on Gracchian lines. However, an unusual clause was added to the effect that every senator had to take an oath that he would oberve what the people had resolved. In the Senate Marius first feigned that he opposed this strange trick, saying that no man in his senses should take this oath. Plutarch, no friend of the consul, wrote that for Marius lying well formed part of virtue and common sense. Marius made this remark because he knew that Metellus would not swear and that this would make the people see in him a mortal enemy. And indeed, Metellus declared that he was not prepared to take the desired oath. A few days later, when the law had been passed and the senators were summoned to swear it, Marius ascended the pulpit and among dead silence declared that he was ready to take the oath in order to obey the law. He was loudly applauded by the populace. All the other senators, terrified as they were, followed Marius' example. Only Metellus, in spite of the entreaties of his family and indifferent to the threats of Saturninus, remained adamant in his refusal. As a consequence, the refractory senator was banished from Rome. He went to Rhodes in order to devote himself to the study of philosophy [178].

f. Marius' political incompetence

The fact that Marius had to leave so much of the machinations to his perfectly unscrupulous stooge Saturninus proves that he was not sure of himself in the field of politics. Plutarch says that he did not show in the popular assembly the same audacity and constancy as he did in battle. Forced to cajole the people, he went against his own nature, since he had to play the gracious popularis. In fact, adds his biographer, this fearless general was afraid of the people [179].

The task of implementing the new Lex agraria fell to Marius. This law touched not only upon the ager publicus in Italy - the object of the Gracchi - but upon all the public lands in the newly acquired provinces, including those recently conquered by Marius in southern Gaul, and even the as yet unconquered Celtic territories north of the Alps. Mommsen believes that, had Marius succeeded, he could have been elected consul year after year and have thus become the 'monarch' of Rome as long as he lived [180]. But this would have asked for a far more able politician than he was. Marius' vacillations between the two classes of society are shown by the following incident. When in the night some optimates came to his house to complain of Saturninus, he let the tribune in through another door without the nobles knowing this. Marius commuted between them, excusing himself, each time that he disappeared, on the plea that he had bowel problems. The only result of this mediation was, says Plutarch, that the parties grew ever more irritated with each other [181]. It must be conceded that the execution of the agrarian law would have demanded superhuman political skill. Senators and knights, although not always seeing eye to eye, became allies in their opposition, because they felt injured in their vested interests, while the Romans were discontented with the fact that the Italians were to have equal rights with them [182].

g. Saturninus' party defeated

Things were coming to a head now. At the end of 100 B.C. Saturninus wanted to be reelected as tribune (which was against the law); at the same time he proposed his comrade Glaucia for the office of consul [183]. There was yet another candidate for this office, a certain Memmius, whose chances were better. The prospective consul and tribune hired a gang of ruffians who, before everyone's eyes, clubbed Memmius to death [184]. With this crime Saturninus overplayed his hand. He lost favour with the people who, according to Appian, wanted to kill him [185]; the comment of Orosius is that Senate and people of Rome trembled before such great evils in the Republic [186].

The Senate issued a senatusconsultum ultimum ordering the tribunes and the praetors to watch over the sovereign authority and the majesty of the populus romanus; they excepted Saturninus and Glaucia from this protection which virtually outlawed them. Citizens were armed, and the command was given to Marius [187]. So he had to fight his own complices. However, he had already taken his U-turn, because he had realized that he was in very bad company with these two. But Marius was not enthusiastic about this unexpected assignment. The party of Saturninus and Glaucia had entrenched itself on the Capitoline hill, but when their water-supply was cut off, they were forced to surrender. Hoping to save the lives of his former cronies, Marius shut them up in the Senate House. But members of the crowd climbed onto the roof and with tiles plucked from it stoned them to death; there were some other victims too [188].

"Very many others were swept out of existence", writes Appian, and he adds ruefully that "freedom, democracy, laws, reputation, official position, were no longer of any use to anybody"; even the office of tribune was no longer sacred and inviolable [189]. It goes without saying that, in 99

B.C., Metellus was recalled from exile [190], in spite of vehement opposition by Marius [191]. Marius found it better to disappear for some time from the Roman scene by paying a visit to Asia Minor [192]; he returned only in 97 B.C. [193]. And of course, not much came of the Lex agraria [194].

17. The Social War

a. The question of citizenship again

The victory of the senatorial class, of the optimates, was not so complete as it seemed. The constant delays in the solution of the social problem, that of the desperate situation of the paupers, only served to aggravate the discontent of the people. There was also constant friction and wrangling between the senatorial and equestrian classes. And not only the Roman plebs were disgruntled, the Italian allies too. They clamoured to acquire rights of citizenship in Rome. But in 95 B.C. the consuls of that year introduced a law preventing the allies from acquiring this right. Rome would pay dearly for this lack of generosity and gratitude : it turned the allies from friends into enemies [195].

The man who had proposed to grant Roman citizenship to the allies was the tribune M. Livius Drusus. In 91 B.C. he fell a victim to an assassin in his home on the Palatine hill; "a shoemaker's knife was found thrust into his hip" [196]. His proposal, says Florus, had split Roman society into two camps, one for, one against, but in spite of his death, the allies "went on demanding the execution of the promises of Drusus" [197]. "In him the allies lost their last hope of reaching a peaceful settlement of their differences with Rome, and now the issue was committed to the final arbitrament of war" [198].

b. A clash inevitable

Guessing correctly that something was brewing among the allies, the Senate sent out agents to investigate [199]. The expected revolt broke out in

Asculum (Ascoli Piceno). A Roman praetor, C. Servilius, got wind that the citizens of this town were taking preparatory measures; in order to prevent this, he addressed them with menacing words, whereupon they killed him, and not only him, but every Roman in town [200]. Immediately many allied towns and nations took up arms against Rome, the Picenians, the Marsi, the Samnites, the Apulians, the Lucanians ... [201]. They all, says Florus ruefully, "rose against Rome, their mother and nurse". He makes the critical remark that the people that was the arbiter of kings and nations was incapable of governing itself, with the result that, although victorious in Europe and Asia, Rome was now attacked by Corfinium (which became the capital of the insurgents - F.) [202]. The war that now began is called the Italian War or the Social War to attenuate its odious character, writes Florus, but, this same author adds, it really was civil war [203].

c. The war with the allies

The rebels, as stated above, made Corfinium, renamed Italia or Italica (no longer existing), into the capital of their confederacy [204]. That the Italians meant business is shown by the special coins minted by the confederacy : they showed the Italian bull goring the Roman wolf [205]. Another token of their strength of purpose was that they mobilized an army of a hundred thousand men, most of them trained soldiers who had seen service in the Roman army.

The rebellion raged fiercest in the central part of Italy. There it had two points of focus : the region of the Marsi just east of Rome, and the Samnite country more to the south-east. In the first phase of the war everything went wrong, although the Romans who could count on the Latins and some other nations that had not joined the rebellion, were numerically superior [206]. Twice, in 90 and 89 B.C., a consul was defeated and slain [207]. In Rome the males laid aside their civilian clothing and went about in military garb [208]. Meanwhile, the revolt spread further, especially in the south.

But, says Florus, "the great Fortuna of the Roman people, always greater in adversity, rose once again in all her vigour" [209]. "Pompeius (Strabo, the father of Pompey the Great - F.), Sulla, and Marius restored the tottering power of the Roman people" [210]. The rebellious nations were attacked one by one. The counter-attacking Romans were not fastidious in the choice of their methods; "they made a general devastation by flames and iron", massacring many. In a revealing passage Florus tells us that there was no end of massacring until Pompeius had destroyed Asculum in 89 B.C. and thus "brought a sacrifice to the Manes (the spirits of the dead) of so many armies and consuls and to the gods of so many pillaged cities - a sacrifice that could at least propitiate them" [211]. Dualistic in thought and action as the Romans were, throughout the whole history of the Republic, they were unable to think of a political solution except in terms of a holocaust.

18. The Senate under fire

Although the rebellion was nearing its end now, the situation of the senatorial class, responsible as it was for its outbreak, was far from comfortable. It was sheer good luck that Mithridates VI of Pontus who was fighting the Romans successfully in Asia Minor, rejected a request by the rebels to come and help them [212]. Then there was still the risk that Etruria would join the rebellion [213]. Finally, one of the tribunes, Q. Varius Hybrida, introduced a law that was directed against all those who were somehow involved in or were known to sympathize with the cause of the Italian allies. The precise aim of this law is not known but doubtless its purpose was "to bring to judgment all those with whose help the allies had taken up arms against the Roman people" [214]. The real aim is revealed by Appian. "The knights ... persuaded Quintus Varius to bring forward a law to prosecute those who should, either openly or secretly, aid the Italians to acquire citizenship [215], hoping thus to bring all the senators under an odious indictment, and themselves to sit in judgment over them, and that when they (the senators) were out of the way they themselves (the knights) would be more powerful than ever in the government of Rome". The proposal met with heavy opposition, but when other tribunes threatened to veto it, they saw themselves surrounded by armed knights [216]. By now, the use of violence had become quite a normal occurrence in Roman public life.

It will be clear that the Lex Varia was to serve as a political weapon against the Senate and its power monopoly. The great majority of the Senate had been, in fact, just as much against Drusus' proposal as Varius Hybrida and his cronies. But this consideration did not carry any weight; any stick to beat the dog would do. The situation has analogies with the one that arose after the attack on Hitler on July 22, 1944, when his 'Gewitteraktion' not only hit those who were directly involved but also countless others who had no idea of the conspiracy but were supposed to be opposed to the regime. As soon as the law was enacted the processes began. Many important optimates were indicted. Many were banished; others went into exile of their own accord [217].

19. The citizenship extended

The Senate had now come under such a heavy barrage that it began to take the measures it should have taken before the Social War began. At the end of 90 B.C. full Roman citizenship was accorded to those allies who had not taken part in the revolt or had laid down arms at an early stage [218]; the Senate also authorized commanders in the field to extend citizenship to non-Roman contingents that had shown exemplary courage [219]. A second law was passed in 89 B.C. that gave full civic rights to all those who lived in federate towns, had been resident in Italy at the time of its enactment, and had registered in Rome with the praetor peregrinus within sixty days [220]. A third law of the same year gave full citizenship to the non-Roman Celts south of the Po, in Gallia Cisalpina Cispadana. The practical result of these laws was that all the inhabitants of Italy were Roman citizens now with equal rights - although, if they wanted to vote, they had to travel to Rome. The number of Roman citizens almost trebled to about nine hundred thousand [221].

There was, however, a restriction that must have dissatisfied the new citizens. "Rome's conduct may seem generous, even if dictated by expediency" [222], but there was a snake in the grass. The Senators had not the intention to change the fabric of power. Rome was not a democracy; the Roman political system did not know universal suffrage, there was no voting per head. Voting in the comitia went per tribe. The word 'tribus' does not denote an ethnic entity, as though the populus romanus were composed of different nations; it indicated a territorial division. The total number of tribes being thirty-five since 241 B.C., there were four of them in Rome herself and thirty-one 'rustici', that is, in the country (Roman colonies); through the tribes taxes were raised and soldiers levied. Since voting went per tribe, there were thirty-five votes in the concilium plebis [223].

The new Italian, Greek, and Celtic citizens were all inscribed in the existing tribes, no new ones being created. But they were not distributed evenly; rather, they were concentrated into only four tribes. This meant that the new citizens were unable to exercize their rights in a proportionate way. "So it often happened", concluded Appian, "that their vote was useless ...; (this) became the source of a new conflict" [224]. The oligarchy that ruled Rome since times immemorial could feel at ease.

We should, however, not overlook the positive side of the extension of the citizenship. It made Italy into some sort of unified state in which all citizens enjoyed equal rights; they all were members now of the civitas romana. "All citizens", thought Cicero, "henceforward had two fatherlands, one by nature (= the birthplace) and one of the civitas (= Rome)" [225]. This instilled such a strong sense of unity into the nations of Italy, that it never fell totally into abeyance, not even in the long centuries of political fragmentation that followed on the dissolution of the Western Roman Empire. The present Italian Republic is, in the last resort, the product of this sentiment.

NOTES TO CHAPTER I

1. Vol. X, Ch. II.11.
2. Livy 1.8.7.
3. Dion.Hal. 2.9.1; Mitchell, Patricians 2.
4. Mitchell, Patricians 4.
5. Dion.Hal. 2.8.1.
6. Dion.Hal. 2.9.3.
7. Dion.Hal. 2.10.1-2.
8. Mitchell, Patricians 5.
9. Scullard, History 65.
10. Livy 1.47.7; Dion.Hal. 4.25.1 en 40.3.
11. Dion.Hal. 4.42.5.
12. Dion.Hal. 4.43.1.
13. Livy 2.9.5-6.
14. Livy 2.21.6.
15. Livy 2.31.
16. Grant, History 63.
17. Some historians doubt whether this event really took place.
18. Livy 2.32.
19. Livy 2.33.1-3. Scullard, History 85, writes : "The origin of the tribuni plebis is obscure; they were not created by the secession of 494, but are to be explained by the growth of the tribal system".
20. Livy 3.54.11-15.
21. Mommsen, Röm.Staatsrecht II.1, 276; on p. 277 he spoke of the tribunate as a 'revolutionäre Gegenmagistratur'.
22. Livy 2.44.9.
23. Livy 3.55.7.
24. Livy 3.33-57. But this too is debatable matter. "No legal code known as the Twelve tables was ever publicly displayed at Rome, in bronze or in wood", writes Mitchell, Patricians 125. Reading such a glib statement I wonder whether the author might have had the opportunity to walk about in early Rome.
25. Livy 3.34.6.
26. Grant, Hist. 65.

27.	Grant, Hist. 65.
28.	Grant, Hist. 67.
29.	Livy 4.6.3; Mitchell, Patricians 127/128.
30.	See for this passage Horst/Günther, Röm.Gesch. 50.
31.	Bleicken, Rom 76.
32.	Another way was adoption by a patrician.
33.	Mommsen, Röm.Staatsrecht III.1, 29-40.
34.	Ferenczy in the title of his book, see Bibliography.
35.	Volkmann s.v. 'patres, patricii', Der kleine Pauly 4, 551/552.
36.	Last, Tiberius Gracchus 2.
37.	Heuss, Röm.Gesch. 43.
38.	Volkmann s.v. 'Nobiles', Der kleine Pauly 4, 142/143.
39.	Vogt, Röm.Rep. 272.
40.	Vogt, Röm.Rep. 272.
41.	The Sempronii were originally a plebeian family, but since members of this family had been consuls, they belonged to the nobility from the fourth century B.C.
42.	Plut. Tib. 1.5.
43.	Cic., Brutus 104 and 211; Tac., De or. 28.
44.	Plut., Tib. 1.7.
45.	Cic., Brutus 104.
46.	Cic., Brutus 211.
47.	Plut., Tib. 4.5-6.
48.	Plut., Tib. 8.9; Vogt, Röm.Rep. 274.
49.	Plut., Tib. 9.1. Appius Claudius was his father-in-law since he had married his daughter Claudia who gave him two sons, Plut., Tib. 4.2-4.
50.	Appian, Rom.hist. Civ.Wars 1.9.
51.	Appian, Rom.hist., Civ.Wars 1.9; Plut., Tib. 8.1-5.
52.	Plut., Tib. 8..6.
53.	Livy, Per. 58.1.
54.	Appian, Rom.hist., Civ.Wars 1.11. Most modern historians agree with Appian that Gracchus' aim was military rather than social. But since every accepted view on whichever aspect of ancient history is combated by at least one historian, this opinion has found its opponent too. The

Israeli scholar Yanir Shochat, Recruitment and the Programme of Tiberius Ghracchus. Collection Latomus, Vol. 169. Bruxelles, 1980, p. 8. sets out to show "the error of the view that Tiberius' aim in distributing land was to increase the number of assidui who could be recruited for the legions, although the reform had both a social and a military aspect, each of them related to a different category within the population. Tiberius' objective with regard to Roman citizens was social rather than military, while his intention to distribute land to the allies derived primarily from his desire to increase the military burden upon them".

55. For the details see Bernstein, Tiberius, Ch. 5 Lex Sempronia Agraria, and Stockton, The Gracchi, Ch. III The Lex Agraria.
56. Appian, Rom.hist., Civ.Wars 1.9-10.
57. Plut., Tib. 9.5-6.
58. Appian, Rom.hist., Civ.Wars 1.2.
59. Appian, Rom.hist., Civ.Wars 1.11.
60. Appian, Rom.hist., Civ.Wars 1.10.
61. Appian, Rom.hist., Civ.Wars 1.9.
62. Appian, Rom.hist., Civ.Wars 1.10.
63. Diod. 34/35.6.1.
64. Appian, Rom.hist., Civ.Wars 1.10.
65. Diod. 34/35.6.2.
66. Plut., Tib. 10.1-3.
67. Plut., Tib. 10.6.
68. Plut., Tib. 10.8.
69. Plut., Tib. 10.8.
70. Plut., Tib. 11.1-2.
71. Plut., Tib. 12.1-4.
72. Appian, Rom.hist., Civ.Wars 1.12.
73. Plut., Tib. 12.5-6.
74. Plut., Tib. 13.1.
75. Stockton, Gracchi 67.
76. Appian, Rom.hist., Civ.Wars 1.13.
77. See the discussion in Bernstein, Gracchus 185-197.
78. Plut., Tib. 13.2-3.
79. Plut., Tib. 10.4-6.

45

80. See Vol. X, Ch. IV.13c.
81. Plut., Tib. 14.1-2.
82. Plut., Tib. 14.3.
83. Appian, Rom.hist., Civ.Wars 1.14.
84. See Vol. X, Ch. II.2.c.
85. Plut., Tib. 14.3.
86. Appian, Rom.hist., Civ.Wars 1.15.
87. Plut., Tib. 17.6-7.
88. Plut., Tib. 18.1.
89. Plut., Tib. 19.4-6; Appian, Rom.hist., Civ.Wars 16.
90. Appian, Rom.hist., Civ.Wars 16.
91. Appian, Rom.hist., Civ. Wars 16; Plut., Tib. 19.6-10.
92. Plut., Tib. 20.1.
93. Plut., Tib. 20.4-5; Vell.Pat. 2.7.4.
94. Plut., Tib. 21.7; Diod.Sic. 34/35.7.3. Scipio quoted Hom., Od. 1.47.
95. Bernstein, Tiberius 225.
96. Stockton, Gracchi 87, applies these words of Thuc. 5.26.3, in the translation of Jowett, to this situation.
97. Appian, Rom.hist., Civ.Wars 1.18.
98. Appian, Rom.hist., Civ.Wars 1.19.
99. Appian, Rom.hist., Civ. Wars 1.19.
100. Vell.Pat. 2.4.4-5; Val.Max. 6.2.3.
101. Appian, Rom.hist., Civ.Wars 1.19.
102. Appian, Rom.hist., Civ.Wars 1.20, says that he was found 'without a wound', but suggests that he was killed or killed himself. Vell.Pat. 2.4.6 says that there were marks 'as though of strangulation on his throat', but leaves the possibility open that his death was due to a natural cause. Carcopino, in his Autour des Gracches, devoted a long essay 'La mort de Scipion Émilien', pp. 83-123, to it. The general opinion of historians is that Scipio's death was accidental.
103. Appian, Rom., hist., Civ.Wars 1.21.
104. Cic., De off. 3.46.
105. Plut., Gaius 2.9-10.

106.	Cic., Brutus 125/126; Plut., Gaius 3.4. According to Livy, Per. 60, he was more eloquent than his brother. Only fragments of Gaius Gracchus' speeches remain; they are to be found in ORF I.48, pp. 174-198.
107.	Diod.Sic. 34/35.24.
108.	Bellen, Grundzüge 96.
109.	Cic., Laelius 41.
110.	ORF I, 48.17.
111.	The chronlogy of the legislation is discussed by Last, Gaius Gracchus IV, The chronology of the legislation.
112.	Plut., Gaius 5.1; Appian, Rom.hist., Civ.Wars 1.21; Vell.Pat. 2.6.3.
113.	Cic., De off. 2.72.
114.	Cic., Tusc.disp. 3.48.
115.	Cic., Pro Sesto 103-104.
116.	ORF I.48.52.
117.	Last, Gracchi XII The judiciary law : the second phase 75.
118.	Plut., Gaius 5.3; Vell.Pat. 2.32.3.
119.	Appian, Rom.hist., Civ.Wars 1.22.
120.	Florus 2.5.3.
121.	Appian, Rom.hist., Civ.Wars 1.23.
122.	Appian, Rom.hist., Civ. Wars 1.23.
123.	Plut., Gaius 12.3-4.
124.	Plut., Gaius 9 and 11; Appian, Rom.hist., Civ.Wars 1.24.
125.	Plut., Gaius 10; Appian, Rom.hist., Civ.Wars 1.23.
126.	Victor, Ars rhet. 1.4 (402).
127.	Plut., Gaius 12.7.
128.	Plut., Gaius 12.8.
129.	Last, Gaius Gracchus 84.
130.	Plut., Gaius 13.1.
131.	Appian, Rom.hist., Civ.Wars 1.25.
132.	Plut., Gaius 13.3-14.1; Appian, Rom.hist., Civ.Wars 1.25.
133.	Appian, Rom.hist., Civ.Wars 1.26; Plut., Gaius 14.5-15.2.
134.	Appian, Rom.hist., Civ.Wars 1.26.
135.	The term is found for the first time in Caesar, Bell.civ. 1.5.3.

136. Cic., Cat. 1.4 and Phil. 8.14.
137. Cic., Phil. 8.14; see also Livy, Per. 61.
138. Plut., Gaius 14.3.
139. Plut., Gaius 14.4; Appian, Rom.hist., Civ.Wars 1.25.
140. Plut., Gaius 16.1-2.
141. Plut., Gaius 14.3.
142. Appian, Rom.hist., Civ.Wars 1.26; Plut., Gaius 16.3-4.
143. According to Appian, Rom.hist., Civ.Wars 1.26, Flaccus took refuge in the workshop of an acquaintance where he was pointed out to his pursuers and killed.
144. Plut., Gaius 16.4-17.3; Appian, Rom.hist., Civ.Wars 1.26; Or. 5.12.7-8.
145. Earlier he had destroyed the rebellious city of Fregellae, Livy, Per. 60.3.
146. Plut. Gaius 18.1.
147. Rumour had it that the man had stuffed the head with lead to make it heavier. Those who had brought the head of Flaccus received nothing, because they were men of low condition, Plut., Gaius 17.4-5.
148. Plut., Gaius 17.7.
149. Appian, Rom.hist., Civ.Wars 1.26.
150. Plut. Gaius 17.6; Appian, Rom.hist., Civ.Wars 1.26; Or. 5.12.9-10.
151. Last, Gaius Gracchus XV The achievement of the Gracchi 92.
152. Doblhofer, Popularen 122/123, points out that we should not see the populares as one homogeneous block; there were several groups among them, different from each other.
153. Last, Wars of the age of Marius 138/139.
154. Vol. X, Ch. VI.2d-3.
155. Weynand s.v. 'Marius (Leben)', PW VI Suppl. 1373.
156. Sall., Bellum Iug. 73.6-7.
157. Plut., Marius 9.2-3.
158. Sall., Bellum Iug. 84.1.
159. Sall., Bellum Iug. 85.
160. Plut. Marius 9.2.
161. Val.Max. 8.14.4.
162. Plut., Sulla 3.7.
163. Plut., Marius 10.5-6.

164. Vol. X, Ch. VI. 1e.
165. Perelli, Populares 118.
166. Vol. X, Ch. I.3.
167. Scullard, Gracchi to Nero 60.
168. A useful 'chronologische Übersicht' of the years 107-100 B.C. is to be found Robinson, Marius 132-134.
169. Plut., Marius 14.11-14.
170. Victor, Vir.ill., 73.1.
171. Diod. 36.15.
172. Plut., Marius 10.6 and 1.
173. Cic., Pro Sestio 101.
174. Appian, Rom.hist., Civ.Wars 1.28.
175. Appian, Rom.hist/, Civ.Wars 1.28; Plut., Marius 29.1-2; Val.Max. 8.7.3.
176. Appian, Rom.hist., Civ.Wars 1.29.
177. Plut., Marius 28.5-7.
178. Plut., Marius 28.9-29.12; Appian, Rom.hist, Civ.Wars 1.29-31.
179. Plut., Marius 28.2-6.
180. Mommsen, Röm.Gesch. II, 202.
181. Plut., Marius 30.3.
182. Mommsen, Röm.Gesch. II, 202/203.
183. Florus 2.4.4.
184. Appian, Rom.hist., Civ.Wars 1.32.
185. Appian, Rom.hist., Civ.Wars 1.32.
186. Or. 5.17.6.
187. Cic., Pro Rab. 7.20.
188. Appian, Rom.hist., Civ.Wars 1.32; Victor, Vir.ill. 73.10; Or. 2.4.16 adds that the corpse of Saturninus was torn to pieces.
189. Appian, Rom.hist., Civ.Wars 1.33.
190. Appian, Rom.hist., Civ.Wars 1.33.
191. Plut., Marius 31.1.
192. See for his visit to Mithridates of Pontus in 99 B.C. Vol. IX, Ch. IV.13f.
193. Plut., Marius 31.2.

194. Cic., Pro Balbo 48.
195. Cic., Pro Balbo 54.
196. Appian, Rom.hist., Civ.Wars 1.37; Diod.Sic. 37.10; Vell.Pat. 2.14.1-2.
197. Florus 2.5.5 and 9.
198. Last, Enfranchisement V The Tribunate of M. Livius Drsus the Younger 183.
199. Appian, Rom.hist., Civ.Wars 1.38.
200. Appian, Rom.hist., Civ.Wars 1.38; Vell.Pat. 2.15.5.
201. Appian, Rom.hist., Civ.Wars 1.39; Diod.Sic. 37.2.4.
202. Florus 2.6.5 and 7.
203. Florus 2.6.1. The oldest names seem to have been Marsic War and Italian War; the name 'Social War' originated only in the second century A.D., Gardner, Enfranchisment VI The first phase of the Social War 185.
204. Vell.Pat. 2.16.4.; Diod.Sic. 37.2.4--5.
205. Scullard, Gracchi to Nero 67.
206. Diod.Sic. 37.2.9; Appian, Rom.hist., Civ.Wars 1..39.
207. Florus 2.6.12.
208. Vell.Pat. 2.16.4.
209. Florus 2.6.13.
210. Vell.Pat. 2.16.4.
211. Florus 2.6.14.
212. Vol. IX, Ch. IV.15e.
213. Appian, Rom.hist., Civ.Wars 1.49.
214. As., In Scaur.or. 22B.
215. In fact, Livius Drusus did not intend to give them full citizenship but only the right of suffrage.
216. Appian, Rom.hist., Civ.Wars 1.37.
217. Appian, Rom.hist., Civ.Wars 1.37.
218. Vell.Pat. 2.16.4.
219. CIL I, 2.709.
220. Cic., Pro Archia 7; Appian, Rom.hist., Civ.Wars 1.49.
221. Bellen, Grundzüge 106.
222. Scullard, Gracchi to Nero 70.

223. The Romans did not believe, like the Athenians, that the popular will could be expressed in the form of a majority obtained by means of a universal and individual vote. This will was expressed by the majority of the corporate tribes. The vote of the tribes was prepared in the comitia centuriata (voting on laws, declaration of war, conclusion of peace, election of consuls), the comitia plebis tributa (election of the tribuni plebis and some other officials), and the comitia populi tributa (election of quaestors and other officials) (see for more information Vol. X, Ch. II.3a). When the voting in the comitia began, non-citizens were ordered out. Then the assembly was divided into tribal groups which were roped off from each other. Within the tribal groups voting was individual; the majority was decisive.

224. Appian, Rom.hist. Civ.Wars 1.49.

225. Cic., De leg. 2.2.5.

CHAPTER II

CIVIL WAR

1. The contest between Sulla and Marius

a. Sulla appears on the political scene

Hardly had Rome begun to breathe more freely after the bloody war against the allies, when news came that eighty thousand Romans and Italians had been massacred in the province of Asia on the orders of King Mithridates VI of Pontus [1]; this king had conquered almost all Asia Minor and stood ready to invade Greece [2]. The Romans, realizing that they had to fight back, entrusted the command to Sulla, one of the optimates.

Lucius Cornelius Sulla was born around 138 B.C. in a patrician family. He served under Marius in the Jugurthine War [3] and later against the Cimbri and Teutones. As proconsul of Cilicia in 96 B.C., he successfully expanded Rome's influence in Asia Minor, being the first Roman official to come into contact with Parthia [4]. Relations between Marius and Sulla had never been cordial, but they became definitely envenomed when, in 91 B.C., King Boccus of Mauretania had a golden statue erected on the Capitoline hill in honour of Sulla whom he considered the real victor of Jugurtha [5]. It embittered the ageing Marius still more that he could only play a secondary role during the Social War (the revolt of the Allies against Rome). "The war ...", wrote Plutarch, "lent as much glory to Sulla as it took away from Marius"; the older general, suffering from nervous disorders and physically exhausted, had become slow and hesitating [6].

b. Sulpicius, Marius' 'organon'

We have seen that Marius was not a great politician. He always needed helpers; this time he found one in a tribune, Publius Sulpicius Rufus. He was a politician in the line of the Gracchi. A nobleman by birth, he originally defended the cause of the nobility, but for some reason or other he went over to the side of the populares at a later stage. He won great fame as a powerful popular orator, 'among other men eminently endowed by nature and adapted for oratory' [7]. He has an exceedingly bad press with the ancient authors : 'second to none in the lowest vices' [8], 'the proper instrument to bring down the state' [9], 'perverse and temerarious' [10], and more in this vein. But, says Van Ooteghem, "does not such a unanimity of the witnesses prove that we have to do here with the tenacious rancour of the (noble) party ..., rather than with truth?" [11].

In 88 B.C. Sulpicius, called by Plutarch 'the organon of Marius' [12], came forward with no less than four bills. The exiles of the Lex Varia were to be called back [13]. His second bill concerned the new citizens. As we have seen, their having been cramped into only a few tribes had made their ius suffragii, their voting rights, almost valueless. Sulpicius now proposed to distribute them evenly over all the thirty-five tribes [14]. "Man for man, the new citizens were to be the equals of the old. And the citizenship of Rome, no longer Roman in anything but name, was to be the citizenship of Italy. In fact, if not in theory, Italy was not to be the territorium of Rome; Rome was to be the capital of Italy. The city-state, in brief, was at an end" [15]. The third Sulpician law struck from the list of senators all those with a debt of more than two thousand denarii [16]; this was aimed directly at Sulla who was deeply indebted. The fourth law, in fact the crowning one, entrusted the command in Asia to Marius [17].

c. On the road to civil war

This legislative program caused an enormous outcry. The old citizens understood that they would be outnumbered by the new ones (the number of voters almost trebled); they fought the newcomers with sticks and stones [18]. The senators were furious too. When the fracas became ever louder, the consuls, one of whom was Sulla, ordered the cessation of public business for a few days [19]. Not to be thwarted, Sulpicius convoked the concilium plebis and ordered six hundred young knights whom he called his 'contra-Senate', to gather in the assembly square, each with a dagger hidden in his cloak; it is said that he held another body of three thousand men in readiness. In the assembly Sulpicius declared the cessation illegal and ordered the consuls to cancel it. When they refused, they saw daggers pointed at them; a son of the consul Cn. Pompeius was killed in the tumult. Both consuls escaped, after which Sulpicius pushed through his legislative progam; Marius got the command in Asia (which he was prevented from assuming) [20].

"When Sulla heard of this he resolved to decide the question by war, and called the army (which stood ready in Nola in Campania for departure to Asia - F.) together to a conference ... Sulla spoke of the indignity put upon him by Sulpicius and Marius and ... urged them to obey his orders" [21]. "His recent experiences", writes Keaveney, "had shown how little protection was offered by his consular dignity alone. If he were to assert himself now, it could only be by force of arms" [22]. However, his superior officers were obviously chips of the old republican block, for they all deserted him and returned to Rome, "because they would not submit to the idea of leading an army against their country" [23].

The Senate dispatched two praetors to Sulla's camp ordering him to proceed to Asia (it is not clear whether or not as commander-in-chief; anyhow, he had to be off). Since these officials adopted a high tone with their general, the legionaries threw themselves upon them; short of killing them, they tore the robes from their body, broke their axes and fasces, and chased them out of the camp [24]. This incident was a turning-point in the history of the late Republic. It speaks volumes that the enraged soldiers broke the axes and fasces of the praetors, for these were the ceremonial emblems carried before every dignitary by the lictors. An attack on them was an affront to the Republic. What the soldiers did signified that, from now on, they would refuse to obey the Senate and were ready to turn against the state. The army no longer was an instrument in the hands of the government; henceforward it was a tool in the service of some ambitious general.

d. Sulla marches on Rome

Sulla did not proceed to Asia but, instead, turned northward and marched on Rome at the head of his legions [25]. When asked what he intended to do in the capital, he replied : "to deliver her from her tyrants" [26]. Nobody stopped Sulla's forces on their way to the imperial city, but as soon as they were within the city gates, fighting began. People threw missiles on the troops from the roofs of their houses, but when Sulla threatened to burn them down, they desisted. The situation got more serious when they arrived at the Esquiline forum which they found occupied by Marius and Sulpicius with hastily collected and armed forces. A battle in due form took place, 'with bugles and standards in full military fashion, no longer like a mere faction fight' [27]. Sulla had to send for reinforcements to overcome them.

     Marius and Sulpicius even promised freedom to the slaves who were ready to join them, but this appeal remained unanswered. They then fled from the city, "together with those of the nobility who had cooperated with them" [28]. It was a momentous day in the history of Rome. For the first time since the Celtic invasion in 387 B.C. Rome had been taken by force. And it had not been Rome against foreign enemies, but Romans against Romans. "To such extremity of evil had the recklessness of party strife progressed among them", sighs Appian [29].

e. Sulla in power

The victorious Sulla posed as the saviour of the Republic. He posted guards throughout the city to prevent looting by his troops. In the early hours of the next morning he called the concilium plebis together and, haranguing it, claimed that he acted from necessity. Measures were announced "for curtailing the power of the tribunes which had become extremely tyrannical", while three hundred prominent citizens were enrolled into the Senate in order to replenish its much shrunken numbers [30]. Then the Senate assembled and outlawed Marius, Sulpicius, and twelve others as public enemies. Marius was already beyond the reach of the victor, since he had escaped to Numidia in an adventurous way, but Sulpicius was caught and killed [31]; all his legislation was declared null and void on the ground that it had been pushed through by force [32].

Sulla's situation was, however, by no standard as comfortable as it may seem. As soon as he had sent his army to Capua for embarcation to Asia, his enemies, the followers of Marius, raised their heads again. They knew that the dictator was to depart soon to assume the command in Asia. The elections for the year 87 B.C. showed that there was still popular support for Marius [33]. It would have displeased Sulla greatly that, while an ineffective adherent of his became one of the consuls, the other was an opponent, a patrician, called Lucius Cornelius Cinna. Sulla was so afraid of him that he wanted him to swear publicly on the Capitoline hill that he would remain faithful to him [34]. Soon after, in the spring of 87 B.C., Sulla left for Asia, in all probability with dire misgivings about the situation in Rome. During his last weeks in the capital he was so apprehensive that he surrounded himself with a bodyguard that kept an eye on him by day and night [35].

2. The struggle of Octavius and Cinna

a. Cinna aspiring to power

As soon as he dared, Cinna declared that the oath he had taken did not bind him, since it was forced on him by Sulla [36]. He immediately took up again the abandoned scheme of Marius and Sulpicius to redistribute the new citizens evenly over the tribes [37]. By doing so he presented himself as the leader of the populares in the absence of Marius. The other consul, Cn. Octavius, was an optimate. So the two consuls belonged to opposite factions. "The hardly extinguished fire", wrote Florus, " flared up again and had its origin in the discord of these two men" [38]. "The more reputable part of the plebeians adhered to Octavius", remarked Appian, meaning those who were against the redistribution of the new citizens [39]. The others sided with Cinna, "even those of the aristocratic party in Rome, to whom the stability of goverment was irksome" [40]. With the same bias Florus described the optimates as "those who preferred peace and quiet" [41]; that is to say, they preferred the status quo which guaranteed the domineering position of the senatorial class.

The tension in Rome grew with every day that passed. A proposal by Cinna to recall the exiles, and in particular, of course, Marius, heightened the tension [42]. Cinna believed he could steer his proposal through with the support of all those new citizens who had been lured to Rome. They "took possession of the Forum with concealed daggers, and with loud cries demanded that they should be distributed among all the tribes". When the majority of the tribunes vetoed the proposals, riots broke out, and these tribunes were assaulted. On hearing this, Octavius ran to the Forum accompanied by a dense mass of his followers, burst into the crowd 'like a torrent', and cleared the square. Many new citizens were killed, others driven out of town. In vain Cinna called upon the slaves to help him, promising them freedom. He then fled to the allied towns in the vicinity, "inciting these all to revolution and collecting money for the purposes of war" [43].

Now there was hell to pay! Having the field to itself now, the Senate deposed Cinna as consul - a very rare move! - on the ground that he had left the city at a dangerous moment; he was also deprived of his citizenship [44]. Nothing daunted, Cinna proceeded to Capua where a Roman army stood. There he performed a great theatrical show in front of the troops, pleading, shedding tears, rending his garments, and even throwing himself on the ground. It helped. He was assured by the soldiers that they still acknowledged him as consul and took an oath to support him. New troops arrived in the camp from allied cities [45].

b. Rome captured by Cinna

Events now took their inevitable course. Octavius heavily fortified the capital, preparing it for a siege; he summoned Gnaeus Pompeius Strabo, the father of Pompey the Great, who stood with another army on the Adriatic, to come to Rome where he encamped just outside the gates. Cinna marched on with his army and took position in front of that of Pompeius. This news was enough to make Marius leave his place of exile and sail to Etruria; with six thousand Etrurians he joined Cinna's forces. The Samnites too were ready to help Marius and Cinna. Since the grain-depots in Latium were in the hands of the insurgents, the imperial city was cut off from its food-supplies. The party of Octavius possessed hardly one competent military leader and was weakened by the desertion of many of its soldiers who disappeared out of town to join the opponents. Pompeius' attitude was ambiguous; furthermore, his troops were thinned out by an epidemic, while he himself was killed in his tent by a stroke of lightning. When the attack began, severe fighting occurred at the Janiculus, with heavy losses on both sides. Then negotiations were opened as the result of which the decree of banishment was rescinded.

The troops of Marius and Cinna were now free to enter the city. "Everybody received them with fear", and not without reason. The invaders immediately began to plunder. And then the killing began; it was to go on for five endless days. Octavius, with some of his party, had retired to the

Janiculus; as a Roman of the old stamp, he refused to fly, even when his horse was brought to him. The hill was captured by his enemies; his head was cut off and suspended on the Forum in front of the rostra - "the first head of a consul to be so exposed". As the days passed, many more heads were placed next to the first; the row grew ever longer. The knights, many of whom were killed too, were not deemed important enough to have their heads exposed in this way; this honour was reserved for the senators. "They (Cinna's men) paraded these horrors (the severed heads) before the public eye, either to inspire fear and terror, or for a godless spectacle ... All Sulla's friends were put to death, his house was razed to the ground, his property confiscated, and himself voted a public enemy. Search was made for his wife and children, but they escaped ... There were banishments, and confiscations of property, and depositions and a repeal of the laws enacted during Sulla's consulship" [46]. It was the dualistic 'either them or us'. When all was over, Cinna was elected consul for the second time and Marius for the seventh time. But Marius was not allowed to enjoy presiding over a city reeking with blood; he died in the spring of 86 B.C. [47], leaving the popular party in the hands of Cinna.

3. Sulla undisputed master of Rome

a. Sulla brooding on revenge

If we may believe certain ancient authors, the greater part of the senators fled Rome and joined Sulla in Asia Minor where they even formed a sort of Senate-in-exile [48]. But Perelli thinks this is an exaggeration since, according to him, many senators preferred staying quietly in Rome (quietly? after what had happened?). All the same, the majority of the Senators were favourably disposed towards Sulla [49].

If Cinna had ever dreamt that Sulla would remain in Asia, he was soon to be disillusioned. Sovereignly ignoring the fact that he had been declared a public enemy, Sulla reported to the Senate what he had achieved in Numidia, his victories over the Cimbrians, and his efforts in the

Social War; "most of all he dwelt upon his recent victories in the Mithridatic War ... In return for this, he said, he had been declared a public enemy ... (But) he would be there (in Rome) presently to take vengeance upon the guilty ones" [50].

b. Cinna's death

During Sulla's absence Cinna had ruled Rome, Italy, and the western provinces as an autocrat [51] - years in which, said Cicero, the state was without law and without any dignity [52]. He took fright at the thought that Sulla was about to return and began to prepare for this emergency [53]. He and his colleague-consul, Cn. Papirius Carbo, assembled soldiers who were to be ferried over to Liburnia on the northern coast of Illyria, for they expected that Sulla's way home would lead through Greece [54]. Only one detachment reached Liburnia; from the rest there were many deserters; those who remained in the camp near Ascona refused to fight against their fellow-citizens. When Cinna attempted to bully them into obeisance, the result was a brawl in which he was killed, leaving Carbo as the only consul for 84 B.C. [55], a man who was to prove himself no match for Sulla.

c. Sulla's return to Italy

The victor of Mithridates was now on his way home "with a large and well-disciplined army, devoted to him and elated by its exploits. He had an abundance of ships and money, and an apparatus suitable for all emergencies, and was an object of terror for all his enemies" [56]. He came with five legions of infantry and six thousand horse. gathering more and more troops while marching through Macedonia and Greece, so that six hundred vessels were needed to ferry his forty thousand men from Patras to Brindisi. He was met by a delegation from the Senate whom he told that he desired to be restored to his former dignity and property; "it was made plain in a single sentence that he would not disband his army, but was now contemplating supreme power" [57].

d. Sulla marches on Rome

Nobody opposed Sulla's landing in the spring of 83 B.C.; having made sure of Lucania and Apulia, he took the Via Appia northward. With the greatest care he avoided doing any damage to the fields and properties of the farmers and citizens, since he wanted to come 'not as the champion of war but as the establisher of peace' [58]. A slave with a mantic spirit prophesied that he would be victorious, but if he did not make haste, he would find the Capitol in flames [59]. South of Capua, however, he found his way blocked by a consular army which he fought and routed; its losses were great and became even greater during the relentless pursuit by Sulla's men [60]. The remnants of the consular army were shut up in Capua while Sulla followed the Via Latina northward.

At Teano he was opposed by a second consular army under the command of Lucius Cornelius Scipio. Knowing that Scipio's men were 'in a state of dejection', Sulla began to negotiate with his opponent. The intended armistice did not come off, but seeing Sulla's army and sensing where the wind was blowing, Scipio's men deserted en bloc to the other side, "so that the consul, Scipio, and his son Lucius, alone of the whole army, were left, not knowing what to do" [61].

Sulla's hope that he would become the master of Rome and Italy in a mainly peaceful way, was dashed because two die-hards, Carbo and Gaius Marius, the son of the seventime consul, became the consuls for the year 82 B.C. [62]. There was heavy fighting in several theatres of war. Feeling that his cause was lost, Marius "hastened to put his private enemies out of the way", several of whom were murdered, their corpses being thrown into the Tiber, "for it was now the custom not to bury the slain" [63]. Since a large part of Italy was hostile to Sulla, he had to work his way to Rome slowly and carefully. Great devastation was wrought since Sulla now considered himself in enemy territory [64]. Because his advance ws so slow, the prophecy of the slave came true : on July 6 the temple of Jupiter on the Capitoline hill went up in flames. It was already November when Sulla finally arrived before the gates of Rome.

But his army had been preceded by another that had arrived during the foregoing night. It consisted of Samnites and Lucanians under the command of the Samnite chief Pontius Telesinus whom Plutarch calls 'a great warrior'. He was, on the surface at least, an ally of the Marians, but in reality he was an enemy of Rome, no matter in whose hands she was. "He hated the very name of Rome", writes Velleius, "and told his troops : 'the last day is at hand for the Romans'", adding : "These wolves that made such ravages upon Italian liberty will never vanish until we have cut down the forest that harbours them". He was, in fact, not fighting the civil war but continuing the Social War. Velleius is of the opinion that Rome had not faced so great a danger since the days of Hannibal [65].

A desperate sally by a number of young Romans against Telesinus only led to severe losses among them. In the town the women hysterically believed that they were already prisoners in Samnite hands. And then all of a sudden Sulla's vanguard of seven hundred cavalry arrived, riding with loose reins. Their commander gave his men a few moments of rest and then made them charge the Samnites in order to push them back from the Porta Collina. Later Sulla arrived with the main body; at four o'clock he went over to the attack. It became a murderous fight. Sulla, on his high-mettled grey, was everywhere. But the Samnites were the toughest of fighters, and there were moments that he thought that the day was lost. It was already dark when the enemy began to withdraw. The next morning he could collect the prisoners; Telesinus was found half-dead and was executed. According to Appian, the pious Sulla believed that the medaillon with the golden image of the Delphic god which he carried on his breast had saved him [66].

e. Sulla dictator

Sulla was master of Rome now. All Italy too was in hands, although two cities with Marian garrisons held out for some time yet. There remained pockets of resistance in Sicily, North Africa, and Spain, but these too were soon reduced. His main opponent, young Marius, committed suicide, while

Carbo was killed in Sicily [67]. With Sulla's entry in Rome the First Civil War was virtually at an end.

Since both consuls were dead, the Empire was now without rulers. The normal procedure was for the Senate to appoint an 'interrex' - which indeed happened, - on the assumption that this interrex would arrange the election of new consuls - which did not happen. For Sulla let it be known that he desired to be appointed dictator - an office that had been in abeyance since the days of Hannibal. The popular assembly did not relish the idea but obeyed. It "chose Sulla their absolute master for as long as he liked", which was inconstitutional, the ordinary time of office being half a year. "Thus", states Appian, "Sulla became king, or tyrant, de facto, not elected, by holding power by force and violence" [68]. Autocracy having been installed, the Republic had had its day.

f. Sulla's revenge on Latins and Italians

The seizure of power by Sulla inaugurated what was propably the most dualistic period in Rome's internal history. It was no longer 'either them or us'; it was 'them' tout court. 'They' had to go. "The dictator sullied the finest of victories by an unequalled cruelty [69]; everybody was shivering with fear and in hiding, or dumb" [70]. His very first act, on November 3, 88 B.C., was to have eight thousand prisoners of the battle of the Porta Collina, mainly Samnites, brought to the Campus Martius where he ordered his men to massacre them with their javelins. The cries of the victims reached the ears of the senators who were assembled in the temple of Bellona. When they showed their horror of this carnage, Sulla bluntly told them to mind their own business [71]; he was only punishing a few rebels, he said [72].

When the beleaguered town of Praeneste at last surrendered, its fate was horrifying. The Marian senators who were found there were executed, while almost the entire citizenship, to the number of twelve thousand, was put to the sword under the eyes of Sulla himself. The town was given over to plunder; its lands were divided among Sulla's veterans

[73]. Other Latin and Italian towns did not fare better at the hands of the victor. The Latin town of Norba could only be taken by treason. The inhabitants preferred killing one another to being butchered by Sulla's ferocious men. "Others closed the gates and set fire to the town; a strong wind fanned the flames, which so far consumed the town that no plunder was gained from it" [74]. It was never rebuilt. Several Etrurian cities resisted for a long time. Volaterrae (Volterra) only capitulated in 79 B.C,; the garrison was promised an unopposed withdrawal but, once out of the town, it was massacred by Sullan cavalry [75].

The dictator fostered a special hatred against Samnium. He said that "he realized that no Roman could ever live in peace so long as the Samnites held together as a separate people"; he would not stop "until he had either destroyed all Samnites of importance or banished them from Italy". Many Samnite cities were reduced to mere villages [76]; their lands were divided among Sulla's veterans [77]. This not only happened in Samnium but everywhere in Italy, especially in Lucania. According to Appian, Sulla, "by plundering the allies, provided one hundred thousand of his men with land and money" [78]. "And now, after thus crushing them with war, fire, and murder, Sulla's generals visited the several cities and established garrisons at the suspected places" [79]. Italy was being treated as a defeated and occupied country; it was as though the days of Hannibal had returned, sighed Valerius Maximus [80].

g. Reign of terror

Not that Rome herself remained a haven of quiet and security. Far from it! "Being made dictator ..., Sulla now wielded with unbridled cruelty the powers which former dictators had employed only to save their country in times of extreme danger" [81]. There seems to have been a strain of madness in him. It had always been there, but now it came to the surface; "he had doubtless always desired to act thus, but revealed himself only in the days of his power" [82]. He even sought to cool his wrath on Marius, now four years dead. His natural death was not enough; he was postumously 'executed'. The corpse of the old general was dug up and his ashes were dispersed into the river Anio (as though the Tiber was too good for them) [83]. All the monuments commemorating his victories in Africa and Gaul were demolished [84]; all his acts were declared null and void [85].

Sulla did not stop at the dead. With countless living men he had an axe to grind. "Of his enemies he could spare none", he declared, "but would visit them with the utmost severity. He would take vengeance by strong measures on the praetors, quaestors, military tribunes, and everybody else who had committed any hostile act after the day when Scipio had violated the agreement with him" [86]; according to him, this was simply military law [87]. Thousands and thousands were set wondering how long their heads would remain on their shoulders. It was as though an oriental despot had descended on the city! Or even worse, "for the deeds of Mithridates, deemed so terrible in slaughtering all the Romans in Asia in one day, were regarded as of slight importance in comparison with the number now massacred and their manner of death" [88].

To execute his orders Sulla gave a free rein to his friends and cronies [89]. This meant that the imperial city fell under the sway of very bad men, even downright criminals, who squared their accounts with their personal enemies many of whom had no problems with Sulla at all [90]. There occurred, as Florus states, 'killing at discretion' [91]. Many innocent people lost their lives too [92]; even partisans of Sulla were not spared [93]. The violence done to women and boys, even of the noblest families, seemed, in the eyes of Dio, the lesser evil, compared with so much blood [94]. The heads of the victims were brought to the Forum and exposed there on the rostra [95]. Soon there was not room enough there; a new place of exhibition was found near the Servilius fountain next to the Forum [96].

Did nobody protest? Yes, indeed, some senators were courageous enough to raise their voices. "When will these evils have an end?", asked C. Caecilius Metellus; "we do not ask you to pardon those whom you have decided to kill, but rather to free of doubt those whom you intend to save". Probably taken by surprise, the dictator evasively answered that he did not know this. "Then tell us at least who are going to be killed", retorted Metellus. Sulla declared himself ready to do this [97].

The result of this short but sharp debate were the so-called 'proscription lists'. Lists with the names of those who were 'proscribed', that is, who were to die, were publicly posted in town; the first day eighty names appeared on them, the second day two hundred and twenty, and on the next another two hundred and twenty. These were all, said Sulla, whom he could write down on the spur of the moment, but more would be added as soon as he hit upon them [98]. Thus, in spite of his promise to the Senate, he left everyone in the direst uncertainty.

Whoever harboured a proscribed person, became one himself, even if he hid his brother or son or mother or father. Slaves were encouraged to kill their masters, sons their fathers. Children and grandchildren of the proscribed were outlawed and their goods confiscated. This happened not only in Rome but in all the cities of Italy. Husbands were murdered in the arms of their wives, children on the lap of their mothers. It was not only for political reasons that people were killed : this one was disposed of because of his fine mansion, another because of his beautiful garden, yet another because of his swimming-pool [99]. One can easily imagine how citizens stood staring nervously at the proscription lists to see whether their names appeared on them, and how they lay awake in the night waiting for the footsteps to come near.

Sulla's persecution mania knew no bounds. Sons and grandsons of the proscribed persons were debarred from all offices; "the sons of (proscribed) senators were compelled to bear the (financial) burdens and yet to lose the rights of their rank" [100]. Confiscated goods were sold by auction in public; Sulla loved to play the auctioneer himself. It became a queer sort of auction since , in spite of higher bids made, he gave away goods for very little or even for nothing at all to his friends; he even presented a beautiful woman with a whole village [101]. Protests he dismissed with the remark that it was all his personal booty [102]. Some of his cronies got exceedingly rich in this way. His arbitrariness reached a culmination-point when he forced women to divorce their husbands and assigned them to his favourites; it did not interest him that one of these women was with child [103].

Only a few persons escaped the proscriptions. One of these was Julius Caesar, barely twenty years of age; he refused to cede his wife Cornelia, fled the town, survived, but lost his family inheritances [104]. When advisers remarked to Sulla that he need not be afraid of such a young chap, he retorted in a fit of prophecy : "Bear in mind that the man you are so eager to save will one day deal the death blow to the cause of aristocracy, which you have joined me in upholding; for in this Caesar there is more than in Marius" [105].

h. The results

When, on June 1, 81 B.C., Sulla finally closed the proscription lists [106], there had been four thousand seven hundred names on them [107], among them forty senators and more than sixteen hundred knights [108]. The knights paid dearly for the fact that the laws of Gracchus and Glaucia had allowed them to sit in judgment over the optimates. By the proscription of their masters a good many slaves became available whom Sulla turned to good use; he set ten thousand of them free and gave them full civil rights, so that they were at his beck and call in the popular assembly [109]. He crowned his achievements by holding a resplendent triumph, officially to celebrate his victory over Mithridates, in reality over his Roman co-citizens. On that day he told the concilium plebis that henceforward he desired to be addressed as 'Sulla Felix' [110], this 'felix' not meaning 'the happy one' but rather that he had been successful in everything he had undertaken. On the Forum a golden equestrian statue of him was erected dedicated to 'Cornelio Sulla Felici dictatori' [111].

j. Sulla's legislation

So far for the negative side of Sulla's activities. Now for the 'positive'side, his legislative work which, for a large part, consisted of destructive measures. The legislative building of the Gracchi was torn down to the last stone. No longer would there be distribution of grain to the citizens. The knights were no longer allowed to judge senators. The power of the tribuni plebis was severly clipped. They lost the right of initiative in legal matters; henceforward they needed the assent of the Senate to propose a bill which made them virtually powerless [112]. Persons who had held this office were debarred from holding any other later, for instance, that of consul, which made 'all men of reputation or family' shun away from it [113]. In proportion as the power of the tribuni and the rights of the knights and the people were weakened and curtailed, those of the Senate were strengthened and increased. He introduced into this body many newcomers, among them persons without any political experience; the total number of senators was raised to six hundred [114]. In this way he made sure that he would not be contradicted in the Senate. Sulla's most remarkable innovation was that he kept his dictatorship after his half year of office.

k. Sulla steps back

Although a dictator, Sulla became one of the consuls for the year 80 B.C., "in order to preserve the pretence and form of democratic government" [115]. A year later, in 79 B.C., he refused to be reelected consul, laid down the dictatorship, and voluntarily retired into private life [116]. He went to his estate near Cumae in Campania and devoted his time, as a country gentleman, to hunting and fishing. This sudden retirement of Sulla has always been an object of wonder and speculation. Perhaps Appian offered the wisest explanation : "he was weary of war, weary of power, weary of Rome" [117]. Weary of himself too? For he began to live a life of debauchery surrounding himself with dissolute women and men of the meanest origin. He took to the bottle and sat drinking with his friends all day long on the low couches. And then all of a sudden, he fell ill and died, not yet sixty years old [118].

1. Who was Sulla?

How are we to assess Sulla? Was he 'the last republican' [119], or was he 'a failed monarch' [120]? Is the question what kind of man he was one of the unsolved cases, as Seneca wrote [121]? Was he, in the words of Drumann-Groebe, 'a riddle for all times' [122]? Perhaps every potentate is a riddle. I am thinking here of a Stalin, a Mao, or a Hitler whom Sulla resembles in more than one respect. They are very difficult to gauge for ordinary persons like ourselves; the principal difficulty is that we feel unable to understand why they sacrifice everything, even their personal happiness, in order to acquire power and to keep it at all costs. At all costs, indeed, for in order to reach the top and stay there, they cover their path with corpses, with thousands, with hundreds of thousands, with millions of dead bodies. They stand apart from the common run of humanity; they are inhuman and, by the same token, they consider themselves superhuman or extra-human, even divine. They pay a price for this : they are incapable of love and, more often than not, they cannot sleep [123]. Shakespeare perfectly understood what this signified when he made his Julius Caesar say that he would have men about him 'such as sleep o'nights'; he found sleepless people dangerous, they think too much [124]. Men like Sulla are opposed to mankind whom, in fact, they hate; Michelet thought that even his sudden abdication was a sign of his prodigious contempt of mankind, because he did something that nobody expected of him [125]. This radical opposition to ordinary people makes them into living cases of dualism.

Of one thing we may be absolutely certain : Sulla may have paved the way for the monarchy, but he did not found one. The Republic had still half a century to go. Is the alternative then that he restored the Republic and revitalized it? However, if he ever fancied that he had ended the civil strife once and for all by destroying the opponents of the optimates, he was wrong. More internecine fighting was to come. Furthermore, he did not restore the fabric of the Republic as it was, say, in 133 B.C., before Tiberius Gracchus appeared on the scene. He pushed things back to a period before the year 287 B.C., when the Lex Hortensia had given such important prerogatives to the tribuni plebis; he abolished all that the people had gained since then. And did he not transgress himself one of the oldest and most fundamental rules of the Republic, to wit that a dictator should remain in function no longer than six months?

Carcopino concludes his monograph on Sulla by stating that he is not ready to absolve him of his crimes. But then, with that curious callousness that we find so often in historians and which makes them the stooges of those very men in power, he goes on to say that we should credit Sulla with the supposition that "he has immolated his victims because he judged their death necessary for the birth of the new times" [126]. Brave new world that was built on so many corpses! I wonder whether, in centuries to come, historians will also hail Hitler as one who inaugurated new times.

What Sulla left behind was a muddle. One need not be a psychologist to sense that countless people were thirsting for revenge. One need not be a deep political thinker to understand the people would soon enough try to recover their lost rights. Nothing, indeed, had been resolved; everything still hung in the balance. Would the optimates be able to preserve their position? Or would it be the turn of the people? Whatever the result might be, the Republic would be the main victim. The hour for a well-balanced solution of the problems of the state was irrevocably past now - if it had ever been there, which I don't believe. It would have required a man of superhuman genius and of impeccable character to save the capsizing ship of state. But the politicians of the ensuing decades were neither geniuses or, if they were, did not possess that quasi-angelic nature. They were generals, men reared in the trade of arms and geared to war, men who were wont to use the hard hand. There was nothing but dualism to come.

4. The anti-Sullan reaction

Hardly had Sulla closed his eyes than the reaction set in. One of the consuls of the year 78 B.C. was M. Aemilius Lepidus, an opponent of Sulla [127]. That he was no friend of the deceased dictator he showed by trying to prevent (in vain) his burial on the Campus Martius [128]. Inveighing against the tyranny of Sulla [129], he inaugurated what Scullard calls 'a counter-revolution' [130]. The subsidized distribution of grain to the populace was restored and all laws of Sulla were rescinded [131]. Still more disturbing was his plan to restore to their dispossessed owners the lands which Sulla had given to his veterans; the citizens of Faesulae (now Fiesole) in Etruria took him at his word, evicted the colonists from their lands, and even killed many of them [132].

In an attempt to halt the anti-Sullan revolution, the Senate despatched an army under both consuls into Etruria. Now, since Lepidus was one of the consuls, this was asking for trouble; understanding this, the Senate forced them to take an oath that they would not undertake any action against one another - this to prevent the renewed outbreak of civil war [133]. Once in Etruria, Lepidus was seen as the great man there; from all sides adherents flocked to him (called by Sallust 'the scum') [134]. Realizing its mistake, the Senate ordered Lepidus back to Rome. He did not obey but, after the end of his term as consul, remained in command as proconsul. With an army at his orders, he put his demands to the Senate, insisting, in particular, on the restoration of the tribunicia potestas and a second consulate for himself [135].

When the Senate gave a non-committal reply, Lepidus marched on Rome [136]. Events became self-repeating : rescinding the laws of the predecessor, recall of the exiles, restoration of confiscated goods, and marching on Rome. Although Lepidus' coming terrified the citizens of the capital greatly, he did not enter the town. Taking drastic action at last, the Senate issued a senatusconsultum ultimum for the defense of the Republic (to be read as : for the preservation of the rights of the oligarchy); two men, an interrex and Catulus, who had been consul with Lepidus and was now proconsul, were given full powers to do what they deemed necessary [137]. Catulus succeeded in defeating Lepidus, who was declared a public enemy by the Senate, before the gates of Rome and driving him back to Etruria [138]. Catulus followed him there; unable to hold his own, the public enemy fled to Sardinia where he, according to Florus, soon died of chagrin [139].

5. Pompey appears on the political scene

Catulus also took a measure that would have far-reaching consequences : he entrusted Pompey with a military command [140]; this man was to play the major role in the late Republic for years to come. The ancients gave him the surname of 'Magnus', the Great'; modern authors also lavish epithets on him : 'builder of Empire' [141], 'the republican prince' [142], 'the Roman Alexander' [143]. Cicero praised him as 'a man of integrity and high moral character' [144]. But Sallust gave something away when he commented that Pompey had 'an honest expression hiding a shameless heart' and that he was 'modest in everything but his lust for power' [145]. As an aspirant to power he was without doubt less ruthless and cruel than other contenders.

Pompey was born in Rome in 106 B.C. as the son of a father who had held important offices in the service of the state. Of his youth next to nothing is known until he, as a seventeen-year-old, began his military career in 89 B.C. under the command of his father. He saw service in the Social War and later took the side of Sulla for whom he fought in Sicily. After the death of Sulla he remained a staunch supporter of the cause of the Senate, or so it seemed. The question is whether the senators really trusted this ambitious young man. And indeed, he did not offer his assistance to the Senate for nothing. When trouble arose in Spain, because of the rebellion of Sertorius, he asked for a proconsular imperium, that is, an important military command with the authority of a consul without being one; the request was granted and the theatre of war to which he was delegated was the Iberian peninsula. But before nominating him, the Senate had hesitated. Being only twenty-nine years of age, he had never been a member of the Senate. Besides, according to the rules laid down by Sulla, his appointment was highly irregular. He had never held any political office, let alone that he had ever been a consul.

6. The Sertorian War

a. Sertorius the rising man

Spain was an unruly country; after 100 B.C. the Romans saw themselves confronted with one rebellion after another. But things came to a head when Sertorius appeared on the scene. Quintus Sertorius was not a Roman or Latin but a Sabine, born as he was at Nursia (now Norcia) in 123 B.C. He was, however, a Roman citizen, of which he was proud; at the same time he was not a nobleman but a 'homo novus' without illustrious forebears. In spite of these handicaps, he aspired to a political career. As Spann, his modern biographer, writes, he was soon to learn that "politics in Rome had become a dangerous game" [146].

He made a fairly good start since he got an appointment on the staff of the proconsul who was fighting the Cimbri and Teutons in Gallia Narbonensis in 105 B.C. He was present at the dies ater at Arausio on October 105 B.C. [147]; he was one of the very few who escaped the wholesale massacring of a Roman army by the Germans by swimming over the Rhône [148]. After this harrowing experience he became a staff-officer of Marius with whom he served for four years, "the school in which he learned the art of war" [149]. When after 100 B.C. Marius began to lose momentum in his political career, Sertorius associated himself with the influential Metellus family. A friend of this clan took him with him in 97 B.C. for service in Spain; Sertorius saw much cruelty and butchering of rebels there. But he himself was not a hair better than the normal Roman commander; he too resorted to mass-murder and selling into slavery [150].

Sertorius had now acquired enough fame to be elected praetor for 91 B.C. in which capacity he acted as governor of Gallia Cisalpina. With the men he had levied and trained there he fought in the Social War. Meanwhile he had become quite a presence in Rome; he was a senator now and on entering the theatre was greeted with applause [151]. Quite a thing for a homo novus! But then Sulla blocked his career by preventing his election as tribune of the people, "for which apparently he became an opponent of Sulla" [152].

He now allied himself with Cinna; by doing so, "he joined the enemy of his enemy (Sulla) and a man who could offer him a future" [153]. But Cinna's reign was short. After his death Carbo and young Marius became the consuls for 82 B.C., heavily criticized by Sertorius who had been no friend of the older Marius. Probably to have him out of the way he was made proconsul of Hispania Citerior (= the eastern regions along the Mediterranean). For the first time he had an independent command [154].

b. Recruiting in Spain

In the winter of 82 B.C. he set out for Spain with his own army, some six thousand men perhaps [155]. His route led through southern France; the passage through the Pyrenees was difficult because of the heavy storms that were raging there, and also because the passes were blocked by Celtiberian tribesmen to whom he paid tribute in order to expedite his passage. His companions "considered it a pestilent thing to render tribute to pestilent barbarians" [156]. Once in Spain, he enlarged his army by recruiting among the Roman settlers and the Celtiberians. The last mentioned had grown hostile to the Empire as a result of 'the rapacity and insolence of the Roman officials'. He succeeded remarkably well in winning the sympathy of the natives, for he was 'mild in the affairs of peace' [157]. From Sulla he had nothing good to expect. Being one of the very few Marian leaders still at large, and greatly feared by him, he stood high on the dictator's proscription lists [158].

c. Sertorius' Odyssey

Sulla sent Caius Annius to Spain as the new governor with a force much larger than that of Sertorius [159]. Then an Odyssey began for Sertorius who embarked at Cartagena with three thousand men. A failed landing in Mauretania caused heavy losses; he was repulsed from the shores of Spain, attempted Ibiza, lost half his fleet in a sea-battle against Annius, sailed with the remnant through the Straits of Gibraltar, got ashore for a while near the mouth of the Guadalquivir, dreamt for a moment of crossing over to the Islands of the Blest, probably Madeira or the Canary Islands, hoping to live there 'in quiet, freed from tyranny and wars that would never end', but finally decided to sail to Africa again, "to give his men some fresh ground for hope and occasion for new enterprise" [160]. In Mauretania he took the side of insurgents who were fighting King Ascalis, defeated him, and became the master of the whole country. He acted with great moderation, did no harm, and could probably have remained there indefinitely [161].

d. The Sertorian War

But then came an invitation of the Lusitanians who lived in what now is Portugal, to come and be their leader in their struggle against Rome [162]. With his arrival in 80 B.C. the so-called 'Sertorian War' began. It was really an historical moment since it was the first time in Rome's existence that a general of the standing of Sertorius chose the side of anti-Roman insurgents. Perhaps the man himself would have declared that he was fighting, not Rome, but Sulla. However, his Lusitanians were fighting Rome, not Sulla. And later developments showed that Sertorius was an authentic revolutionary.

Sertorius landed in Spain with only two thousand six hundred Romans and six hundred Mauretanians, but he soon enrolled thousands of Lusitanians and Celtiberians [163], while in 77 B.C. the remnants of Lepidus' army were shipped to him from Sardinia [164]. It will serve no purpose to describe the campaign in detail. Brilliant commander as he was, and tactful in the handling of his troops, he was for years highly successful [165]. Soon enough he had conquered almost all of Spain.

e. The 'counter-Rome'

Many opponents of Sulla who had succeeded in escaping his reign of terror joined Sertorius. This suggested to him an idea that is the most interesting part of his story. He founded a council of his own, consisting of three hundred of his friends, and called it 'the Roman Senate in derision of the real one'. He also appointed quaestors and praetors, 'making all such arrangements in accordance with the customs of his country' [166]. Osca (Huesca) became his capital where a school was opened for the sons of Celtiberian chiefs, to all intents and purpose to provide him with educated 'Nachwuchs'. The boys went about in purple-bordered togas, as if they were vintage Roman youngsters [167]. There is a strongly dualistic element in all this; Spann is certainly correct when he writes, that "the Sertorian Senate ... was ... politically anti-Roman, seeking independence from or the destruction of Rome" [168]. Anyhow, the Senate in Rome became alarmed and already saw Sertorius marching on Italy, like another Hannibal [169]. It really had reason for fear, for Sertorius, a very capable commander, had strong forces at his disposal and possessed a powerful base in Spain.

It is at this point that we link up again with the story of Pompey who was ordered to fight Sertorius. What exactly was he going to combat? An insurgent general? Certainly! Rebellious nations? Surely! But what he really would fight was an idea - the idea of a 'counter-Rome', the blasphemous supposition that Rome was not all-comprising, not universal, so that there was room for other realms, for other empires.

f. Sertorius defeated

In 76 B.C. Sertorius was in a very strong position. He had sixty thousand infantry under his command and eight thousand cavalry, and "all the advantages : interior lines, easy access to supply and reinforcement, knowledge of the terrain and numerous, aggressive troops, now organized and disciplined by Roman military science. At most, as all parties were well aware, there was nothing between Italy and his sixty thousand men but an ambitious Roman eques (Pompey) and a relatively inexperienced army" [170]. However, a Roman commander, Metellus, still stood in the south of Spain with twenty thousand men.

Pompey marched to Spain through southern France and crossed the Pyrenees; he arrived in the Iberian peninsula in the spring of 76 B.C. Once again, it serves no purpose to recount the vicissitudes of the Sertorian War. There was much hard fighting; Pompey had no easy task. In 75 B.C. the conjunction of the two Roman armies took place near Segovia - bad news for Sertorius who said : "As for this boy (= Pompey), if that old woman (= Metellus) had not come up, I should have given him a sound beating and sent him back to Italy" [171]. Pompey's tenacity slowly but certainly wore out the stamina of his opponent. Town after town was lost, while one Celtiberian tribe after another understood that it had better conclude a pact with the man who obviously would be the victor.

In 72 B.C. Sertorius' second-in-command, Perperna, became jealous of his chief and organized a conspiracy against him [172]. During a banquet the conspirators fell upon him and killed him [173]. This sealed their own fate, for without its really great commander the Sertorian army was no match for the Pompeian forces. Soon it was all over. After his last defeat, Perperna fell into the hands of Pompey and was executed; other conspirators who were taken prisoner also lost their heads [174]. In 71 B.C. the victorious Pompey returned to Rome. In the Pyrenees, on the Col de Pertus, he erected a monument to commemorate his capture of eight hundred and seventy-six towns (Metellus' name was not mentioned) [175].

7. Pompey an ineffectual consul

The great prize for Pompey was that he was elected consul for the year 70 B.C. Politically he was now on the side of the populares. His colleague in the consulate, M. Licinius Crassus, was not exactly a friend of Pompey, since he had supported Sulla and the optimates. Neither of the consuls had dismissed his army; both were encamped near Rome (Crassus had fought the slaves with his). The people feared an outburst of hostilities but with some difficulty a public reconciliation was arranged between the two rivals, after which their armies were disbanded [176]. As a consequence, the renewed outbreak of the civil war was postponed for some time. After his election Pompey inaugurated his political career on December 10, 78 B.C. by haranguing a crowd just outside the town-walls. He promised the plebs that he would restore the tribunicia potestas, and the knights that he would give them back their place in the judiciary. This populist program, which also touched on a series of other matters, was greeted with loud applause [177].

Pompey, 'a military rather than a political animal' [178], soon showed his lack of experience and interest in public affairs. The only point of his program that he fully realized was the restoration of the power of tribunes [179]. For the rest he did not perform much. No democrat at heart, he shunned contact with the plebs and rarely appeared on the Forum; when he came there, "he encompassed his presence with majesty and pomp" [180]. His difference with Crassus became ever more apparent [181]. Pompey's first consulate fizzled out like a damp squib.

He came into his own again in 67 B.C., when he was entrusted with the command against the pirates who infested the eastern Mediterrean and the Aegean. Their "power extended over the whole of the Mediterranean Sea, making it unnavigable and closed to all commerce" [182]. What Pompey got was a proconsular command which made him virtually independent [183]. Protests against conferring so much power upon one man became loud; Q. Hortensius, a senator, complained that such a law would entrust everything to one single commander [184]. Other optimates addressed the popular assembly in the same vein, because they "thought that such unlimited and absolute power ... was ... a thing to be feared".

The only one who did not speak out was Julius Caesar who advocated the law, "not because he cared in the least for Pompey, but from the outset he sought to ingratiate himself with the people and win their support. The rest vehemently attacked Pompey. One of the consuls told him that if he emulated Romulus (= by attempting to become king), he would not escape the fate of Romulus (= who disappeared in a mysterious way)" [185]. The law was passed, and Pompey got what he wanted : an army of one hundred and twenty thousand soldiers and five thousand cavalry, together with five hundred ships [186].

8. Pompey's great victories

It need not be repeated how thorougly and how quickly Pompey fulfilled his task [187]. In less than three months time he cleared all the seas from pirates, defeated and destroyed their fleets, captured their strongholds, and took twenty thousand prisoners. For a change they were not massacred but settled, most of them in Cilician towns [188]. How greatly he thought of himself is shown by the fact that, in true Alexandrian fashion, he rebaptized one of these towns, Soloi, as 'Pompeiopolis' (no longer existing) [189]. This successful expedition added enormously to his fame and bettered his political chances in Rome.

    The reward for this success was a still more grandiose assignment : the command in the war against Mithridates. The victorious Pompey was still busy touring the cities of Cilicia , when in 66 B.C., one of the tribunes, C. Manilius, proposed to entrust him with the command in Asia [190]. He would keep his fleet, take over the Asian army, and become governor of the provinces of Bithynia and Cilicia. Plutarch could not restrain himself from remarking that "this meant the placing of the Roman supremacy into the hands of one man" [191] to which Appian adds that "all these powers had never been given to one general before" [192]. The aristocratic party was of the same opinion, for "they were ... displeased at the power given to Pompey which they regarded as establishing a tyranny". But again the law was passed, and "Pompey, in his absence, was proclaimed master of all the powers which Sulla had exercised after subduing the city in armed warfare" [193]. The difference with Sulla was, of course, that Pompey had grown thus powerful without fighting his own compatriots.

    There is no need to recount all that I have already related in Volume X [194]. Mithridates was definitively defeated. Pompey marched right through Armenia and reached the foothills of the Caucasus range, then turned southward, conquered the remnants of the Seleucid Empire, and making his way through Syria, penetrated into Judaea where he captured Jerusalem. New provinces were established, others enlarged; many kings became clients of Rome.

When, after an absence of five years during which he worked wonders, Pompey returned to the capital, this caused "much commotion there, because it was thought that he would straightway lead his army against the city, and that a monarchy was to be securely established". But nothing of this kind happened. To everybody's surprise he disbanded his army as soon as it had got ashore in Brindisi at the end of the year 62 B.C. The victor came home as if he was a private person returning from a trip abroad [195]. Obviously he fostered no revolutionary plans; he declared that he had always attached the greatest significance to the opinion of the Senate - which, according to Cicero, put him on the side of the optimates [196].

9. Pompeius Magnus

All this does not imply that Pompey thought meanly of himself. On September 29, 61 B.C., one day before his forty-fifth birthday, he celebrated the greatest triumph Rome had ever seen [197]; kings and sons of kings walked in his procession. Riding on his chariot, he wore a mantle that had once adorned the shoulders of Alexander the Great [198]; he was greeted with cries of 'magnus, magnus', as though he were Alexander redivivus, the conqueror of the orbis terrarum [199]. Pompey the Great even acquired mythical proportions; for speaking of his victories, Pliny wrote that "they equalled in brilliance the exploits of Alexander the Great and virtually of Heracles himself" [200]. Henceforward, he wore the laurel wreath on all public occasions [201]. Pompeius Magnus had assumed more than human dimensions.

10. Pompey frustrated

Pompey soon ran into difficulties with the Senate which now took a critical attitude towards him; very probably the senators found him too powerful and tried to take him down a peg or two. They endlessly temporized with two important requests of his : that the Senate should ratify the order he had established in the East, and that lands should be granted to forty thousand of his veterans. When these requests were presented to the comitia, they were sucessfully obstructed there. "But before long the Senate discovered that it must pay heavily for the luxury of teaching Pompey a lesson" [202]. Frustrated in his designs, Pompey now turned for help to Caesar; once again he took his distance from the senatorial camp and made common cause with the populares.

11. The rising star of Julius Caesar

The star of Julius Caesar was quickly rising. The bearer of this name was born in 100 B.C. into a noble family; he was a nephew of Marius and himself married a daughter of Cinna, Cornelia. Through these family ties he was associated with the popular party. This meant that he had trouble to remain out of the claws of Sulla [203]. Later he was received back into the favour of the dictator; after Cornelia's death in 68 B.C. he married Sulla's granddaughter Pompeia. Perhaps he was betting on two horses at once, since this marriage meant a relationship with the optimates. However, he divorced his second wife in 63 B.C., and this severed his links with the optimates for good.

Caesar saw military service in Asia and at sea against the pirates, studied for a while in Rhodes, busied himself with Roman politics, and found the time to dally with many women and to endebt himself heavily. His creditors were constantly at his heels.

12. The First Triumvirate

In 61 B.C., when Caesar was propraetor in Spain [204], he felt that the time had come to make a bid for power; hastily he returned to the capital and shamelessly bribed his way into the consulate for 59 B.C. [205]. Since he placed little faith in the affections of the Senate, he made an alliance with Pompey who had been made sour by the treatment he had received. Caesar showed his diplomatic gifts by reconciling Pompey again with his enemy Crassus who in the past had opposed the former's requests. He "made a compact with both of them, that no step should be taken in public affairs which did not suit anyone of the three" [206]. With this pact the so-called 'First Triumvirate' came into being. A perspicacious Roman observer might have concluded that one of these three would become the first autocratic ruler of the Empire. He would have no problem in eliminating Crassus as rather ineffectual. Faced with such a choice, he would probably have opted for Caesar as the most ruthless of the three.

Caesar's colleague-consul Bibulus was the first to suffer from his harshness. He terrorized the poor man so thoroughly that he did not even venture to leave his house [207]. "From that time on Caesar managed all the affairs of the state alone and after his own pleasure" [208]. But what about Pompey? Pompey was in this period without an official function, except that he was a senator. But his alliance with Caesar was further cemented by his marrying Julia, Caesar's daughter, in 59 B.C. [209]. The consequence was that Pompey was six years older than his father-in-law. He was dependent on his new relative for steering his two laws, ratification of the eastern settlement and land for the veterans, through the legislative assemblies. The passage of these acts was greatly helped by the presence in town of a great many of his veterans whom he ordered to come there [210]. On that occasion Caesar acquired the governorship of Gallia Cis- and Transalpina which would enable him to conquer the rest of Gaul. Triumphantly he declared that he would henceforward walk on the heads of his opponents [211].

13. The strategy of the Triumvirate

The political scene in Rome in the years after 59 B.C. was as unruly as a sea lashed by a violent storm. Or shall we say that it was a lair where vicious snakes tried to bite each other with their poisonous fangs? Caesar fought in Gaul [212] but returned in the winters in order to make his presence felt and to defend his imperium, his command. Pompey and Crassus were as hostile to one another as ever, but Caesar knew how to reconcile them. It is not necessary to describe all the petty intrigues that poisoned Roman politics. Pompey and Crassus, 'les frères ennemis', became the consuls for the year 55 B.C. Some months earlier the Triumvirate had convened in Lucca to plan its strategy. Crassus got the command in Asia, Pompey that in Spain, while Caesar's imperium in Gaul was to be prolonged for five years [213]. Caesar was the money-lender of the party; his days of penury and debt were over now that he was enriching himself in the most scandalous way in Gaul [214]. All Pompey's friends, and probably Pompey and Crassus themselves too, became financially dependent on him [215]. In this way Caesar built up a large clientele.

14. Pompey sole consul

While Caesar was away in Gaul, covering himself with fame and training his armies for what was sure to come, Pompey stayed in Rome. He did not take up his command in Spain but, instead, sent his legates there. Was it out of love for his young wife, as was rumoured in Rome, or was Julia so deeply enamoured of her husband that she pressed him to stay? Plutarch cynically states that "his mature age did not invite such devotion" [216]. Or did he want to keep an eye on developments in Rome as the man on the spot? Anyhow, whether or not he inspired the devotion of his wife, he missed the chance of winning the devotion of battle-hardened legionaries.

His family tie with Caesar was suddenly severed when Julia died in childbed in 54 B.C. [217]. Immediately the situation grew more tense; "the city became at once a tossing sea, and everywhere surging tumult and discordant speeches prevailed, since the marriage alliance which had hitherto veiled rather than restrained the ambition of the two men, was now at an end" [218]. Add to this that Crassus, who had gone to Asia, fell in the disastrous Battle of Carrhae against the Parthians in 53 B.C. [219]. Plutarch laconically remarks that "what had been a great hindrance to the breaking out of civil war was removed; for through fear of him both Pompey and Caesar had somehow or other continued to treat one another fairly" [220].

Rome's political life ran riot. "The magistrates were chosen by means of money and faction fights, with dishonest zeal, with the aid of stones and even of swords. Bribery and corruption prevailed in the most scandalous manner." According to Appian, Pompey secretly hoped that this state of affairs would lead to his becoming dictator [221]. And indeed, people were already talking that way, saying that "the only remedy for existing evils was the authority of a single ruler", by which they thought of Pompey [222]. Even the Senate wanted to make an end of the anarchy by appointing a dictator, but in the end Pompey was made sole consul in 52 B.C., that is, without a colleague - a strange device constitutionally. "By ruling alone he might have the power of a dictator without having the responsibility of a consul" [223].

Pompey, who had allied himself with the rich Crassus family by marrying Crassus' widowed daughter-in-law Cornelia [224], inaugurated without delay a program of reforms which soon enough yielded considerable results [225]. When this program was nearing its completion, Pompey made Cornelia's father Metellus Scipio his colleague in the consulate for the five remaining months of 52 B.C. [226]. When, at the end of the year, he was no longer consul, Pompey remained "none the less the supervisor, and ruler, and all-in-all in Rome. He enjoyed the good-will of the Senate, particularly because they were jealous of Caesar, who did not consult the Senate during his consulship, and because Pompey had so "speedily restored the sick commonwealth" [227]. It might look, therefore, that the new monarch would be Pompey, rather than Caesar.

However, there were a few factors to be reckoned with. The political stance of Pompey had never been wholly clear, least of all to himself. He had chosen the side of the populares for reasons of expediency but had never been a man of the people at heart. He was now moving back to the optimate party. Van Ooteghem thinks that the social group he really belonged to was that of the knights [228]. Further more, Pompey was not an accomplished politician; rather he was a general, a man born for battles in the field but not for those in the political arena [229]. Yet a third factor should be taken into consideration. In the summer of 50 B.C. Pompey fell gravely ill at Naples [230]; Van Ooteghem guesses that it was a severe attack of malaria [231]. An Italian author, E. Ciaceri, believes that this malaria became so chronic that he suffered every year from it [232]. Certainly Cicero wrote that Pompey was dangerously ill every year [233]. Ciaceri thinks that the bad state of his health greatly impaired his energy and his will-power [234], so that in the end he proved no match for that bull of a Caesar.

15. Caesar marches on Rome

In 51 B.C. Caesar, being victorious in Gaul, had his hands free and was about to return to Rome. With or without his army? It was Pompey's idea that his rival "should lay down his arms and return to private life" [235]; the Senate shared this opinion. Greatly fearing a Caesar returning at the head of his armies, it made plans to deprive him of his command [236]; "the victorious army ought to be disbanded" [237]. This was naive. "Caesar was on no account inclined to become a private citizen after holding so important a command and for such a long time, and in particular he was afraid of falling into the power of his enemies. Therefore he made preparations to stay in office in spite of them, collected additional soldiers, gathered money, provided arms, and administered affairs in such a way as to please all" [238].

Caesar cleared his way to Rome by the publication of his report on his campaigns in Gaul, the 'Commentarii de bello Gallico'. It is evident that he intended to show that as a military commander he was on a par with

Pompey. He was very popular, indeed, in Rome and in all Italy, but so was Pompey. What Caesar wanted concretely was the consulate, but of course not with Pompey as his colleague. Opposition against this in the Senate was strong. "The one leader (Pompey) seemed to have the better cause, the other (Caesar) the stronger; Pompey was armed with the authority of the Senate, Caesar with the devotion of his soldiers" [239]. In the Senate "Marcus Cato insisted that they (the senators) should fight to the death rather than allow the Republic to accept a dictate from a mere citizen (= Caesar)" [240].

Caesar was on his way back from Gaul now. Coming from there, he proceeded to Ravenna, the town nearest to Rome that still fell under his imperium; he had five thousand infantry with him and three thousand horse, rather than his whole army [241]. On the first day of the year 49 B.C. the newly elected consuls (Pompey not being one of them) received a letter from Caesar. He was ready, he wrote, to disband his legions and give up his command, if only Pompey would do the same. But in case his rival should retain his command, he would not lay down his own; he had no wish to become exposed to his enemies. He would come, and come quickly, and "avenge his country's wrongs and his own" [242].

Unwillingly, but pressed by Mark Antony, the consuls made this letter public [243]. When it was read in the Senate, "it was considered a declaration of war" [244]. Scipio, Pompey's father-in-law, brought forward a proposal that Caesar had to disband his troops before the first of July; if not, he would be considered a rebel against the state [245]. This motion was carried almost unanimously. A few days later, on the 7th of January, the Senate issued a senatusconsultum ultimum ordering the public officials to take care that the Republic should not incur any damage; this was, writes Van Ooteghem, 'tantamount to a declaration of the state of siege' [246].

War was now inevitable. Pompey was full of optimism. "In whatever part of Italy I stamp upon the ground, there will spring up armies of foot and horse" [247]. The Senate ordered Pompey to levy an army of one hundred and thirty thousand men throughout all Italy; the necessary funds were taken from the public treasury [248]. Cicero, while praising the efforts made, found it rather late in the day [249]. And he was quite right : Caesar was already on his way to Rome.

Caesar had decided not to wait for his troops to arrive from Gaul. In the night of January 11, 49 B.C. he crossed the frontier river Rubicon, thus leaving the confines of his imperium, and a few hours later occupied by surprise Ariminium (Rimini) with five cohorts; another five cohorts were directed to Arretium (Arezzo) [250]. It was at this Rubicon that Caesar spoke the words that became proverbial : "iacta alea est", the die is cast [251]. A few days later his forward troops were in Arretium and Ancona. Rome was directly threatened now; it was the fifth time in forty years that a Roman army marched on the capital (to say nothing of the conspiracy of Catilina, a disgruntled patrician, who in 63 B.C. planned to conquer Rome).

16. Pompey evacuates Rome

There was panic in Rome, and there was panic in the country-side. "People did not look for any moderate treatment from Caesar ... On the contrary, inasmuch as the greater part of his army consisted of barbarians, they expected that their misfortunes would be far greater in number and more terrible than the former ones (= those inflicted on them by Marius and Sulla - F.)" [252]. "Nearly all Italy was in commotion ... Those who dwelt outside the city came rushing in hurried flight from all quarters into Rome, and those who dwelt in Rome were rushing out of it" [253]. The town resembled an ant-heap that someone was poking with a stick. Portents were seen everywhere; people flocked to the temples to pray [254]. The magistrates were no longer obeyed [255].

Pompey knew he had no chance to defend Rome; he had only two legions at his disposal, and since these had served under Caesar, he did not trust them. Large scale recruiting south of Rome proved impossible as the whole region was insecure [256]. Not that he trusted the Romans any better : many were on the side of Caesar and showed this openly [257]. He therefore caused the Senate to declare the state of war [258], with which the Second Civil War officially began.

He then decided to leave the city, departing in the evening of January 17, ordering all senators to follow him and declaring that "he would regard as a partisan of Caesar anyone who remained behind" [259]. But return he would, he said. "If Sulla could make it, I can make it too" [260]. In the next days the consuls and the majority of the Senate followed his example [261]. There was a great uproar in Rome, what with packing and loading of waggons and running to and fro and saying farewell and kissing the ground [262].

The rallying-point of the fugitives was Capua where Pompey arrived on the 19th [263]; he immediately began levying troops [264] and furthermore, there were two legions stationed in Apulia. There was a last-minute attempt at reconciliation; messengers went to and fro. But when Pompey demanded of Caesar that he should evacuate all the towns in Italy he had conquered so far, his adversary refused [265].

17. Caesar fails to catch Pompey

Caesar was in no hurry to capture Rome, for "the capital, he knew, lay as a prize before the victors" [266]. What he also knew was that his rival was concentrating his army, now some six legions strong, at Brindisi; from this harbour he intended to cross to the Balkans and carry on the war from there. "Caesar, accordingly, was anxious to join issue with Pompey before he could sail away and fight the war in Italy, if he could but overtake his adversary while he was still at Brundisium" [267]. Had Caesar succeeded in defeating him at Brindisi, he would have become the sole master already in 49 B.C. There was a real chance for Caesar to arrive in time, since Pompey had not enough ships to ferry his men over in one haul [268].

Caesar arrived before the walls of the town on March 9. He proved incapable of preventing the transfer of the Pompeian troops. Once again Pompey showed himself a brilliant tactician. Manning the walls with his most experienced veterans, and barricading all the streets of the town, he managed to bring the last cohorts aboard ship, and finally even the men on the walls. In the evening of March 17, Pompey himself sailed out of the harbour. When Caesar dared to enter the city, he found no troops there. Once again the die was cast [269].

18. Caesar in Rome

A few days later Caesar entered Rome; nobody offered any resistance. "In sixty days he had become master of all Italy, without shedding any blood" [270]. He made it perfectly clear who was boss now. He sent out one of his underlings to take possession of Sicily where Marcus Cato was governor. When Cato asked who had given these orders, the new governor replied : "The master of Italy has sent me on this business". Caesar also "hewed down the bars of the public treasury, and when ... one of tribunes tried to prevent him from entering threatened him with death. He took away money hitherto untouched" [271]. But all things considered, his position was not really enviable. Master of Italy he was indeed, to which we may add Gaul, his recent conquest; in Spain and North Africa, however, the Pompeians were strong, while the whole East, with all its resources of money and fleets, lay at the feet of Pompey. Plutarch states that Caesar "greatly feared a protraction of the war" [272]. And indeed, what came was what Cicero called 'a world-convulsion' [273].

Caesar was prudent enough to act with moderation in Rome. "He found the people shuddering with the recollection of the horrors of Marius and Sulla, and he cheered them with the prospect and promise of clemency" [274]. Seeing how the land lay, many senators returned to the capital, so that Caesar assembled some sort of government, although he had no consuls [275]. He did not conjure up the spectres of the past by having himself appointed dictator. At the end of the year, however, he became one of the consuls for 48 B.C. [276].

19. The Second Civil War

It is not necessary to recount the history of the Second Civil War in detail; a broad outline may suffice. After having occupied Sardinia and Sicily [277], Caesar "placed Aemilius Lepidus in charge of the city of Rome, and Mark Antony in charge of Italy and of the army guarding it" [278].

a. The conquest of Spain

With respect to the military situation it must be stated that Caesar had lost the initiative : he "was at a loss which way to turn or from what point to begin the war" [279]. Since the seas were controlled by Pompey - "his navy was simply irresistible" [280] -, Caesar was as yet unable to cross the Adriatic and, instead, marched to Spain. In the early morning of April 6, 49 B.C., Caesar departed for the Iberian peninsula; since Pompey had taken all the ships with him, he had to travel through Gaul (for exactly the same reason he was unable to follow his opponent to the Balkans) [281]. In Gaul he had to spend a month before Massilia which was under the control of the Pompeians; being incapable of capturing the town, he left the siege to one of his commanders and hastened on to Spain [282]. In his first encounters with the Pompeian forces he was far from lucky, so much so that many Romans gave up his cause as lost and some of his senators even deserted to Pompey [283]. But Caesar was a brilliant general, as he had proved so often already. He succeeded in turning the tables on his adversaries by defeating them; in less than three months he became master of the Iberian peninsula. He behaved with remarkable leniency. Not one of the prisoners was put to death; he sent the officers home and took the rest into his service. "By this course both his reputation and his cause profited not a little; for he won over all the cities in Spain and all the soldiers there" [284].

On his return journey through southern Gaul, he arrived before Massilia that was still holding out; seeing Caesar coming, however, the town capitulated. Nobody was put to death, but Massilia was robbed of its fleet, "and later of everything else except the name of freedom (= its autonomy)" [285]. Late in the year 49 B.C. Caesar was back in Rome; it was now time to fill the political vacuum. He was appointed dictator on the proposal of Lepidus (very probably at his own instigation) [286]. Although the people trembled at the very word 'dictator' [287], Caesar "committed no act of terror while holding this office". The exiles were called back, while the children of those proscribed by Sulla got back their political rights [288]. His first dictatorship was of short duration, only eleven days, since he resigned the function when he was elected consul [289].

b. Caesar's quasi-legal authority

Even before the beginning of his term of office as consul, Caesar left Rome for the campaign against Pompey himself. His situation at that particular moment was considerably better than it had been at the beginning of the year; he now had Italy, Gaul, and the Iberian peninsula behind him, but not yet North Africa where his subcommanders were fighting the Pompeians. Dio characterizes Caesar's position very aptly by stating that he did not need the title of dictator at all, "since he had quite all the authority and functions of the position constantly in his grasp. For he exercised the power afforded by arms, and also received in addition a quasi-legal authority from the Senate that was on the spot (i.e. of those senators who happened to be in Rome - F.), in that he was granted permission to do with impunity whatever he might wish" [290]. Could it be stated more clearly that the Republic was at an end?

c. Pompey's government in Thessalonica

When Pompey in March 49 B.C. had sailed out of Brindisi harbour, he came ashore in Dyrrachium (Durazzo, Dürres in present-day Albania) [291]. From there he led his five legions along the Via Egnatia to Thessalonica. There, in the capital of the province of Macedonia, a great many Roman officials, Cicero among them, were with him or came to join him, "since they believed that he had more justice on his side and would conquer in the war [292], ... all the nobility, countless senators, ex-praetors, ex-consuls, and victors in the great wars" [293]. Because there were about two hundred senators in Thessalonica, Pompey could take the view that this town was the provisional seat of government as long as the capital was in the hands of the usurper. Using his authority as proconsul, he proclaimed that "the capital was in the hands of his enemies and that they themselves were the Senate and would maintain the form of government wherever they should be" [294].

But, as Dio remarks, this was only a façade of legality, for "in reality it was Pompey and Caesar who were supreme, with for the sake of good repute the legal titles of consul and proconsul; yet their acts were not those which these offices permitted, but whatever they themselves pleased" [295]. The scene was wholly dominated by the two bulls that would ferociously charge at each other. For the time being the Empire had two capitals and two governments that were dualistically opposed. It should be noted, however, that the split in the Empire ran along the East-West line. In consequence, we have to do, and this for many years to come, not only with the dualism of the optimates and populares and that of Caesar and Pompey, but also with that of the eastern and western worlds.

d. Caesar's predicament

According to Dio, Pompey disposed of five hundred men-of-war [296], and according to Appian, as many as six hundred, with additionally 'a great number of transports and ships of burden' [297]. His land forces grew to nine legions, while he expected two more from Syria [298]. Add to this seven thousand picked horsemen [299], three thousand archers and two cohorts of slingers [300]. His soldiers loved and respected him [301]. From all over the East vassal-kings came to pay their homage to the prospective victor [302]. For who could doubt to whom the final victory would fall? There was, however, one man who had no doubts : Caesar.

e. Pompey defeated in Greece

The dare-devil Caesar, having collected enough transports, crossed the Adriatic from Brindisi and got safely ashore in southern Epirus on January 5, 48 B.C. with seven legions [303], profiting from the fact that his adversary believed him still far away [304]. A few days later he occupied Apollonia, more to the north, which he found unguarded, so that he was now provided with a base on the coast [305]; in April Mark Antony arrived with five more legions [306]. Although Caesar now had a large army, nevertheless in the first encounters Pompey was more successful. In a battle near Dyrrhachium Caesar lost almost a thousand infantry and had to leave thirty-two standards in the hands of the enemy. Because of this victory Pompey was given the title of 'imperator' [307]. Caesar had every reason to believe that the end of his perilous adventure had come, but Pompey did not press on [308]. "To-day", said Caesar, "the victory would have been with the enemy if they had had a victor in command" [309].

All the same, this result made the Pompeians believe that they were already the victors [310]. Pompey's entourage "was so elated that they were eager to have the issue decided by battle". Pompey, more prudent, tried to restrain them, but when his opponent, plagued by lack of supplies, left the coast and marched inland, Pompey gave in [311]. He began by using Fabian tactics, following Caesar on his heels, harassing him as much as he could, but studiously avoiding battle [312]. But his friends and his army would not have it so; they pressed him to give battle "as though it were already won. Many of them adorned their tents with laurel branches, the insignia of victory". At last Pompey yielded to their entreaties, against his better judgment, "as though he were no longer commander but under command" [313]; Plutarch says he "was a slave to fame and loath to disappoint his friends" [314]. But full of dire forebodings he remarked to them that "whichever side should conquer, that day would be the beginning of great evils to the Romans of all future time" [315].

In the plain of Pharsalus, in Thessaly, he found Caesar. On August 8, 48 B.C. battle was joined. As usual, the numbers given for the combatants on both sides vary wildly, but both hosts were large, with Pompey's forces the stronger by far, especially his cavalry [316]. Pompey trusted that his horsemen would decide the issue [317]. Some philosophically minded persons, Greeks and Romans, who were present, realized what was the background of all this. They "began to reflect upon the pass to which contentiousness and greed had brought the sovereign Roman state. For with kindred arms, fraternal ranks, and common standards, the strong manhood and might of a single city in such numbers was turning its own hand against itself" [318].

When the hostilities were opened, Pompey's far superior cavalry proved unable to cut through Caesar's serried ranks [319]; repulsed, the Pompeian horsemen "ingloriously took to flight" [320]. Seeing his forces getting routed by the enemy, Pompey lost heart; "most like a man bereft of sense and crazed, who had already forgotten that he was Pompey the Great, and without a word to anyone, he walked slowly off to his camp", muttering verses of Homer to himself [321]. There he sat in his tent, speechless. When at the end of the day enemy troops spurred on by Caesar himself reached the camp, he threw himself on a horse and fled [322].

f. The fugitive

While Caesar, who had entered Pompey's tent, sat eating the supper prepared for his opponent, the fleeing man morosely reflected "how in a single hour he had lost the power and the glory gained in so many wars and conflicts" [323]. He passed through Larissa and the Vale of Tempe after which he reached the coast of the Aegean. After having rested a few hours in a fisherman's hut, at early dawn he boarded a river-boat cruising along the coast, until he found a Roman merchant-man that ferried him across the Aegean to Mytilene where he was united with wife Cornelia and his son.

Meanwhile the fugitive had recovered somewhat from his nervous breakdown. He knew that his considerable sea-forces were still intact; in Attaleia, on the south-coast of Asia Minor (the present-day Antalya), some ships of the line loaded with soldiers arrived, while he was also joined by some sixty senators [324]. But the Greek cities along the coast, the vassal-kings of Asia Minor, Syria, Rhodes, Cyprus, did not prove eager to help him, what with Caesar's giant shadow looming on the horizon. However, North Africa and Egypt suggested a solution; with the whole coast firmly in Pompeian hands it might be feasible to invade Italy from there. The unhappy man was cheered up by the news that Cato with a fleet and an army was crossing to Africa [325].

g. Death on the Nile

Pompey now sailed to Cyprus. There he borrowed money with which to pay his soldiers, for he levied some two thousand men in the island [326]. With this small force he crossed the sea and anchored before Pelusium in eastern Egypt. There the once so great man humbly asked the thirteen-year-old Pharaoh Ptolemy XIII for asylum in Alexandria [327]. But this boy-king was as wax in the hands of his council, which reasoned that if they were to grant Pompey his wish, they would make Caesar into an enemy; it was thought more advisable to curry favour with him [328]. By killing Pompey, "they would gratify Caesar and have nothing to fear from Pompey". Theodotus, the man who proposed this noble plan, said cynically : "A dead man does not bite" [329].

So a boat was sent to row Pompey ashore; since this was only a simple fishing-boat and no state-barge, suspicions were aroused. But in spite of the entreaties of his friends, he stepped into the boat. There reigned profound silence during the short trip; Pompey immersed himself in repeating the speech he would deliver to the king. When he had stepped ashore, he was run through by three men in turn. His wife Cornelia was able to witness the horrid scene from aboard her ship. The murderers cut off their victim's head [330] and brought it to Caesar who had already arrived in Egypt by then; shuddering, he turned away from the sight. He gave orders to burn and entomb its ashes [331]. Pompey's naked corpse was left lying on the shore; his faithful freedman Philip made a funeral pile and burned it; the ashes were taken to Cornelia who gave them burial [332].

h. Caesar's situation at the end of the year 48 B.C.

With Crassus and Pompey out of the way, Caesar was, at least in theory, the sole ruler of the Empire now. But the reality was different : in many parts of the Roman world Pompeian forces were still holding out. After his victory at Pharsalus he first of all went to Egypt. In Volume X I have extensively narrated how Caesar, virtually acting as a Pharaoh, had great trouble at first of maintaining himself at Alexandria, how he had his love affair with Queen Cleopatra IX, and how he finally managed to bring the country under his control. Nominally Egypt remained independent but only as a vassal-kingdom of Rome [333].

Although Caesar could by no means feel sure of his position at Rome, where his enemies agitated against him and his veterans were unruly [334], he was at least secure of his legal status. In October 48 B.C. he had been made dictator for an unlimited period; he made Mark Antony his 'magister equitum', his Master of Horse, that is, and his deputy in Italy while he was away [335].

j. Victories in Asia Minor and North Africa

In Asia Minor everything hung in the balance once again. News arrived that Pharnaces, the son of Mithridates VI, making use of the confusion in the Empire, had invaded his ancestral kingdom and reconquered it. He seemed intent on reestablishing the power sphere of his father, for he also occupied Bithynia and Cappadocia and threatened Lesser Armenia. Caesar hastened thither with three legions and destroyed Pharnaces' army in the Battle of Zela on August 2, 47 B.C. He had acted quick as lightning, which he summarized in three words written to a friend : 'Veni, vidi, vici', I came, I saw, I triumphed [336].

After this victory he passed through Rome where he was elected consul for the third time, for the year 46 B.C. [337]. He then had to speed on to Africa where strong Pompeian forces posed a threat. On April 6, 46 B.C. Caesar won a decisive victory over them at Thapsus in Tunisia (now in ruins). The sequel was bloody in the extreme. Caesar coolly states that his veterans massacred the Pompeian infantry to the last man, to the number of ten thousand [338]. The last bastion of the Pompeians was Utica on the coast, where Marcus Cato commanded; this stronghold was captured, after which Cato committed suicide [339].

k. Triumphs and honours

When back in Rome, in the last days of September 46 B.C., Caesar celebrated not one but four triumphs, for his victories in Gaul, Egypt, Pontus, and North Africa respectively [340]. Incredible amounts of money, in gold and silver, were carried along in the procession, together with 2282 golden crowns dedicated to the imperator, the total weight of all this metal being 1585 tons [341]. Caesar himself rode on his chariot surrounded by a greater number of lictors than any official before him [342]. He lavishly distributed money; every officer and soldier of his army received a generous sum, while a smaller amount was given to every plebeian citizen. Various spectacles were offered : mock infantry and cavalry engagements, and even a naval combat for which part of the Campus Martius was hollowed out and filled with water. There was a spectacular fight of twenty elephants against twenty others. On the last day of the festivities, October 1, Caesar treated the Roman populace to a dinner at twenty-two thousand tables. The host was present in person; afterwards, he was accompanied home by the people by the light of torches carried on elephants [343]. Never before had Rome seen such a splendour.

Not everybody, however, was pleased with all this pomp. It was considered less than tactful that Arsinoe, once a Pharaoh of Egypt, a woman, a queen [344], had to walk in the procession in chains, while the excessive number of lictors was found offensive. He was blamed for the great number of slaves and captives killed in the sham fights, as though, it was said, he had not already shed blood enough. Protests became loud against the money squandered on all these displays - money the imperator had obtained unjustly [345].

1. The defeat of the Pompeians in Spain

Caesar had much to attend to. The Iberian peninsula was once again virtually in the hands of the Pompeians; Caesar's legates on the spot were not equal to the situation [346]. The imperator had to take things in hand himself; in December 46 B.C. he arrived in Spain. His main opponent was Cneius Pompeius, the oldest son of Pompey the Great, with thirteen legions under his command. The decisive battle for the possession of the peninsula took place on March 17, 45 B.C. near Munda (now Montilla near Cordoba). At first Caesar's men had the worst of the fighting; their ranks began to fall back under the fierce impact of the Pompeians. But their supreme commander threw off his helmet, seized a shield from one of the legionaries, cried "Let this day be the end of my life!", and ran ahead of his troops till some ten feet from the enemy; from all sides missiles were raining on him. Then his own battle-line rushed on so that he finally won the victory although with the greatest difficulty. He said that he had often fought for victory, but this time he had fought even for his existence [347]. The losses of the Pompeians were enormous, those of his own troops only slight. Pompeius himself took to flight but was overtaken and killed [348].

After having completed the pacification of Spain, the victor returned to Rome to celebrate his fifth triumph [349]. The painful thing was that what he celebrated was not a victory over foreign enemies but one of Romans over Romans; this had never happened before.

20. The road to the end

a. Still more honours

By now Caesar was the undisputed master of the Roman Empire. Already before his departure for Spain the process of his magnification, even of his deification, had set in, mainly orchestrated by himself. He was made consul for the fourth time for 45 B.C., this time 'sine collega' [350]. When back from Spain, he was appointed dictator for life [351]. Not much was left now of the venerable constitution of the Republic with its careful system of checks and balances. The Senate heaped one honour after another on him : he became consul for ten years [352] and censor for life [353]. He was proclaimed 'pater patriae' [354], and what is very telling, the title of 'imperator' too was to be added to his name as a hereditary possession; Dio comments that this signified that he would permanently exercize supreme power [355]. All the Roman rulers after him called themselves 'Imperator' as well as 'Caesar' [356]. It is well known that modern terms like 'emperor' and 'empereur' are derived from 'Imperator' just as 'keizer' (Dutch), 'Kaiser', and 'czar' from Caesar. Add to this that Caesar was to remain pontifex maximus (which he was already) for life (which office would devolve upon an eventual son [357]), and it will be clear that all the highest political, military, and sacral functions were henceforward concentrated in one hand.

That the idea of political sovereignty had undergone a considerable shift was made clear in several ways. Caesar was effectively screened off from political attacks by making him, just like the tribunes, inviolable [358]; "if anyone insulted him by deed or word, that man should be an outlaw and accursed" [359]. All his future decrees were declared legally valid in anticipation [360]; in other words, he could do what he wanted. Roman magistrates wore the toga pretexta as their robe of office; Caesar, however, was given the right of wearing the triumphal garment, the toga purpurea, whenever and wherever he wished [361]; its colour must have reminded the Roman public of a royal garb. He wore the laurel crown continuously, which suited him well since he was getting bald [362], 'a disfigurement which troubled him greatly' [363]. When acting officially, Roman officials were seated in an ivory seat; Caesar was allowed to sit in a golden chair which was placed higher than those of the other magistrates [364].

b. A royal magistrate

All these honours, bestowed on him by a subservient Senate, show that Caesar was not only a very important magistrate but an exceptional one at that, of a sort the Republic had not seen before. No wonder that many were reminded of the long ago days of the Roman monarchy. Caesar was enjoying royal distinctions when he got the right to stamp his image on the coinage, and this would equally the case when it was decreed that his birthday would be celebrated each year, just like the royal anniversaries in the Netherlands and Great Britain [365]. And just like a king, he would have his own bodyguard, consisting not of ordinary soldiers but of senators and knights [366]. Finally, the fifth month of the year, the Quintilis [367], was renamed 'Julius', a name it has kept in our modern calendar [368]. Caesar made no secret of it that, in his opinion, the Republic was now incarnate in his person : "the state", he said, "was nothing, a mere name, without body or form" [369]. This crude utterance signified a fundamental mutation in the political fabric of the Roman state. "L'état, c'est moi', obviously. Political power which had hitherto been invested in a system, now became embodied in a person.

c. Signs of deification

Perhaps people's thoughts, or suspicions, went even farther than the Roman monarchy, namely to the East where kings had always been almighty and even divine. Had Caesar not made his Egyptian paramour come to Rome and installed her in his own gardens where she - shamelessly, said the Roman public - kept court [370]. And wasn't she a queen and a godlike Pharaoh? And wouldn't it be fitting that her amant should become king too, perhaps even a divine one? Her protector had a golden statue of Cleopatra placed in the temple of Venus Genitrix, next to that of the goddess [371], as though she was divine herself, the equal of Venus. This temple was a new one, erected on the orders of Caesar, for the veneration of the goddess whom he considered the ancestor of his race [372], evidently to point out that he had a divine origin himself.

Suspicions that Caesar was aiming at downright deification were not wholly unwarranted. Perhaps he did not deliberately strive for this, and perhaps popular enthusiasm was responsible for pressing marks of divinity on him, but the fact of the mater is that he did not repudiate this adulation. The Senate had already declared him a demi-god. Now a bronze statue of his would be placed on the Capitol, facing that of Jupiter [373]. During the ceremonial procession at the games in the Circus a chariot with his statue would appear, together with those of the gods; another image of his would placed in the temple of Quirinus, the ancient protecting deity of Rome, with the revealing inscription 'To the invincible god' (Caesar, however, ordered this text to be erased, although the statue itself remained where it was); finally another statue was placed on the Capitol, next to those of the Roman kings [374].

d. Caesar and Roman dualism

The question which must occupy us now is not whether this self-adulation aroused opposition - which it did - but whether Caesar, as the sole and almighty ruler of the Empire, would have been able to lay the two great Roman dualisms to rest : the imperial dualism on the one hand, and the internal dissension on the other, which had plagued the Republic for a century. I understand by the first dualism, the imperial one, the zest for conquest which had dominated Roman life for six centuries and which had led to the destruction of states and the subjection of nations, frequently even to their total extinction. The Romans had never recognized the rights of political entities other than their own.

Caesar, for his part, had not the slightest intention to make an end of all this. Quite the contrary! In the last months of his life he was planning an enormous campaign in which he would out-Alexander Alexander. A punitive expedition against the Parthians would be undertaken. After their defeat, of which there could be no doubt, he would push on through the Caucasus, march westward through Russia, subject the Balkans and Germany, and then return triumphantly to Rome. Thus, for the first time in history, all the lands between the Atlantic and the Caspian would be united in one Empire. Extensive preparations were made, but nothing came of the campaign since Caesar was murdered in March 44 B.C. That nobody took up these plans to execute them in his place proves that the heyday of Roman imperialism was already over.

With regard to that other dualism, the internal one, the great question was whether Caesar would succeed in overcoming the deep and fierce dissensions which had been the bane of the Republic for a hundred years. Of course, it was his aim that the optimates would no longer fight the populares, or the reverse, or that any ambitious general would be free to march on Rome to establish his rule there, only to be combated by another equally ambitious general. Probably he felt that the concentration of all power in his hands would be henceforward sufficient to prevent all this. Many people, especially Romans of the old stamp, hoped that he would restore the Republic to its old splendour [375]. And indeed, Caesar posed as the second founder of Rome, the second Romulus.

It cannot be denied that he treated his Pompeian opponents with great moderation; the 'clementia Caesaris' became more or less proverbial. In 44 B.C. he proclaimed a general amnesty for all Pompeians who had fought him; some of them he even promoted to offices [376]. He made important reforms in the management of the provinces; Carthage and Corinth were to be rebuilt and repeopled [377]. He also tackled some of the worst problems of the Republic, in particular of the capital itself. Some eighty thousand proletarians received land in the provinces; new colonies were founded [378]. In this, wrote Adcock, he acted as the heir of the Gracchi [379]. He gave land also to his veterans so that they would not swell the moneyless masses in Rome [380]. Measures were taken to alleviate the plight of the pauperized 'plebs urbana' [381]. A lasting reform was that of the Roman chronology by which the so-called 'Julian calendar' was introduced, a considerable improvement which remained in use till a second reform by Pope Gregorius XIII in 1582.

e. Caesar's undoing

All these measures, and others which I have not mentioned, were no doubt salutary. But up to 44 B.C. Caesar had spent almost all his life in the field where he had been a merciless, often cruel general, crushing enemies all around the Mediterranean - all this wholly in accordance with the tradition of Roman imperialism. Wouldn't it ask for a totally different man if he wanted to be the great pacifier? We have already seen that Caesar was in haste with his policy of reconciliation and his legislative program. What he really desired was to depart for the great new campaign that would keep him away from Rome for years. Did politics bore him? And then, Caesar was ambitious; he wanted more for himself than any Roman before him had ever acquired, more power, more fame.

A line of Willam Blake comes to my mind here : "The strongest poison ever known came from Caesar's laurel crown". Caesar's lust for power was slowly poisoning him; he lost sight of what was reasonably possible. Those who hoped that he would restore the Republic to its former glory had probably overheard what he had said to the Senate already in 49 B.C. : that he would govern the state 'per se', that is, by his own authority, and nobody else's [382]. Not only were all the public functions concentrated in his own person, he also ruled - and this was quite new - with a kind of personal cabinet, a 'cabala', as the Italians later called this sort of government; intimate friends of the dictator individually managed a 'department' and disposed of staff for this [383].

Caesar felt that the stability of the state depended solely on him. "He was wont to declare that it was not so much to his own interest as to that of his country that he remain alive; he had long since had his fill of power and glory; but if aught befell him, the commonwealth would have no peace, but would be plunged in civil strife under much worse conditions" [384]. And for this reason he found that in the field of politics everything was permitted to him. Cicero mentions a quotation from Euripides' 'Phoenician women' [385] that was repeatedly on Caesar's lips, to the effect that if what is right must be violated, it should be because of reigning (power); in all other things one should observe piety (morality) [386]. He made a clear, dualistic distinction between the domain of the gods and that of ordinary life and of politics. It was this uncontrolled zest for power that conjured up exactly those evils that Caesar wanted to exorcize.

We cannot be wholly sure that he intended to make himself king, but his opponents saw that hateful word REX already rising above the horizon [387]. True enough, when he was hailed by the plebs as king, he retorted : "I am Caesar and no king". And when Mark Antony at the Lupercalia feast several times attempted to place a crown on his head, he refused as many times. But, as Suetonius remarks, "he could not rid himself of the odium of having aspired to the title of monarch". He himself fortified this suspicion. When someone placed a laurel wreath on his statue, with a white fillet attached to it - which was an emblem of royalty -, and two tribunes ordered to take this away, he was angry [388]. It even came so far that a senatorial friend of his proposed that Caesar should indeed be given the title of king - to be used not in Italy, but elsewhere in the Empire -, since it was found in the Sybilline books that Parthia could only be conquered by a king [389]. The day of the formal liquidation of the Republic seemed near.

f. The Ides of March

Many influential Romans, old-fashioned republicans as well as those whom Caesar had frustrated, grew hotly indignant about the course Caesar was taking. Some sixty persons who dubbed themselves 'republicans' became involved in a conspiracy against Caesar's life; its main leader was Quintus Servilius Caepio Brutus, once a personal friend of Caesar. This Brutus was a descendant of Lucius Iunius Brutus who had toppled the monarchy in 509 B.C., and also a nephew of that republican par excellence, Marcus Porcius Cato [390]. There were rumours that in the Senate a proposal would be brought forward to grant Caesar the title of king on March 15, 44 B.C.; the conspirators appointed this day for their assault on their enemy. He did not heed the warnings he received from several sides : "Caesar, beware the Ides of March!". He took his seat in the Senate as usual but was fallen upon by the conspirators who stabbed him to death. Brutus raised his bloody dagger above his head and loudly proclaimed that freedom had been regained [391].

21. The aftermath

a. Antony's emergency measures

Caesar's death became the immediate cause of a renewed outbreak of the civil war. It is as Heinz Bellen wrote : "Caesar had set so much in motion, but he had not found a way out of the dilemma in which the state was caught" [392], in other words, not even he had been able to overcome the internal dualism. "The chaos is inextricable", sighed Cicero, "when he with his genius did not find a way out, who can?" [393]. If the conspirators had expected that political power would fall into their lap like a ripe apple, they had reckoned without Antony, Caesar's most faithful friend. After a few hours of panic he came to himself again and began to act. In the night of March 15 to 16 he had the state treasury brought into his house, together with Caesar's private treasury and his papers, which the murdered man's widow Calpurnia had entrusted to him [394]. In his function as consul he convened a meeting of the Senate on March 17 [395]; the murderers did not turn up [396]. Manoeuvring very cleverly between the pro- and anti-Caesar factions, he succeeded in preventing any declaration to the effect that Caesar had been a tyrant, while at the same time he ensured that an amnesty was granted the murderers [397]. In the session of the next day the senators "gave a vote of thanks to Antony for having stopped an incipient civil war" [398].

b. Octavian appears on the scene

However, the reading of Caesar's testament created new trouble. It was opened in Antony's house on March 19; it was a great disappointment for him since the main beneficiary was not he (he got nothing at all) but the dictator's great-nephew, a grandson of his sister Julia, Gaius Octavius [399], who was to become the Emperor Augustus; in this will Caesar adopted the fatherless young man as his son. Born in 63 B.C. Octavius was nineteen years old; he had accompanied Caesar, who had no son of his own, during the campaign in Spain. He was not present at the reading of the will because his adoptive father had sent him to the Balkans to help prepare the campaign against the Parthians; on hearing what had happened, he hastened to Rome as quickly as possible [400]. There was a halo around the sun, when he entered the city, says Pliny [401].

c. The funeral speech

On that same 19th of March the Senate decreed that Caesar should have a public funeral at which occasion his will would be read in public [402]. The scenes that took place on that day are immortalized by Shakespeare in his 'Julius Caesar'. A great mob assembled on the Forum to hear Antony delivering the funeral speech; Brutus had been imprudent enough to grant him this privilege. When the people heard that Caesar had given his gardens to them as a public park and that every citizen in town would have seventy-five drachmas, they became enthusiastic but at the same time angry when they were told that their benefactor was accused of tyranny. Emotions were already running high, people were wailing and lamenting, when Antony began his famous funeral speech [403].

Speaking with 'a severe and gloomy countenance', he extolled the deceased dictator as 'the peerless protector of his country', even as superhuman, sacred, and inviolable. Standing before the bier 'like one inspired', he "hymned the dead man as a celestial deity, raising his hands to heaven in order to testify to Ceasar's divine birth". He then uncovered the corpse and "lifted the robe on the point of a spear and shook it aloft, pierced with dagger-thrusts and red with the dictator's blood". Then somebody raised a wax image of Caesar above the bier and turned it around and around so that everyone could see the twenty-three wounds. Now "the people could no longer bear the pitiful sight presented to them". They rushed away and set the Senate-house on fire. Having done this, they returned, made a funeral pile from the benches on the Forum, and burned the corpse on it. A few days later "the murderers fled from the city secretely" [404].

22. Postumous deification

The divinisation of Caesar was a development that was of the greatest importance for the prestige of the Roman emperors. Already begun during his life, the process was continued after his death [405]. According to Helga Gesche, it was the population of Rome that saw a god in him [406]. Soon after his death, an altar was erected at the spot where he was killed, on which sacrifices were brought 'as to a god' [407]. Dio enumerates all the honours awarded to the dead Caesar. A shrine dedicated to his name was erected at the Forum; his image, together with that of his dea protrectrix, Venus, was to be carried in the ceremonial processions in the Circus Maximus. Rome's warfare was henceforward put under the aegis of Caesar, for thanksgivings would be offered to him for all future victories. His birthday would be celebrated each year. There were still more honours of this kind [408]. There can be no doubt that Caesar was considered to have taken his place among the gods [409].

23. Octavian and Antony

The one who profited from this was, of course, Octavius, or rather Octavianus, as he is called usually [410], who in this way became 'filius divi', which gave him some sort of precedence over his competitors. He appeared like a meteorite on the Roman scene, a man of singular purpose, determined and merciless to the point of cruelty, and even beyond. When he arrived in Italy, he added the name of Caesar to his own name [411]. There can be no doubt that he saw himself as Caesar's successor. In November 44 B.C., addressing the people, he swore, pointing to the statue of Caesar, that "he would acquire the honour of his father" [412].

To Mark Antony, however, he proved far from welcome. Up to that moment, the consul was master of the situation. His enemies had taken to their heels; the Senate ate out of his hand [413]. But he showed himself petty as well as imprudent when, on the arrival of Octavian, he did not go to meet him nor did he send anyone to salute him in his name; he had nothing but contempt for the young man [414]. A few days later the two men met in a house in the gardens of Pompey; Antony showed his displeasure by letting Octavian wait at the vestibule [415]. During the interview that followed they fell out entirely when Antony refused to hand over Caesar's private funds to his adoptive son. When the young man asked for the money, the older man "was astonished at his freedom of speech and his boldness, which seemed much beyond the bounds of propriety and of his years. He was offended by his words, because they were wanting in the respect due to him, and still more by the demand for money". Octavian in his turn was irritated by the patronizing manner in which the older man addressed him [416].

24. Preparations for war

In October Antony discovered that some of his bodyguards were plotting against his life; he saw the hand of Octavian behind this. Whether true or not, this made the breach between the two complete [417]. Already in April 44 B.C. Cicero had prophesied that it would come to fierce conflicts between Antony and Octavian [418]. Now the first steps towards civil war were taken. Antony seemed to have the best point of departure. The dualistic character of the coming struggle was quite clear to him; "alone the victor will remain alive", he declared [419]. He thought, of course, that the young upstart would prove no match for him. In April and May he had travelled through Campania in order to secure himself the sympathies of Caesar's veterans. When Cicero, who was in Puteoli then, heard this, he wrote : "we are heading for war" [420]. In June he got permission, from the comitia, not from the Senate, to transfer the five legions that stood ready in Macedonia for the Parthian campaign to Italy [421]. Furthermore, he managed to change his govenorship of Macedonia that was allotted to him for 43 B.C. for that of Gallia Cisalpina, a province that was 'very powerful in soldiers and money' [422]. Since Antony was now riding roughshod over the prerogatives of the Senate, there arose great friction between him and that august body [423].

Octavian did not sit still either. He sent agents around to work on the populations of the colonies that were founded by Caesar, in particular on the veterans who were living there. By paying them handsome hand-outs - he had succeeded in raising money -, he could enlist some three thousand of them in Campania [424]. And when four of the five legions from Macedonia had arrived in Brindisi, he lured two of them away to his side by offering more than Antony [425].

It will be evident that Antony was losing ground. He had no longer the support of the Senate which he had antagonized; he was in control of an army now, composed of Caesarian veterans and Macedonian legions, but could only keep them from mutiny by the most severe and even cruel measures [426]. And then, the sympathy of the masses was with 'that rash boy', as Antony contemptuously called him [427], rather than with himself [428]. The situation was confused. "The citizens were still at peace and yet already at war; the appearance of liberty was kept up, but the deeds done were those of a monarchy." The only question was who would become the monarch. "To a casual observer Antony ... seemed to have the best of it ... But (the masses) were displeased at the great power of Antony" [429].

25. The Third Civil War : the first Italian phase

a. Antony's defeats

In the autumn of 44 B.C. the two armies began to move. Antony directed part of his troops northward along the Adriatic coast towards Ariminium (Rimini); with another part he marched on Rome and entered it. It was there that he heard that two of his legions had defected to Octavian [430]. With new levies and with the fifth legion that meanwhile had arrived from Macedonia he continued his march northward in order to take the place of Decimus Brutus [431], one of Caesar's murderers, who was governor of Gallia Cisalpina but who refused to cede his post to Antony [432]. On the coming of his rival Brutus threw himself into the heavily fortified Mutina (Modena) to which Antony laid siege [433].

Octavian was somewhat at a loss what to do. He could neither fight both Antony and Brutus at one time nor did he feel inclined to join one of the two. But when he had entered Rome, with his army of four legions encamped outside the city walls, a great prize was conferred on him. As Appian states, "he desired to take the lead in humbling Antony" [434]. However, he was still no more than a private person, but now the influential Cicero helped him to become a public one. At his instigation [435] a hesitating Senate - the debates lasted three days [436] - appointed the young man as propraetor with imperium, his first real office [437]. This happened on January 2, 43 B.C.

Although the Senate did not yet formally declare war on Antony, two consular armies marched northward, eight legions strong between them, with the still too young and inexperienced propraetor under the command of one of the consuls. On April 14, 43 B.C., Antony was heavily defeated near Forum Gallorum (no longer existing, near the present-day Castelfranco) [438]. A week later, on the 21st, a second battle took place, now near Modena, as a consequence of which the siege of the town was raised. Having lost almost all his infantry, Antony fled to the Alps [439].

b. Rewards and triumphs

These opening scenes of the Third Civil War had important consequences. Firstly, the Senate now declared Antony a public enemy [440], in this way legitimizing the preceding military events. Secondly, it awarded Octavian the title of 'imperator'; true enough, the consuls received this distinction too, but both had fallen, an exceptional occurence in the history of the Republic. This led to the third consequence. Who is surprised to hear that Octavian now wanted to become consul? The Senate must have agreed with what Marcus Brutus wrote to Cicero's pen-friend Atticus that it would prove hard to keep Octavian under control; once he had thrown down Antony's tyranny, he would certainly establish one of his own; it was, therefore, imprudent of Cicero to dote so much on him [441].

It was not Octavian who was allowed to celebrate a triumph, but Decimus Brutus, the Caesar-murderer, who had defended Mutina against Antony [442]. What was more, this same Decimus Brutus was made commander-in-chief in the war against Antony [443]. "Of Octavian not a word was said" [444]. No wonder that little love was lost between Brutus and Octavian! "Nature forbids that I should even look at Brutus or hold any conversation with him" [445].

c. Octavian master of Rome

Being thus rebuffed by the Senate, Octavian began to make friendly approaches to Antony who had recovered from his defeats. He stood in Gallia Cisalpina with several legions, while Lepidus, the governor of Hispania Citerior, came to his assistance with no less than seven legions [446]. Octavian, on his part, did not march out against this host, but took the exactly opposite road. Turning southward, his army of eight legions marched on the capital [447]; it was the sixth time in forty-six years that Rome saw a Roman army approaching. His coming created panic in the city. "The Senate was struck with consternation since they had no military force in readiness ... Cicero, who had so long been in evidence, was nowhere to be seen" [448]. On August 43 B.C., Octavian, leaving his army outside the gates, but accompanied by his bodyguard, entered the city; Cicero came forward to greet him and was ironically called 'the last of his friends' by the victor [449].

So the imperial city, the capital of the ancient world, was totally in the hands of a young man of twenty! Octavian got what he wanted : he was elected consul [450], and the Senate rescinded the decrees against Antony and Lepidus. Octavian wrote to them promising his assistance against Decimus Brutus and received a friendly answer [451]. Brutus, who had so suddenly fallen from his high position, took to flight. In Gallia Cisalpina he was captured by a Celtic chief. He informed Antony who ordered to kill him [452]. With this event the Italian phase of the Third Civil War was over.

26. The Second Triumvirate

The incipient understanding between Antony, Lepidus, and Octavian led to the 'unholy alliance' [453] that is called 'the Second Triumvirate'. There was no friendship between them, they did not even trust one another, but they needed one another, because the East was still firmly in the hands of the republicans. In the autumn Octavian went north with his army and met the two others near Bologna. On a small islet in the river Lavinius (Lavino) the three sat conferring for two long November days, without anybody else being present. So great was their mutual distrust that "they searched one another carefully, to make sure that no one had a dagger concealed" [454]!

Sitting together and eyeing each other suspiciously, these three worthy gentlemen concocted a plan that was quite a nouveauté in Roman history. Octavian was made to step back from the consulship, because this gave him an undue advantage over the two others who had no functions at all. Then they created a brandnew magistracy which they would hold in common for five years, a kind of dictatorship, although it was not called so. They arrogated to themselves the power to appoint the urban magistrates for a period of five years. Finally, they divided the western half of the Empire among themselves. Octavian would have Africa, Sardinia, Corsica, and Sicily, Lepidus the Iberian peninsula and Gallia Narbonensis, and Antony the rest of Gaul. "Only the assignment of the parts beyond the Adriatic was postponed, since these were still under the control of Brutus and Cassius, against whom Antony and Octavian were to wage war" [455].

The great question who was to have Rome and Italy was more or less left open. Lepidus would be consul in 42 B.C., probably because his two friends were less afraid of him than of one another. He would stay in Rome and govern his provinces by proxy; he would have three legions at his disposal to guard the capital, whereas the two principal contestants were to have twenty each [456].

27. Terror in Rome

After the conclusion of this pact the triumviri marched on Rome - the seventh march on the capital by ambitious men - and entered it at the end of November, "giving the impression that they were all going to rule on equal terms, but each having the intention of getting the entire power for himself" [457]. A day later the proscriptions began by the public posting of a list of one hundred and thirty names of people who must forfeit their lives. As Charlesworth wrote, "the hunt was up" [458]; the days of Sulla had come back. Most of the men who found their names on the list were optimates, senators, Pompeians. The city looked as though it had been captured. "Many were killed in their houses, many even in the streets and here and there in the fora and around the temples." To the first batch another hundred and fifty were added, while some were killed by mistake. Those who hid a proscribed person were liable to the same penalties. There were many suicides.

The heads of those murdered were exposed on the rostra on the Forum. The most conspicuous of these, put on a stake, had belonged to Cicero. Expecting nothing good, the famous orator had fled the town in a small boat, but became sea-sick and was put ashore. Soldiers were searching the country for him in squads until somebody pointed out his hiding-place to a patrol. A centurion rushed in and cut off his head, and after that the hand with which he had written against Antony, to whom the head was brought. "It is said that even at his meals Antony placed the head of Cicero before him, until he became satiated with the horrid sight" [459]. Once let loose, the wild soldatesca for a long time went on looting and killing of their own accord [460].

28. The Third Civil War continued

a. The Greek phase

While Lepidus remained in Rome, Antony, as commander-in-chief, and Octavian proceeded to Greece with no less than twenty-eight legions [461]. They marched straight across the Balkans to Thrace where they found the army of their opponents near Philippi (now only a field of ruins) [462]. Both sides threw about nineteen legions into the battle [463] the first part of which took place on October 43 B.C. It was Antony's brilliant generalship that carried the day; the losses on both sides were great [464]. After the defeat Cassius committed suicide [465]. The next day Antony engaged the remaining enemy host under Brutus and triumphed [466]. Finding no way of escape and with his officers declining to resume the fight, Brutus too killed himself [467]. This double suicide deprived the Triumvirate of its two most formidable opponents; Macedonia and Greece were safely in their hands now.

b. Antony under the spell of Cleopatra

After Philippi, Octavian and Antony parted ways; the first mentioned returned to Italy, the second proceeded to the East. In the beginning of 42 B.C. Mark Antony arrived in Ephesus; he lived in royal splendour and acted as though he were 'the uncrowned king of Asia' [468]. In his grandiose manner he regulated the affairs of the East. But when touring the eastern provinces, he met Cleopatra and fell under her spell. In Volume X [469] I have told in extenso the story of Antony's fatal relationship with the Egyptian queen - fatal because he spent so much time, energy, and attention on it that it left Octavian a free hand in preparing his bid for power. But perhaps, as I wrote there, he would happily have left the West to his competitor, if only he had been able to become the divinized ruler of a large Kingdom of the East.

c. The Perusine War

Once back in Italy, Octavian had to face a coalition of a motley character : victims of the proscriptions, runaway slaves, survivors from Philippi, Pompeians, republicans, proletarians, landowners who were dispossessed in order to make place for Octavian's veterans, all those who found the young man's presence a threat to their own interests, and in particular, Sextus Pompeius, the great man's only surviving son, Lucius Antonius, Antony's brother, and Fulvia, Antony's wife.

Fulvia and Lucius managed to assemble no less than eight legions. Octavian, now twenty-three and every day coming more into his own, rushed northward. He was wise enough not to attempt to storm the city of Perugia which was their main stronghold, but, instead, built 'a line of palissade and ditch', with fifteen hundred wooden towers on it, around the hill on which Perugia stands and reduced it by famine. On January 1, 40 B.C., Lucius made a valiant attempt to break out which failed after desperate fighting. In February he unconditionally surrendered. Octavian pardoned him, with an eye on the fact that the defeated man was the brother of Antony whom he did not want to antagonize. The victor revenged himself on the town councillors whom he put to death, and on the town itself which was set ablaze. A strong wind fanned the flames so that Perugia, 'renowned for its antiquity and importance', was reduced to ashes; many inhabitants perished in the fire [470]. This 'Perusine War' is one of the many bloody incidents with which the interminable civil wars are punctuated. It left Octavian the undisputed master of Italy and virtually of all the West, since Antony was still in the East, while he had nothing to fear from the fainéant Lepidus.

29. Antony and Parthia

a. The rise of Parthian power

Antony's task in the East was neither to dally with Cleopatra nor to form an Eastern Empire controlled by him, but to fight Rome's most dangerous enemy, Parthia. The Parthian Empire, situated roughly in the area between the Euphrates and the Indus in the time of its greatest expansion, was the inheritor of the Persian Empire with its imperialistic claims, but also of the Seleucid Empire which had once stretched almost to the Indus. Its civilization was mainly Iranian but contained many Hellenic elements, among them a wide-spread use of the Greek language. The continuous decay of the Seleucid Empire had created a vacuum into which many tribes penetrated, one of these being the Indo-European Parthians. They settled in what now is the Iranian province of Khorasan, called Parthia after them. From there they began to extend their influence, eastward towards Bactria and westward towards the Seleucid Empire. From 250 B.C. the Seleucid rulers saw themselves confronted with a mighty power block on their east flank [471].

The situation became really dangerous when in 163 B.C. Mithridates I [472] became the Parthian prince, a scion of the Arsacid dynasty, who is considered the real founder of the Parthian Empire. Blow after blow he dealt to his neighbour, the Seleucid Empire. In 160 B.C. he conquered Media, followed by Mesopotamia in 141/140 B.C., where he triumphantly entered the Seleucid capital, Seleukeia on the Tigris; opposite this town he founded a new capital, Ctesiphon. Mithridates assumed the ancient Achaemenid title of 'Great King' or 'King of kings'. This meant that aspirants to imperial power in the East had to reckon with a self-assured competitor. When attempts by the Seleucid king Antiochus VII to restore the situation in Mesopotamia had dismally failed in 129 B.C., the Euphrates definitely became 'the frontier of Europe'.

b. The first clashes between Rome and Parthia

When Rome became powerful in Asia Minor, her relations with Parthia were at first peaceful; the Euphrates served as frontier between the two zones of influence. But Armenia presented a problem. The Parthian rulers saw it as an annex of their own empire; they had incorporated part of it. It was because of Armenia that Parthia came into contact with Rome. Mithridates II made Tigranes II in 95 B.C. his vassal-king of that country. But this Tigranes, as I have related earlier, had an agenda of his own [473]; he combined forces with Mithridates VI of Pontus, proclaimed himself 'King of kings', began to conquer right and left, and founded a shortlived Armenian Empire. Romans and Parthians realized that they had common interests, which led to the recognition of the Euphrates frontier by Rome in 66 B.C.

This meant that two great empires, each with its imperialistic aspirations, had a common boundary; this did not bode well for the future. After Rome had defeated Tigranes, installed herself in Syria and by doing so assumed the inheritance of the now defunct Seleucid Empire, constant friction with the Parthians was the result. In 53 B.C. Crassus, one of the Triumvirate, got it into his head to attack Parthia; there was no good reason for this aggression except that this old and deaf man wanted to make himself the equal of Caesar and Pompey by means of a resounding victory. But what he got was a resounding defeat. In the Battle of Carrhae in 53 B.C. his army was destroyed almost to the last man; Crassus himself lay among the dead, without his head which was brought to the Parthian ruler [474]. This defeat was one of the reasons why Caesar planned to undertake a campaign against the Parthians.

c. The Roman world divided

Since Mark Antony considered himself the real ruler of the East, the task of avenging Carrhae fell naturally to him. But first of all he wanted to regulate his relations with Octavian whom he deeply suspected (their suspicions were mutual; their respective armies came very near to an armed clash).

When the Perusine War was over, Antony crossed to Brindisi where he met his rival in October 40 B.C. Lepidus, who was not present, was treated as a 'quantité négligeable'; he was transferred from Spain to Africa. In the Pact of Brundisium the two potentates divided the Roman world among themselves along the old dividing line, with the East for Antony and the West for Octavian. Fulvia now being dead, Antony cemented his alliance with Octavian by marrying his sister Octavia [475].

30. Pompey's son in action

There was great rejoicing everywhere since the danger of civil war seemed to have been averted; Virgil expressed his hope for the future in his famous Fourth Eclogue. The star of Octavian rose ever higher; since the Pact of Brindisi he called himself 'Imperator Caesar Divi Iulii Filius'; in 36 B.C. the Senate allowed him to wear the laurel crown whenever he wanted [476].

He had, however, to reckon with a formidable opponent, Sextus Pompeius, the son of Pompey the Great, who, after the Perusine War, had not abandoned his aspirations; like his father, he wore the surname 'Magnus'. He commanded an army of his own, composed of proscribed men, runaway slaves, deserters, and pirates. In the autumn of 43 B.C. he had made himself master of Sicily [477]. Three years later he succeeded in occupying Sardinia too [478] - since it was a kind of 'seaborne empire', he considered himself 'the son of Neptune' [479]. Disposing of a considerable navy, he threatened to cut off the corn transports to Italy (both islands were great grain exporters). Famine broke out in Rome [480] which led to rioting, during which the statues of Antony and Octavian were overthrown, with the consequence that "these two against their will were forced to make overtures to Sextus" [481]. The result was the Treaty of Misenum, concluded in 39 B.C.. Sextus was officially made governor of Sicily, Sardinia, and Corsica, on the condition that he would no longer block the transport of grain to Italy [482]. There was great rejoicing in Rome [483].

But the problems were by no means over. Sextus' pirates could not sit still and went on marauding; he did not evacuate his strongholds on the coast of Italy [484]. With Antony gone to the war in the East, the task of reducing Sextus fell to Octavian who succeeded in assembling a considerable fleet [485]. The offensive was very carefully prepared; Octavian engaged the assistance of Lepidus. The decisive attack began on July 1, 36 B.C., the first day of the month of Julius [486]. The story has a mythical nature since Octavian was the son of Divus Iulius and Sextus of Neptune.

Coming from Africa, Lepidus landed with twelve legions in Sicily and was soon master of half the island [487]. In August Octavian followed with a landing in the east near Tauromnium (no longer existing) [488]. Here he almost met his end. Sextus fell suddenly on him with his combined land- and sea-forces and destroyed his navy. Octavian, who had been in command, reached the shore of Italy accompanied by only one man; he was so utterly dejected that he asked his companion to kill him [489]. But he recovered and set to work again. His three legions in the island held firm so that he could think of a conjunction with Lepidus [490]. In a second sea-battle on September 3, near the north-eastern point of the island, Octavian's admiral Agrippa inflicted a heavy defeat on the enemy's naval forces [491].

After this Sextus' adventure was doomed. His infantry in the island began to surrender so that he lost his ground-forces too. In Messina he loaded a ship with his treasures and with this and another sixteen vessels sailed to Mytilene on the Aegean coast of Asia Minor [492]. Collecting enough men for an army of three legions [493], he offered his services to Antony as well as to the emperor of Parthia. But Antony found him loathsome and despatched a legate against him [494]. Most of his troops deserted to Antony. He himself tried to get eastward through Bithynia with a small force [495]. There Sextus was captured and brought to Milete to be executed in that town in 35 B.C. [496].

31. Lepidus disposed of

Having thus got happily rid of the Pompeian party, Octavian saw himself saddled with yet another problem. Not entirely without reason Lepidus found that it was he who had conquered Sicily, and not Octavian; in consequence, he claimed the governorship of the island [497]. But Octavian was just as expert in handling troops as his adoptive father had been and succeeded in enticing Lepidus' men away from his rival, twenty-three legions in all and much cavalry. Octavian deprived the now powerless man of his command and sent him to Rome to live as a private citizen [498]. On the orders of Octavian, who did not find him dangerous, he was left in peace [499].

32. The sinking star of Antony

a. The Duumvirate

With these events the Third Civil War came to an end. The Triumvirate had become a Duumvirate. For the time being the relations between Antony and Octavian were superficially peaceful; the Roman world had been carefully divided between them. Octavian, now twenty-eight years of age, had come out of the affair extremely well. He had no competitor in the West any more, while he disposed of immense armed forces, forty-five legions of infantry, twenty-five thousand horsemen, forty-thousand auxiliary troops, and six hundred war-ships [500]. When he was back in Rome, "the Senate voted him unbounded honours"; a golden image of his was placed in the Forum with this inscription : 'Peace, long disturbed, he reestablished on land and sea' [501].

b. Antony campaigning against the Parthians

Meanwhile the star of Antony began to sink. He saw himself as the heir to Caesar's plans; furthermore, he had to avenge the defeat of Carrhae. Hostilities with the Parthians began in 37 B.C., but it was only in the following year that Antony himself was ready to march out against them, with almost a hundred thousand men under his command. First he crossed the Euphrates and went to Armenia whose king became his ally

[502]. From there he invaded the Parthian Empire but achieved nothing because his large siege-train was destroyed by the enemy [503]. As a consequence he was deserted by his Armenian ally [504]. In the autumn he decided to return; on his road back to Syria he lost no less than thirty-two thousand men through hunger, exhaustion, and constant harassing by the enemy [505]. In 34 B.C. Antony was again in the field, but although he could avenge himself on his treacherous Armenian ally, he again achieved nothing against Parthia [506].

c. The dream of Empire

In Volume X I have described how Antony planned to become the imperial ruler of the whole East, in the tradition of the oriental kings. I spoke there of his 'abortive Empire of the East', while Tarn called it 'the dream of Empire' [507]. The habits of the East were far more to his taste than those of republican Rome. Married to Cleopatra, he was close to the source of divine kingship. He was Dionysos, she was Isis. The title 'King of kings' was revived for the Egyptian queen and for her and Caesar's son Caesarion. Alexandria seemed to have become the new capital where triumphs were held even, to the horror of all authentic Romans. They hated Antony for a self-glorification which had the effect of making Octavian shine as the true guardian of Roman identity and as the guarantor of the indivisibility of the Empire.

  The dualism of the situation became apparent in Antony's very person. To his Roman friends and to his Roman troops he remained Marcus Antonius, Roman magistrate. But to Greeks and Asiatics he was a divine oriental monarch. However, it was not Antony's intention to acquiesce in the permanent division of the Empire and leave the West to his rival. On the contrary! He desired to become the ruler of Rome too.

d. Preparations for the showdown

With every day that passed people in Rome became more displeased with Antony's behaviour. Octavian made good use of this mood; with his speeches he inflamed the plebs against his rival daily more. Everybody in the East and West understood that this would lead to an armed clash. Both sides made their preparations for the showdown that seemed unavoidable. But the war of 32-30 B.C. was not be called the Fourth Civil War which in fact it was; civil strife was supposed to have ended once and for all with Caesar's return to Rome. It was advertised as a war against a foreign enemy, Cleopatra, whose Egyptian kingdom was nominally independent still. That it would be a dualistic struggle along the East-West line is proved by the fact that Octavian could count on none of the eastern provinces and vassal-kingdoms which followed Antony, whereas Italy and the western provinces of Africa, Spain, Sicily and Sardinia, and Gaul all swore allegiance to the future emperor.

e. Antony's end

On September 2, 31 B.C., the final showdown took place in the Battle of Actium, on the western Greek coast, the greatest sea-battle of all Antiquity. The issue hung in the balance for hours on end. But Cleopatra, whose fleet played a major role, lost nerve and sailed away with sixty ships. Then Antony followed her leaving the victory in the hands of Octavian. In the summer of 30 B.C. the victor entered Egypt from Syria. In the first encounter, on August 1, Antony's troops deserted him. He fled to Alexandria and took his own life there. When Octavian entered the Egyptian capital, Cleopatra too committed suicide [508].

NOTES TO CHAPTER II

1.   Vol. X, Ch. IV.17d.

2.   Vol. X, Ch. IV.17a-c.

3. Vol. X, Ch. VI.1f.
4. Vol. X, Ch. IV.16d.
5. Plut., Marius 32.4.
6. Plut., Marius 33.1-2.
7. Cic., De or. 1.99.
8. Plut., Sulla 8.1.
9. Plut., Marius 35.1.
10. Vell.Pat. 2.18.5-6.
11. Ooteghem, Marius 279/280.
12. Plut., Marius 35.1.
13. Livy, Per. 77..1; (Cic.), Ad Her. 2.45, states that Sulpicius first was against this measure but later changed his mind and proposed the same law under another name.
14. Appian, Rom.hist., Civ.Wars 1.55, adds spitefully that Marius, using Sulpicius as his instrument, hoped to use the new voters 'as loyal servants for his own ends'.
15. Gardner, Enfrachisment VIII The Leges Sulpiciae, and the first capture of Rome, 202.
16. Plut., Sulla 8.2.
17. Livy, Per. 77.1; Vell.Pat. 2.18.6.
18. Appian, Rom.hist., Civ.Wars 1.55.
19. Appian, Rom.hist, Civ.Wars 1.55.
20. Appian, Rom. hist., Civ.wars 1.56; Plut., Marius 35.1-5, Sulla 8.1-8; Vell.Pat. 2.18.6.
21. Appian, Rom.hist., Civ.Wars 1.57.
22. Keaveney, Sulla 62.
23. Appian, Rom.hist., Civ.Wars 1.57.
24. Plut., Sulla 9.3-4.
25. Plut., Sulla 9.5.
26. Appian, Rom.hist., Civ.Wars 1.57.
27. Appian, Rom.hist., Civ.Wars 1.58.
28. Plut., Sulla 9.10-14; Appian, Rom.hist., Civ.Wars 1.58.
29. Appian, Rom.hist., Civ.Wars 1.58.
30. Appian, Rom.hist., Civ.Wars 1.59.

31. Appian, Rom.hist., Civ.Wars 1.61-62.
32. Appian, Rom.hist., Civ.Wars 1.59.
33. Appian, Rom.hist., Civ.Wars 1.63; Plut., Sulla 10.4-8.
34. Plut., Sulla 10.6-8.
35. Appian, Rom.hist., Civ.Wars 1.64.
36. Sulla, fr. 1.26 M.
37. Appian, Rom.hist., Civ.Wars 1.64.
38. Florus 2.9.9.
39. Appian, Rom.hist., Civ.Wars 1.64.
40. Appian, Rom.hist., Civ.Wars 1.66.
41. Florus 2.9.10.
42. Vir.ill. 69.2; Florus 2.9.9.
43. Appian, Rom.hist., Civ.Wars 1.64-65; Cic., Cat. 3.24; Livy, Per. 79.1; Florus 2.9.10; Vell.Pat. 2.20.2-3.
44. Appian, Rom.hist., Civ.Wars 1.65; Livy, Per. 79.2; Vir.ill. 69.2.
45. Appian, Rom.hist., Civ.Wars 1.65-66.
46. Appian, Rom.hist., Civ.Wars 1.66-74, from whom the quotations are; Florus 2.9.13-17; Plut., Marius 41-44.
47. Appian, Rom.hist., Civ.Wars 1.75; Vell.Pat. 2.22.1-2.
48. Plut., Sulla 22.1; Vell.Pat. 2.23.3.
49. Perelli, Populares 134.
50. Appian, Rom. hist., Civ.Wars 1.77 and Mithr.Wars 51 and 60.
51. Plut., Caesar 1.1 literally speaks of 'Kinna tou monarchêsantos'.
52. Cic., Brutus 227.
53. Appian, Rom.hist., Civ.Wars 1.76.
54. Appian, Rom.hist., Civ.Wars 1.77.
55. Appian, Rom.hist., Civ.Wars 1.78.
56. Appian, Rom.hist., Civ.Wars 1.74.
57. Appian, Rom.hist., Civ.Wars 1.79.
58. Vell.Pat. 2.25.1.
59. Plut., Sulla 27.11.
60. Plut., Sulla 27.7-10; Vell.Pat. 2.25.2-3.

61. Appian, Rom.hist., Civ.Wars 1.85.
62. Vell.Pat. 2.26.1.
63. Appian, Rom.hist., Civ.Wars 1.88.
64. Appian, Rom.hist., Civ.Wars 1.86.
65. Vell.Pat. 2.27.1-2.
66. Front., Strat. 1.11.1; an account of the battle in Plut., Sulla 29-30; Appian, Rom.hist., Civ.Wars 1.93; Vell.Pat. 2.27.3.
67. Livy, Per. 89.2.
68. Appian, Rom.hist., Civ.Wars 1.98-99.
69. Livy, Per. 88.1.
70. Appian, Rom.hist., Civ.Wars 1.97.
71. Appian, Rom.hist., Civ.Wars 1.93; Livy, Per. 88.2; Plut., Sulla 30.3-4.
72. Seneca, De clem. 1.12.1.
73. Plut., Sulla 32; Appian, Rom.hist., Civ.Wars 1.94; Cic., De leg.agr. 2.78.
74. Appian, Rom.hist., Civ.Wars 1.94.
75. Licin. 36.8.
76. Strabo, Geogr. 5.4.11.
77. Livy, Per. 89.12.
78. Appian, Rom.hist., Civ.Wars 1.104.
79. Appian, Rom.hist., Civ.Wars 1.95.
80. Val.Max. 9.2.1.
81. Vell.Pat. 2.38.2.
82. Dio, fr. 109.2.
83. Val.Max. 2.9.1.
84. Suet., Caesar 11; later they were restored by Caesar.
85. Vell.Pat. 2.43.1.
86. Appian, Rom.hist., Civ.Wars 1.95. This breaking of an agreement referred to the moment in 83 B.C., when Scipio had taken up arms against him.
87. Florus 2.11.3.
88. Dio fr. 109.8.
89. Plut., Sulla 31.1.
90. Plut., Sulla 31.1.

91. Florus 2.9.25.
92. Vell.Pat. 2.28.4.
93. Or. 5.21.1.
94. Dio fr. 109.11.
95. Dio fr. 109.21.
96. Sen., De prov. 2..7; Cic., Pro Sexto 89. Cicero compared the slaughter in Rome to that at Lake Trasimene in 217 B.C., while Seneca mentions thousands of dead.
97. Plut., Sulla 31.2-4.
98. Plut., Sulla 31.5-6.
99. Plut., Sulla 31.7-10.
100. Vell.Pat. 2.28.4.
101. Plut., Sulla 33.3.
102. Cic., In Verr. 3.81.
103. Plut., Sulla 33.4.
104. Plut., Caesar 1.2-3.
105. Suet., Caesar 1; Dio 43.43.4.
106. Cic., Pro Sexto 128.
107. Val.Max. 9.2.1.
108. Appian, Rom.hist., Civ.Wars 1.95; Florus 9.2.25.
109. Appian, Rom.hist., Civ.Wars 1.100.
110. Plut., Sulla 34.1-2.
111. Appian, Rom.hist., Civ.Wars 1.97; CIL I.584.
112. Livy, Per. 89.4; Vell.Pat. 2.30.4.
113. Appian, Rom.hist., Civ.Wars 1.100.
114. Appian, Rom.hist., Civ.Wars 1.100; Dion.Hal. 5.77.5.
115. Appian, Rom.hist., Civ.Wars 1.103.
116. Appian, Rom.hist., Civ.Wars 1.103.
117. Appian, Rom.hist., Civ.Wars 1.104.
118. Val.Max. 9.3.8; Plut., Sulla 35.5-36.4.
119. The subtitle of Keaveney's book on him, see Bibliography.
120. The subtitle of Carcopino's book on him, see Bibliography.

121. Seneca, De cons. 12.6.
122. Quoted by Carcopino, Sylla 10.
123. Both Hitler and Mao were horrible sleepers. Mao, a mass murderer if there ever was one, slept badly even with pills and not at all without them.
124. William Shakespeare, Julius Caesar, Act. I, Scene II.
125. Quoted by Carcopino, Sylla 240.
126. Carcopino, Sulla 245.
127. Plut., Pomp. 15.1.
128. Plut., Pomp. 15.3. Opponent or not, but Lepidus had profited financially from the proscriptions, Sall., Or.Lep. 18.
129. Sall., Or.Lep. 7 sqq.
130. Scullard, Gracchi to Nero 88.
131. Lic. 36.33-35.
132. Lic. 36.35-37.
133. Lic. 36.38-41; Appian, Rom.hist., Civ.Wars 1.107.
134. Sall, Or.Phil. fr.1.77.7 (M).
135. Sall., Or.Phil., fr. 1.77.14-15 (M); Florus 2.11.3; Plut., Pomp. 16.2.
136. Florus 2.11.5; Plut. Pomp. 16.2; Appian, Rom.hist., Civ.wars 1.107.
137. Sall., Or.Phil., fr. 1.22 (M).
138. Florus 2.11.6-7.
139. Florus 2.11.7; Plut., Pomp. 16.4; Appian, Rom.hist., Civ.Wars 1.107.
140. Plut., Pomp. 16.1.
141. Van Ooteghem, Pompée le Grand. Bâtisseur d'Empire (see Bibliography).
142. Greenhalgh, Pompey. The Republican prince (see Bibliography).
143. Greenhalgh, Pompey. The Roman Alexander (see Bibliography).
144. Cic., Att. 11.6.5.
145. Donatus, Form. 170.
146. Spann, Sertorius 5.
147. See Vol. X, Ch. VI.3b.
148. Plut., Sert. 3.1. See Vol. X, Ch. II.3b.
149. Spann, Sertorius 17.

127

150. Plut., Sert. 3.3-5. Marius had enlisted a great number of slaves; later these were looting and murdering in Rome on their own account. In 86 B.C., "when the slaves were all encamped together, he (Sertorius) had them shot down by javelins, and they were as many as four thousand", Plut., Sert. 5.5; Or. 5.19.24 even speaks of eight thousand slaves.

151. Plut., Sert. 4.1-3.

152. Plut., Sert. 4.3.

153. Spann, Sertorius 29.

154. Plut., Sert. 6.2.

155. Appian, Rom.hist., Civ.Wars 1.108.

156. Plut., Sert. 6.3.

157. Plut., Sert. 6.4-6.

158. Or. 5.21.3.

159. Plut., Sert. 7.1-2.

160. Plut., Sert. 7.2-9.1.

161. Plut., Sert. 9.2-3 and 5.

162. Plut., Sert. 10.1.

163. Plut., Sert. 12.2.

164. Plut., Sert. 15.1; Appian, Rom.hist., Civ.wars 1.108.

165. Or. 5.24.16; Appian, Rom.hist., Civ.Wars 1.108.

166. Plut., Sert. 22.3-4.

167. Plut., Sert. 14.2-3.

168. Spann, Sertorius 87.

169. Appian, Rom.hist., Civ.Wars 1.108.

170. Spann, Sertorius 92; Or. 5.23.9; Sall. fr. 2.98.9 (M).

171. Plut., Sert. 19.6.

172. Plut., Sert. 25.1.

173. Plut., Sert. 26.4-6.

174. Plut., Pomp. 20.4, Sert. 27.3-4; Appian, Rom.hist., Civ.Wars 1.115.

175. Pliny, HN 3.18.

176. Appian, Rom.hist., Civ.Wars 1.121.

177. Cic. 1Verr. 15.45.

178. Greenhalgh, Pomp.Al. 68.

179. Livy, Per. 97.6.
180. Plut., Pomp. 23.3.
181. Plut., Pomp. 23.1-2.
182. Plut., Pomp. 25.1-2.
183. Plut., Pomp. 25.3; Cic., De imp. Cn.Pomp. 52.
184. Cic., De imp. 52.
185. Plut., Pomp. 25.3-4.
186. Plut., Pomp. 26.2.
187. I described the war against the pirates shortly in Vol. X, Ch. IV.18.
188. Plut., Pomp. 28.4.
189. Strabo, Geogr. 14.3.1.
190. Appian, Rom.hist., Mithr.Wars 91.
191. Plut., Pomp. 30.2.
192. Appian, Rom.hist., Mithr.Wars 97.
193. Plut., Pomp. 30.3-5.
194. Vol. X, Ch. IV.24.
195. Dio 37.20.6; Plut., Pomp. 43.2-3.
196. Cic., Att. 1.14.1.
197. Eutr. 6.16; Appian, Rom.hist., Mithr.Wars 116-117.
198. Appian, Rom.hist., Mithr.Wars 117.
199. Dio 37.3.
200. Pliny, HN 7.26.
201. Dio 37.4.
202. Cary, First Triumvirate 511/512.
203. Suet., Caesar 2-3.
204. Suet., Caesar 18.1.
205. Suet., Caesar 19.1.
206. Suet., Caesar 19.2.
207. Suet. Caesar 20.1.
208. Suet., Caesar 20.2.
209. Suet., Caesar 21; Plut., Pomp. 47.6.

210. Plut., Pomp. 48.1-2.
211. Suet., Caesar 22.1-2.
212. See Vol. X, Ch. VI.5-12.
213. Suet., Caesar 24.1; Plut., Pomp. 51.4 and 52.3.
214. Vol. X, Ch. VI.10a.
215. Plut., Pomp. 51.3; Suet., Caesar 26.2 and 27.1-2.
216. Plut., Pomp. 51.4-52.2.
217. Plut., Pomp. 53.4.
218. Plut., Pomp. 53.5; Appian, Rom.hist., Civ.Wars 2.19.
219. See Vol. V, Ch. I.2b.
220. Plut., Pomp. 53.6.
221. Appian, Rom.hist., Civ.Wars 2.19.
222. Appian, Rom.hist., Civ.Wars 2.20.
223. Appian, Rom.hist., Civ.Wars 2.23; Plut., Pomp. 54.3-6.
224. Plut., Pomp. 55.1-2; Cornelia's first husband, Publius, the son of Crassus, had also found his end at Carrhae. Cornelia was still young which prompted one of Plutarch's caustic remarks that her youth "made her a fitter match for a son of Pompey".
225. Plut., Pomp. 55.4; Appian, Rom.hist., Civ.Wars 2.23-24.
226. His real name was Publius Cornelius Scipio Nasica but he had been adopted by Quintus Caecilius Metellus Pius, and henceforward called himself Quintus Caecilius Metellus Pius Scipio. This marriage gave Pompey family ties with two influential noble families, the Cornelii and the Metelli.
227. Appian, Rom.hist., Civ.Wars 2.25.
228. Van Ooteghem, Pompée 643.
229. Van Ooteghem, Pompée 644/645.
230. Plut., Pomp. 57.1.
231. Van Ooteghem, Pompée 495.
232. E. Ciaceri, I febbri di Pompeo. Il mondo classico, May/June 1931, 39-45, quoted by Van Ooteghem, Pompée 627.
233. Cic., Att. 8.2.3, 17.II.49 B.C.
234. Ciaceri (see note 230) quoted by Van Ooteghem, Pompée 627.
235. Dio 40.59.4.
236. Dio 50.49.1.

237. Suet., Caesar 28.2.
238. Dio 40.60.1.
239. Vell.Pat. 2.49.2.
240. Vell.Pat. 2.49.3.
241. Appian, Rom.hist., Civ.Wars 2.32.
242. Dio 41.1.4; Appian, Rom.hist., Civ.Wars 2.32.
243. Dio 41.1.2.
244. Appian, Rom.hist., Civ.Wars 2.32.
245. Plut., Caesar 30.4; Caesar, Bell.civ. 1.2.6. The date in question follows from Caesar, Bell.civ. 1.9.2.
246. Van Ooteghem, Pompée 311.
247. Plut., Pomp. 57.5; Caesar, Bell.civ. 29.5-6.
248. Appian, Rom.hist., Civ.Wars 2.34.
249. Cic., Fam. 16.11.3.
250. Plut., Caesar 32.1. It is not exactly known where this Rubicon is to be found; the choice is between the Pisciatello, the Fiumicino, and the Lusio, see Van Ooteghem, Pompée 514, note 5.
251. Suet. Caesar 32; Appian, Rom.hist., Civ.Wars 2.35. In his own Bellum civile Caesar does not mention these words.
252. Dio 41.8.5-6.
253. Plut., Pomp. 61.1-2.
254. Appian, Rom.hist., Civ.Wars 2.36; Plut., Caesar 33.1.
255. Plut., Caesar 33.2.
256. Caesar, Bell.civ. 1.14.4.
257. Plut., Caesar 33.3-4.
258. Plut., Pomp. 61.3.
259. Plut., Pomp. 61.3; Appian, Rom.hist., Civ.Wars 2.37.
260. Cic., Att. 9.10.2.
261. Appian, Rom.hist., Civ.Wars 2.37.
262. Dio 41.9.1.
263. Caesar, Bell.civ. 1.10.1.
264. Cic., Att. 8.11b.2.
265. Caesar, Bell.civ. 1.10-11.

266. Dio 41.10.1.
267. Dio 41.12.1.
268. Dio 41.12.1.
269. Plut., Pomp. 62.2-4; Dio 41.12.2-3; Caesar, Bell.civ. 1.25-28.
270. Plut., Caesar 35.3.
271. Appian, Rom.hist., Civ.Wars 2.40.
272. Plut., Pomp. 63.2.
273. Cic., Fam. 2.16.4.
274. Appian, Rom.hist., Civ.Wars 2.41.
275. Dio 41.15.
276. Appian, Rom.hist., Civ.Wars 2.48.
277. Dio 41.18; Caesar, Bell.Civ. 1.20.2.
278. Appian, Rom.hist., Civ.Wars 2.41; Dio 41.18.3.
279. Appian, Rom.hist., Civ.Wars 2.40.
280. Plut., Pomp. 64.1.
281. Caesar, Bell.Civ. 1.29.1-30.1.
282. Dio 41.19; Caesar, Bell.Civ. 1.34-36.
283. Dio 41.20.1-21.2.
284. Dio 41.23-24.
285. Dio 41.25.
286. Caesar, Bell.civ. 2.21.5; Dio 41.36.1. It is not quite clear by whom he was appointed, by the populus, Appian, Rom.hist., Civ.wars 2.48, or by the Senate, Plut., Caesar 37.2.
287. Appian, Rom.hist., Civ.Wars 2.48.
288. Appian, Rom.hist., Civ.Wars 2.48; Plut., Caesar 37.2.
289. Plut., Caesar 37.2.
290. Dio 41.36.4.
291. Plut., Pomp. 42.2-4.
292. Dio 41.18.4.
293. Eutr. 6.20.3.
294. Dio 41.18.5-6. In Thessalonica the consuls could not convoke the comitia centuriata, so that at the end of the year no new magistrates could be elected. The way out that was found was that the acting

officials would continue in their offices as proconsuls, propraetors, and proquaestors. Dio 41.43.3.

295. Dio 41.43.5.
296. Dio 41.52.2.
297. Appian, Rom.hist., Civ.Wars 2.49.
298. Caesar, Bell.civ. 3.4.1 and 3.
299. Plut., Pomp. 64.1.
300. Caesar, Bell.civ. 3.4.2-3.
301. Appian, Rom.hist., Civ.Wars 2.49; Plut., Pomp. 64.2.
302. Plut., Pomp. 64.3.
303. Dio 41.44.3-4; Appian, Rom.hist., Civ.Wars 2.54; Caesar, Bell.civ. 3.6.
304. Dio 41.44.1.
305. Dio 41.45.1.
306. Caesar, Bell.civ. 3.35-38.
307. Caesar, Bell.civ. 3.71.1-3.
308. Caesar, Bell.civ. 3.70.
309. Plut., Pomp. 65.5.
310. Caesar, Bell.civ. 3.72.1.
311. Plut., Pomp. 66.1-3.
312. Plut., Pomp. 66.1-3.
313. Appian, Rom.hist., Civ.Wars 2.69.
314. Plut., Pomp. 67.4.
315. Appian, Rom.hist., Civ.Wars 2.69.
316. Appian, Rom.hist., Civ.Wars 2.70.
317. Plut., Caesar 42.3.
318. Plut., Pomp. 70.1-2.
319. Appian, Rom.hist., Civ.wars 2.78.
320. Plut., Pomp. 71.4-5.
321. Plut., Pomp. 72.1-2.
322. Appian, Rom.hist., Civ.Wars 2.81.
323. Plut., Pomp. 73.1.
324. Plut., Pomp. 76.1.

325. Plut., Pomp. 76.2.
326. Caesar, Bell.civ. 3.103.1.
327. Caesar, Bell.civ. 3.103.2.
328. Appian, Rom.hist., Civ.Wars 2.84.
329. Plut., Pomp. 47.4.
330. Plut., Pomp. 78.1-80.1.
331. Val.Max. 5.1.10; Vir.ill. 77.9.
332. Plut., Pomp. 80.2-6. I have also related this sad scene in Vol. X, Ch. V.3b and 4a.
333. See for all this Vol. X. Ch. V.4.
334. Appian, Rom.hist., Civ.Wars 2.92.
335. Dio 42,21; Plut., Ant. 8.4-5.
336. Plut., Caesar 50.
337. Plut., Caesar 51.
338. Caesar, Bell.civ. 2.42.5. Bell.Afr. 86.1.
339. Plut., Caesar 54.1-2.
340. Livy, Per. 115.1.
341. Appian, Rom.hist., Civ. Wars 2.102; Vell.Pat. 2.56.2.
342. Dio 43.19.3.
343. Dio 43.19; Appian, Rom.hist., Civ.Wars 2.102; Suet., Caesar 37-39.
344. See Vol. X, Ch. V, note 88.
345. Dio 43.19.3-4 and 24.1.
346. Dio 43.28-29.
347. Appian, Rom.hist., Civ.Wars 2.104; Plut., Caesar 56.4.
348. Appian, Rom.hist., Civ.Wars 2.105.
349. Suet., Caesar 37.1.
350. Plut., Caesar 56.1.
351. Plut., Caesar 57.1.
352. Dio 43.45.2.
353. Dio 44.5.3.
354. Appian, Rom.hist., Civ.Wars 2.106.
355. Dio 43.44.2.

356. Dio 43.44.3.
357. Dio 44.5.3.
358. Appian, Rom.hist., Civ.Wars 2.106.
359. Dio 44.5.3.
360. Dio 44.6.1.
361. Dio 43.43.1.
362. Dio 43.43.1.
363. Suet., Caesar 45.2.
364. Dio 44.6.1 and 11.2. It was, in fact, an ivory seat which was gilded.
365. Dio 44.4.4.
366. Dio 46.6.1.
367. The Roman year began on March 1 so that September still means the seventh month, October the eight, and so on.
368. Appian, Rom.hist., Civ.wars 2.106.
369. Suet., Caesar 77.1.
370. See Vol. X, Ch. V.3e.
371. Dio 51.22.3.
372. Appian, Rom.hist., Civ.Wars 2.102.
373. Dio 43.14.6.
374. Dio 43.44.2-4.
375. For instance Cicero, Pro Marcello 27 : "ut rem publicam constituas".
376. Dio 43.50.1-2.
377. Dio 43.50.3.
378. Suet., Caesar 42.1.
379. Adcock, Dictatorship 707.
380. See for details Adcock, Dictatorship 705-7-7.
381. Suet., Caesar 41.3.
382. Caesar, Bell.civ. 1.32.7.
383. Cic., Fam. 6.12.2; Bellen, Grundzüge 146.
384. Suet., Caesar 86.
385. Euripides, Phoinissai 526-527.
386. Cic., De off. 3.82; Suet., Caesar 30.5.

387. In Vol. X, Ch. II.2c I have described how the Romans came to loathe this very word.
388. Suet., Caesar 79.
389. Suet., Caesar 79.3.
390. Suet., Caesar 80.4; Dio 11.4-12.1.
391. Cic., Phil. 2.28.
392. Bellen, Grundzüge 149.
393. Cic., Att. 14.1.1. The author began his letter with this sentence, without mentioning Caesar's name. It is just : HE. This reminds one of how Mussolini in the top regions of the Italian Fascist Party was always called LUI = he.
394. Appian, Rom.hist., Civ.Wars 2.215. Five weeks later Antony paid off his private debts out of the public money, Cic., Phil. 2.93.
395. Appian, Rom.hist., Civ.Wars 2.126.
396. Appian, Rom.hist., Civ.Wars 2.127.
397. Appian, Rom.hist., Civ.Wars 2.135.
398. Plut., Brutus 19.3.
399. Suet., Aug. 4.1.
400. Suet., Aug. 8.3.
401. Pliny, HN 2.98.
402. Appian, Rom.hist., Civ.Wars 2.136.
403. Appian, Rom.hist., Civ.Wars 2.143.
404. Appian, Rom.hist., Civ.Wars 2.144-148.
405. Meyer, Caesars Monarchie 503/508.
406. Gesche, Caesar 169.
407. But the consuls were displeased with this and overthrew the altar, Dio 46.51.1.
408. Dio 47.18-19.3.
409. The usual date for the official granting of the title 'divus Iulius' to Caesar is January 1, 42 B.C. Gesche. Caesar 171, however, argues that we should rather think of a somewhat later date.
410. 'Octavianus' means that he belonged to the gens of the Octavii. It is not quite clear who gave him this name. He himself? Or was it Cicero who repeatedly called him so? See Bellen, Grundzüge 150, note.
411. Appian, Rom.hist., Civ.Wars 3.11.

412. Cic., Att. 16.15.3.
413. Bengtson, Marc.Ant. 87.
414. Appian, Rom.hist., Civ.Wars 3.13.
415. Appian, Rom.hist., Civ.Wars 3.14.
416. Appian, Rom.hist., Civ.Wars 3.15-21.
417. Appian, Rom.hist., Civ.Wars 3.39; Suet., Aug. 10.3, held Octavian for guilty.
418. Cic., Att. 14.10.3 (19.IV.44).
419. Cic., Phil. 3.27 and 5.21.
420. Cic., Att. 14.21.2.
421. Appian, Rom.hist., Civ.Wars 3.27 and 30.
422. Dio 45.9.3.
423. Appian, Rom.hist., Civ.Wars 3.30.
424. Dio 45.12; Cic., Att. 16.8.2 and 11.6; Appian, Rom.hist, Civ.Wars 3.40 and 42.
425. Appian, Rom.hist., Civ.Wars 3.43-45; Dio 45.13.3.
426. Appian, Rom.hist., Civ.wars 3.43.
427. Appian, Rom.hist., Civ.wars 3.43.
428. Dio 45.11.2.
429. Dio 43.11.2.
430. Appian, Rom.hist., Civ.wars 3.45.
431. Not to be confused with the main conspirator, Quintus Brutus.
432. Appian, Rom.hist., Civ.wars 3.46.
433. Appian, Rom.hist., Civ.wars 3.49; Dio 46.29.
434. Appian, Rom.hist., Civ.Wars 3.51.
435. Cic., Phil. 11.20.
436. Cic., Phil. 6.3.
437. Res gestae 1.
438. Appian, Rom.hist., Civ.Wars 3.67-70; Cicero desribed the battle in a letter to Galba, 16.IV.43 B.C., Fam. 10.30; Frontinus, Strat. 2.5.39.
439. Appian, Rom.hist., Civ.wars 3.71-72.
440. Cic., Phil. 14.6-8; Livy, Per. 119.4.
441. Cic., Corr. no. 856, Brut. 1.17.

442. Livy, Per. 119.6; Vell.Pat. 2.62.4.
443. Appian, Rom.hist., Civ.Wars 3.74.
444. Vell.Pat. 2.62.5.
445. Appian, Rom.hist., Civ.Wars 3.73.
446. Plut., Ant. 17-18; Appian, Rom.hist., Civ.Wars 3.83-84.
447. Appian, Rom.hist., Civ.wars 3.88.
448. Appian, Rom.hist., Civ.wars 3.89.
449. Appian, Rom.hist., Civ.wars 3.92.
450. Appian, Rom.hist., Civ.Wars 3.95.
451. Appian, Rom.hist., Civ.Wars 3.96.
452. Appian, Rom.hist., Civ.wars 3.97-98.
453. Charlesworth, Avenging 20.
454. Dio 46.55.1.
455. Appian, Rom.hist., Civ.Wars 4.3.
456. Appian, Rom.hist., Civ.Wars 4.3; Dio 46.55-57.
457. Dio 47.1.1.
458. Charlesworth, Avenging 20.
459. The whole story, with the text of the proscriptions, is told in extenso by Appian, Rom.hist., Civ.wars 4.7-31; Dio 47.2-13.
460. Appian, Rom.hist., Civ.wars 4.35.
461. Appian, Rom.hist., Civ.Wars 4.86.
462. Appian, Rom.hist., Civ.wars 4.87.
463. Appian, Rom.hist., Civ.wars 4.88.
464. Appian, Rom.hist., Civ.Wars 4.107-112.
465. Appian, Rom.hist., Civ.wars 4.113.
466. Appian, Rom.hist., Civ.Wars 4.128-129.
467. Appian, Rom.hist., Civ.Wars 4.130-131.
468. Bengtson, Mark.Ant. 157.
469. Vol. X, Ch. V.5.
470. Appian, Rom.hist., Civ.Wars 5.27-49; Dio 48.14.
471. Vol. V, Ch. 2.

472. It is somewhat confusing that rulers of both Pontus and Parthia were called Mithridates; they should be kept carefully apart.
473. See Vol. X, Ch. IV.22.
474. See Vol. V, Ch. I, 2b.
475. Dio 48.28; Appian, Rom.hist., Civ.Wars 5.64-65.
476. Dio 49.15.1; Bellen, Grundzüge 158.
477. Dio 48.17.4-6.
478. Dio 48.30.
479. Dio 48.19.2.
480. Dio 48.18.1.
481. Dio 48.31.5-6; Appian, Rom.hist., Civ.Wars 5.67-68.
482. Appian, Rom.hist., Civ.Wars 5.71-72.
483. Appian, Rom.hist., Civ.Wars 5.74.
484. Dio 48.45.7.
485. Dio 48.49.
486. Appian, Rom.hist., Civ.wars 5.97.
487. Appian, Rom.hist., Civ.Wars 5.98.
488. Appian, Rom.hist., Civ.Wars 5.108.
489. Appian, Rom.hist., Civ.Wars 5.110-111; Suet., Aug. 16.
490. Appian, Rom.hist., Civ.Wars 5.116.
491. Appian, Rom.hist., Civ.Wars 5.118-121.
492. Appian, Rom.hist., Civ.wars 5.122 and 133.
493. Appian, Rom.hist., Civ.wars 5.137.
494. Appian, Rom.hist., Civ.Wars 5.138-139.
495. Appian, Rom.hist., Civ.wars 5.140.
496. Appian, Rom.hist., Civ.wars 5.143; Dio 49.17-18.
497. Appian, Rom.hist., Civ.Wars 5.123.
498. Appian, Rom.hist., Civ.Wars 5.124-126.
499. Appian, Rom.hist., Civ.Wars 5.131; he never again played a role in Roman politics and died in 13 B.C.
500. Appian, Rom.hist., Civ.Wars 5.127.
501. Appian, Rom.hist., Civ.Wars 5.130.

502. Plut., Ant. 37.2-3.
503. Plut., Ant. 38.1-2.
504. Plut., Ant. 39.1; Dio 49.25.5.
505. Plut., Ant. 41-51.
506. Appian, Rom.hist., Civ.Wars 5.145; Dio 49.39-40.
507. Vol. X, Ch. V.5; Tarn, War of the East 76.
508. I am quoting myself more or less verbatim from Vol. X, Ch. V.5e-j.

CHAPTER III

THE EMPIRE OF THE EMPERORS
AND ITS END

1. A new era

a. Honours for Octavian

After having regulated the affairs of the East, Octavian, now consul for the fifth time, returned to Rome in August 29 B.C. Who was sole boss now was made clear by a senatusconsultum of January 1, 29 B.C. stating that all Octavian's actions would be legal [1]. Since he wanted to pose as the prince of peace, it pleased him immensely that the doors of the Ianus temple were to be closed, doors that since times immemorial had been open only in wartime [2]. The senators heaped honour after honour on him, many of which pointed in the direction of deification. When praying on behalf of Senate and people, the priests had to include him in their prayers; in all public and private banquets libations were to be poured to him, just as they were to the gods [3]. In several Asiatic cities temples were dedicated to his name [4]; Dio cautiously remarks that in Rome itself and in Italy no emperor ever dared to do this [5]. Octavian did not forget his deified adoptive father : on August 18, 29 B.C., the Templum Divi Iulii in the Forum was consecrated [6].

b. Augustus

That a new era was being inaugurated is shown by the fact that Octavian's name was changed into 'Augustus' which signifies 'majestic, venerable, worthy of honour'; it is preserved in the English word 'august'. This name was given to him by a senatorial decree of January 16, 27 B.C. Octavian himself "was exceedingly desirous of being called 'Romulus'", since he considered himself the second founder of Rome. "But when he perceived that this caused him to be suspected of desiring the kingship, he desisted from his efforts to obtain it, and took the title of 'Augustus', signifying that he was more than human; for all the most precious and sacred objects are called 'augusta'" [7]. Dio, whom I am quoting here, adds that "in this way the power of both people and Senate passed into the hands of Augustus, and from his time there was strictly speaking a monarchy; for monarchy would be the truest name for it" [8]. All emperors, beginning with Augustus, were 'imperator' for life, no matter whether they had won a victory or not, "and this displaced the titles 'king' and 'dictator'" [9].

c. The end of the Republic?

Officially, the Republic never ceased to exist. For some centuries to come it is known as the 'Principate'. Augustus and his successors were the 'princeps civitatis', the first man in the state, which indicated that they were neither kings nor dictators, but the 'primi inter pares'. By this device it was possible to imagine that the Republic continued to exist. Augustus, wrote Tacitus, "organized the state, not by instituting a monarchy or a dictatorship, but by creating the title of First Citizen" [10]. This was not an official title and it was not conferred on the emperors by the Senate. Augustus modestly belittled the power he really had by stating that "although I came before all others in authority, I had absolutely not more power than the others who were my colleagues in the magistracy" [11]. Republican appearances were carefully saved.

In practice Augustus and his successors wielded an almost unlimited power, such as no previous official had ever possessed. They had 'the foremost place of authority', wich gave them the right to declare war and conclude peace, while at the same time they also conducted foreign affairs. The provinces of the Empire were divided under two heads, provinces of the Emperor, and provinces of the people; the most important belonged to the Emperor, who ruled them through legates and procurators. Perhaps most important of all, the princeps was given "the right and power to do all such things as he may deem to serve the interest of the Republic and the dignity of all things divine and human, public and private" [12].

d. From Principate to Dominate

It will be self-evident that this stipulation opened the door to an authoritarian regime, even to absolutism. True enough, the ruler's freedom of action was limited by the words 'the interest of the Republic'; the imperial power was meant to be of a public, not of a personal kind. But, as Ennslin wrote, "this limitation lost importance, inasmuch as he (the Emperor) was left to judge whether the condition was fulfilled ... This provision, that state interests should be regarded, ... was not a barrier strong enough to prevent self-willed men from setting up an autocratic régime ... The auctoritas of the first princeps was not merely founded on his political supremacy, but was supported by the attribution of innate supernatural and superhuman capabilities and characteristics, which made him seem god-send and his actions divinely inspired" [13]. Already during the Principate the emperorship was distancing itself more and more from the republican order and coming ever nearer to the ideology of kingship that had been prevalent in the Hellenistic East, in particular in Egypt.

A first step towards a new phase in the status of the Roman emperor - which is called the 'Dominate', because it made the ruler into a dominus, an overlord - was taken by Septimius Severus (193-211). This Emperor came from a Roman family but was born in Leptis Magna in North Africa in 146. As a young man he went to Rome and made a quick career in the public service. In 187, after the death of his first wife, he married Julia Domna, a member of a priestly family in Emesa (the present-day Homs in Syria). This marital union gave Severus an intimate link with ideas of priest-kingship and divine kingship which were current in the East, not the least in Emesa and in Julia's family [14].

In the year 195 Severus took a very unusual step : he proclaimed himself to be the son of the Emperor Marcus Aurelius by calling himself the son of 'the divine Marcus Pius' and telling the world that he was the cognate of the Emperors Nerva, Trajanus, Hadrianus, Antoninus Pius, and Commodus, all of them 'divine' [15]. Hasebroek stated that this (pseudo)-adoption (for Marcus Aurelius had died way back in 180) took place under the influence of Julia Domna. It "had above all a religious tendency and was meant for the divine veneration of the dynasty", a veneration which was introduced in this way into the public order [16]. From then on the process of deification steadily gathered momentum. The Emperors came to be called 'invictus', which was the epithet of the invincible oriental Sun-god, the 'Sol invictus'; on coins they appear in the company of divinities.

We may safely state that, with the emperorship of Diocletian (284-305), the Principate had definitely changed into a Dominate : the Emperor was now 'dominus et deus'. An inscription found near Dyrrhachium speaks blandly of Diocletian and his co-emperor Maximinian as 'born gods and creators of gods (= their sons), our lords the invincible Augusti' [17]. It was only natural that the court ceremonial became oriental in character, copied from that of the Persian emperors, and that Roman rulers went about 'arrayed in garments embroidered with gold and jewelry' [18].

Jupiter became the patron deity of the dynasty which was called 'Iovian', because the Emperors identified themselves with the supreme godhead; a 'nimbus', a halo around the imperial head appeared on coins as a token of 'divine illumination'. The sacred person of the prince was kept away from the public gaze; he who approached him had to go down on his belly, in the 'proskynêsis', so well-known from the East [19]. "Here is the beginning of that 'imperial liturgy', the strange mixture of civil and religious rites which was preserved with scrupulous care at the court of the Byzantine Caesars" [20]. Thus a new dualism had found its way into the fabric of the Empire, that of the ruler, who was divine, and the subjects (no longer citizens), who were only human, a dualism such as had existed in Egypt between Pharaoh and his subjects [21].

2. The Roman dualisms overcome?

The great question now was whether, with the coming of the Principate, of one-man rule in the Empire, an end would come to both the determining Roman dualisms, the external and the interior ones. Let us look back for a moment. Century after century, almost since the foundation of Rome, conquest had been the dominating motivation of Roman public existence. In consequence, the Roman power sphere had become ever more extended. For a very long time the fabric of the state had been able to carry the enormous weight of the imperialistic policy. It was even strong enough to solve the conflict between the patricians and the plebeians either with the means it had at its disposal or by creating new ones, like the tribunician office.

Around the middle of the second century B.C., however, the weight of Empire had become so great that the political fabric began to crack. After all, the constitution had been designed for a city-state of very moderate size, but it had come to serve an Empire stretching over Europe, Africa, and Asia. When new problems arose, such as the conflict between the optimates and the populares, the wealthy and the dispossessed, the old devices no longer worked. Instead, their appliance made the conflict only worse.

Perhaps we might put it in this way. According to Gödel's theorem, which I described in the Preface of Volume IX of this work [22], every arithmetical system may contain contradictions and anomalies. No such system is capable of solving its own problems in their entirety; it cannot make itself wholly consistent. To achieve this it is necessary to appeal to the next higher system. Of course, Gödel was speaking of arithmetical propositions, but perhaps we might (metaphorically) apply his theorem to a political system too. The extension of the Empire meant a relative weakening of the power centre; it could no longer cope adequately with its internal problems. A kind of implosion took place. The external dualism - the lust for conquest, the zest for war, the need for subjecting, the urge towards destruction - turned inward because the power centre, the political fabric, had become too feeble to ward it off by directing these forces to the fringes of the power sphere. The outwardly directed dualistic impulse, now turned inward, that had always been the domineering element in Roman politics, became stronger than internal cohesion. Now the Romans began to fight one another, and the great prize of conquest no longer was some foreign kingdom but Rome herself.

But already during the tragic and bloody events of the civil wars a solution was suggested. In Gödelian terms, the next higher system came in sight, or in historical terms, one-man rule became ever more probable. From general to general, from Marius to Sulla, from Sulla to Caesar, from Caesar to Antony, from Antony to Augustus, we see this posibility growing and growing until with Caesar and definitely with Augustus with whom the Principate began, it became the political, the historical reality.

It is not my intention to relate the whole history of the Principate and of the Dominate that followed it. There is, however, one question that fits into the general framework of this book. Did Augustus, did his successors, succeed where Caesar failed? Did they make an end of the two great dualisms of Roman history, the external and the internal ones?

a. The external dualism

In the days of Augustus (30 B.C.-14 A.D.) the Imperium Romanum had two sore spots, the Rhine frontier and the Euphrates frontier, or the Germanic question and the Parthian question. In Volume X I have described how Rome attempted to solve the Rhine problem by conquering Germany [23]. Under the command of Augustus' stepsons Drusus and Tiberius, Roman armies had been campaigning beyond the Rhine from 12 B.C. onward. In A.D. 5 they seemed entirely successful, having broken through to the Elbe.

However, in A.D. 9 a Roman army of three legions under the command of P. Quinctilius Varus was completely destroyed in the dark woods of Germany. All the conquests beyond the Rhine were lost. There were no new attempts to subject Germany.

Quite the contrary! In his testament of A.D. 14, Augustus advised his countrymen "to be satisfied with their present possessions and under no conditions to wish to increase the Empire to any greater dimensions. It would be hard to guard, he said, and this would lead to danger of their losing what was already theirs" [24]. This was a world-historical decision because now, after some seven centuries, the Roman machinery of conquest stopped moving; the heyday of imperialism was past. But since Rome's policy had always been geared to conquest, and since nobody else had envisaged anything other than going relentlessly forward, Augustus' decision must necessarily entail that no defensive policy would ever succeed, so that, then or later, the Empire would begin to crumble.

There were, however. two more conquests in Europe, that of Britain in the period A.D. 37-85 [25], and that of Dacia (Romania) in the early second century A.D. [26]. In the East, Armenia, Assyria, and Mesopotamia in 115 A.D. became provinces, but remained so only temporarily and intermittently; these regions became part of the struggle with the Parthians and the Persians. Although in the early period of the Principate Rome's foreign policy had ceased to be dualistic, this does not mean that the Romans were now rid of all dualistic tendencies. On the contrary, the struggle with Parthia and Sasanian Persia assumed dualistic dimensions. We shall have to return to this.

b. The internal dualism

And now for that other dualism, the internal one. The advent of Augustus to the throne was hailed by the peoples of the Empire as the inauguration of an era of peace. "Aeneas Caesar (= Augustus), son of a god, shall again set up the Golden Age", words of Virgil written by him in 19 B.C. [27]. Two years later, in 17 B.C., the emperor celebrated the 'secular games', the 'ludi saeculares', to commemorate and stress the fact that a 'saeculum', an era, had ended and a new one begun. This celebration had a catharctic, a purifying character, since all the misery of the bygone days, those of the civil wars, was done away with, so that Roman society could make a new start. The festivities began on June 1 with prayers and sacrifices brought by the Emperor himself. The religious ceremonies lasted three days, followed by eight days of games and scenic performances. On June 3, a choir of twenty-seven boys and as many girls, none of them an orphan, sang a hymn that was composed by Horatius, his 'carmen saeculare' : "Grant, o ye gods, to the young a spirit to learn and righteous conduct, to the old peace and calm, grant to the race of Romulus wealth and offspring and all glory ... Now Faith and Peace and old-time Modesty and neglected Virtue have courage to come back, and blessed Plenty with her full horn is seen" [28]. And whichever god might be involved, Mars is never mentioned [29].

The fire of the civil wars had always flared up in Rome itself, as a consequence of the opposition of two socio-political factions; from the capital it had spread all over the Empire. This fire had been quenched for ever. A few pages back I applied the Gödelian thesis to the political system in Rome : a one-higher system was needed to resolve the anomalies and contradictions of the first system. Principate and Dominate, acting as this one-higher system, succeeded in solving the problems of the original system, the Republic. Its socio-political system became a thing of the past.

Gödel taught us that the one-higher system is not exempt from contradictions and anomalies itself. In the imperial families there were problems about the succession; there were ambitious generals desiring to ascend the throne. Armies proclaimed their favourite commanders as emperor; the third century A.D. was the epoch of the 'soldier-emperors' of whom there were more than fifty in less than a hundred years. But we cannot say that these problems assumed a dualistic character.

c. Another abortive Empire of the East

However, the problems Rome had with subjected nations were not rarely of such a nature. I shall return to this in Chapter IV. And then, there was a threat looming ever more darkly over the Roman Empire, the danger of an East-West split that finally, indeed, was to materialize; this too is a subject for a later chapter. An ominous prelude to the falling apart of the Empire occurred towards the end of the second century A.D. On March 28, 193 the Emperor Pertinax was murdered. Soon after the governor of Syria, Caius Pescennius Niger, was proclaimed emperor in Antioch by his troops; he was also the favourite of the Roman populace. The whole East, Egypt included, ranged itself behind him. Antioch became the capital and the imperial residence of this Empire of the East.

But almost at the same time Septimius Severus was proclaimed emperor by his army in Pannonia, and he got the West behind him. After he had made himself master of Italy and Rome, he marched through the Balkans to Asia Minor; from there he wanted to proceed to Syria. On his way thither he was met, in the autumn of 194, on the plain of Issus by the host of Niger which he defeated; his rival was killed in his flight. The precarious unity of the Empire was restored. For the time being [30].

3. The co-regency

a. During the Principate

Soon enough the burden of government, the weight of the Empire, proved too much for the shoulders of one man. Already Augustus had chosen a 'co-regent' [31] to help him, his lifelong friend M. Vipsanius Agrippa who in 18 B.C. received the tribunicia potestas on which his authority was based, 'and many privileges almost equal to his own (the emperor's)'. It was the wish of Augustus that there should be no vacuum in case he was killed (fearing assassination he wore a breastplate under his dress) [32]. Already in 23 B.C., when seriously ill, he had handed Agrippa his signet-ring, therewith designating him, not as his successor but as his lieutenant [33]. At the same occasion he granted Agrippa an extraordinary imperium; he was sent to the East, with Mytilene as his basis, to act as the Emperor's lieutenant there, with supreme control of the imperial as well as the senatorial provinces. In this measure we see already vaguely outlined the future division of the Empire along the East-West line.

Agrippa died in A.D. 12. A year later Augustus' adoptive son Tiberius was really made co-regent by a law allotting him the administration of the provinces together with the Emperor.

For a long time the Principate remained the apanage of one single family, first the dynasty of the Iulii, then that of the Flavii. After the death of the last of the Flavian Emperors, Domitian in 96, there followed a long series of Emperors who had been adopted each by his predecessor, all of them outstanding rulers, Nerva, Trajan, Hadrian, Antoninus Pius, Marcus Aurelius. So far so good. But the situation that there was no natural successor to the throne, no prince with an undisputable claim, implied a risk. "When the Principate had ceased to be the possession of a single family, the enlargement of the field in which candidates might be sought inevitably increased the number of those who might see to press their own claims, possibly by force" [34]. Marcus Aurelius avoided the risk of a renewed outbreak of civil war by taking a colleague, a socius, as soon as he had ascended the throne in 161; this socius was his own brother Lucius Verus. Without exaggeration we may say that the Empire had two 'augusti' then; "Marcus for the first time made the Principate continuous" [35]. Verus died in 166; in 177 Commodus, a son of Antoninus Pius, became socius and succeeded Marcus in 180.

b. During the Dominate

I have already mentioned Diocletian as the real founder of the Dominate. He was also important in another respect. He was certainly not a pleasant man, but he had a deep insight into the problems of the Empire. When he came to the throne in 284 the Empire had decades of disorderliness behind it. One soldier-emperor after another had been hoisted onto the throne by his own troops, soon to be chased away again by the next one. Local troops and provincial governors had become power factors; the coherence of the Empire had considerably weakened.

The new Emperor realized that the Empire was too unwieldy and its problems too great to be governed by one man from one centre. To remedy this, he appointed a co-regent, a real one this time, an authentic co-emperor, Maximinian, who was made 'Augustus' as well as Caesar. Diocletian was to rule the East and Maximinian the West. In 293 both Augusti appointed each a socius, a Caesar, Galerius for the East and Constantius for the West. The East-West division was becoming ever more visible.

This new institution is called the 'Tetrarchy', the four-man rule. Of course, the four Caesars were not supposed to go their separate ways; they had to collaborate according to the Concordia Augustorum. Diocletian, a man not be trifled with, remained the supreme ruler. The Tetrarchy had a good start, since the four rulers were "brave, wise, kindly, all of one mind towards the commonwealth, very respectful to the Roman Senate, moderate, friends of the people, earnest, and pious, and, in fact, such emperors as we had always desired" [36].

In 305 Diocletian abdicated (he died in 313), and Maximinian, against his will, with him. A second Tetrarchy followed, Constantius I (Chlorus), now senior Emperor, became the Emperor of the West, while Galerius held the East as Augustus; both Augusti had their own Caesar. But soon enough the Tetrarchy broke down; again there was fighting for the throne. In 313 Constantine I the Great emerged from the struggle as the victor. He too had a co-emperor, Licinius, who ruled the East, and he himself the West. Each had his Caesar, the third Tetrarchy. What perspicacious observers may long have expected now happened : the two rulers fell out. Their disagreement ultimately led to open warfare. In two battles in the Balkans of unprecedented magnitude, Constantine, in 324, defeated his colleague who was captured and executed [37]. Once again, but almost for the last time, the Empire had only one ruler, a 'rector totius orbis'.

4. A new capital

It was a very important thing for the development of the Empire as well as for the history of Europe that Constantine was thinking of a new capital. His first idea was Ilion, the site of ancient Troy which, according to Roman legend, had been the cradle of Aeneas. But later he had another idea and decided upon the old Hellenic town of Byzantium as the site for a new foundation [38]. Why did Rome fall out of favour and why was the site of Byzantium chosen? Constantine seems not to have loved Rome, perhaps because it was a heathen city where the old pagan rituals were still being celebrated [39]. Or maybe he wanted to have a city of his own, one that would bear his name, Constantinopolis, and that would be the equal, or more, of the old capital [40].

The new site had great advantages, such as the splendid harbour of the Golden Horn; and Byzantium lay on the crossroads between the Black Sea and the Mediterranean, and between Europe and Asia (nowadays it is the only city in the world that is situated in two continents). Located on a peninsula, it could be more easily defended than Rome that, as history had amply proved, was not hard to approach. Byzantium already had its walls, but the Emperor had a new one built, more to the west and running from the Black Sea coast to that of the Sea of Marmara (the Propontis) [41]. But possibly the most fundamental reason for displacing the seat of government was that, after the conquest of the Hellenistic East, the centre of gravity of the Empire was to be found there, and not in the West. Caesar and Antony had been aware of this [42], as well as the chief-emperors of the Tetrarchies who had reserved the eastern half for themselves.

5. Two empires

After the death of Constantine the Great his three sons, just like the sons of Charlemagne, divided the Empire between them : Constantine II got Gaul and Spain, Constans Italy, North Africa and the Balkans, and Constantius II Egypt and Asia Minor. The brothers fought among each other;

Constantine II fell, and Constans laid his hands on Gaul and Spain in 340. Ten years later a rebellious general. Magnentius, a Frank in Roman service, had great success; he occupied Italy and Constans lost his life. But coming from the East, Constantius drove the usurper back; the latter took his own life. In 353 Constantius II was sole ruler of the Empire.

His successors Julian the Apostate (361-363) and Jovinian (363-364) governed alone, but Valentinian I (364-375) made his brother Valens his co-emperor in the eastern half. When Theodosius I was emperor (379-395), most of the time he had co-emperors in the West. After his death his two sons succeeded him, Honorius (395-423) in the West, and Arcadius (395-408) in the East; it was a sign of the times that both had a Germanic wife. The year 395 marked the definitive division of the Roman Empire; it never again had a single ruler. During the fifth century there were, by all accounts, two Empires, the Western Roman Empire which collapsed in 476, and the Eastern Roman Empire, commonly called the Byzantine Empire, that survived, ever more precariously, until 1453. Its capital, Constantinople, the present-day Istanbul, was called 'the second Rome'.

6. Rome's problems in the East

Rivers are dubbed 'natural frontiers' but in fact they are not hard to cross. Wide deserts and high mountain ranges offer a far better protection. The river frontiers of the Empire, the Rhine, the Danube, and the Euphrates, were weak spots; the Rhine and part of the Danube were covered by the limes, the fortified defence line [43], and the lower course of the Danube by Dacia (Romania) which served as a glacis [44]. But the Euphrates had no special protection at all, although the danger of foreign invasions always loomed very large here.

a. A dualistic struggle

The existence of two great imperialistic empires, the Roman and the Parthian, later the (Neo-)Persian Empires, with only the Euphrates between them, was a source of constant friction, since both empires claimed to be the heirs to the great and age-old imperial traditions of the East. Neither of them felt inclined to cede even an inch to its competitor; so their rivalry always had a dualistic character. As we have seen, Caesar's great avenging campaign against Parthia did not materialize; we have also seen that Augustus had no intention of expanding the Empire [45]. "He felt - instinctively perhaps, but none the less truly - that it was an Empire based on the Mediterranean, and that that was the basis of its strength and the condition of its existence" [46].

b. The problem of Armenia

The existence of Armenia, a poor and mountainous country, with a population that had always caused headaches to those who wanted to rule it, constituted a problem. Situated as it was between Parthia and the Roman Empire, it could be coveted by both. However, it lay beyond the Euphrates so that Augustus had no cause to be interested in it [47]. But loud voices clamoured for action, especially when in 30 B.C. all the Romans in this country were massacred [48]. The least that Augustus could do was to demand that Parthia should restore the standards and the prisoners captured at Carrhae, the scene of Crassus' catastrophic defeat in 53 B.C. [49]. Staging military manoeuvres in Asia Minor in 20 B.C., he got the Parthian king so far that he handed over the standards and those prisoners of war who were still alive [50]. "I compelled the Parthians", wrote the proud Emperor, "to restore the spoils and standards of three Roman armies and as suppliants to implore the friendship of the Roman people" [51]. Anyhow, Tiberius could now invade Armenia without having to fight and instal a vassal-king there, which turned the country into a Roman client-state [52]. With Armenia virtually under Roman control and Parthia effectively cowed, Rome could count on a period of peace. Or should we rather say, of armistice?

In A.D. 34 the second emperor, Tiberius, had become an old and embittered man who sat brooding in his villa on Capri. King Artabanus

(A.D. 12-39) of Parthia saw his chance. He installed his own son Arsaces on the Armenian throne, thus turning the country into a Parthian client-state. "At the same time, he referred in boastful and menacing terms to the old boundaries of the Persian and Macedonian Empires, and to his intention of seizing the territories held first by Cyrus and afterwards by Alexander" [53]. However, the Parthian nobles, discontented with Artabanus' autocratic style of government, sent an embassy to Rome asking the Senate to send them a Parthian prince who happened to live in Rome as king [54]. But although the Roman candidate with Roman help made his way to Ctesiphon, he was unable to hold out there and was compelled to retire to the Roman side of the Euphrates. Nevertheless, the Romans succeeded in putting a puppet of their own on the throne of Armenia [55]. This episode ended in a compromise. Artabanus accepted the fact that Armenia was to be a Roman client-state, and Rome recognized him as the legitimate ruler of Parthia. However, he had to send his son Darius to Rome as a hostage [56]; the name of the young man proves what high hopes were vested in him.

c. Warfare because of Armenia

During the years of the Emperor Claudius (A.D. 41-54), whose control of affairs was not very firm, there was trouble again in Armenia. Profiting from the Emperor's weakness, the Parthians invaded Armenia and in 53 put their man in charge there [57]. It was now the turn of the Romans to tip the balance again. In the first days of Nero's emperorship (54-68), a delegation from Armenia arrived to plead, as it was said, the interests of its people [58]; by 'people' very probably the interests of the Romanizing party must be understood [59]. Nero who clearly wanted to show that he, in spite of his age of sixteen years, was an energetic ruler, immediately began to plan a large-scale attack on Parthia (he was advised, among others, by Seneca). Legions were set moving eastward; the military engineers began building bridges over the Euphrates [60]. The command was given to Domitius Corbulo [61]. But the quality of the troops put at his disposal was so low that he first of all had to train and thoroughly harden his men.

It was only late in 57 that Corbulo could invade Armenia. It was winter and so cold that the sentries froze to death at their posts. There were, of course, many deserters but Corbulo stopped the flight from the colours partly by his manly example - he went about without winter clothing -, partly by a very stern discipline [62]. In the spring of 58 the Roman commander led his army deeper into Armenia. His enemy evaded an open encounter but resorted to guerilla warfare [63]. The strong fortress-town Volundum was taken by the now well-disciplined and trained legionaries in a few hours' time; its whole garrison was slaughtered to the last man and its inhabitants sold into slavery [64]. Then came the turn of one of the two Armenian capitals, Artaxata (no longer existing). Terrified by the fate of Volundum, its inhabitants let the Romans in. Since Corbulo had no men to spare for garrisoning the town, it was put on fire and razed to the ground. Rome rejoiced, and Nero was proclaimed 'imperator', although he had not left the capital [65].

Corbulo's next goal was Tigranocerta, the second Armenian capital, on the upper Tigris, which he reached in 59 after a difficult march over the mountains. When the Armenians made ready to defend the town, Corbulo had an Armenian nobleman who had fallen into his hands beheaded and sent his head, by means of a catapult, straight into the Armenian war council; the officers understood what this meant and delivered the town to him [66]. In 60 the affair was rounded off by putting a client of Rome on the throne of Armenia; he was given a small Roman force to lean upon [67].

d. Romans humiliated

During these campaigns there had been no reaction at all from the part of the Parthian King Vologases, crippled as he was by risings in his own country. But in 61 he was provoked into action by an Armenian invasion into his country (which could hardly have taken place without Roman acquiescence) [68]. In 62 he decided to place his own man on the Armenian throne again; his troops entered Armenia, while he even threatened Syria [69]. It was a kind of shadow-war since neither Rome nor Parthia was ready for open warfare. Concentrating on the defence of Syria, Corbulo asked for a special commander to protect Armenia [70]; the Emperor sent Caecennius Paetus, an incompetent man [71]. This Paetus proved ineffectual against the Parthians; he was defeated, and his army was made prisoner by the Parthians. An armistice was arranged, and the Roman puppet-king of Armenia retired with his Roman garrison to Cappadocia. For the umpteenth time Armenia received a new king, this time from the Parthians [72].

For Vologases this was not yet enough. Wanting a lasting monument of his victory, he had his Roman prisoners build a bridge over the Euphrates. Running the gauntlet, the legionaries, on their way to the bridge, had to pass between two rows of Parthian soldiers who robbed them of their arms and clothes; these, together with the corpses of the fallen, were thrown onto a heap as a demonstration of the Roman defeat. When the Romans had crossed the bridge, King Vologases waded after them through the river, seated high on an elephant [73]. Abandoning their wounded, Paetus' flying men covered forty miles in one day. The day of the Caudine Forks seemed to have returned [74].

e. The agreement of 66

When Rome realized what had happened, Nero decided on war. Paetus was relieved of his command, and Corbulo was made commander-in-chief [75]. He assembled four war-hardened legions, much cavalry, and a great number of auxilaries, invaded Armenia in the spring of 63, and created panic there. Both Tiridates, the Armenian king, and Vologases (whose grip on Parthia was not firm) seem to have realized that they were unable to resist a Roman attack in due form. Tiridates asked for a meeting with Corbulo; on being received by the Roman, he even stated that he was ready to go to Rome, 'as an Arsacid in the role of a suppliant' [76].

It was only in 66 that Tiridates arrived in Rome after a journey of nine months. Rome made much of the occasion; he was lavishly entertained. When he met Nero in Naples, he had, however, to kneel down before him, call him master, and do him obeisance. Later, in Rome, the Emperor himself set the royal diadem on his head. "The entire city had been decorated with lights and garlands" [77]. Of course, the Romans did not care a straw for Tiridates; what they celebrated was the humiliation of Parthia. But the frolocking Roman public overlooked one thing : Tiridates was not their choice, but that of King Vologases. Nero might put as many crowns on the head of his new vassal as he wanted - and it certainly was a great triumph for him -, but when all was said and done, Tiridates, himself an Arsacid, was and remained Vologases' man. The public "hardly realized that the prize paid was the virtual abandonment of Armenia to Parthia. The Arsacids were now recognized as the legitimate rulers of that harassed country which really became ... an appanage of the Parthian crown; and Rome's right of enfeoffment left her only a shadow of the authority she had claimed for a century" [78].

f. The agreement broken

For decades the situation remained unchanged; neither of the parties concerned seemed anxious for a showdown. Nevertheless, under the Flavian Emperors Rome was steadily strengthening her grip on the eastern half of Asia Minor and fortifying the Euphrates line. That Trajan proved to be a warlike emperor, which he showed by his exploits in Dacia [79], made the Parthians feel uneasy. In 113 the Parthian Great King Osroes, for one or another reason that still remain obscure to us, deposed the then reigning king of Armenia and, without informing Rome, put a candidate of his own on the throne there. This was an open breach of the agreement of 66 which had given Rome a say in the nomination of the Armenian kings. The Roman Emperor, not a friend of half measures, decided to react uncompromisingly.

g. Trajan annexes Armenia

"The war of Trajan against the Parthians is perhaps the largest military enterprise of the Roman 'haut-empire'; the destinies of the two powers that then seemed to divide the world between them were dependent on its success which proved far from happy for Rome; it gave the Roman conquest its greatest expansion : for the first time the legions saw the Persian Gulf" [80]. Thus wrote Julien Guey, and he added that of all the Roman wars this is one of the least known. Trajan left Rome in the autumn of 113, probably on October 27 [81]. Travelling via Brindisi, Athens, and Ephesus, he crossed the length of Asia Minor and was in Antioch at the end of 113 or the beginning of 114 [82]. Here he found the legions stationed in Egypt, Syria, and Palestine concentrated, five in all; another five legions, coming from the Danube or stationed in Asia Minor, he found at Melitene (now Malatya, in Cappadocia), when he had gone there [83].

With this impressive force of ten legions Trajan invaded Armenia and, without encountering resistance, reached the important town of Elegeia (now Ilidsha). There he met the king of Armenia, Parthamasiris. When the two rulers were face to face, the Armenian "took the diadem from off his head and laid it at his (the emperor's) feet; then he stood there in silence, expecting to receive it back. This would have signified a return to the agreement of 66 which implied that Armenian kings were to be enthroned by the Roman emperor." The soldiers began to cheer already because they saw the king, an Arsacid, 'standing before Trajan without a diadem like a captive'. Alone with the Emperor, Parthamasiris was confronted with Trajan's refusal to accede to his wish. Flying in a rage, he fled from the Roman camp but was brought back. "He spoke with great frankness, declaring among other things that he had not been defeated or captured, but had come there voluntarily, believing that he should not be wronged and should receive back the kingdom, as Tiridates had received it from Nero". But Trajan peremptorily retorted that "he would surrender Armenia to no one; for it belonged to the Romans and was to have a Roman governor". In other words, Armenia was annexed and became a Roman province (A.D. 114) [84].

h. Trajan's invasion of Parthia

Elated by this easy success, Trajan and his troops then invaded Mesopotamia, that is, they entered Parthia proper. Without scarcely any fighting the whole northern half of the land between the rivers was occupied in the course of the year 114. It is not wholly clear where the Emperor spent the winters of 114/115 and/or 115/116 -, the chronology is confused - whether in Antioch or in Edessa on the Euphrates; anyhow, he left his conquests well garrisoned. Probably in the spring of 115 the Roman offensive was resumed. Trajan now headed straight for the Parthian capital, Ctesiphon; in order to get there, he had to cross the Tigris. He effected a crossing indeed, but this time he had to overcome very heavy resistance [85].

While he was marching towards Ctesiphon, another Roman force, coming from the Euphrates, penetrated into Babylonia as far as Babylon itself [86]. Very probably to his great surprise, Trajan could take Ctesiphon without much figthing [87]. His Parthian colleague Osroes had fled but his daughter and his golden throne fell into Trajan's hands [88]. What a triumph! And so easily obtained! The Senate granted the victor the titles of 'imperator' and 'Parthicus'. He himself had his medallions stamped with the words 'Parthia capta' [89]. The great days of the Empire seemed to have returned. The crowning event was, of course, the annexation of Mesopotamia as a province, probably in 115 [90]. Now the Tigris had to serve as 'the frontier of Europe'.

In the winter of 115/116 the victorious emperor sailed down the Tigris and finally reached the Persian Gulf. When he saw a ship departing for Asia, he said : "I should certainly have crossed to the Indi, if I were still young"; he found Alexander a lucky man, since the Macedonian had been in the prime of his life during his famous campaign. Alexander's exploits obviously were on his mind, for he declared "that he himself had advanced farther than Alexander" [91]. In Babylon he offered sacrifice to the spirit of the Macedonian conqueror in the room where he had died [92].

j. The tables are turned

But suddenly the tables were turned on the Romans. "During the time that he (Trajan) was sailing to the Ocean (the Persian Gulf) and returning from there again, all the conquered districts were thrown into a turmoil and revolted, and the garrisons placed among the various peoples were either expelled or slain" [93]. To make things worse, a Parthian force coming from Media, invaded Armenia and Assyria, and after having occupied these regions, entered Babylonia. With much fighting and much burning of cities the Romans succeeded in recovering Mesopotamia [94]. The situation in Armenia could only be restored by ceding part of it to the Parthians [95].

But in other parts of Asia Minor too revolts broke out, and Trajan, an old and weary man now, hardly knew where to turn first. In order to keep his hands free, he detached the southern part of Mesopotamia from the new province and set it up as a vassal-kingdom under an Arsacid client-king [96]. This meant that the Romans remained only nominally in control there. Trajan then left Parthia to fight insurgents on the fringes of Arabia, without success [97]. Feeling ill and exhausted, he decided to return to Rome, but died on his way back in August 117 at Selinus (no longer existing) [98].

Trajan's Parthian expedition had been a shortlived adventure. Rome proved incapable of extending her power beyond the Euphrates. Already Trajan's successor Hadrian allowed the Armenians to have a king of their own [99]. Historically, it is not clear whether the Romans were able to keep control over Assyria, the northern part of Mesopotamia. Probably not, for we find that Hadrian did not claim from the Mesopotamians the tribute that his predecessors had imposed on them [100]. Once again 'the frontier of Europe' rolled back to the Euphrates.

k. A new Great King

For more than a century all remained quiet on the eastern front. But after 226 a new and formidable threat arose. In 208 a Parthian vassal, a member of the Sasanian House, a certain Ardashir, rose against his suzerain, King Artabanus V, conquered province after province, and, when his overlord marched against him, defeated him in 224 in a battle in which the king fell. Two years later the victor was crowned as Ardashir I and assumed the ancient title of 'King of Kings'. At this point the history of the Persian Empire under the Sasanian dynasty began.

Soon enough the new ruler made it clear that he considered Armenia and Mesopotamia as integral parts of the Parthian heritage. However, the one in power in Armenia was Osroes, who was an Arsacid and a relative of the last Arsacid Great King. The son of the fallen ruler had fled to him. For the time being, Ardashir was unable to conquer Armenia, but, nevertheless, the Romans grew nervous of him, for "he boasted that he would win back everything that the ancient Persians had once held, as far as the Grecian Sea (= the Aegean), claiming that all this was his rightful inheritance from his forefathers" [101].

In 231 Ardashir began to threaten the Roman border fortresses on the Euphrates. The Roman Emperor of these days was Severus Alexander (222-235). He judged the situation so serious that he went to the East in person; he gathered around him a great number of troops from the whole area between Egypt and the Black Sea. When the proud Ardashir refused to enter into negotiations, Alexander marched against him in 232 starting from Antioch. With considerable forces he penetrated far into Armenia, but was then stopped by Ardashir. Another Roman column that was marching on Ctesiphon, the Sasanian capital, was defeated and suffered heavy losses. The Romans had to retreat but Ardashir was unable to invade Roman territory [102]. The positive result seems to have been that Rome was temporarily in control of Mesopotamia again. But not for long. For a time Ardashir was occupied with campaigns in the east. In the last year of the Emperor Maximinus Thrax (235-238), Ardashir succeeded in recovering Mesopotamia [103].

1. 'King of Kings of Iran and non-Iran'

Both the Roman and Sasanian Empires got new rulers at about the same time : Gordian III (238-244) and Shapur I (241-272). With the last mentioned "there had come to the throne a man who represented even more energetically than his father and with more resolute determination the imperialism of the New Persian Empire. The struggle with Rome was immediately resumed" [104].

Already in 241 Shapur had invaded Syria and even threatened its capital Antioch [105]. But a year later Gordian opened the doors of the Janus temple in Rome which was to indicate that there was a war on, a war against the Persians [106]. A considerable Roman force marched through the Balkans and Asia Minor to Syria, drove the enemy successfully back over the Euphrates and reconquered Nisibis on the Tigris [107]. But there Timesitheus, the man who had the real command over the army, rather than the Emperor, who was a minor, died, leaving the boy-emperor helplessly alone; as Praetorian Prefect this Timesitheus was succeeded by an ambitious and unscrupulous man, Philip the Arabian [108]. At his instigation the mutinous troops assassinated Gordian and proclaimed Philip emperor (243-249). The new Emperor, who wanted first of all to secure his position in Rome, immediately abandoned the victorious campaign and concluded peace with Persia [109]. The terms of this treaty are not given but it is evident that Mesopotamia and Armenia remained under Roman control [110].

For the time being a Roman vassal, who could lean on a Roman garrison, was king in Armenia. But when in 252 this man was murdered, Persian troops appeared who chased the king's young son and successor away and put Shapur's candidate on the throne. The Roman garrison had to leave the country [111]. "The loss of Armenia meant for Rome the collapse of the Empire's eastern defences" [112]. The other bulwark was

Mesopotamia. Attacks on this country and on Syria and Cappadocia followed the Persian conquest of Armenia [112]. From now on there was a state of continuous warfare between Rome and Persia, with the Sasanian ruler on the offensive. At one time or other - Zonaras and Zosimus give different dates - he captured Antioch, 'the metropolis of the Orient', sacked it thoroughly, killed a number of its inhabitants, drove others away, and burnt the town down, without anybody offering resistance [113]. The proud Shapur then changed his title from 'King of Kings of Iran' into 'King of kings of Iran and Non-Iran'. The Romans could take this to heart!

It was then that Valerian (253-260) became Emperor. He simply had to retaliate. In the devastated Antioch where he had his headquarters [114] he heard that Shapur I had invaded Mesopotamia and that, in 260, he had laid siege to the important town of Edessa (the modern Urfa) [115]. Valerian, who was no great warrior [116] and who saw his legions being depleted by an epidemic [117], offered Shapur a sum of money if he was ready to end the war. The Sasanian answered that he wanted to meet his counterpart in person. Inadvertedly, Valerian went to the encounter with only a small escort; he was overpowered and led away in captivity [118].

What a catastrophe! A Roman emperor taken prisoner, a Roman emperor in the hands of 'barbarians'! Shapur did not even use him as a political tool for obtaining the most favourable peace conditions. He held Valerian in captivity until he died. Later the most gruesome stories circulated in the West of how Shapur had treated his prisoner. It was asserted that he had used the poor man as a stirrup; after forcing Valerian to kneel down, Shapur climbed on his back in order to mount his horse [119]. What is certain is that the Roman POW's were used as a work-force to build a dam near Shoshtar; this dam still exists and is called 'Band-e-Kaisar', the Emperor's dam (the Emperor being Valerian) [120].

m. An unexpected intervention

That the Romans did not lose an inch of ground beyond the Euphrates was due to the ruler of Palmyra, Septimius Odaenathus. Palmyra was a vassal-kingdom or protectorate of Rome in the north-east of Syria (the town no longer exists). Shapur, after his victory over Valerian, had triumphantly crossed the Euphrates, plundered Antioch again, and invaded Cappadocia. But Odaenathus had a strong army of archers and cavalry; he overtook the Persians, defeated them, and drove them back over the Euphrates [121]. The grateful Romans overwhelmed him with resounding titles : dux Romanorum, imperator, corrector totius orientis. In all probability he was not entirely disinterested; his aim may have been to make his kingdom independent of Rome. And no doubt he saw in the Persian aggression a real danger to himself and his principality. That he too styled himself 'King of kings' meant that he considered himself the equal of Shapur I, the Great King [122].

In 262 Odaenathus attacked again with Roman and Palmyran forces. He crossed the Euphrates, recaptured Carrhae and Nisibis, defeated Shapur, and laid siege to Ctesiphon [123]. He besieged the Persian capital again in 267 [124]. The result was that Mesopotamia came again under the control of the Romans [125] and perhaps Armenia too [126]. But it was humiliating for the Romans to realize that they had to thank one of their vassals for this. A few years later they had their revenge. Under their famous Queen Zenobia the Palmyrans had succeeded in incorporating Egypt and the southern half of Asia Minor into their realm. The Roman Emperor Aurelian (270-275), finding that this went too far, marched on Palmyra, captured it in 274, and took Zenobia with him to Rome as his captive. All this goes to show that the Romans were losing their grip on the East.

n. A look at the general situation

In 288 a kind of peace treaty, or rather a 'gentleman's agreement', was concluded between the two empires. It proved only temporary. A general remark is necessary. The situation in Mesopotamia in the period under consideration was always labile and confused; the sources do not make us much the wiser. The problem is that the land between the rivers served as a glacis, from the Roman viewpoint as a first line of defence against the Sasanian Empire, and, from the Persian side, as fulfilling precisely the same function against its Roman counterpart. So both parties coveted the same area.

In the decades we are speaking of it is never quite clear who was really in control of Mesopotamia (and Armenia). So if we say 'under the control of Rome' or 'annexed by the Persians', we should always cautiously add : more or less, to a certain extent, or, for the greater part. The point is that neither Rome nor Persia was able to realize its innermost desire, that of the Romans to finally revenge Carrhae, by throwing down the Sasanian Empire, that of the Persians to become the true successors to the Achaemenids by conquering Asia Minor. But each had its own insuperable problems standing in the way of these sweeping designs. Rome was harassed by Germanic invasions in the West and by one rebellion after another - so that the historians speak of 'the crisis of the Empire'; the Sasanians too had their revolts. So neither of them was able to mobilize sufficient force for the knock-out blow to its rival.

o. Diocletian's offensive

In 286 Diocletian became Emperor (286-305). Since the Roman Empire was in a critical state, his co-emperor Maximinianus went west to cope with the rebellions and invasions there, while Diocletian himself went eastward. The Great King, Wahram (Bahram) III sensed that he meant business and sent him an embassy; since he in his empire was beset with the same problems as the Romans in theirs, he wanted to make an end of the prevailing state of phoney war. The embassy came offering rich presents. Some kind of agreement was reached; the Euphrates remained the official frontier [127]. Diocletian had to acquiesce in this because the bulk of the Roman forces was engaged on the Rhine frontier. He even had to leave the East in order to come to the assistance of Maximinianus.

But the Roman Emperor must have remained convinced that a definitive settlement with Persia was necessary, which meant in practice that Mesopotamia and Armenia had to be brought under Roman control again. Real or alleged Persian breaches of the agreement of 288 were used as an excuse. In 298 two Roman armies attacked; one invaded Armenia, the other, led by the Emperor himself, Mesopotamia. Both offensives were highly successful; the two armies met in Nisibis on the Tigris which fell into Roman hands. The result was a peace treaty which was favourable for the Romans. Armenia (with a Roman vassal-king) and Mesopotamia came under Roman rule again; henceforward the Tigris would be the Roman-Persian frontier [128]. For the time being Rome was safe from Persian aggression; the Romans, however, did not possess the means to go further.

p. The struggle of Constantius II and Shapur II

The situation in the East remained unaltered for almost forty years. But during the last years of Constantine the Great the peace was disturbed by Persian raids on Mesopotamia; the Emperor sent his son Constantius there. He himself took up the time-honoured plan of Roman eastern politics, a decisive campaign against Persia [129]. This obviously proved enough for the Persians to send an embassy which made excuses. In 337 Constantine died, bequeathing the eastern provinces to his son Constantius II (337-361, co-emperor since 324). The whole eastern front came into movement; in Armenia the Persian party assumed control, while King Shapur II (310-379) threatened Mesopotamia; he besieged Nisibis but was unable to capture it [130].

Mesopotamia became a no man's land. Every spring the Persians came and raided it; then came Constantius to restore the situation. But although he had a strong cavalry the horses of which were protected by armour, he achieved nothing decisive; as soon as the enemy appeared, he beat the retreat. The orator Libanius even accused him of being, so to speak, in league with the Persians. It seems as though Constantius was deadly afraid of his opponents and infected his troops with his fear. "So deeply ingrained was the dread of the Persians that had grown during many years, that you might say that they (the Romans) might not look at pictures of them without a shudder" [131]. So there was no decisive engagement.

Not that the Persians fared much better. In 350 Shapur II planned a daring stroke, a great migration of people, including women and children, with the intention of settling them in Roman territory in order to make this once and for all Persian [132]. To realize this, he had to take Nisibis first, but however hard he tried, performing, as he did, the most ingenious feats of engineering, storming it with elephants, he was incapable of capturing it and retired [133].

There was a lull in the never ending fighting until 358. When the Emperor was in Sirmium (no longer existing) in the Balkans, he received a Persian embassy bringing a letter. This letter was a response to one sent by Constantius to Shapur in which he proposed to conclude a definite peace at last. In this way, writes Ammianus, he could dispose of a stubborn opponent; he had troubles enough in the west [134]. Of course, the Persian ruler interpreted this request as a tacit admission of weakness. In consequence, he adopted a high tone in his answer. He styled himself 'King of Kings, companion of the stars, brother of the sun and the moon'; in other words, he presented himself as a cosmic ruler. He called to mind that his forefathers had ruled an empire that stretched to the frontiers of Macedonia. What he demanded in practice was less grandiose : the restitution of Armenia and Mesopotamia. In the event his request was denied, he intended to open the offensive after the winter [135]. Constantius sent two embassies in the hope of persuading Shapur to change his plans but to no avail [136].

It was 359 before Shapur was ready to attack; he had assembled an army of a hundred thousand men [137]. The Roman East was largely depleted of troops; most legions had been relocated to the West [138]. In the summer Shapur's troops crossed the Tigris and invaded Mesopotamia; the Romans retaliated with a scorched-earth policy : between the two rivers they burned all the crops [139]. Shapur's plan was to cross the Euphrates too and invade Syria, but against the advice of his strategists he laid siege to Amida (now Diyarbakir) on the upper course of the Tigris. But the strong

Roman garrison defended the town heroically; it cost Shapur thirty thousand men and seventy-three days before he could take it. The Roman commanders were crucified; many inhabitants were massacred, the rest enslaved. The Roman historiographer Ammianus Marcellinus was present in the town during the siege of which he left us a graphic description [140]; as one of the few he managed to escape [141]. Shapur was beside himself with anger because it was now too late in the year to continue the campaign [142]. In the next year he went on with the conquest of Mesopotamia; he captured some towns but stormed others in vain and finally retired beyond the Tigris [143].

Of course, Constantius was forced to react. With a number of legions he crossed the Euphrates later in 360, came to Amida - the sight of its ruins made him break out in tears -, and then laid siege to the town of Bezabde on the Tigris (no longer existing) but in spite of all his efforts he was unable to take it. The rainy season had begun and the disheartened Romans retired to Asia Minor [144]. For both parties Mesopotamia proved a nut too hard to crack. Constantius died on November 3, 361, in Mopsukrene (Mopsuestia in Cilicia, no longer existing).

q. The offensive of Julian the Apostate

Constantius II was succeeded by the twenty-nine-year-old Julian (361-363) [145]. When he, on December 1, 361, heard that the Emperor was dead, he was in Naissus (now Nisj in Serbia). Ten days later he was in Constantinople [146]. He reminds me of John F. Kennedy, a still youthful man on whom great hopes were built but who, after a short career, met a violent death. He spent a lot of time on his religious policy, favouring paganism to the disadvantage of Christianity, but in the winter of 362 he went eastward and arrived in Antioch [147]. He was there mainly to prepare a campaign against the Persians. A Persian embassy came to negotiate a peace treaty, but this time it was the Emperor's turn to send it back with empty hands [148].

On March 5, 363, he left Antioch for his fateful journey to Mesopotamia [149]. We may be sure that the Emperor "had now begun consciously to imitate Alexander" [150]. "Alexander was dear to you", said his friend Libanius [151]; he even saw himself as the incarnation of the great conqueror [152]. Seldom had a Roman ruler fostered more grandiose plans with regard to Persia than Julian. His campaign would simply mean the end of the Sasanian Empire. "We expected the whole Empire of Persia to form part of that of Rome, to be subject to our laws, receive its governors from us and pay us tribute" [153]. Not everybody was as sanguine about the outcome as he was; during the march of the army to the Euphrates, the Emperor received a letter from Sallust, the governor of Gaul, imploring him to desist from his plans, or else he would effect his own destruction. The Emperor paid no heed to this advice and marched on [154].

In the middle of March Julian crossed the Euphrates with his army [155]. A few days later he was in Carrhae, the scene of the never forgotten Roman defeat of 53 B.C. "Here dreams disturbed the night's rest of the ruler and prophesied a sad fate to him" [156]. From there he directed part of his army towards the Tigris to join hands with the forces of the king of Armenia [157], while he with sixty-five thousand men [158] marched to the south and there entered enemy territory [159]. Having conquered the fortresses he found on his way, he reached the Tigris just opposite Ctesiphon; here he allowed his troops a time of rest [160]. 'So far everything went according to plan" [161].

After the rest period the army succeeded in crossing the Tigris and in scaling the steep opposite bank. There the Romans defeated the ironclad horsemen and the elephants of the Persians whom they drove back into Ctesiphon. The legionaries might even have entered the capital but the Emperor, himself wounded in the shoulder, forbade it, because he feared that his men would be crushed in street-fighting [162]. Since the position of Ctesiphon was extremely strong and since it was feared that Shapur was approaching with a large army, the idea of besieging the town was abandoned. But Julian did not give up his grandiose plan to destroy the Persian Empire. After eight days before the capital he turned his back on the Tigris and marched inland. The weather was stiflingly hot, and the air was infected with enormous swarms of flies and mosquitoes. Far and wide the Persians had destroyed the harvests; the legionaries suffered horribly [163]. But despite the protests of his troops, their stubborn commander refused to retreat.

On the 16th of June 363 the army began its daily march at a very early hour. Then the vanguard saw a dust-cloud rise into the air. What might that be? A troop of wild donkeys? Or perhaps troops coming from Armenia to their assistance [164]? The legions spent a starless night in a state of nervous apprehension. When the sun rose, they saw that Shapur's army was near. In the unbearable heat of the summer the Romans continued their march with the Persians on their heels. On the 18th it was necessary to give the exhausted men some days of rest. They had constantly to beat off attacks by the harassing Persians. In the morning of the 26th the Romans saw themselves confronted by an enormous enemy army. The Persians were clad in iron so that they seemed to be men of metal. The sight of the gigantic, loudly trumpeting combat-elephants made the legionaries feel very nervous. But once Julian had given the order to attack, the legions succeeded in breaking through the enemy lines and in continuing their march [165].

Because the losses of the Persians had been considerable, there followed three days of armistice. There was very little to eat; the Roman soldiers went about with empty stomachs. In the night Julian dreamed that the Genius of the Roman state appeared to him, but he did not speak and went away with his face covered [166]. On the 27th the march was resumed. Once again the Persians attacked, and the vanguard was thrown into disorder. Julian, who because of the heat did not wear his armour, rode thither. When he came into the front-line, he was hit by a javelin that pierced his side and remained stuck in his liver. He was brought to a tent, but the haemorrhage could not be stopped, and the Emperor died of his wounds. He was only thirty-two years old; his reign had lasted no longer than twenty months [167].

After the death of Julian the commander of the imperial guard, Jovian (363-364), was proclaimed emperor [168]. He ordered the retreat to Roman territory. Shapur, whose army had suffered considerably losses, unexpectedly offered peace negotiations. The peace talks lasted four days; Jovian had no choice but to accept the conditions proposed to him by Shapur. The Romans had to evacuate every strip of land beyond the Tigris and also a large part of Mesopotamia with the important town of Nisibis. They were also forced to agree that they would no longer assist and protect the king of Armenia - a fatal decision, says Ammianus, for later this king was taken prisoner by the Persians who annexed a large part of his realm [169]. Valens, who was Emperor from 365 to 378, repeatedly attempted to recover Armenia but having too many wars on his hands at the same time, he was unable to do anything decisive.

r. The regulation of the Armenian problem

In the course of 384 a Persian embassy, sent by King Shapur III to the Emperor Theodosius I, arrived at Constantinople to speak of a settlement of the Armenian problem [170]. The negotiations lasted a long time but in 387 peace was concluded : the Persians were to have the larger part of Armenia and the Romans the smaller part. This time the agreement lasted. Apart from some incidents, peace prevailed on the Roman-Persian frontier for more than a century. The upshot of the whole story is that, in spite of the situation being clearly dualistic, both parties wanting to defeat the other for good, neither of them was able to do so. Thus the situation along the Euphrates remained virtually unaltered for centuries. The problem of the eastern frontier became the heritage of the Byzantine Empire.

7. Rome's problems in the West

Before we turn our attention to the western half of the Roman Empire, that is, to the Germanic problem, a preliminary remark must be made. Whereas the situation in the East was clearly dualistic, this was not the case in the

West. The invading Germanic tribes did not want to throw down the Roman Empire and put a Germanic Empire in its place. What they wanted was land within the frontiers of the Empire. A broad outline of the Germanic invasions (which, after all, became the undoing of the Western Empire) may suffice therefore.

a. Pressure on the frontier

Since the second century B.C. the Germans had been exterting pressure on the frontiers of the Empire. In Vol. X I have described how Marius succeeded in warding off the dangerous invasions of the Cimbri and the Teutons [171]. In the same volume I have also related how the Roman attempt to settle the Germanic question once and for all by conquering Germany misfired as the result of Varus' catastrophic defeat in A.D. 9 [172]. To protect the Empire against new incursions a strong defensive line, the limes, was built along the Rhine and the Danube, while Roman Dacia served as a glacis in front of the Balkans [173].

b. Osmosis

There was osmosis on both sides of the Rhine, mainly through commercial activities. Regularly groups of Germans crossed the Rhine and with Roman permission installed themselves in Roman territory; Augustus allowed ninety thousand Germans to come in and Nero a hundred thousand. The Germans living within the Empire became gradually romanized; in the course of the centuries many of them reached high positions in the army and administration, so many, indeed, that it was sometimes asked whether the Western Empire was not becoming germanized. Until the middle of the third century the Romans had the situation fairly well in hand. There was no German Empire; the German tribes knew no solidarity or cooperation and fought each other instead of Rome. Tacitus prayed fervently that this might last : "Long may the barbarians continue, I hope, not to love us, but at least to hate each other, for the destiny bears hard upon us, and fate has no greater bounty in store than disunion among our enemies" [174].

c. The gathering storm

The first harbinger of the gathering storm were the so-called 'Marcoman Wars' which began in 166 and lasted until 180. Since the days of the Cimbri and the Teutons there had never been such an onrush on the frontiers. The point is that the Romans had to do with a collectivity of tribes - but it was not a regular coalition - of which the Marcomanni and the Quades were the leading elements; perhaps some twenty-five tribes were involved.

We find the Marcomanni themselves north of the Danube in what now is Bohemia. Inside Germany there was a permanent moving of tribes looking for land; around the middle of the second century the Goths migrated southward from their habitat along the Baltic and began to exert a strong pressure on nations further south. These tribes wanted to move too but were kept back by the limes. In 166, however, the defence line was largely depleted of troops, since all legions had been reallocated to the Parthian front. Attempts by the Marcomanni and other tribes to cross the Danube into the Empire led to large-scale and prolonged fighting with the Romans in which these did not always come off best. In 168 the Marcomanni crossed the Alps and invaded Italy; they came as far as Aquileia (near present-day Venice). Panic in Rome! But Marcus Aurelius took energetic counter-measures and drove the enemy back over the Danube. The limes was safe again in 172. But the war broke out anew in 178 and cost the Romans another three years of hard fighting. In 180 the status quo along the Danube was restored. It is important to note that Marcus Aurelius had, to a large extent, to rely on Germanic troops to fight the Germans.

d. The Aleman storm

After this the Romans got another century of respite. That there was brewing something is shown by the fact that in 213 the Emperor had to fight a short war against the Alemanni near the Main in which he remained victorious. Shortly before 260 the great 'Aleman storm' began. 256 was a catastrophic year. The Alemanni, followed by the Franks, broke through the limes on the stretch between Rhine and Danube; all the fortresses fell into their hands. All Roman territory east of the Rhine was abandoned. The raids of the Franks reached as far as Spain, while the Alemanni plundered Auvergne, crossed the Alps, and invaded Italy. Some of their bands were already nearing Rome, when the Emperor Gallienus succeeded in crushing their main force near Milan in 258 or 259. But in spite of this success the plundering forays of the Alemanni into Gaul continued. Two things emerge very clearly now : the Germans had become the aggressors, and the Romans were no longer able to hold the limes. "The political centre of gravity shifted naturally to the new forces beyond the frontiers, and thereby rendered inevitable the birth of Germano-Roman states" [175].

e. Dacia abandoned

The situation on the Danube front did not look brighter. There the Goths were active. Time and again they invaded Dacia and the Danube provinces. In 253 they entered Asia Minor and came as far as Ephesus. This exploit was repeated more than once. Marauding Gothic bands spread all over Greece, and even Byzantium was plundered. The pressure exerted by the Goths was so great that, probably in or after 259, Dacia had to be abandoned. The Roman Empire began to shrink. Diocletian, an energetic man, succeeded in stabilizing the situation along Rhine and Danube for a time.

f. Continuous pressure

The picture remained unchanged for decades. Germanic tribes constantly threatened the Empire along the whole northern front, but when there was a powerful ruler, the Romans could breathe more freely for a time. Valentinian I stayed for years in the north, cleaning northern Gaul of marauding Germanic bands, and in 368 even invaded 'Alemannia' without being able to recover the lost Roman territories. Further east, the Romans were unable to resist the onslaught of the Visigoths; they defeated a Roman army and killed the Emperor Valens in the Battle of Adrianople on August 9, 378. The result was that the Goths had come to stay. Within the frontiers of the Empire autonomous Gothic states were erected in Hungary and Bulgaria.

g. The 'Great Migration of Peoples'

The final blow fell on December 31, 406, when the 'Great Migration of Peoples' began. Of course, this was not really an unexpected event; we have seen how shifting the situation beyond Rhine and Danube had been in the last one-and-a-half centuries. The Huns, a Mongolian nation, kept back by the Chinese Wall, had not succeeded in entering China. Looking for land, they turned westward, chasing other nations before them. The Ostrogoths began to move westward too and appeared in northern Italy. Huns and Ostrogoths precipitated a real avalanche of tribes : Vandals, Alans, Alemanni, and others hurried westward in great masses of land-hungry people.

On the last day of 406 they crossed the frozen Rhine near Mainz and then flooded all over Gaul, cutting off Britain from Rome. The vanguard of the migration, the Vandals, reached the Pyrenees in the autumn of 409 and crossed into Spain. Finding this barren country not rich enough (they made effectively an end of the Roman presence in the Iberian peninsula), they invaded North Africa in 429 and established an independent kingdom there.

I have already related how, after the Battle of Adrianople, Visigothic kingdoms came into being in the Balkans. For their energetic King Alaric this was not enough; he put his people on the march again and thoroughly plundered Greece. In 401 he entered Italy at the head of his hords. After two abortive attempts he captured Rome on August 24, 410; for the first time in exactly eight centuries the 'caput mundi' saw a foreign enemy within its walls. In three days' time the town was robbed of everything that had value. No wonder that people thought that the end of the world had come! Being unable to cross to North Africa, Alaric marched northward with his booty-laden men but died in 410 at Consentia (Cosenza) in Bruttium. The bed of the river Busento was laid dry to have his tomb built into it, after which it was covered by the flowing waters. The scene has been immortalized by Felix Dahn in his once famous historical novel 'Die Könige der Germanen'. The Visigoths then crossed the whole length of Italy and entered Gaul and from there Spain where they established their kingdom. At first they still recognized the suzerainty of the Roman Emperor but in 475 their King Euric declared his realm totally independent.

A coalition of Germanic tribes, called 'the Franks', had been infiltrating the Empire already since 355; they lived with official permission in Roman Toxandria (Dutch and Belgian Brabant). But after 425 they began to extend their territory still further southward till in 478 it comprised the northern half of France, Belgium, Luxemburg, the southern half of the Netherlands. and south-west Germany. Smaller Germanic kingdoms were those of the Burgundians in the Provence, and that of the Alemanni south of the Main and on both sides of the upper Rhine. Britain was invaded and conquered by Anglosaxon tribes; the last Roman garrison was withdrawn in 407. What remained of the Western Roman Empire in the second half of the fifth century was Italy alone (Sicily, Sardinia and Corsica being in the power of the Vandals).

h. The end

Very little was left now of the prestige of the Roman Empire, and of Rome in particular. Honorius in 404 had made Ravenna the imperial residence, because he felt more secure there, leaving Rome virtually to the care of the Popes. In 455 a Vandal army from North Africa under King Geiseric landed on the coast of Middle Italy and appeared on the 2nd of June before the gates of Rome where it was met by Pope Leo I. Leo, who knew the city to be defenceless, succeeded in making the Vandal king desist from massacre and arson. It was not really Geiseric's intention to slaughter the inhabitants and then to burn down the city. What he really wanted was the metal of every sort which the city contained and which was used for public decoration. For fourteen long days his men took off the gold, bronze and iron coverings of all kinds of buildings with the utmost care, together with all the metal statues. To make good use of all this metal he took with him several thousands of artisans. It is evident that he intended to shift the physical weight of the Empire to his own capital that, by a stroke of historic irony, was called Carthage. That the Empire had lost its significance is proved by the fact that he took the imperial insignia with him.

We have no idea what Geiseric needed the insignia for; we have no indication that he wanted to found a Vandal counter-empire of the West. The French historian Christian Courtois was probably right when he wrote that all these barbarian conquerors, whether they were Visigoths, Franks, Vandals, or whatever, had 'an insatiable ambition of things' [176]. What they wanted was land for their tribesmen, grain for their populations, metal to make their armies strong, and money to enrich themselves. But no grandiose imperial designs entered their heads.

Even without insignia the emperors kept succeeding one another in the rump-Empire that was Italy. In 475 an ambitious man, Orestes, raised his young son to the throne in Ravenna; it was again an irony of history that the boy wore the names of the two founders of the Empire, Romulus Augustulus - little Augustus because he was still young. In August 476 a Germanic commander in Roman service, Odoacer, deposed the Emperor but did not nominate a new one. Instead, he styled himself 'King of the Germans in Italy' (476-489); Romans and Italians had evidently become second choice. What became of the deposed Emperor is not known; nobody was interested in him. With his deposition the Western Roman Empire is held to have come to an end.

NOTES TO CHAPTER III

1. Dio 51.20.1.
2. Dio 51.20.4.
3. Dio 51.19.7.
4. Dio 51.20.7.
5. Dio 51.20.3.
6. Dio 51.22.2.
7. Dio 53.16.7-8.
8. Dio 53.17.1.
9. Dio 53.17.4.
10. Tac., Ann. 1.9.
11. Res gestae 34.
12. ILS 244 (the Lex Vespasiani); further Strabo, Geogr. 17.25.
13. Ensslin, End of the Princ. 352/353.
14. Babelon, Imp.syr., Ch. III Julia Domna et la Syrie.
15. CIL V, 4868, VIII, 9317 and 24.004.
16. Hasebroek, Untersuchungen 92.
17. Dessau I, 629.
18. Ensslin, End 337.
19. Ensslin, End 387/388.
20. Epilogue of CAH XI, 784.
21. Vol. IV, Ch. I.4.
22. Vol. IX, Preface 9b.
23. Vol. X, Ch. VI.14.
24. Dio 56.33.5.

25. See Vol. X, Ch VI.15.
26. See Vol. X, Ch. VI.18.
27. Virgil, Aeneid 6.792.
28. Hor., Carm.saec. 45-48 and 57-60.
29. Res gestae 22; Suet., Aug. 31.5; Dio 45.18.2. Description of the ceremonies in Zosimus 2..5. See M.P. Nilsson s.v. 'saeculares ludi', PW IA (Stuttgart, 1914), 1696-1720; Jones, Princeps, CAH X (1939), 150/151; Nock, Rel.Dev. CAH X (1939), 477-479.
30. Dio 73.11.1-74.8.3. See Wilhelm Reusch s.v. 'Pescennius Niger', PW XIX (Stuttgart, 1938), 1086-1102.
31. The term is not wholly adequate but there is no better.
32. Dio 54.12.2-4.
33. Dio 53.30.1-2.
34. Last, Principate 415.
35. Last, Principate 415.
36. Carinus 18.4 in Script.Hist.Aug.
37. Zos. 2.18-28.
38. Zos. 2.30.1-2.
39. Zos. 2.29.
40. Eutr. 10.8.1.
41. Zos. 2.30.
42. Vol. X, Ch. V.4g and 5e.
43. Vol. X, Ch. VI.17.
44. Vol. X, Ch. VI.18.
45. Vol. X, Ch. VI.14e.
46. Anderson, Eastern frontiers 256.
47. Res gestae 27.
48. Dio 51.16.2.
49. Dio 53.33.2.
50. Dio 54.8.1.
51. Res gestae 29.
52. Dio 54.9.4.
53. Tac., Ann. 6.31.

54. Dio 58.26.1.
55. Tac., Ann. 6.32-36; Dio 58.26.2-4.
56. Tac., Ann. 12.50.
57. Tac., Ann. 12.50.
58. Tac., Ann. 13.5.
59. Anderson, East.front. 758.
60. Tac., Ann. 13.7.
61. Tac., Ann. 13.8.
62. Tac., Ann. 13.35.
63. Tac., Ann. 13.37.
64. Tac., Ann. 13.39.
65. Tac., Ann. 13.41.
66. Front., Strat. 2.9.5; Tac., Ann. 13.24.
67. Tac., Ann. 13.26.
68. Tac., Ann. 15.1.
69. Tac., Ann. 15.2-3.
70. Tac., Ann. 15.3.
71. Tac., Ann. 15.6.
72. Dio 52.21.3; Tac., Ann. 15.14.
73. Tac., Ann. 15.15.
74. Vol. X, Ch. II.11b.
75. Tac., Ann. 15.25.
76. Tac., Ann. 15.29. The Arsacids were the ruling Parthian dynasty; Tiridates was the brother of King Vologases.
77. Dio 63.2-6.
78. Anderson, East.front. 773.
79. Vol. X, Ch. VI.18.
80. Guey, Essai sur la guerre 11. See also Lepper, Parth.War 1. It is a great pity that Appian's Parthica, with a full description of this war, is almost completely lost.
81. For the reconstruction of the date see Guey, Essai 39-42; Lepper, Parth.War 28-30.
82. Dio 68.17.2-18.1.

83. Guey, Essai 50.
84. Dio 68.19.2-20.1.
85. Dio 68.26.1-3.
86. Dio 28.26.4.
87. Dio 68.28.2; Guey, Essai 107-109.
88. Longden, Wars of Trajan 247.
89. Guey, Essai 118; Lepper, Parth.Wars 223.
90. Guey, Essai 78-80.
91. Dio 68.28.3-29.1.
92. Dio 68.30.1.
93. Dio 68.29.4.
94. Dio 68.30.2.
95. Dio 68.30.3.
96. Dio 68.30.3.
97. Dio 68.31.
98. Dio 68.33.
99. Spartianus, Vita Hadr. 21.11.
100. Spartianus, Vita Hadr. 21.12.
101. Dio 80.3.3-4.
102. Lampridius, Alex.Sev. 55-57. Lampridius celebrates this encounter as a Roman victory, but according to Herodian, who has a low opinion of the military capacities of the emperor, it was a downright defeat, Herod. 6.2.3-6.1.
103. Zonaras 12.18.
104. Ensslin, Sass.Persia 130.
105. Iul.Cap., Gord.Tert. 27.5. The communication that Antioch was already lost is not correct.
106. Iul.Cap., Gord.Tert. 26.3. Since the emperor was only fifteen years old, it was his Praetorian Prefect Timesitheus, who was also his father-in-law, who had the command, but Gordian marched along with the army, see Iul. Cap., Gord.Tert. 27.3.
107. Iul.Cap., Gord.Tert. 27.4-6.
108. Iul.Cap., Gord.Tert. 28.1; Zos. 1.18.2-3.
109. Zos. 1.19.1.

110. Ensslin, Sass.Persia 131.
111. Zonaras 12.21A.
112. Ensslin, Sass.Persia 132.
112. Zos. 1.27.2.
113. Zos. 1.27.2; Zonaras 12.23.
114. Zos. 1.30.1-32.2.
115. Zos. 1.36.1; Zonaras 12.23.
116. Zos. 1.36.2.
117. Zos. 1.36.1.
118. Zos. 1.36.2.
119. Orosius 22.4.
120. Ensslin, Sass.Persia 137.
121. Zonaras 12.23.
122. Alföldi, Crisis 175/176.
123. Zos. 1.39.1-2; Orosius 7.22.12.
124. Orosius 7.39.2.
125. Eutr. 9.10.
126. Alföldi, Crisis 175.
127. This must be concluded from the Latin sources which do not state that the Persians ceded territory to Rome, Pan. 2.9.2 and 10.6.
128. Patricius, Historia 3.
129. Rufus Festus, Brev. 26.
130. Julian.Ap., Or. 1.18; Rufus Festus, Brev. 27.
131. Libanius Or. 591-593 (18.206-211).
132. Julian.Ap., Or. 1.27; Zonaras 13.7.
133. Rufus festus, Brev. 27; Zos. 3.8.2; Zonaras 13.7; Iul.Ap., Or. 1.27B).
134. Amm.Marc. 16.9.3-4.
135. Amm.Marc. 17.5.1-8.
136. Amm.Marc. 17.5.9-15.
137. Amm.Marc. 19.6.11.
138. Amm.Marc. 18.5.2.
139. Amm.Marc. 18.7.2-4.

140. Amm.Marc. 19.1-9.
141. Amm.Marc, 19.8.5-12.
142. Amm.Marc. 19.9.9.
143. Amm.Marc. 20.6-7.
144. Amm.Marc. 20.11.
145. Constantine the Great was his uncle. He owed his nickname the Apostate to his religious policy, but this need not occupy us here.
146. Amm.Marc. 22.2.4.
147. Amm.Marc. 22.9.13-15.
148. Libanius, Or. 18.164.
149. Amm.Marc. 23.2.6.
150. Athanassidi, Julian 192.
151. Libanius, Or. 17.7.
152. Socrates 3.21.7.
153. Libanius, Or. 18.282.
154. Amm.Marc. 23.5.4-5.
155. Amm.Marc. 23.2.6-7.
156. Amm.Marc. 23.3.3.
157. Amm.Marc. 23.3.5.
158. Zos. 3.13.1.
159. Amm.Marc. 23.5.1-4.
160. Amm.Marc. 24.6.1-3.
161. Amm.Marc. 24.6.4.
162. Amm.Marc. 24.6.
163. Amm.Marc. 24.7.
164. Amm.Marc. 24.8.
165. Amm.Marc. 25.1.
166. Amm.Marc. 25.2.
167. Amm.Marc, 25.3.
168. Amm.Marc. 25.5.
169. Amm.Marc. 25.7.
170. Orosius 7.34.8.

171. Vol. X, Ch. VI.4.
172. Vol. X, Ch. VI.15.
173. Vol. X, Ch. VI.18.
174. Tac., Germ. 33.2.
175. Alföldi, Invasions 164.
176. Courtois, Les Vand. 213.

CHAPTER IV

UNDERPRIVILEGED GROUPS
PART I SUBJECTED NATIONS

1. The protectorate of the world

Let us listen to Cicero. "As long as the Empire of the Roman people maintained itself by acts of service (beneficiis), not of oppression, wars were waged in the interests of our allies or to safeguard our supremacy (de imperio); the end of our wars was marked by acts of clemency or by only a necessary degree of severity. The Senate was a haven of refuge for kings, tribes, and nations; and the highest ambition of our magistrates and generals was to defend our provinces and allies with justice and honour. And so our government could be called more accurately a protectorate of the world (patrocinium orbis) than a dominion (dominium)" [1]. In these words Cicero unambiguously stated that the Romans were the protectors of the whole world (orbs). The Roman people, writes Paul Veyne, was a kingly people, and its relations with the nations it ruled were those of a king with its subjects. A king must be obeyed because he is a king, and for no other reason [2].

So there were Romans and others - which makes a world of difference. The question is whether the 'others' were ready to join in Cicero's laudatio, whether they too saw Roman rule as an unmixed blessing. We shall see that the Romans often had to cope with unrest and resistance in the provinces, even with serious and dangerous rebellions. Two of the fiercest insurrections, those of the Jews in A.D. 67-70 and 135, will be dealt with in a later part of this volume. Not rarely such rebellions became a (dualistic) struggle between Roman universalism and the particularism of nations and tribes; what they felt to be at stake was their identity which they wanted to preserve in the face of Roman imperialism.

2. Roman opinion of 'the others'

Like the Greeks, the Romans took a low view of all those who did not speak their own vernacular. The language of such people was unintelligible; what they spoke was understood as 'bar-bar-bar' [3]; hence the term 'barbarus'. Ovid makes somebody say : "I am a barbarian understood by nobody" [4]. This also meant that such people were considered somewhat less than fully human; Ovid added in disgust : "You may loathe the sight of their bodies covered with hides and long hair" [5]. The quality of full humanity remained reserved for Romans only. As irony would have it, in the eyes of the Greeks the Romans too were barbarians since they did not have Greek as their maternal language.

Originally the Romans found everyone who did not speak Latin a barbarian; they liberally applied this term to members of foreign nations, high civilized ones among them, like the Parthians. In the fourth century A.D. Ammonius, a Roman living in Egypt, wrote to his friends that they should not think of him as 'a barbarian or a non-human Egyptian' [6]. Indeed, there came a point when the Romans overcame their feelings of inferiority to the Greeks, although acknowledging that the Greeks had been their teachers. "Greece, the captive, made her savage victor (Rome) captive and brought the arts into rustic Latium" [7]. But they also began to feel that the centre of civilization had shifted from Athens to Rome, even that the Romans now outshone the Greeks.

"In their own creations the Romans have everywhere shown more wisdom than the Greeks; where they borrowed from the Greeks they perfected everything they thought worthy of their efforts. In our manners and in our customs, in the management of our homes and affairs we have assuredly the better and also more brilliant organization; with regard to the government of the state, our ancestors have doubtless arranged this by means of the better institutions and laws." Cicero, whom I am quoting again, concludes his self-praise by stating that neither the Greeks nor any other people could be compared to the Romans as long as one was referring to character and not to study. Having thus effectively put the Hellenes in their place, he could readily admit that they had the lead in general culture and literary achievements, but in this respect he excused his countrymen by saying that they were latecomers [8].

3. The absorption of 'barbarians'

Once they were the hub of the world themselves, the Romans were willing to admit others to the orbit of their Latinitas. The populations of the provinces, living under the Roman aegis and protected by the Emperors, were no longer seen as barbarians. This term was only applied to the 'gentes externae non foederatae', the Romans that lived outside the Roman pale and had no treaty (foedus) with Rome. The frontiers of the Roman Empire presented, in consequence, a line of dualistic distinctions. But barbarians who were admitted into the Empire and settled there, became foederati and were no longer considered hopelessly barbarian. Generally, however, the Romans did what they could to keep the barbarians out. They were 'aliegeni', of an alien race. Although there was some commercial exchange along the frontiers, the laws of the Empire forbade the export of 'strategic goods', like wine and oil, let alone arms, to barbarian countries. Barbarians who were made prisoner on Roman soil became ipso facto slaves. A law of 365 forbade Roman citizens to marry persons of barbarian nationality. But try what they might, the Romans could not stem the barbarian tide. They settled as colonists; more and more barbarians, once having become foederati, entered the ranks of the army. They became officers and generals and manned the palace guard; some even became consuls [9].

4. 'Materia victoriae

But when all was said and done, it still remained that barbarians were the enemies of culture and as such had to be fought, writes Vogt, and he continues : "The imperial government did what it could to proclaim the idea of the victorious power of the Empire over the inferior barbarian world" [10]. If the barbarians refused to accept the blessings of the Pax Romana, 'bestial and obtuse of mind' as they were, they were no more than 'materia victoriae', stuff for victory [11]. It is as though fighting barbarians were identical with destroying vermin. Since Constantine the Great the Emperors called themselves 'debellator gentium barbararum, victor omnium gentium', the subduer of barbarous nations, the victor of all peoples [12] - this in flagrant contradiction to the fact that the Empire sorely needed the barbarians, because its population was dwindling. This also meant that it employed barbarians to fight barbarians. But what the grateful Romans really thought of 'barbarians' fighting Rome's battles is revealed by Claudian when he wrote of the Battle of Polentia in 402 in which the Roman commander Stilicho, a German, triumphed over Alaric's Ostrogoths : "Our great profit in battle is twofold when barbarians are put against barbarians and both fall" [13].

It was only in the last century of the Empire that Roman public opinion became somewhat more positive with regard to 'barbarians'. They were now seen as the subjects of Roman 'philanthropy'. In the year 370 the orator Themistius, who spoke Greek, said some highly revealing things. "There is in every human being a barbaric kernel ... of recklessness and insatiable desires that oppose sensible reasoning, just as Scyths and Germans (oppose) the Romans ... Whoever uselessly fights boldly behaving barbarians only turns himself into the king of the Romans, but who triumphs over them and spares them, he knows himself to be the king of all men, and above of all those he has saved, although it had been possible totally to destroy them." And then the rhetor said something that showed how shallow his philanthropy was. He told his hearers that elephants and lions and hippopotami were spared too, and "therefore should we also spare a race of humans, barbarians admittedly, but humans after all, that submits itself to us and puts itself under our protection, instead of annihilating it completely" [14]. This is vintage Roman dualism : there is nothing between subjection and destruction.

5. Discontent always smouldering

"The native revolt is an omnipresent social movement in the history of imperialism." We find these words which are also true for Roman imperialism in Dyson's essay on native revolts in the Roman Empire [15]. The general causes of these regularly recurring revolts are twofold. Firstly, there is the displeasure of proud and formerly independent nations for having been subjected and incorporated against their will into an alien political fabric. A second cause of widespread discontent was Rome's mismanagement of their affairs. Roman rule was often harsh, oppressive, and even cruel. Roman officials not rarely saw their governorship of the provinces as a means to fill their empty purses. Taxation was heavy, often amounting to downright extortion. A famous, or rather infamous, case is that of Verres who was proconsul for Sicily in 73-71 B.C. in which capacity he shameslessly plundered the inhabitants, not even sparing the Roman citizens living on the island. Cicero, however, succeeded in having him indicted and condemned - this, however, was exceptional.

After the Social War, which resulted in Roman citizenship for the Italian allies, Italy always remained the quietest part of the Empire. But this granting of citizenship did not mean at all that Italy, as a political entity, came on a par with the imperial city itself. As Heuss wrote, the Imperium Romanum was 'originally the dominion of Romans over non-Romans, and this it remained conceptually also in the time of the Emperors" [16]. The Italians were privileged subjects, but subjects. It made little difference if the authority over them lay in the hands of the consuls in Rome, or in those of a proconsul or propraetor as in the provinces [17].

6. Violent outbreaks of discontent

Since Rome had asserted her dominion over Gallia Cisalpina (northern Italy, the plain of the Po) after the Second Punic War, she had no trouble with the Celtic tribes living there; Roman citizenship was extended to them in 49 B.C.. Sicily remained pacified, but both Sardinia and Corsica were unruly. There were regular outbreaks of revolt, although never on a great scale, but it is not always possible to distinguish clearly between guerilla warfare and ordinary brigandage.

Dyson calls Spain 'a unique and agonizing experience in Roman history' [18]; it is one long story of resistance to Roman rule. Shortly after 200 B.C. heavy taxation led to a revolt that spread over the whole peninsula. When it seemed to have been suppressed, it flared up again. Fighting went on for decades. After 150 B.C. it even became extremely fierce after a Roman massacre of Lusitanians. With the capture of the great Iberian stronghold of Numantia in 133 B.C. most of the resistance broke down.

The years after 100 B.C. again saw much native unrest, once again going on for decades. In the years 56 to 49 B.C. the Romans were confronted with the rebellion of quite a number of tribes, while the rebellion of Sertorius which I described in Chapter III, occurs in this period. "The continued resistance of Sertorius would not have been possible if there had not been deep resentment against Rome" [19].

During the reign of Augustus there were new eruptions of armed discontent. Rebellion after rebellion had to be beaten down. When the Cantabri rose in 19 B.C., Rome could only quell the revolt by 'destroying nearly all of the enemy who were of military age' [20]. Then at last, after two centuries of rebellion, a kind of peace descended over the harassed peninsula, although small revolts were still recurring regularly.

The Romans had their problems with North Africa too. Of the Gaetulians and other tribes which rose in A.D. 7 Dio writes that they were "scorning the thought that they should be ruled over by the Romans" [21]. Dyson sums up the history of the African rebellions in these words : "throughout the next two centuries North Africa remained one of the most disturbed areas of the Empire in spite of considerable efforts of the Emperors to pacify it ... The North African frontier was one where the Romans were unable to stop completely the revolt cycle" [22].

Morocco - Mauretania in Roman days - has always been a difficult province for its occupants, for the French no less than for the Romans. The nomadic tribes that lived there were not pleased with Roman rule. In 19 B.C.

a revolt broke out that later found a response in Numidia (Algeria). It caused the Romans endless trouble; the Mauretanian War went on for decades. It was only after some sixty years, in A.D. 44, that Rome was master of the situation. But in the days of the Emperor Hadrian Rome had to beat down a series of revolts and then again when Marcus Aurelius was emperor. In fact, it never became really quiet in North Africa; the third and fourth centuries saw endless rebellions. When in 427 the Vandal King Genseric arrived in Africa, the Mauretanians instantly choose his side.

The pacification of Gaul by Caesar was soon followed by a series of revolts lasting until 12 B.C. Financial exactions and administrative abuses were the general cause [23]. "The Gauls were restive under their slavery", says Dio [24]. During the first and second centuries A.D. there occurred repeatedly larger and smaller outbreaks of rebellion, now here, now there, so that Dyson refers to a 'revolt cycle' [25].

During the same centuries unrest was endemic in Britain too. Large forces were needed to keep the population under control. The same factors as elsewhere were operative here, the anger at heavy taxation and passive resistance against the policy of Romanization.

Pannonia (Hungary) was a restless region where in the second century A.D. the Romans had to cope with one revolt after another. In the Balkans "the Macedonia-Thrace area was another zone of frequent rebellion especially in the period before a strong, permanent frontier was established on the Danube. Here again a combination of an open frontier, rugged terrain and warlike tribes produced a suitable background for rebellion" [26].

7. The great Batavian insurrection

a. The Batavians

We shall now have to speak of one of the greatest and most dangerous rebellions that hit the Roman Empire, the revolt of Julius Civilis [27]. Julius Civilis forms part of the Dutch national myth since he is seen as a Dutchman avant la lettre, with the same urge to freedom in his veins as characterized the

Dutch in their war against Spain. During that war Rembrandt painted a large canvas representing Civilis conspiring with his friends in the darkness of the Germanic woods. Civilis was a Batavian, a member of a small Germanic tribe. If we may believe Tacitus, the Batavians formed part of the larger tribe of the Chatti, but "on account of a rising at home", he continues, "they broke away and found their way into land across the Rhine" [28]. Caesar, who was the first to mention them, says they occupied the 'insula Batavorum', the island of the Batavians [29]. This 'island' is not really an island, situated as it is in the Netherlands between the rivers Rhine and Waal; it was named 'Batavia' after the inhabitants [30].

The Batavians too entered the Dutch national myth as the ancestors of the Dutch people (which they weren't). Their name lives on in the region they inhabited, the Betuwe. When on March 12, 1619, Jan Pietersz Coen founded a Dutch town on the ruins of the ancient Jacatra in the island of Java, he baptized it 'Batavia' [31]. When the revolutionary French arrived in the Netherlands in 1795, they came with a 'Batavian legion' composed of anti-Orange exiles. In that same year the venerable Republic of the United Netherlands was dissolved; the founders of the new state, harking back to the past, called it the 'Batavian Republic' (1795-1806) [32].

The ancient Batavi were allies of Rome; it was probably Drusus who succeeded in befriending them. Since then they kept loyally the Roman side, mainly as auxilia of Legio XIV Gemina [33]. A considerable part of the tribe was later stationed elsewhere in the Empire, as auxiliary troops; for instance, the name of the town of Passau on the Danube, the ancient Batavia Castra, still points to them. What remained of the tribe in the Betuwe was submerged by the invading Franks and disappeared from the historical stage.

b. The outbreak of the revolt

Let us now return to Civilis. Tacitus says that he was of ancient royal stock [34] and that he had great influence with his people [35]. Most male Batavian tribesmen were Roman auxiliaries; Civilis too entered Roman military service, about A.D. 45, and soon became a 'praefectus cohortis', the commander of a cavalry unit (the Batavians were excellent horsemen). During the emperorship of Nero he and his brother Paulus were suspected of planning a revolt; Paulus was decapitated and Julius was sent to Rome in chains. Although nothing is known of his feelings then, it is not hard to imagine them. Meanwhile Nero in A.D. 68 was succeeded by Galba who set him free. Civilis returned to his unit [36].

On January 1, 69, the legionaries of the Rhine army were to swear allegiance to the new emperor, Galba, but they refused and protested that they wanted Vitellius, their own commander, for emperor. He was indeed proclaimed as such [37]. The soldiers seized the opportunity to get rid of a number of unpopular officers, one of whom was Civilis whom they probably saw as a favourite of Galba. They clamoured for his head but Vitellius refused, since he needed the eight Batavian cohorts, if ever he wanted to achieve the throne in Rome [38].

According to Tacitus, our only source for these events, Civilis now had enough of the Romans. He "was cunning beyond the average barbarian and bore himself also like Sertorius or a Hannibal, since his face was disfigured like theirs (i.e. he had only one eye)". For the time being, he hid his discontent. Vitellius unwittingly came to his assistance by being rash enough after the Battle of Betriacum in northern Italy, where he had fought his rival Otho, to send back his Batavian cohorts. Tacitus remarks that "the Fates were already the sources from which both civil war and foreign war would spring" [39]. Later in this same year, when he was emperor in Rome, he was threatened by Vespasian who before the end of the year effectively ousted him. Because he sorely needed troops, Vitellius ordered his officers to recruit men among the Batavians which they did in the most harsh and brutal way.

Civilis and his co-conspirators now decided to strike, profiting from the resentment the levying was causing. He "called the leaders of his tribe and the boldest of the common people into a sacred grove [40] under the pretext of giving a banquet, and when he saw that the night and the revelry had fired their spirits", he began exhorting them to rise [41]. Everyone present acquiesced enthusiastically. The Cannenefates, with Brinno as their leader, were ready to join in, just as the Batavian cohorts which had returned from

Italy and were now stationed in Moguntiacum (Mainz) [42]. Soon enough Civilis disposed of a considerable army, especially when he got the cooperation of the Bructeri and Tencteri in western Germany. He did not yet, however, throw off his mask of loyalty and made all his forces swear allegiance to Vespasian [43].

c. The first hostilities

Meanwhile Brinno, who was a rash man, had already started hostilities against the Romans in the Betuwe so that they withdrew to their fortresses. Somewhat later Civilis himself engaged them in a battle which he won, since the Germanic auxiliaries in the Roman forces and the Batavian rowers in the river fleet deserted to him; indeed, the whole fleet of twenty-four vessels fell into his hands [44]. The immediate result was that the victor gained the support of many Germanic and Celtic tribes. He now no longer pretended that he was either for Vitellius or for Vespasian but, as Tacitus declares, he "was preparing, should his plans prove successful, to gain the kingship over the strongest and richest nations" [45].

Civilis' first aim was to conquer Castra Vetera (Xanten, on the Rhine) which had a garrison of two Roman legions; he laid siege to it. The Roman commanders further south hastily assembled a relieving army (although the soldiers were unruly) and marched to Castra Vetera with it. The commanding officer did not, however, succeed in raising the siege but retired, after heavy fighting, to Novaesium (Neuss), while the siege of Castra Vetera went on [46].

d. Civilis' heyday

The result of this was that "the power of Civilis was being increased by huge reinforcements from all Germany" [47]. With every day that passed the situation of the Romans along the Rhine became more precarious; the legionaries were undisciplined and not to be trusted while "the Gallic provinces were hesitating and Germany was ready to revolt" [48]. The whole Roman position north of the Alps seemed at risk. It was believed among the

195

Gauls that "the end of our (Roman) rule was at hand" [49]. Optimistic rumours flew from mouth to mouth that "the Roman people were wild with discord, that the legions were cut to pieces, Italy laid waste, and Rome at that moment being captured [50], and that all the Roman armies were occupied each with its own wars; if they (the Gauls) but held the Alps with armed forces, the Gallic lands, once sure of their freedom, would only have to decide what limits they wished to set to their freedom" [51].

The situation was highly dramatic; an independent 'Imperium Gallicum' seemed possible. With Castra Vetera finally reduced in the beginning of 70 [52], and with Cologne [53], Neuss, and Mainz in his hands [54], Civilis obviously felt himself on top of the world. He "had dyed his hair red and let it grow long from the time he first took up arms against the Romans, but once the massacre of the legions was finally accomplished, he cut it short" [55].

e. The turning of the tide

But the tide was going to turn. The Gauls were not massively and wholeheartedly on the hand of Civilis because he did not aspire at all to an 'Imperium Gallicum' but to an independent Germanic kingdom [56]. In Rome Vespasian, a competent ruler, was now master of the situation. Nine legions were being assembled to beat down the revolt [57]. Part of this force was directed towards Upper Germany, while the rest, under the command of an experienced general, Petilius Cerialis, crossed the Alps and marched down the valley of the Rhine. He reached Mainz without meeting resistance and from there marched on Trèves; he defeated the enemy force that attempted to block his advance and entered the town [58]. Cerialis' force came near destruction when Civilis made a night attack on his camp. There was desperate fighting on the Moselle bridge along which the legionaries were already flying; without his armour - he came straight from his bed - Cerialis succeeded in restoring order and driving off the assailants [59].

Now many Gallic tribes began to return to obedience, while Civilis fell back on Castra Vetera [60]. A first attempt by Cerialis to storm the town dismally misfired [61]. A second attempt almost went the same way, but then a Batavian deserter showed the Romans a path through a marsh so that their cavalry could attack the enemy from the rear. This decided the issue and Civilis retired to the Betuwe [62].

f. The end of the revolt

Civilis still felt strong enough to go on harassing his enemy [63]; at one moment Cerialis himself only narrowly escaped being taken prisoner [64]. But at last the Romans succeeded in forcing the Batavians out of the Betuwe and made them retire farther westward. With no allies left, their plight was hopeless. Civilis, hearing his men murmuring against him, resolved to contact his opponents and ask for a conference. The two commanders met on a bridge on the river Nabalia; the middle part of this bridge was taken away, and the men stood each at one end. Civilis was the first to take the floor, but his speech breaks off in the middle of a sentence. We have reached the abrupt end of Tacitus' 'Histories' [65].

We have no idea of what happened to Civilis; he is never mentioned again. Anyhow, the rebellion, one of the most dangerous Rome ever had to cope with, was over. The Batavians were received back into favour : Rome could use their cavalry cohorts only too well. "They are reserved for war", says Tacitus; in exchange for this they paid neither tribute nor taxes [66].

8. Conclusion

As this overview shows, hardly a province of the Empire was spared a revolt, especially in the western half; Egypt, Greece, and Asia Minor remained relatively quiet. Dyson concludes that the patterns of revolt "reveal a degree of social unrest in the Western Roman Empire which has been underplayed by historians both ancient and modern". My own impression is that historians are so fascinated by the idea of the Pax Romana that they tend to overlook the fact how unhappy many Roman subjects were within it. In the Empire "injustice and discontent are a continuum". The very "process of Romanization produced severe social and economic tensions which drove the native populace to repeated expressions of rebellion" [67]. A revealing comment on Roman policy with regard to their subjects is what Dio wrote of the 'constitutio Antoniniana' by which the Emperor Caracalla in 212 granted Roman citizenship to all subjects [68]. This author states somewhat cynically that "nominally he was honouring them, but his real purpose was to increase his revenues by this means, inasmuch as subjects did not have to pay most of the (special) taxes" [69].

PART II THE SLAVES

1. Slavery not a part of the original human condition

Slavery was an integral and constitutive part of the ancient world. If a more enlightened ruler than we can imagine had suddenly abolished it and told the slaves that they could go their own ways, the economic and social fabric would have collapsed at once. Even if the great majority of the emancipated slaves had remained in the service of their former masters for a comparatively reasonable salary, the catastrophe would have been complete since the costs of production had always been dependent on the cheap labour of the slaves who received no pay and were kept at a low level of subsistence.

It was a general notion among Greeks and Romans that slavery had not formed a part of the original human condition; in the Golden Age of humanity all people had been free. Annually in December the Romans celebrated the Saturnalia, the festival of Saturn, the god of the Golden Age. It was an occasion of general jollity; the wine flowed freely. The most characteristic trait of this feast was the general equality between masters and slaves. "During the Saturnalia, the slaves are allowed the most complete liberty" [70]. The 'libertas Decembris' [71] even permitted the slaves to say unpleasant things to their masters. They dined together with their masters [72]; the children of the masters then had to serve the slaves [73]. The idea behind all this was that in the Golden Age nobody had possessed anybody else as a slave, while private property did not exist [74]. But as soon the

Saturnalia were over, everything returned to normalcy : masters were masters and slaves were slaves again.

2. What is a slave?

In the second century A.D. a Roman jurist categorically stated that "the principal distinction made by the law of persons is this that all human beings are either free men or slaves" [75]. This confronts us at once with a dualistic distinction since we must expect that a slave counts as far less than a free man. This impression is fortified when we read that slavery is characterized as "an institution of the common law of peoples by which a person is put under the ownership of somebody else, contrary to the natural order" [76]. A slave, by this definition, is not really a human person but rather a thing, a possession. Slaves are wholly subject to the power (potestas) of their masters; these have the right of life and death over their slaves. This does not mean that a master might arbitrarily kill a slave; he must have a solid reason to execute one. If he has no such reason, he will liable to punishment himself [77].

A slave could not contract a marriage in the normal legal way [78]. He might have a consort and offspring but not in his own right; both the woman and the children belonged to the master for whom this often was a cheap way to acquire new slaves. Slaves were not entitled to possess property of their own. If they acquired or inherited goods, these automatically and immediately became the property of their owners [79]. So much for the legal position of a slave, although it is evident that he or she hardly had a legal position, apart from protection against arbitrary brutality (female slaves should not be sold to brothel-keepers; sick or maimed slaves were not to be disposed of by killing them).

3. The better-off and the worse-off slaves

By far the best position a slave could have in Roman society was that of a Greek who became the pedagogue of the children of a well-to-do Roman. Such a man lived in the house of his master and shared its amenities. He was well clad and well fed and his services were appreciated. A 'custos' or 'tutor' did not actually teach himself but supervised the studies of the children, especially of the boys; he brought them to school and home again and was in particular responsible for teaching them manners and morals [80]. His task fulfilled, the tutor, more often than not, was set free. Of course, the relationship between the tutor and the boys might easily become confidential. But even then, as Vogt remarks, it remained an 'unequal educational team' [81]. "Are you my slave or am I yours", snaps young Pistoclerus at his tutor in one of Plautus's plays [82].

There were also, as will go without saying, harsh and unjust masters, such as those who took attractive young slave-girls to their beds. But on the whole the situation of a household slave in Roman society was considerably better than that of their counterparts in Hellenic society [83] or that of an agrarian slave on the latifundia. There are examples of slaves who went with their masters through thick and thin, sometimes even following him into death [84].

From this point we follow a descending line through the various forms of slavery until we reach the bottom where the agrarian slaves are found. "The Italians who were engaged in agriculture purchased great numbers of slaves, all of whom they marked with brands, but failed to provide them sufficient food, and by oppressive toil wore them out" [85]. "Chattel slavery ranked at the bottom of the scale insofar as the sheer rightlesness of slaves and their masters' expectations of their total obedience to authority were concerned. Chattel slavery was an extreme type of compulsory labour" [86].

The impression may have created by now that slaves were owned by individual persons, heads of families, housefathers, and also, of course, by commercial and industrial employers, and, on a large scale, landlords. This is not correct since slaves could also be public property; there were state-slaves, municipal slaves, and, later, imperial slaves. It is impossible to say how great the percentage of slaves was in the total population, but it must have been considerable. I don't think it was possible to go very far, either in a town or in the country without meeting a slave - with this proviso that they were not directly recognizable since they did not wear a distinctive garb.

4. A source of tension in Roman society

In case we might have a too rosy picture of the condition of the estimated household-slave, Bradley reminds us that "slavery itself always remained a form of <u>compulsory</u> (his underlining) labour", and this implies two things : that the slaves were unwilling 'to remain in servitude if an alternative were available', and that the owners had 'to exercice continuous coercion' [87]. This meant that there was always tension in Roman society, most of the time subdued, but sometimes leading to violent outbursts. When Larcius Marcedo, a senator, was killed in his bath by some of his slaves in his villa near Formiae, Pliny the Younger commented that "lenity and good treatment did not offer any security from the villanies of the servants" [88].

As all the chapters of Volumes X and XI will have shown, the establishment of balanced human and social relationships was not the principal 'Anliegen' of those who gave leadership to Roman society. It will, therefore, not surprise us to find this pilot idea in the preamble of Diocletian's edict on maximum prices : "Experience teaches us that fear is the most effective regulator and guide for the performance of duty" [89]. And although this was directed at every citizen, it applies most of all to slaves.

It was perfectly normal for slaves to be punished by flogging and shackling, and in the case of capital punishment, by crucifixion. Seneca complained that slaves were treated "not as if they were men, but as if they were beasts of burden" [90]. It was even so the case that, when a private owner wanted to execute a slave, because of theft for instance, the authorities could put the necessary implement, such as a cross, at his disposal [91]. Bradley concludes that "it is thus indisputable that physical coercion from the owner played a large part in servile life in one way or another and that subjection to brutality was a basic component of slavery". He adds that "all slaves were under the constant pressure of exposure to punishment and that such pressure formed another aspect of the servile mentality" [92].

No wonder then that there were slave-risings. From time to time the concentrated tension discharged itself. "In individual households heavy-handed arrogance paves the way for plots of slaves against masters and terrible uprisings against the whole state. The more power is converted to cruelty and lawlessness, the more the character of those subject to that power is brutalized to the point of desperation. Anyone whom fortune has set in low estate willingly yields place to his superiors in point of gentility of esteem, but if he is deprived of due consideration, he comes to regard those who harshly lord it over him with bitter enmity" [93].

5. The sources of slavery

What were the sources of slavery in the Roman world, apart from natural increase in households with slaves? One answer has been given over and over again in Volume X : it was war. Since the Romans were endlessly warring, there was, as a consequence, a never ending stream of prisoners of war. The Romans were convinced that soldiers of a defeated army or the inhabitants of a conquered town had forfeited their right to freedom. Tens and tens of thousands of men, women, and children were sold into slavery. This is well illustrated by an example I quoted earlier [94] : in 167 B.C. the Roman commander Aemilius Paullus enslaved one hundred and fifty thousand inhabitants of seventy cities in Epirus [95]. If somebody had protested, the Romans would have retorted that these people might be glad that they were not massacred (which, in fact, happened often enough).

Slave-dealers followed the the Roman armies on their heels with bags full of money in order to buy POW's. There were several great slave-markets where any quantity of slaves might be bought; the biggest of these was in the island of Delos where, according to Strabo, "tens of thousands of slaves could be received and despatched on the same day" [96]. Then there were smaller retailer-markets in the towns and the provincial centres.

For some decades piracy too was a lucrative source of slaves. Pirates not only looked for goods but also for persons who could be sold. During the second century B.C. and part of the first, a sea-voyage was really a hazardous enterprise. The crew and the passengers of a merchant-man might easily end up in a slave-market. Travelling became much safer after Pompey had swept the seas. Not that a traveller on land, however, was sure to arrive where he wanted to be. On the roads, even in Italy, free persons might be kidnapped and sold in a slave-market.

Foundlings, that is children abandoned by their parents, became slaves by right, if they were taken by somebody into his household. There were even dealers who bought new-born babies from their fathers who were not able to raise them (a minor was just as much the property of his father as a slave was of his master) [97]. Contrary to what might be expected, debt-bondage at an early date ceased to be a source of slavery. The idea that a Roman citizen could be enslaved because of his debts became increasingly abhorrent to Roman public opinion. Early in the Republic a debtor might still be sold 'across the Tiber', that is, outside the city boundaries. Later this practice fell in abeyance too.

6. Slavery as a dualistic institution

It strikes one's attention that slavery is a thoroughly dualistic institution. It is a matter of two groups of people, opposed to each other, of which one is distinctly inferior to the other, since the difference is one between being authentically human and less than human. This dualism is of a relative sort since both parties are dependent on each other. This gives the position of slaves some hidden strength. If the slaves had been able to withdraw from society and organize themselves in their own way, their masters would be nowhere. There were attempts in this direction.

It is not hard to imagine the state of mind of slaves. Suppose one is a well-to-do Corinthian business-man serving as an officer in the army of his town. He is taken prisoner by the Romans, sold to a slave-dealer, shipped to Delos, sold again to another slave-dealer, transported to the slave-market of Rome to be exposed there with a placard on his breast mentioning his qualities. A Roman patrician buys him and puts him to work in the management of his commercial and financial affairs. However businesslike the relation with his master may be, or however friendly it may become, will this man ever forget that he is there entirely against his will? And will his master ever forget that his man is a slave for whom he paid a handsome sum of money?

Or imagine a free Numidian farmer, a man with a well-paying homestead. As a cavalry-man in the army, he too is made prisoner, sold in Italy to some big landowner, and put to work on one of those large latifundia. Will he, badly fed, badly clad, poorly housed, bullied by the overseers, not bitterly deplore his cruel fate? It will be clear that all over the Empire there were great quantities of dynamite ready for an enormous explosion. But much depended on the way slaves were treated.

Short of rebellion, slaves had many means for revenging themselves : treason, poison, snares and traps. "Think of those", writes Seneca, "who have perished through plots in their own homes, slain either openly or by guile; you will then understand that just as many have been killed by angry slaves as by angry kings" [98]. "Believe me, slaves devour more masters than the dogs!", this was the opinion of the play-wright Terence [99]. Hence the saying : "as many enemies as you have slaves", to which Seneca adds this comment : ""They are not enemies when we acquire them; we make them enemies" [100].

7. Early slave-risings

The very first slave-revolt took place way back in 501 B.C., when the slaves were still small in number. "Their agreed plan was to seize the heights (= the Capitol) and to set fire to the city in many places." But the consuls got wind of the conspiracy; the conspirators were caught, scourged, and after having been tortured, crucified [101].

A year later another plot was discovered. It was hatched by the poorest people in town who were joined by 'unprincipled slaves, beguiled by hopes of freedom'. These people were embittered against their masters because of the way their comrades had been treated the year before. Once again they aimed at seizing the Capitol. But the plot was revealed to the consuls so that, when the conspirators came together for the execution of their plans, they were rounded up by armed citizens and put to death [102].

In 461 B.C. the slaves showed what they could do if they were led by an able man. This man was Appius Herdonius, a Sabine 'of no obscure birth'. The incident took place during the war with the Volsci and the Sabines. Herdonius assembled an army of exiles and slaves to the number of twenty-five hundred according to Livy and four thousand according to Dionysius of Halicarnassus. He armed them and sailed the Tiber with them, landing near the Capitol which he seized, together with the citadel. Herdonius' intention was "to summon the slaves to freedom and to promise the needy an abolition of their debts". "Men's fears were many and various; above all the rest stood out their dread of the slaves. Everybody suspected that he had an enemy in his own household." The consuls decided to wage formal war on the invaders. It was only after three days of hard fighting, in which one of the consuls perished, that the militia was able to take the strongholds of their enemy. Herdonius fell under the missiles of the militiamen; his corpse was found on top of 'an incredible heap of dead bodies'. The captured slaves were crucified, the others beheaded [103].

In 419 B.C. "the slaves conspired to set fire to the city at points remote from one another, and while the people would be busy everywhere with rescuing their homes, to seize the citadel and the Capitol with armed force". But the plan was betrayed and nothing came of it [104]. It will be evident that the slaves every time aimed at the very centre of Rome's might.

In 198 B.C. there was an incident in which, as Wallon expresses it, "captive Carthage failed to surprise the proud victor" [105]. In Setia, in the vicinity of Rome, a group of Carthaginian hostages was lodged; they had a large number of slaves at their disposal. In the town there were also many Carthaginian prisoners of war bought by Setians 'out of the booty'. These two groups of slaves began a conspiracy; they succeeded in overpowering Setia. A praetor starting from Rome forced everybody he found in his way into his army and captured Setia with his two thousand men. When he heard that the remnant of the slaves was in Praeneste, he marched thither and executed five hundred people [106].

Two years later a great danger arose in Etruria where the slaves rebelled. A Roman praetor needed two legions to subdue them. Many slaves lost their lives; their leaders were crucified [107]. In 185 B.C. it was the turn of Apulia where a big slave-rising took place; it was mainly runaway shepherds who infested the roads. Their number seem to have been some seven thousand many of whom were executed [108]. Clearly the scene had shifted from Rome to the countryside. The Republic had become strong enough to guard its capital. Later in the second century the scene shifted again, from Italy to Sicily.

8. The First Sicilian Slave-War

a. The beginning of the revolt

Sicily was a grain-growing island, one of the granaries for Rome's population. To work the fields, it harboured an enormous number of agrarian slaves. A great majority of these men came from Syria; sharing the same background and the same language gave them a sense of solidarity. Many slaves had escaped the hard hand of their masters and devoted themselves to brigandage [109]. Others, "distressed by their hardships and frequently outraged and beaten beyond all reason, could not endure their treatment. Getting together as opportunity offered, they discussed the possibility of revolt, until at last they put their plans into action" [110].

In Henna, the exact centre of the island, called by Cicero 'the navel of Sicily' [111] (the place still exists as Enna), there lived in 135 B.C. a certain Antigenes, the owner of a Syrian slave with the name of Eunus. Although Diodorus speaks denigratingly of this man's uncommon gifts, he must have had a charismatic personality. This ancient author admits "there never was a sedition of slaves so great as that which occurred in Sicily" [112]. Since Eunus was the leader of the revolt, he must have been a man of exceptional abilities. He came from the city of Apamea on the Orontes with a reputation of being a magician and a miracle-worker, a fortune-teller and a visionary, and even a fire-eater. He claimed that the Syrian goddess Atargatis regularly appeared to him, foretelling him that he would become king [113].

It was only a small incident that sparked off the revolt. "There is no indication that a grand uprising of slaves in Sicily as a whole was contemplated at the outset" [114]. In Henna there lived a wealthy slave-owner called Demophilus; he and his wife Megallis had a bad reputation for treating their slaves brutally and sadistically. Their victims, planning to murder them, resorted to Eunus, whom they considered their natural leader, to ask "whether their resolve had the favour of the gods". It had. Then they assembled four hundred armed men and, under the leadership of Eunus, fell upon the city of Henna. They went around killing the masters and not even sparing the babes; all the time more men joined them. Demophilus and Megallis were found in their garden outside the city, bound, and dragged away. But the rebels spared the couple's daughter who had always been friendly to the slaves. The idea was to give Demophilus a regular trial but before it could come so far, he and his wife were already disposed of by persons in the crowd.

b. King Eunus

Eunus was now proclaimed king and supreme commander, and his wife, also a Syrian, became his queen. He went about in full royal garb with a diadem on his head. His first work was to have the whole citizenry of Henna executed, with the exception of the armourers. He killed his master Antigenes with his own hands. By now he had six thousand armed men under his command, recruiting every day more; in the first encounters with Roman generals he came off best. These victories made his ranks swell to more than ten thousand [115].

Then a second rising began near Agrigentum where a certain Cleon, who came from Cilicia in Asia Minor, mobilized five thousand men. The Romans obviously hoped that the two bands would destroy each other, but instead they joined hands; Cleon was even wise enough to put himself under the command of Eunus. Soon enough the rebel army numbered twenty thousand men [116].

The rebel ranks kept swelling all the time. When Diodorus gives us a grand total of two hundred thousand, this may be exaggerated, but it proves that there must have been enormous masses of slaves in the island. News of the success spread like wildfire; there was a small revolt in Rome itself, a larger one in Attica, and still more in Delos and other places. It seemed as though the whole socio-economic fabric of the Empire was beginning to totter. In the homeland of the revolt the insurgents proved steadily stronger than the Romans. "Cities were captured, and many armies were cut to pieces by the rebels" [117].

c. The revolt beaten down

At last the Roman forces in the island were put under the command of one of those ruthless Roman generals, Publius Rupilius, the consul for 132 B.C. He besieged Tauromenium (Taormina) and captured it; Diodorus says that the defending slaves were reduced to cannibalism. The citadel of the town was delivered to him by treason. Rupilius had all the slaves he had caught tortured and then thrown over a cliff [118]. Henna too was first besieged and then captured by treason. Cleon was found dead. Eunus fled with his bodyguard to the mountains where the survivors killed one another. When Eunus was caught by the Romans, he had still four men of his court with him, a cook, a baker, a massagist, and a buffoon. King Eunus was thrown into the prison of the no longer existing Morgantina where he rotted away. Then Rupilius cleared the islands of the last nests of resistance [119]. As usual, the captive slaves were crucified [120].

9. The Second Sicilian Slave-War

a. The cause of the revolt

A generation after this war the island of Sicily was turned upside down by a similar event, the Second Sicilian Slave-War. It began in 104 B.C. The Senate had decreed that Bithynians who had been enslaved by Roman tax farmers had to be set free (since Bithynia was still a nominally independent country where Roman tax gatherers should not operate). Apparently quite a number of Bithynians slaves were to be found in Sicily, for its governor, P. Licinius Nerva, freed some eight hundred persons [121]. Perhaps he went even further than this, since Dio reports that he "sent round a note that all who had any charges to bring against their masters should come to him and accuse their masters" [122]. Of course, because of this high hopes were raised among the slaves so that the notables exercized great pressure on Licinius to make him desist from this policy. He acquiesced, and the slaves who had come to him were rebuked and sent back to their masters [123].

b. The outbreak of the revolt

The disappointed slaves began to think of revolution. Two very wealthy brothers in the region of Halicyae, some twenty miles east of Lilybaeum (Marsala), had a considerable number of slaves. Led by one of them, a certain Varius, they killed the brothers in their sleep and went about in the night to collect support; at dawn they had a band of one hundred and twenty men who were joined in the course of the day by eighty more. Their number was not great but they occupied a strongly fortified position - so strong that when Licinius came he was unable to reduce it. Once again it was a traitor who showed him the way. Most of the defenders were dead already; the rest threw themselves off the cliff [124].

The assault troops had been disbanded already when news came of a new rising. A Roman knight had been killed by a band of eighty slaves who were steadily recruiting new adherents. Soon enough they numbered two thousand. The rebels gained a first victory over a Roman force of six hundred which provided them with many arms. Only a few days later they were six thousand strong [125].

c. King Salvius

The rebels held an assembly in which they made a certain Salvius their king. He was a flute-player who proved to be an able organizer. Raids all around provided the rebels with enough horses for two thousand cavalry; Salvius had also twenty thousand infantry whom he subjected to a thorough military training. When he had laid siege to Morgantina, Licinius came with ten thousand men to relieve it but was completely routed. He lost six hundred dead and four thousand prisoners. And the ranks of King Salvius kept swelling [126].

In the island the confusion became complete. Poor free men took to the countryside to steal and plunder. "Impelled alike by poverty and lawlessness, (they) streamed out into the country in swarms, drove off the herds of cattle, plundered the crops stored in the barns, and murdered without more ado all who fell in their way, slave or free alike." A state of anarchy prevailed [127]. In the west of the island there was a second rising, led by a certain Athenion, another Cilician, an astrologist, who in a short time came to dispose of ten thousand men, But his attack on Lilybaeum misfired [128].

King Salvius, now commanding no less than thirty thousand picked men, summoned Athenion to him, 'as a king might summon a general'. The hopes of those who thought that these two would come to blows were deceived : Athenion accepted the leadership of Salvius. A place called Triocala (perhaps the modern Caltabellota in the south-western half of the island) became Salvius's capital; he had a royal palace built there. In everything he played the Roman, clad as he was in a toga bordered with purple and in wide-bordered tunic; lictors with axes went before him [129].

d. The Roman reaction

Of course, the Romans simply had to react. If they let Sicily go, their oldest province, what might follow? A consul was dispatched to the island with more than seventeen thousand men. They won an initial victory over the rebels but failed to take Triocala. Then Salvius died and Athenion succeeded him as king. It was the same period in which Rome had to battle with the Cimbri and the Teutons. In 101 B.C. Marius, consul for the fifth time, sent Gaius Aquilius to Sicily to make an end of the rebellion.

Aquilius succeeded where all others had failed. He won a great victory and killed Athenion with his own hand. Then one after another he captured the rebel strongholds. At last only a force of thousand slaves remained in the field, under the command of a certain Satyrus. These surrendered themselves on parole. They were sent to Rome to serve as gladiators in the arenas. But instead of fighting the wild beasts, they killed one another. Satyrus killed the last man and then took his own life. "Such was the dramatic conclusion of the Sicilian Slave-War, a war that lasted about four years" [130].

10. The rising of Spartacus

a. Who was Spartacus?

The greatest slave-rising that Rome ever witnessed had its origin in the training school for gladiators at Capua. "It was Capua in the first century B.C. that served as the main entrepôt for the training and housing of Roman gladiators" [131]. There able-bodied men were schooled to fight one another and wild beasts and to kill and be killed in the arenas of Rome for the amusement of a bloodthirsty public. In 73 B.C. a man by the name of Spartacus was an inmate of this Capuan institute [132]. His name has become almost a household word in modern history. To the 'Bildungsbürgertum' of the nineteenth century he seemed the figure-head of all antifeudal movements. Karl Marx found him "the most terrific fellow that the whole of ancient history had to show, ... the real representative of the antique proletariat" [133]. In the early years of the twentieth century there was in Germany a revolutionary organization, the 'Spartakusbund', that in 1919 became the German Communist Party [134]. And even in our days he is a favourite subject for spectacular movies.

Who was this Spartacus? To be honest : we don't know. Next to nothing is known of his life before he initiated the great slave-rebellion "which is generally called 'the War of Spartacus'" [135]. On one point the ancient authorities agree : he came from Thrace [136]. Mommsen believed that he came from noble, even royal stock [137], but there is no basis for this in the ancient sources. It is not known how he fell into Roman captivity [138]. Anyhow, he had become a prisoner and had been sold as a gladiator. He is described as a man "of great courage and strength, in sagacity and culture superior to his fortune and more Hellenic than Thracian" [139]. From the beginning his person was enveloped in myths [140].

b. The origin of the revolt

The owner of the training school at Capua was a man by the name of Lentulus Batiatus; the inmates were mostly Gauls and Thracians. This Lentulus is said to have been a harsh man who kept his men 'through no misconduct of theirs in close confinement' [141]. It must have been a large school, for about two hundred of the trainees planned to get away [142], but their plans transpired and finally only some seventy of them, led by Spartacus, made good their escape [143]. During their flight they held up a waggon train loaded with weapons; this provided them with a better armament; other fugitive slaves and even free men joined them as they went [144]. The band of slaves established themselves on some twenty miles from Capua on the slopes of Mount Vesuvius from where they plundered the neighbouring countryside [145]. It is possible that already then Spartacus was the one in command but he had two subcommanders, Venamaus and Crixus [146]. From far and wide slaves flocked to the Vesuvius to share in the rebellion and in the booty. They were strong enough to repulse the soldiers sent after them from Capua [147].

c. The first successes

As usual, the Romans at first badly underrated the seriousness of the situation. An official, probably a propraetor, C. Claudius Gaber, was dispatched from Rome with three thousand men; he found his enemy ensconced on a steep hill with only one difficult road of ascent which he barricaded. But the slaves wove ladders from the branches of the wild vine that grew abundantly on the top of the hill and along these descended the steep face of the cliff. They then fell upon the unsuspecting Romans and put them to flight. This success encouraged many herdsmen and shepherds of the region to join them, sturdy men who proved to be distinct assets [148].

Then a praetor, Publius Varinius, marched out against the insurgents but he and his legates were badly mauled by them. Varinius had to leave his horse in the hands of Spartacus - "so narrowly did the very general of the Romans escape being captured by a gladiator" [149], while his legate was almost caught when bathing in the sea, and later fell when his camp was overrun by the rebels [150]. The slaves now came in their thousands and thousands to join Spartacus' army; Appian even says that it grew to seventy thousand men [151].

In spite of these successes, Spartacus, who was a prudent man, seems to have been convinced that he would never be able to beat the regular forces of the Republic. What he intended to do was to make his way through the Apennines to the Alps and to lead his men back to their home countries in Gaul and the Balkans. But his men, elated by their victories, would not hear of it, and "full of confidence ... went ravaging all over Italy" [152].

d. Between north and south

By now the Senate was alerted enough to bring consular armies into the field. The spring of the year 72 B.C. saw the beginning of the northward march of the slave-army. Differences of opinion between the commanders made things easier for the consuls. Crixus intended to remain in Italy and turned southward, going to Apulia with ten thousand men, mainly Gauls and

Germans. Near Mount Garganus (the present-day Monte Sant' Angelo) he was overtaken by a Roman army. His force was almost completely destroyed and he himself fell [153].

Spartacus revenged himself for the death of Crixus and so many of his comrades by making some hundred Roman prisoners of war fight one another to death as gladiators, so that "those who had been the objects of the spectacle, now were the spectators" [154]. On his way to the north he was stopped near Mutina (Modena) by the governor of Gallia Cisalpina, C. Cassius Longinus, whose force of ten thousand regulars he defeated [155]. The slave-army now was in the position to cross the Alps, but the men preferred to stay in Italy. So Spartacus was forced to turn south again. Crossing the whole length of Italy on his way southward, he defeated another Roman army in Picenum; many of the regulars were so afraid of the slaves that they threw away their arms and fled for their lives [156]. In the deep south he captured Thurii and with its surrounding hills turned it into a stronghold. The Romans could not prevent him from plundering all around [157]. As a result of this success the number of his soldiers reached impressive proportions, the lowest estimate being sixty thousand [158], the highest one hundred and twenty thousand [159]. No wonder the Romans thought that the days of Hannibal had returned [160].

e. The Roman counter-offensive

In the autumn of 72 B.C. the Senate recalled the ineffective consuls and placed the supreme command in the hands of M. Licinius Crassus; as proconsul he had six newly raised legions under his command plus those of the two consuls, probably ten in all [161]. In the south Crassus first of all decimated a force of ten thousand Spartacists; next he triumphed over Spartacus himself [162]. The rebel chief now retired still further southward into Bruttium, the toe of the boot. He hoped to be able to ferry his army to Sicily in order to rekindle the slave-war there; he paid Cilician pirates to put his men across but they pocketed the money and disappeared [163]. A desperate atempt to cross the Straits on rafts misfired because of the rapidity of the current [164].

While Spartacus was encamped near Rhegium, Crassus cut off his line of retreat by building a wall across the peninsula [165]. During the winter of 72/71 B.C. Spartacus made repeated attempts to break out; in a dark, snowy night he succeeded indeed in getting a third of his force across [166]. According to Frontinus, he filled the ditch along the wall with the corpses of prisoners and animals [167]. Crassus feared his opponent might march on Rome now [168] but, instead, the rebel chief planned to march through Lucania and Calabria to Brundisium in order to esacape from there to the Balkans. Little hope was left of maintaining himself in Italy, since not only Crassus was in the field but now also Pompey, while Lucullus was to arrive in Brundisium from Macedonia [169].

f. The end

Once again part of Spartacus' army seceded from him and went its own way, only to be destroyed by Crassus near Paestum in Campania; the losses of the slaves were enormous, ten thousand killed or more. They fought bravely, says Plutarch admiringly [170]. Crassus was in haste now to make an end of the war, so that the victory should not fall to his rival Pompey. When Spartacus heard that Lucullus was landing in Brundisium [171], he must have understood that all was lost. Retiring to Bruttium in the spring of 71 B.C., he was overtaken by Crassus near Petelia. Battle was joined. The slaves had no chance. Spartacus fought manfully; although wounded in the thigh, he kept on fighting but was killed at last, as an 'imperator', a true general, writes Florus [172].

"The remainder of his army was thrown into confusion and butchered in crowds. So great was the slaughter that it was impossible to count them" [173]. Those who escaped, perhaps some five thousand [174], ran into the arms of the approaching Pompey and were massacred [175]. Orosius gives the total number of fallen slaves as sixty thousand, while six thousand were captured. Many more were killed by pursuing generals who combed the country for fugitives [176]. Short work was made of the six thousand captives who were crucified along the Via Appia between Capua and Rome [177].

11. The easing of the dualistic tension

Within a period of seventy years Rome had had to overcome three great slave-risings. The most dangerous of these was that of Spartacus, for although he did not intend to found a free state for his slaves, the whole episode showed the Romans that they were living on a volcano. It is a remarkable fact that after 70 B.C. there was never again a slave-rising. Both sides had been taught a lesson. The slaves now knew that, in the long run, they did not stand a chance against regular Roman armies; the sight of the long, long row of crosses along the public road would have demonstrated to them how it would end. To escape from their fate, they had to resort to minor means, like flight.

Although the fundamental position of the slaves was not changed, slave-owners began to treat their servants more humanly. An important device for easing the tension was the 'manumissio', the emancipation of slaves. In the time of the Emperors so many slaves were set free that there originated a whole class of them, the 'libertini', or freedmen. Many of these reached positions of importance in Roman society. 'Manumissio' made the dualism of the master-slave relationship less severe, or less hopeless. As Bradley writes, "through observation of freedmen and freedwomen around them, all slaves could consequently see that slavery and freedom were extremes across which a path could be or might be negotiated. The conferment of freedom on some slaves of necessity encouraged its prospects in others" [178].

Finally, it is probable that Stoic and other philosophical notions of humanity and Christian ideas of neighbourly love also played a role in the softening of the relations. A fine example of a change of attitude is that Clement of Alexandria angrily protested against the habit of calling a slave's attention by the snapping of fingers; not to speak to them was 'to deny them their humanity' [179].

PART III THE WOMEN

1. Which women?

The women of the Roman Empire, what about them? They vary from the Empress to Celtic shepherdesses in Yorkshire, from Athenian society ladies to pagan priestesses in Syria, from country women in war-stricken Armenia to Numidian embroiderers. A motley crowd if there ever was one, and a crowd that comprised just half the population of the Empire. Is a description of 'the women of the Roman Empire' possible? "There is no such thing as an ordinary Roman woman", concludes Verena Zinserling [180]. But history, or rather non-history, comes to our assistance. For of by far the greater part of these women, of almost all groups and categories, we know next to nothing or absolutely nothing at all.

2. Female slaves

Were those women existing solely to serve their husbands, to bear them children, preferably male ones, to work hard in the fields? There is a tendency today to view them in this way. Yet even if this picture is correct, we simply do not possess the sources to corrobarate it. Moreover, the condition of the men was not in general particularly enviable either. Most of the inhabitants of the Empire lived on the land and from the land, eking out a meagre existence by drudging away from sunrise to sundown. The condition of the female slaves was, of course, essentially different from that of free women of whatever class. But it is perfectly possible that the personal attendant of a wealthy Roman lady had a far more comfortable life than a free artisan's wife in some small town deep in the province. Once freed, a former female slave "might be more highly educated and enjoy greater economic security than the freeborn poor" [181].

This does not take away the fundamental fact that masters owned slaves in order to exploit them, to do the work for them and perform the tasks they themselves shunned. Female slaves, as may be expected, were particularly prone to sexual exploitation. "The master had access to all his slave-women ... Cato the Censor, who was an authority on Roman virtue, was visited nightly by a slave-girl after his wife had died [182], and the Emperors Augustus [183] and Claudius [184] consorted with numerous slave girls with their wives' explicit approval."

Sarah Pomeroy, whom I am quoting here, has still other things to relate. Owners of female slaves also could exploit them in the sex business. "Exposed baby girls and daughters sold by their parents were raised for this trade." We find such girls and women working as prostitutes, to the profit of their owners. Some were trained to perform in what we would call porno-shows; "actresses sometimes appeared in the nude and performed sexual acts on stage" [185]. During the Republic the husband, the master of the house, was sexually dominant, which meant in practice that not only his wife but also his female slaves and the slave-boys had to submit to his desires.

3. Companions worthy of respect

However, under the Emperors, although themselves not always paragons, a new ethics came into being. Now the man had to be 'sexually respectable', as Eva Cantarella expresses it [186], that is, he had to contain his erotic impulses. This heightened the prestige of the women, of course, who, instead of occupying the position of, so to speak, legalized prostitutes, now became companions worthy of respect. Indeed, many doctors of the first centuries of our era were convinced that sexual activity of whatever kind was unwholesome and had better be avoided. "Control of lust, and if possible, abstinence, became the new sanitary rule, the panacea for evils" [187].

It is important to note that "the aspiration to continence is not born with Christianity" - as is the fable convenue - "but was already present in pagan society". Slowly spreading through all sectors of society, this tendency of "combating desire and vanquishing temptations in order to liberate the soul from the tyranny of the flesh was already present in Orphic thought and in that of the Pythagoreans [188], in the philosophy of Plato [189], and in Neoplatonism" [190].

4. Love and divorce

Was there personal agreement, in other words, was there love between husband and wife [191]? Our information on this point is very scanty; of the lower classes we know hardly anything, and of the higher ones only a little more. There is a great lack of ego-documents. We know that divorce was quite frequent, with subsequent remarriage, both for men and women. "By the last century of the Republic the reasons for divorce were often trivial; often in the highest classes of society at Rome they were a matter of political manipulation and intrigue" [192]. But just as in our own days, a high rate of divorce does not imply that there was no genuine love, no personal attachment, in married couples. In his book on Roman women Balsden saw fit to include a chapter on happy marriages [193].

5. The 'Roman model'

Eva Cantarella has convincingly proved that the condition of free Roman women differed substantially from that of Greek women [194], so much so that she could even speak of the 'Roman model'. There were, it goes without saying, resemblances. Neither Greek nor Roman women had political rights; politics everywhere were the sole domain of men. And both categories of women were equally dependent on a male tutor, their father or their husband. Both categories had a primary task in common, that of the reproduction of the human race.

But whereas the task of Greek women remained virtually restricted to this, that of their Roman sisters was far wider. These "had to transmit to their sons the values of the fathers, to form their personality and their character, and to implant in them the virtues that would make them cives romani". This made their lives far more gratifying than those of Hellenic women; "although not endowed with political rights, they felt themselves, nonetheless, participating in the state" [195].

Viewing it from the standpoint of dualism, we cannot say that the man-woman relationship in marriage was dualistic; there was no unbridgeable gap between the sexes since the women complied with the man in what they had to do. One could call this relationship a 'social pact' for the welfare of the state. Peter Brown illustrates this by directing our attention to the reliefs on the sarcophagi of Italy and Asia Minor in the second and third centuries. "In them, the wife was shown standing attentively, or sitting, in front of her husband, as he raised his right hand to make a point, while in his left hand he displayed the servet which represented the superior literary culture on which he based his claim to outright dominance, in society at large as in marriage ... (His wife) would not be left to her own devices, free to go to seed in the women's quarters. She had been swept, by her cultivated husband, into the charmed circle of a shared exellence" [196]. This also points out the difference between Roman matronae and the ladies of Athenian society who remained confined to their households and in no way participated in the public life of their husbands.

6. A paradox?

True enough, the typical feminine duties were established and defined by men. If Roman women lived up to these duties - of being chaste, pious, homely, and, in addition, good weavers -, they would enjoy the respect of all, of their husbands and sons and of public opinion [197]. Is this a dualistic situation? Not really, I think. Nonetheless, Eva Cantarella discovers a 'Roman paradox'. "The values Roman women transmitted, of which they were the most secure guardians, were the values of a society as patriarchical as possible, in its juridical and social organization as well in its mentality ... Roman women reproduce, from generation to generation, the culture of a world of males who, while keeping power solidly in their hands, left to the women the honour, the fame, and the fake liberty : the liberty of one who accepts and makes into her own and reaps the advantages of rules which others have dictated" [198].

But was it really 'paradoxical'? To us it seems so, no doubt. But what was the attitude of Roman matrons? We should not forget that the Roman state was a machinery geared to war, that Roman society was a fighting machine. Century after century Rome fell from one war into another.

Roman males were fundamentally soldiers, those of the higher classes generals and officers. Can we expect Roman women to take an entirely different, even contrary attitude? Can we imagine that Roman women were convinced pacifists? This would be to ask for the impossible. If there was one ancient society to which that of Rome may be compared, it is that of Sparta. And in Sparta too women shared the ethos of the men. It seems to me that, on this special point, the common attitude to war and the military was perfectly homogeneous; there was nothing dualistic in it.

NOTES TO CHAPTER IV

1. Cic., De off. 2.8.26.
2. Veyne, Humanitas 377.
3. The Dutch verb 'brabbelen' = to jabber, to talk gibberish, comes very near to this.
4. Ovid, Tristia 5.10.37.
5. Ovid, Tristia 5.10.32.
6. Oxyrrh.Papers XV.1681.
7. Hor., Ep. 2.1.156-157.
8. Cic., Tusc.Disp. 1.1-3.
9. For this passage I have been relying heavily on the article of G. Humbert, 'barbari', in Dict.ant.grec. et rom. I.1, 670-672.
10. Vogt, Kulturwelt 12. See also Saddington, Race Relations. Aufstieg II.3, 112-137.
11. An anonymous rhetor, speaking of the Emperor Constantine the Great, ao. 313, Paneg.lat. II, 9.22.4.
12. Quoted by Vogt, Kulturwelt 13.
13. Claudian., Pan.Honorio 221-222.
14. Themistius 10.131b-132a and 140a.
15. Dyson, Native Revolt 138.
16. Heuss, Röm.Gesch. 366.
17. Heuss, Röm.Gesch. 367.
18. Dyson, Native Revolt 146.
19. Dyson, Native Revolt 151.

20.	Dio 54.11.5.
21.	Dio 55.28.4.
22.	Dyson, Native Revolt 166.
23.	Dyson, Native Revolt 154.
24.	Dio 54.32.1.
25.	Dyson, Native Revolt 161.
26.	Dyson, Native Revolt 170.
27.	When I first heard of him, in primary school, he was referred to as 'Claudius Civilis'. In older editions of his 'Histories' Tacitus calls him 'Claudius' indeed; this, however, is a mistake that, in more recent editions, has been corrected into 'Julius', as Tacitus himself writes in Hist. 1.59.
28.	Tac., Germ. 29.1. The first historical date I learned in primary school was '100 B.C. the Batavians arrive in our country'. However, we do not know when they arrived.
29.	Caesar, Bell.Gall. 4.10; Pliny, HN 4.15 (101) also mentions the Cannenefates as inhabitants of this region. As schoolboys we thought that Cannenefates meant 'konijnenvatters' = catchers of rabbits.
30.	Dio 55.24.7.
31.	In 1949, when Indonesia became a sovereign state, it got back its ancient name, in the form of Jakarta.
32.	In more recent times we had the shipping company the 'Batavier Line', 1830-1958, the oldest steamship company of the Netherlands, and a bicycle mark called 'Batavus'. Royal Dutch Shell had its origin in the 'Bataafse Petroleum Maatschappij' (1907).
33.	Tac., Hist. 4.12.
34.	Tac., Hist. 4.13.
35.	Tac., Hist. 1.59.
36.	Tac., Hist. 4.13.
37.	Plut., Galba 22.1-23.1.
38.	Tac., Hist. 1.59 and 4.13.
39.	Tac., Hist. 2.69.
40.	Dutch national myth has it that this grove was somewhere in the wooded hills of the Veluwe just north of the Rhine.
41.	Tac., Hist. 4.14.
42.	Tac., Hist. 4.14.

43. Tac., Hist. 4.21.
44. Tac., Hist. 4.16.
45. Tac., Hist. 4.17-18.
46. Tac., Hist. 4.21-28.
47. Tac., Hist. 4.27.
48. Tac., Hist. 4.49.
49. Tac., Hist. 4.54.
50. The legions of Vespasian indeed captured Rome in December 69.
51. Tac., Hist. 4.55.
52. Tac., Hist. 4.60.
53. Tac., Hist. 4.63-65.
54. Tac., Hist. 4.59.
55. Tac., Hist. 4.61.
56. Tac., Hist. 4.61.
57. Tac., Hist. 4.68.
58. Tac., Hist. 4.71-72.
59. Tac., Hist. 4.77-78.
60. Tac., Hist. 5.14.
61. Tac., Hist. 5.15.
62. Tac., Hist. 5.16-18.
63. Tac., Hist. 5.20.
64. Tac., Hist. 5.22.
65. Tac., Hist. 5.26. There is absolutely no saying which stream may be meant with this 'Nabalia'; its name occurs only here. It may be guessed that we should not read 'Nabaliae fluminis pons' but 'navalis fluminis pons' in which case we should have to do with a pontoon-bridge the middle part of which was taken away, see Alfred Franke s.v. 'Nabalia', PW XVI (Stuttgart, 1935), 1450.
66. Tac., Hist. 5.29.
67. Dyson, Nat.Revolt 171/172.
68. This is called 'Antoniniana' because Caracalla's official name was Marcus Aurelius Severus Antoninus; 'Caracalla' is a surname given to him because he used to wear a 'caracalla', a Celtic or Germanic mantle.

223

69. Dio 78.9.5.
70. Macrobius, Sat.Conv. 1.7.26.
71. Hor., Carm. 2.7.4.
72. Macr. 1.11.1.
73. Ath., 14.639B.
74. Just. 43.1.3.
75. Gaius, Inst. 1.9.
76. Iust.Inst. 1.3.2.
77. Gaius 1.52,53.
78. "Marriage between slaves, and hence the existence of a slave family, was technically a legal impossibility." This did not prevent the slaves from having consorts and children, see Bradley, Slaves, Ch. II The Slave Family, pp.48 sqq.
79. Gaius 2.86-87.
80. Vogt, Ancient Slavery 111.
81. Vogt, Ancient Slavery 112.
82. Plautus, Bacchides 162.
83. See Vol. II, Ch. IV.4i-j.
84. See the chapter (VII) on 'The Faithful Slave' in Vogt, Ancient Slavery.
85. Diod. 34/35.32.
86. Bradley, Slaves 139.
87. Bradley, Slaves 139.
88. Pliny, Ep. 3.
89. Quoted by Bradley, Slaves 114.
90. Seneca, Ep. 47:5.
91. Bradley, Slaves 122.
92. Bradley, Slaves 122/123.
93. Diod. 34/35.33.
94. Vol. X, Ch. IV.6.
95. Strabo, Geogr. 7.7.3
96. Strabo, Geogr. 14.5.2.
97. Cod.Theod. 5.101, quoted Greek and Roman slavery, 118/119.

98.	Seneca, Ep. 4.8.
99.	Terentius, fragment from 'Synephebus', ed. Riese p. 220.
100.	Seneca, Ep. 47.5.
101.	Dion.Hal. 5.51.3.
102.	Dion.Hal. 5.53-57.
103.	Livy 3.15-18; Dion.Hal. 10.14-16.
104.	Livy 4.45.1-2.
105.	Wallon, Esclavage II,290.
106.	Livy 32.26.
107.	Livy 33.36.1-2.
108.	Livy 39.29.8-9.
109.	Diod. 34/35.2.2.
110.	Diod. 34/35.2.4.
111.	Cic., Verres 2.4.106.
112.	Diod. 34/35.2.25.
113.	Diod. 34/35.2.5-9.
114.	Bradley, Slavery 57.
115.	Diod. 34/35.2.10-16.
116.	Diod. 34/35.2.18.
117.	Diod. 34/35.2.19.
118.	Diod. 34/35.2.19-21.
119.	Diod. 34/35.2.21-23.
120.	Florus 2.7.7-8.
121.	Diod. 36.3.2.
122.	Dio 27.93.1.
123.	Dio 27.93.2-4; Diod. 36.3.3.
124.	Diod. 36.3.4-6.
125.	Diod. 36.4.1-3.
126.	Diod. 36.3.4-6.
127.	Diod. 36.5.11.
128.	Diod. 36.4.5.
129.	Diod. 36.7.

130. Diod. 36.10.
131. Bradley, Slavery 85.
132. I was unable to lay my hands on the book of Cathérine Salles, Spartacus et la révolte des gladiateurs. Bruxelles, 1990.
133. Karl Marx, Letter to Friedrich Engels, 27.II.1861, quoted Günther, Aufstand 5.
134. During World War II there existed in the Netherlands an underground Communist League Spartacus; after the war no more was heard of it.
135. Plut., Crassus 8.1.
136. Plut., Crassus 8.3; Appian, Rom.hist. 1.116.
137. Mommsen, Röm.Gesch. III, 84.
138. Appian, Rom,hist. 1.116, said that he had seen service as a soldier with the Romans.
139. Plut., Crassus 8.2.
140. Plut., Crassus 8.3.
141. Plut., Crassus 8.1. Giulia Stampacchia, Tradizione 15/16, lists all the sources on Lentulus and his school.
142. Plut., Crassus 8.1.
143. Plut., Crassus 8.21. The number of the escaped varies from 'thirty or more' in Florus 2.8.3 to seventy-eight in Plutarch, with all kinds of numbers in between, Stampacchia, Tradizione 16/17.
144. Appian, Rom.hist. 1.116.
145. Appian, Rom.hist. 1.116.
146. See the discussion on the leadership in Stampaccchia, Tradizione 17-20; in some sources Venamaus and Crixus figure as of equal rank with Spartacus.
147. Plut., Crassus 9.1.
148. Plut., Crassus 9.1-3.
149. Appian, Rom.hist. 1.116.
150. Plut., Crassus 9.4-5.
151. Appian, Rom,hist. 1.116. See the discussion on the numbers in Stampacchia, Tradizione 35-39. From some sources it may be deduced that members of the rural proletariat also took part.
152. Plut., Crassus 9.5.6; Appian 1.117.
153. Plut., Crassus 9.7; Appian, Rom.hist. 1.117.

154. Orosius 5.24.3; Florus 2.8.9. Both authors speak of three hundred men who were sacrificed in this way (see also Appian 1.117). Stampacchia, Tradizone 45/46.
155. Plut., Crassus 9.7.
156. Plut., Crassus 10.1-3.
157. Appian, Rom.hist. 1.117.
158. Eutr., Brev. 6.7.2.
159. Appian, Rom.hist. 1.117.
160. Eutr. 6.7.2.
161. Appian, Rom.hist. 1.118; Orosius 5.24.5. See Stampacchia, Tradizione 62/63.
162. Appian, Rom.hist. 1.118.
163. Plut., Crassus 10.3-4.
164. Florus 2.8.12.
165. Plut., Crassus 10.4-5.
166. Plut., Crassus 10.6.
167. Front., 5.1.20.
168. Plut., Crassus 11.1.
169. Appian, Rom.hist. 1.119; Plut., Crassus 11.2.
170. Plut., Crassus 11.3.
171. Appian, Rom.hist. 1.120.
172. Florus 2.8.14.
173. Appian, Rom.hist. 1.120.
174. Plut., Pomp. 21.2.
175. Plut., Crassus 11.7.
176. Orosius 24.4.7-8.
177. Appian, Rom.hist., Civ.Wars 1.120.
178. Bradley, Slavery 129.
179. Clem.Al., Paid. 2.7.60. See Brown, The Body 127.
180. Zinserling, Women 53.
181. Pomeroy, Goddesses 191.
182. Plut., M.Cato 24.2.
183. Dio 58.2; Suet., Aug. 71.1.

184. Tac., Ann. 11:29.
185. Pomeroy, Goddesses 192.
186. Cantarella, Vita delle donne, Storia di Roma 576.
187. This is the exact opposite of modern opinion that considers sexual activity the panacea for all evils.
188. See Vol. I, Ch. IV.11 On body and soul.
189. See Vol. IV, Ch. III. 6 and 8.
190. Cantarella, Vita delle donne, Storia di Roma 4, 577/578.
191. There is not much to be found in modern literature on Roman marital love, even in female authors. See for instance the chapter on 'Marriage' in Jane Gardner, Women in Roman Law. It carries sections on the legal requirements for marriage, such as marriageable age, and the formal procedures of marriage, but not on love.
192. Balsden, Roman women 216.
193. Balsden, Roman women, Ch. IX.
194. See for this subject Vol. II, Ch. IV.4.
195. Cantarella, Vita delle donne, Storia di Roma 4, 606-608.
196. Brown, Men, Women 13/14.
197. Emily Hemelrijk, Women's demonstrations 217, writes : "Chastity, frugality, domesticity, industry and loyalty to her husband and family were the main traditional virtues of the Roman matron. These ideals are frequently attested in Roman literature and on numerous epitaphs Roman women are praised for living up to these standards".
198. Cantarella, Vita delle donne, Storia 4, 606-608.

CHAPTER V

THE JEWS IN CONFLICT WITH ROME

PART I THE JEWS IN THE HELLENISTIC WORLD

1. The numerical range

As in all similar cases in Antiquity, estimates as to numbers vary widely. How many Jews were there in Palestine before the catastrophes? Juster finds the number given by Harnack and Eduard Meyer, namely seven hundred thousand, 'inadmissible", that is, far too low, and thinks himself of some five millions, a great many of whom perished in the rebellion of 66-70 [1]. It is still more difficult to state with a reasonable exactitude how many Jews lived in the Diaspora, that is outside Palestine [2]. Beloch calculates the total population of the Empire in the time of Augustus as fifty-four millions, and Meyer as fifty-five, which, according to Juster, is too low. On the basis of these totals Harnack figures out the number of Jews as some four or four and a half millions which makes about 7 % of the grand total. Juster, while agreeing with this percentage, but arguing from a larger total population, arrives at a total number of Jews, before A.D. 70, of six to seven millions, which would mean that, according to him, only one to two millions lived in the Diaspora. He quotes the Jewish author Bar-Hebraeus to this effect; this author wrote that the Emperor Claudius made a census of the Jews in his Empire from which it appeared that there were 6.940.000 of them [3]. To these we must add the tens of thousands of Jews who lived in Mesopotamia, particularly in Babylonia, and in Media, who were not citizens of the Roman Empire [4].

Louis Feldman thinks that "the position of the Jews was certainly strengthened by their great numbers, constantly increasing through highly successful proselytism". To the question whether or not there really was such proselytism we shall have to return in Chapter II of Volume XII. And then this author presents a somewhat bold conjecture. "If the ... great revolts against the Romans had not occurred and if Christianity had not lowered the price of admission, so to speak [5], Judaism might have become the major religion of the Roman Empire" [6]. Feldman forgets that the Gnosis too was a serious competitor for the first place.

2. The dispersion of the Jews

A considerable number of the Jewish population lived outside the Holy Land in what is called the 'Diaspora', a Greek word signifying 'dispersion'. In his famous and seminal work on the Jews of the Roman Empire Juster [7] prints a long list of countries outside Palestine where Jews were to be found, in Italy for instance in Rome, in Milan, Bologna, and Ravenna, in Naples, Pompeii, and Tarento, and in many other towns, in Sicily, in Syracuse and Messina and in various other centres, in Sardinia, in Spain in Cordoba and Toledo, in France in Marseille, Arles, Bordeaux, Lyons, Poitiers - a list that is far from exhaustive -, in Germany in Cologne and Bonn, in Britain, Austria, Hungary, Croatia and Dalmatia, in Thrace and as far as the Crimea, in Macedonia and in Greece where Delphi, Athens, and Corinth are mentioned, in all the Aegean islands, in Rhodes, Crete, and Cyprus, in Asia Minor in a great number of towns, in Syria for instance in Antioch, in Armenia, Assyria and in Babylonia, in Nisibis and Ctesiphon, in Arabia and Egypt with the very important Jewish colony in Alexandria, in Ethiopia and Libya, in Numidia and Mauretania. Juster lists a great many more towns than I have mentioned here. The general conclusion is that the Jews were omnipresent [8].

3. Concentrations of Jews

The Jews of Babylonia, where the Babylonian Talmud originated [9], formed the oldest great concentration of Jews outside Palestine. We find a second great concentration in Egypt, especially in Alexandria; the total number of Egyptian Jews is estimated at one million, about 12 % of the total population. A third, but smaller, concentration was to be found in Rome, some fifty or sixty thousand on a population of perhaps eight hundred thousand [10].

It should be added, however, that there were important differences between the groups of the Diaspora. Those west of Palestine spoke mainly Greek as the translation of the Old Testament into Greek testifies; those east of the mother country used mainly the Aramaic language, like their brethren in the Holy Land itself. It is a curious thing that the difference between western and eastern Jews has persisted throughout the Ages as the distinction between Sephardim and Ashkenazim. Josephus, quoting Strabo, summarizes the overall situation as follows. "This people has already made its way into every city, and it is not easy to find any place in the habitable world which has not received this nation (phulon) and into which it has not made its power felt" [11]. Modern authors think that Josephus exaggerated a little with regard to the influence of the Jews. But it will not surprise the reader that the presence of so many Jews, especially in greater concentrations, could become a source of friction, if they were felt to be 'foreign'. Pleading for Flaccus in 59 B.C., Cicero mentions "the great number of Jews turbulently present in our assemblies which should be held in contempt for the sake of the Republic" [12]. Although we may wonder what the orator may have meant with the presence of Jews in the assemblies, it is evident that he is referring to Diaspora Jews, in all probability in the capital itself, and that their presence was a source of irritation to him.

PART II THE SITUATION OF THE JEWS IN THE EASTERN DIASPORA BEFORE THE ROMANS CAME

My idea is that we should first of all restrict ourselves to the pagan world and leave the Christian attitude aside for the time being. In the attitude of the pagans vis-à-vis the Jews three elements may be distinguished : the official policy of the state, the attitude of the intellectuals, that is, of those who wrote and published, and public opinion. Beginning with the official policy, we must again make a distinction, the policy regarding the Jews of Palestine, and that regarding those of the Diaspora. Let us begin with the Jews of the Diaspora in the period before the arrival of the Romans, and, for the moment, restrict ourselves to official attitudes.

1. On the level of the state

On the whole, governemental attitudes towards Jews and Judaism were not hostile in the period under consideration. "The governments, with few exceptions, did not wish to antagonize so large and important a group and maintained the privileged position of the Jews" [13]. This certainly obtains for the line followed by the Hellenistic Pharaohs of Egypt. In the last period of the Ptolemies we find Jews in high positions, even as commanders of armies, which naturally signifies that they were trusted [14].

This is also true of the Seleucid rulers who, on the whole, did not bother the Jews for religious reasons. The one great exception is, of course, the policy of King Antiochus IV respecting the Jews and their religion, which led to the War of the Maccabees and the foundation of the Hasmonaean kingdom [15].

Perhaps this is still more true of the Persian Great Kings who were very tolerant of all religions. We know how their king Cyrus was applauded in the Old Testament as the Anointed of the Lord because he had made an end of the Babylonian captivity. Those Jews who preferred to stay in Media and Mesopotamia - probably a majority of the exiles - were not bothered because of their creed and religious activities. We have, however, the strange episode that is related in the Book of Esther.

2. The story of Esther

The scene of the story is the court of the Persian Emperor Ahasuerus (= Artaxerxes) at Susa. Having repudiated his wife who did not obey him, he organized a beauty contest for the girls of his realm; the most beautiful of all would become his new consort. A Jewish girl, called Esther, became Miss Persia; she was an orphan in the care of her uncle Mordecai. She dutifully took the place of Ahasuerus' ex-wife. One day Mordecai overheard two officials who were plotting against the Emperor's life. He duly notified his niece, and she warned her husband. The two conspirators were hanged.

A very important man at the king's court was Haman. When he remarked that Mordecai did not do obeisance to him, as the king had ordered, he planned to destroy, not only Mordecai, but all the Jews of the Empire. He won the approval of the Emperor for this plan. "Deal with them as you wish", he said [16]. So orders went out to all provincial governors that they should annihilate all the Jews in their resorts on a certain day. Mordecai realized that the only one who would be able to save the Jews was Esther. She took the risk of approaching the king unannounced but found favour with him. The only thing she asked was that he would invite Haman to a banquet with her husband and herself.

Haman was highly pleased, of course, with this invitation. He even went so far that he had a gallows erected on which Mordecai would come to hang. But in that night the king could not sleep and ordered an attendant to read the annals to him. When he heard the story of the failed conspiracy, he also came to know that Mordecai had not been remumerated for having discovered the plot. Thereupon the king summoned Haman and ordered him to lead Mordecai on a horse through the town, proclaiming everywhere that this was the man whom the king wanted to honour. This Haman did, in every probability with a very sour face.

At the banquet Esther accused Haman of planning to destroy the Jews. The king flew into a rage and ordered Haman to be hung on his own gallows; Mordecai inherited the functions of Haman. And now the roles were reversed. Ahasuerus gave the Jews permission to defend themselves and destroy their enemies on exactly the same day that was destined for their own destruction. The number of those killed by the Jews is given as seventy-five thousand.

3. The problems posed by this book

The Book of Esther presents modern exegetes, Jewish and non-Jewish alike, with considerable difficulties. The main body of the text is in Hebrew but there are a number of Greek insertions which are of a later date. It is a curious thing that in the main Hebrew text the name of God is not once mentioned. It was at a comparatively late date that the book was incorporated into the biblical canon. The final redaction of the Hebrew text may date from the second century B.C. and probably mirrors the situation of the Jewish people when it was oppressed by the Seleucids. But the original core may be an ancient story about the plight of the Jews in the Persian Empire; this is supported by the fact that the story presents a fair number of accurate historical details of life at a Persian court. It may have been known to and been adapted by a later author for a special purpose.

Mordecai says to his niece when she hesitates to approach her husband : "Who knows whether you have not been elevated to the royal dignity exactly for his occasion" [17]. This is the theological objective of the book : God's providence will always find means to save his people, even if this must be by means of a beauty contest. The book has also an important liturgical function. It is one of the five 'megillot' or 'festival scrolls', destined to be read during Jewish feasts. 'Esther' was (and is) read at the Purim feast. The name of this feast is derived from the Hebrew word 'pur' = lot, for the day for the attack on the Jews was determined by the drawing of lots [18]. 'Esther', therefore, is an aetiological story explaining the origin and the significance of the Purim feast [19].

That the Book of Esther gives precise historical information does not say that it is historical itself, that is, that it relates something that really happened. For instance, who is this King Ahasuerus? The Greek rendering of his name as 'Artaxerxes' does not make us any the wiser since there have been more Achaemenid emperors of this name; there is no telling which one is meant. That a Persian Great King would raise a Jewish girl to the position of First Lady is highly improbable. Admittedly he does not know that she is Jewish, but he was acquainted with her uncle Mordecai, and who would not know that this man was Jewish to the core?

A very queer picture is given of the king's policy with regard to the Jews. At the very first instigation of Haman he is quite prepared to condemn them all to death - which was completely at variance with the usual religious policy of the Persian government. A few days later he is just as quick, at the request of Esther, to rescind his orders. And not only that, for he gives the Jews permission to launch what is in fact a civil war. All this is inconceivable. But the Book of Esther, just as the other megillot (the Song of Songs, the Lamentations, Ruth, and Ecclesiastes), is not meant to be read and understood as history.

The book has three aims : on the highest level a theological one, on the middle level a liturgical one (both of which I mentioned), and on the down-to-earth level a secular one. It gives us the general or basic reason why Jews are persecuted; in other words, it explains a form of radical dualism. Haman felt insulted because Mordecai did not bow to him. The reason why Mordecai refused to do this is given in the Greek text : "I did it so that I might not hold a man in greater honour than God; I will not bow for any but you (God - Mordecai is praying)" [20]. Haman rightly suspects that Mordecai's refusal had a religious ground. When he complains to the king, he does not mention his enemy at all, but immediately generalizes his accusation by involving the whole Jewish nation. In his eyes they are obviously all of the same ilk as Mordecai. "There is a certain nation, dispersed among the many peoples in all the provinces of your kingdom, who keep themselves apart. Their laws are different from those of every other people; they do not keep your majesty's laws. It does not benefit your majesty to tolerate them" [21].

This is a seminal text. It mirrors the situation of the Jews in the Diaspora : 'dispersed among the nations'. And it explains why there is persecution of Jews : they are different, they keep themselves apart. And they are suspected of civil disobedience for religious reasons. The reaction of the authorities is : let us destroy them. We are in the presence here of the first 'Final Solution'; it is the sheerest dualism of 'either them or us'. The Greek text adds, in the form of an official letter of the king, : "This nation stands alone in its continual opposition to all men, ... thus undermining the security of the Empire ... Those persons who have long been disaffected shall meet a violent death in one day so that our government may henceforth be stable and untroubled" [22]. A world with Jews can never be a safe world. Hitler did not think and act differently.

All our sympathies could be with the Jews but for the end where it is related how they paid their enemies back in kind. This is repellent to the modern mind. The Greek text excuses it by saying that the Jews acted in self-defence [23]. The Dutch professor Wildeboer writes that the Book of Esther shows Israel in its natural state; this is also exemplified by the curious fact that the name of God does not occur in the older Hebrew text [24]. In its 'natural state' Israël did not leave the revenge to God, as it should. In Volume IV [25] I spoke of an inconsistency in the biblical presentation. There are two strands, or two levels, in the history writing of the Old Testament, a divine one and a historical, secular, and natural one, which do not tally with each other and are even (dualistically) opposed. The secular level is that of the punitive expeditions, of the destruction of towns, and of the extermination of their inhabitants. On the divine level we see, however, that King David is not allowed to build the Temple, because he has shed too much blood. The Book of Joshua imputes without blushing the orders to root out the Canaanites to God - to the same God who said : "Thou shalt not kill". This is an inconsistency, but not one in Jahve; it is one in mankind, in Israel that still has to understand the full impact of the divine law in all its consequences. The retaliation of the Jews in Esther is not attributed to God; it is imputed to the earthly ruler. Perhaps the name of God is never mentioned in the Hebrew text to make it possible to leave God entirely out of this.

The Book of Esther is an important paradigm of the natural order. Feeling threatened, the Jews retaliate. This is presented as what they are expected to do, what they should do in the natural order; wherever Jews are attacked they should defend themselves. "Cet animal est très méchant; quand on l'attaque, il se défend" [26]. There is no consolation in the fact that the described events did not happen at all, since we know of several instances in which Diaspora Jews fell upon their compatriots and killed a great many of them.

4. Relations on the polis-level

Naturally the Jews in the Hellenistic towns of Asia Minor and of Egypt stuck together in order to preserve an identity which was determined by their religion. In many greater and smaller towns there existed Jewish communities centred around the synagogue and with their own (religious) leadership. That the Hellenistic town councils saw nothing special in the existence of such communities appears from the fact that there is no special Greek term for them. The Jews of the city were simply referred to as 'Jews' or 'Jews resident in the city'. Their community was called a 'politeuma' or a 'katoikia' or some similar term. There was nothing unique in this since there were politeumata or katoikiai of many other groups of people, for instance of mercenaries who had settled somewhere. These terms were used to indicate the recognition of some measure of self-administration or autonomy. The fact that specific ethnic, social, or religious groups looked after their own affairs eased, of course, the administrative task of the authorities [27].

Tcherikover characterizes the situation of the Jewish communities as follows. "No politeuma could be organized without the special permission of the king, or of a high official representing him. No more could the Jewish communities, of course, be formed solely on their own initiative ... The Jewish community did not exceed the restricted limits of the city or village, and these lacked any political power, because it was too small. Yet within these restricted bounds it enjoyed complete freedom in all matters of religion, observance and law. The right 'to live according to its ancestral laws' meant the right to build synagogues, to maintain independent courts of justice, to educate the youth in the spirit of the Torah, to set up communal institutions and to elect officials and the like" [28].

The Hellenistic authorities, either on the state level or lower, did not interfere in the religious (and administrative) affairs of the Jews - with the notable exception, of course, of the anti-Judaistic policy of Antiochus IV of Syria in Judaea. Radin concludes that "the attitude of Greek states toward the Jewish communities in their midst was certainly not uniformly hostile". But none the less, a certain irritation on the side of the Hellenistic authorities may also be discerned. This was the consequence of the special grants accorded to Jewish communities, making them exempt from the local laws of 'asebeia' = godlessness. The monotheistic Jews were not asked to venerate the local divinities. Sometimes the town authorities seem to have regretted the existence of this privilege, but since it was based on a royal grant, they had to accept it [29]. Yet the privileged position of a Jewish community could easily become a source of friction between Jews and non-Jews. Not that the pagan inhabitants too desired to possess the privilege of exemption from the asebeia law. They were quite ready to pay homage to their local divine protectors. But we should not forget that a Greek polis was first and foremost a sacral fellowship with a communal cult. The fact that some people refused to share in it was considered not only impious but also dangerous.

5. Jewish citizenship?

Jews in Egypt and in the eastern Hellenistic states were, as a matter of fact, always immigrants, that is, aliens. This means that basically they were everywhere non-citizens without any political rights whatsoever. Did Jews, as a group or individually, come to enjoy citizenship in Hellenistic towns? Tcherikover is categorical on this point. "The Jewish community as a whole stood juridically outside the Greek city, and the Jews who lived in it had no civic rights there ... (But) isolated Jews could acquire civic rights there" [30]. The problem, however, is that Josephus mentions a number of cities in which Jewish communities were accorded civic rights, the most important of these being the community in Antioch. Josephus is our only source for his; no pagan author supports his claim. For Tcherikover this is a sufficient reason to dismiss him [31]. Schürer is inclined to give Josephus some credit, but he too concludes that "without clear documentary evidence on either side, the question must be left open" [32]. I feel that we may safely infer that as a rule Jewish communities did not enjoy citizenship; if civic rights were sometimes granted, this was not the general policy [33].

PART III THE OFFICIAL ROMAN POLICY

1. The policy of the Roman government with regard to the Diaspora Jews

a. How Rome dealt with foreign religions

When we now turn to the official relations of the Roman state with Jewry, it is first of all necessary to define Rome's general attitude to the religions of non-Roman nations. The Greeks, who were no conquerors and did not found an empire (that of Alexander was a Macedonian one), did not feel obliged to define their relationship to other peoples' creeds, at least not politically. The Romans, on the contrary, annexed the countries of numerous peoples, inluding the homeland of the Jews. They not only annexed the territory but the local gods. These gods might be angry that the city they had protected was destroyed; for this reason, it was thought safer to house them in Rome under imperial control. This made it abundantly clear who was the victor, militarily but also spiritually.

This was pregnantly expressed by the Roman dictator Camillus when he captured Rome's old enemy, the Etruscan city of Veii, in 396 B.C. "You, Queen Juno, you who now lives in Veii, I implore you, follow our victorious troops into the city that is ours, and will soon be yours, where a temple worthy of your majesty will receive you" [34]. The fact may be legendary, but the spirit is not [35].

When Scipio Africanus in 146 B.C. was on the point of storming Carthage, he recited a doubtless old and hallowed prayer. "Whoever you are, whether god or goddess, in whose ward the people and the city of Carthage are, and you above all, who accepted the wardship of this city and this people, I implore you, I beseech you, that you will desert the city and the people of Carthage ... and graciously come to Rome, to me and my people ..., and that you may become the lords of myself, the Roman people, and my soldiers ... If you do so, I solemnly promise to erect temples in your honour and establish festal games" [36]. But when Pompey on October 10, 63 B.C. entered the Holy of Holies of the Jerusalem Temple, he found it empty. There was simply no god there whom he could invite to follow him to Rome. The Yahve of the Jews was beyond the religious conceptions of the Romans.

Generally speaking, the Romans did not meddle with the religious affairs of their subjected nations, as long as these did not serve as a cloak for anti-Roman activities. Polytheistic as they were, they did not care about a divinity more or less. They were quite content if the nations - wherever they lived - were ready to acknowledge Jupiter Capitolinus as the highest imperial god. But it will be evident that here a problem arose for the strictly monotheistic Jews, and later also for the Christians.

b. The Jews as a special problem

The presence of so many Jews dispersed all over the Empire presented the Roman government with a special problem. Whereas all other ethnic communities lived within the borders of their own territories, the Jewish nation was only partly based on its own soil; for the rest, it was at home among other nations, even in Rome itself, here and there in considerable numbers. The Jews of the Diaspora, just like their co-religionists in Palestine, practised 'apartheid'. They distinguished themselves from others by following a very detailed code of behaviour; they kept aloof from others, the Gentiles, the 'goyim', because of their rules of purity and their food taboos. They did not intermarry with non-Jews, and, if possible, stuck together in certain quarters of a town. They were religiously different too. They did not acknowledge the polytheistic pantheon of the ancient world; they were strictly monotheistic and venerated a God who did not figure among the divinities of the world of

Antiquity. For this reason they were not prepared to pay homage to the imperial godhead, Jupiter Capitolinus.

c. The official regulations

We find the first evidence of a legal regulation of Jewish affairs in Josephus who mentions eight documents, dating from the year 49/48 B.C., concerning the position of the Jews in the cities of Asia Minor [37]. Jews were to be exempted from military service because they are not permitted to do work on Sabbath days. Furthermore, they were given the right freely to assemble for religious purposes, to build houses of prayer, to observe the Sabbath days, and, in general, to live according to their own laws. These were important concessions, especially, of course, given the number of Jews, the exemption from military service. It must be remarked that this favourable regime was imposed on the cities by the imperial government often against their wish; it impinged on their communal right to order their own affairs, even with regard to cult [38]. The city of Tralles, for instance, was 'dissatisfied with the decrees concerning the Jews' and would not allow them to live according to their customs; it had to be forced into obedience by the proconsul of the province [39].

The short rule of Julius Caesar proved very favourable to the Jews. He was grateful to them because they had come to his assistance, when he was in an almost hopeless position during the Alexandrian War [40]. He granted the Jews of the Diaspora a Charter of Jewish Rights which safeguarded their status of apartheid. What until that time had been 'an unwritten convention' now became law : their religion became a religio licita, an authorized cult, which meant that the Jews were to enjoy religious liberty. This implied that they were absolved from the obligation to do homage to the imperial supreme godhead. They were also exempted from military service because of the problems the dietary laws posed to a Jewish conscript [41]. These rights and exemptions were also granted to the Jews of the homeland [42]. In exchange, "sacrifices of two lambs and a bull were to be offered daily in the Temple to

God for the emperor's well-being, to replace the offering of sacrifices to the emperor himself in other provinces" [43].

The High Priest in Jerusalem (the office was hereditary) became the 'ethnarch' of the Jews; in matters concerning the mode of life of all the Jews, in Palestine as well in the Diaspora, the decision rested with him [44]. This meant that all Jews, wherever they lived, came under one single authority; it also implied that they might live according to their own laws. Furthermore, they were officially recognized as a separate ethnos, even if they lived in the Diaspora in the midst of other nations. On top of all this, Caesar granted the Jews the right to rebuild the walls of Jerusalem [45]. There would be no auxiliaries levied in Judaea nor would Roman legions be quartered there for the winter [46]. A month after the death of Caesar in 44 B.C. these decrees were not rescinded but, on the contrary, confirmed by the Senate [47].

In line with this benevolent policy, we see Augustus acting as the high protector of the Jews, when the cities of Asia Minor and Cyrenaica tried to prevent the Jews living there from sending money to the Temple in Jerusalem; the Emperor decreed that this was their right and that it should not be violated [48].

d. Collusion between Romans and Jews

With regard to the relations of the Diaspora Jews with the Roman authorities and the reverse, we are allowed to speak of collusion. Realizing that others were jealous of them and did not wholeheartedly welcome them into their cities, the Jews knew that they were dependent on the government for protection against evil-intentioned people and for the maintenance of their special status. Josephus reports a long speech by a certain Nicholas of Damascus, a Jew, in favour of the Jews of Ionia [49] which is summarized by Juster as follows. "The Romans are superior to all; therefore, all are equally subject to Rome. In consequence, the subjects should not lord it over each other; from this it follows that none other than the Romans have the right to regulate the affairs of the Jews" [50]. The Jews, knowing the Roman authorities to be their protectors, were loyal to the Empire and could, therefore, be seen as a unifying element. On their part, the government realized how touchy the Jews were with regard to their religion and cult; they wanted to avert the danger of Jewish seditions [51].

e. Toleration and irritation

The official policy of the Roman government with regard to the Jews was a mixture of toleration and irritation. In general, Rome was tolerant for ethnic religions, "but the Jews could not respond to this tolerance with the same attitude ... (They) were not prepared to recognise other forms of cult and life as equal to their own" [52]. To live as they desired to live the Jews needed privileges which the authorities were ready to grant them. In doing this the Romans remained true to the line followed by the Ptolemaeans and the Seleucids. But of course, these very privileges were a source of jealousy and made the Jews hated by their pagan compatriots. "Granting such privileges meant deferring to the incomprehensible obstinacy of a separate population group that itself showed no deference to others" [53].

f. The Jews of Rome in difficulties

For the Jews of Rome the outlook became less bright during the reign of Tiberius who succeeded Augustus in A.D. 14. He made Aelius Sejanus his praetorian prefect, "leaving him virtually in charge of affairs in Rome during the Emperor's self-imposed exile from the capital city" [54]. When this man was in power, writes Philo, "matters in Italy became troublesome"; he even accused him of desiring to do away with the whole Jewish nation [55]. This ancient author speaks of a policy of aggression against the Jews that was initiated by Sejanus [56].

According to Josephus, the following incident was the cause of anti-Jewish measures. A high-ranking Roman matrona, Fulvia, was a Jewish proselyte. She became the victim of four Jewish crooks who persuaded her to send purple and gold to the Temple in Jerusalem; they embezzled these valuables. The deceived woman complained to her husband Saturninus [57] who, in his turn, informed his friend the Emperor. The enraged Tiberius "ordered the whole Jewish community to leave Rome". Four thousand of them were drafted for military service and sent to Sardinia; when a great number of them evaded this measure for fear of being forced to break the Law, they were punished. This happened in A.D. 19. Josephus rounds off his story by stating that "because of the wickedness of four men, the Jews were banished from the city" [58].

It is somewhat hard to believe that the fact that a Roman matrona was swindled by some Jewish scoundrels was a sufficient reason for such drastic measures. Rather we should think of a latent animosity against the Jews which was not foreign even to the highest authorities. The incident with Fulvia may have activated this animosity. Anyhow, the background was not racial but rather social and religious [59]. Tacitus, who ascribes the decree in question not to the Emperor but to the Senate, speaks of 'the proscription of the Egyptian rites' (with which the Isis cult is meant), and of 'superstition' and 'impious ceremonial' (which refers to Judaism). He adds the cynical remark (whether from himself or made by the Senate) that, "if they (the mobilized Jews) succumbed to the pestilential climate (of Sardinia), it was a cheap loss" [60]. Suetonius goes even further by stating that this military service was only a pretext for expelling young Jews to insalubrious regions [61]; if this is correct, then there is doubtless an element of genocide in this measure.

Dio gives as an additional reason that the Jews were proselytizing in Rome and made many converts there [62]. If this is correct too, then the Emperor and/or the Senate may have found that the Jews, by extending their ethnos, were overstepping their bounds. Very probably Radin is right when he writes : "This much ... seems established : an attempt was made to check both the spread of Judaism and of Isis-worship" [63].

As long as Sejanus lived, the situation of the Roman Jews remained precarious, but when he died in A.D. 31, Tiberius reverted to the policy inaugurated by Caesar. The hateful measures were not rescinded but forgotten; once again the Jews might live according to their established customs [64]. Dio states that in A.D. 41 they were numerous again in Rome [65]. Giulio Firpo sums up the affair by saying that we should conceive of it neither as a change in the status of the Jews nor as the beginning of a persecution, but rather as a police-action for the protection of the public order and the 'mores antiqui' [66]. True enough, but all the same, the authorities felt that the Jews were capable of threatening this order and those mores.

g. Caligula and the Jews

An incident revealing the thoughts a Roman Emperor might harbour took place when Philo came to Rome with an embassy to plead the cause of the Jews in Alexandria (of which I shall speak later). The Emperor of those days was Caligula (37-41). To the extreme merriment of his Greek cronies, he asked the Jews why they did not eat pork. Obviously he found the Jewish food taboos perfectly ridiculous. He took leave of the embassy with the following words. "They (the Jews) seem to me a people unfortunate rather than wicked and to be foolish in refusing to believe that I have got the nature of a god" [67].

Later this same irresponsible ruler hit on the idea of having his statue erected in the Temple of Jerusalem [68]. Nothing, of course, was better calculated to create considerable disturbance among the Jews, a nation which Caligula considered 'his worst enemy' [69]. The murder of this Emperor prevented this sacrilege.

This turns our attention to Jerusalem and to Judaea. For it was not in the Diaspora but in the Jewish homeland that the relations between Rome and Jewry grew most problematic.

2. The Jewish homeland

a. The first contacts between Rome and Judaea

The very first contact between Rome and Judaea dates from the year 163 B.C. Under the impression of the resounding victories of Judas the Maccabee, King Antiochus V of Syria conceded the Jews the right to live according to their ancestral laws and customs. Two Roman legates, Quintus Memmius and Titus Manius, sent a letter to the Jews in which they expressed their approval for these Syrian concessions; they asked the Jews to send ambassadors to Rome [70]. In this way Palestine became an element in the Roman power game. Rome had already been repeatedly at war with the Seleucid Empire; she was quite content with the Jewish rebellion which blocked the Syrian southward expansion.

The second step came two years later, in 161 B.C. Judas, having heard how powerful the Romans were, sent two ambassadors to Rome in order to conclude a treaty of friendship with the Empire; these ambassadors were even admitted into the Senate House. A treaty of mutual assistance and friendship was concluded. The Senate even wrote to King Demetrius I of Syria in a menacing tone to tell him that he had to leave the Jews alone [71].

b. Hasmonaean conquests

During the Wars of Maccabees the Jews of Judaea fought themselves free . These wars lasted, all in all, more than twenty years [72], but in 140 B.C. Simon the Maccabee might rightly consider himself as the man who had liberated his people from the rule of the Syrian Seleucids. In that year a popular assembly acknowledged Simon as ethnarch, as the chief of his people, as supreme commander, and as High Priest, so that he combined in his person the highest political, military, and religious functions [73]. The rule of the Seleucids had been exchanged for that of the Hasmonaeans, the clan name of the Maccabees.

The Hasmonaean regime was expansionist. Already Judas the Maccabee and his brother Simon had campaigned far beyond the frontiers of Judaea. The High Priest Johannes Hyrcanus (135-104 B.C.), the successor of Simon, appeared at the head of his army in Samaria in 129 B.C. where he conquered several cities, the ancient Sichem, for instance, and Mount Garizim, where he destroyed the temple, the centre of the Samaritan cult [74]. After this he penetrated into Idumaea (the ancient Edom, to the south of Judaea) which he subjected; the inhabitants were forcefully judaized, circumcision and all. "And from that time they have continued to be Jews" [75]. It is said that Hyrcanus hated the Samaritans because of the way they had injured the Jewish cause during the wars of liberation; in 107 B.C. he besieged the capital Samaria which capitulated to him after a year [76]; he then razed it to the ground [77]. For about a half century Samaria remained a Hasmonaean possession.

Another Hasmonaean conquest was the territory just east of the Dead Sea and the Jordan, known as Peraea (which means 'the land beyond the Jordan'). The High Priest Alexander Jannaeus (103-76 B.C.) forcibly judaized the non-Jewish population he found there [78]. In Jesus' days it had a tetrarch of its own, a Herodian. As Schürer remarks, "since the three provinces (Judaea, Galilee, and Peraea) were also frequently divided politically, they were regarded as in certain respects different lands" [79]. A Talmudic Rabbi defined this as a difference in quality too, Judaea being the grain, Galilee the straw, and Peraea the chaff [80].

c. The Hasmonaean High Priest a Roman vassal

For about a century hardly anything was heard of Roman-Jewish contacts. There was as yet no need for Rome to take an official stance with regard to Jewry before the middle of the first century B.C. But then Pompey arrived and conquered the whole of Palestine which meant the end of the Hasmonaean kingdom. This happened in 65 B.C. [81]. Pompey detached Samaria from Judaea and combined it with the province of Syria [82]. He did not think of respecting the independence of Judaea. "An independent Judaea was only necessary for Rome as long as the Syrian Empire existed". i.e. in order to block Syrian expansion southward. "What is more : the existence at the (southern) frontier of the new Roman province (Syria) of an independent Jewish state that, during a whole century, had stubbornly defended its right to freedom and had never for a moment stopped pursuing its fight against a far mightier opponent, might in the future lead to undesirable complications" [83]. Considerations such as these sealed the fate of Judaean independence. Making use of disagreements in the bosom of the Hasmonaean family, Pompey intervened in the affairs of the country. In Vol. X I have described what happened. Pompey had to besiege the Temple Mount which he conquered in

63 B.C.; the number of victims was enormous. The victor made one of the Hasmonaeans, Hyrcanus II, High Priest with political authority; henceforward the High Priests were vassals of Rome [84]. Although under firm Roman control, Judaea (with Galilee) retained a modest measure of autonomy; it was not attached to Syria, although the Roman governors of this province intervened at will in Judaea [85].

d. Rome and the Herodians

In the following two decades Judaea was torn apart by civil strife and became the sport of ambitious men during the last phase of the civil wars in the Empire. In this struggle the last Hasmonaean, Antigonus, played a fatal role. In 40 B.C., during a Parthian invasion, Syria was temporarily occupied; the Parthians even entered Jerusalem where they were welcomed as liberators. Antigonus was made King and High Priest of the Jews; according to Josephus, he promised the Parthians a thousand talents and five hundred women if they were ready to give him the throne [86]. It goes without saying that his rule could only last as long as the Parthians were at hand. Moreover, a powerful claimant was waiting in the wings, Herod I the Great, who, at the instigation of Mark Antony and with the approval of Caesar, had been proclaimed King of the Jews by the Senate [87]. Once the Parthians had been successfully expelled from Syria and Palestine, Herod, with a Roman army and troops of his own, marched on Jerusalem where Antigonus held out till 37 B.C. Then he was made captive and beheaded; with this event every form of Hasmonaean rule came to an end [88].

Herod, king from 37 to 4 B.C. (under his reign Jesus was born) was a strange mixture of the tendencies of the time : he was 'an Edomite (Idumaean) by race, a circumcised Jew by profession, and mainly a pagan by culture' [89]. Although he greatly extended his realm and although he built a new and magnificent Temple, he was hated by the Jewish populace which saw in him an alien and was extremely critical of his life-style. It is important to note that he was king but not High Priest. And as king he was a client of Rome, of course [90].

The Senate had never promised to make Herod's rule hereditary; so, when he died in 4 B.C., Augustus could do what he thought fit. Several delegations from Judaea appeared at his court, one of them from the Jewish population, which advocated making Judaea into a Roman province, rather than having to receive Herod's son Archelaus as king [91]. The Emperor acquiesced in their wish in so far as Archelaus did not become king but 'ethnarch'. Galilee was detached from Judaea and became a separate Tetrarchy under Archelaus' brother Antipas [92]. Archelaus succeeded in making himself so immensely unpopular that Augustus had no choice but to depose him in A.D. 6 [93].

e. Judaea made into a province

The time had come to solidify Rome's grip on Palestine, which was an important strategic link between Syria and Egypt, between Asia and Africa. No new king or ethnarch was nominated; instead, Judaea was turned into a province [94] under a procurator 'with full powers, including the infliction of capital punishment' [95]. Judaea was, as Millar states, 'a second-rank province', under imperial (not senatorial) supervision; no legions were to be stationed in it but only auxiliary troops. The governors were appointed and dismissed by the Emperor. Their official residence was Caesarea on the coast, a heathen city that Jews preferably did not enter [96]. The procurators disliked Jerusalem with its fanatical and, in their eyes, superstitious population. However, every year at the Passover festival, the procurator came to Jerusalem because then an outbreak of unrest was always feared. For the same reason the Holy City had a permanent garrison, which was exceptional for a provincial city; it was stationed in the Antonia, the Roman fortress bordering on the north-west corner of the Temple complex. From its walls the sentries could overlook the Temple square [97].

The very unruly Galilee, where fanatical Zealots were active against foreign rule, was governed by Antipas until his death in A.D. 9; after a short interlude with another ruler, the Emperor Claudius in A.D. 44 dissolved the Tetrarchy and placed Galilee under the jurisdiction of the procurator of Judaea. So much for the political allegiance of the Jews of Palestine. There are elements in this situation which may explain why Judaea became the platform where the Jewish rebellion of A.D. 66 originated.

3. Messianic expectations

a. Herod's fear of a Messiah

As vassal-king of Rome, Herod I the Great constantly feared the appearance of a Messiah, false or true, a real Jewish king who would oust him. He had every reason to do so. He was no descendent of King David, and as an Idumaean, that is, as one of the hated nation of Edom [98], he was not Jewish [99]. There was a prophecy current, spread by the Pharisees, that "by God's decree Herod's throne would be taken from him, both from himself and from his descendants ... These things were reported to the king" [100]. The position of the king was sufficiently insecure to make him afraid of a Messiah [101].

b. Mutual distrust in Palestine

Messianic expectations were part of a larger context, that of the fundamental relationship of the Roman Empire and Judaism. The background of Roman policy with regard to Judaea and Galilee is that Rome was and remained distrustful of the loyalty of the population. The Romans knew, of course, how strongly the Jews felt about their presence. They left them a fair measure of autonomy; above all, they did not interfere in their religious affairs. On the whole, they tried not be provocative, always afraid as they were of a sudden outburst of what they considered 'religious fanaticism'. It cannot be said that, certainly in the first decades of the province, the Romans treated the Jews badly; perhaps they were more lenient to them than to other subjected nations.

But when all is said and done, in the eyes of the Jews the Romans were guilty of an unforgivable crime : they, pagans as they were, should simply not tread the sacred ground of the Holy Land; they soiled it with their presence. The orthodox and pious population had only one wish : out with them! Whether this was to be achieved by direct violence, as the Zealots wanted, or whether one would have to wait for the promised Messiah, as the Pharisees thought, makes only a difference of degree. But the basic attitude of the Jewish people with regard to the Roman occupation must be dubbed dualistic.

Emil Schürer defines this dualism in the following words : "The rule of aliens in the land of Israel constituted a glaring contrast between the ideal and reality. The land was the property of the chosen people. Only Israelites could own territory there. Even the renting of houses and fields to the Gentiles was, according to the rabbis, prohibited. Yet Gentiles had taken possession of the whole land. Thus, on the one hand, Gentile customs exerted a strong influence, and on the other, a very stout dividing-wall was erected against them" [102].

c. A dualistic distinction

In the eyes of the orthodox and the Pharisees Herod the Great was no more than a stooge of the Emperor. It was Augustus (and his successors) who stood for everything they abhorred. Roman paganism was, they found, the sheerest blasphemy. Orthodox Jewry believed that Israel was the chosen people, the beloved of Jahve, the nation that was providentially destined to bring forth the promised Messiah, the Redeemer. He would be King, the King of all nations; his coming would inaugurate a realm of universal peace. But this is exactly what the Roman Empire pretended to do, with its Pax Romana, its universal peace for all mankind. Rome too understood her mission as a religious one; she was the delegate of the gods on earth which gave her the right to rule all nations and subject them to her benevolent and salutary dominion.

It will be evident that we are in the presence here of a clear-cut dualistic distinction. Rome was not ready to accept the pretensions of the Jews; for orthodox Jews it was equally unthinkable to acquiesce in the politico-religious concept of the Romans. Josephus, himself a Jew, but not a nationalist, castigates his compatriots for their shortsightedness. "The power of the Romans is irresistible ... Nothing has escaped them ... Fortune is on their side, and God, who makes the imperium circulate from one nation to another [103], has now lodged it in Italy ... God is with the Romans ... You (the Jews) should know that you not only wage war on the Romans but on God himself" [104]. Could the real issue be expressed more clearly [105]?

4. Rebellious movements in the Jewish land

a. Rebellions throughout Galilee, Peraea and Judaea

Unrest was brewing at every point in the Jewish land. After the death of Herod the Great in 4 B.C. there were several insurrections. In Sepphoris in Galilee Judas, a brigand-chief who had already been at odds with Herod, with a considerable number of followers plundered royal arsenals; his aim seems to have been completely independent power, for he attacked all potential rivals, says Josephus [106]. In Peraea a royal slave, Simon, an imposing man, even assumed the diadem, as if he was king. He plundered far and wide and burnt down the royal palace at Jericho; with many of his adherents, he met his end at the hands of regular troops [107]. The next was, as Josephus writes, 'a mere shepherd', called Athongaeus, who also donned the royal diadem. He too employed an armed band, the principal objective of which "was to kill Roman and royalists (= Herodians)". His rebellion was beaten down by regulars, but meanwhile he had succeeded in 'making the whole of Judaea the scene of guerilla warfare' [108]. We may safely state that the period up to A.D. 66 was one of sudden and violent anti-Roman outbursts [109].

b. Uproar in Jerusalem

A far more serious outbreak took place in Jerusalem after the death of Herod. Its outbreak was caused by the arrival in town of the procurator of Syria, Sabinus, 'a shining example of the self-important minor official' [110]; this man wanted to lay his hands on the royal treasure, for which end he armed a band of slaves. The Jews must have seen this treasure as national property. It was just at the time of the feast of Pentecost so that great masses of believers were in the city. They rose and encircled Sabinus and his mob on the Temple Mount. There was a bloody fight in the Temple with many victims and much burning of porticoes, but the Roman succeeded in stealing the Temple treasure to the amount of four hundred talents.

This made the Jews so furious that they besieged Sabinus in the royal palace [111]. The desperate Sabinus asked the help of Quinctilius Varus, the governor of Syria (the one of the Teutoburgerwald [112]), who came with a large regular force. Without much difficulty he relieved Sabinus; Judaea was thoroughly searched for what Josephus calls 'turbulent individuals', two thousand of whom were crucified. In Galilee the city of Sepphoris was burnt to the ground and its inhabitants sold into slavery [113]. The revolt, which had proliferated all over Palestine, survived in Jewish memory as 'the War of Varus' [114].

c. No mortal masters

When after the short reign of Archelaus Judaea became a Roman province in A.D. 6, the Roman tax system was introduced. Judas, a Galilean [115], found the obligation of paying tax to Rome a reason for revolt; those who paid taxes were cowards in his eyes. Jews should not tolerate mortal masters since God was their lord [116]. This man who, according to Josephus, was a scholar, a sophist, became the founder of the sect of the Zealots, the most fanatical anti-Roman movement of those days [117]. In the view of the Zealots Rome was the ultimate enemy; without her destruction there would never be a Messianic kingdom. The man at the head of this utterly pagan Roman Empire was a godless tyrant, the Emperor, a devil in human shape, the opponent of the Messiah; he persecuted the pious and crucified them. Rome's power would be destroyed by the Israelite host of the last days under the leadership of the Messiah; he would annihilate the enemy in a miraculous way. The downfall of Rome would usher in the dominion of God which, by the same token, would be the dominion of Israel [118]. The Zealots, therefore, incorporated the dualistic tendencies of Judaism in these decades.

d. Bad incidents

Although the Jews of Palestine enjoyed the same privileges as their co-religionists in the Diaspora, they were a far greater problem for the Romans than their brethren of the Dispersion. "Grave disturbances in Judaea signified inacceptable risks, in an always strategically delicate sector ... This required the maintenance of order and control at any cost" [119]. In the first decades of Judaea as a province they had behaved with tact, with the notable exception of Sabinus, but after A.D. 50 there was a dramatic and fateful change. Then the hard-fisted manner in which Roman governors maintained order was perfectly calculated to incite the people to rebellion, 'as if by secret arrangement, systematically and deliberately' [120].

Every now and then, Roman underlings behaved in an insulting way. Around A.D. 50, during the Passover festival, when tension was always at its most acute, a Roman legionary, standing guard near the Temple square, committed an indecency (he showed the crowd his privy parts [121]). The indignant Jews rushed to the procurator, Ventidius Cumanus, to ask for excuses and satisfaction. The governor tried to calm them and asked them not to make an uproar during the festival. But he was howled down whereupon he became nervous and sent in the military. These restored order at the price of thousands and thousands of dead. So this Passover ended in blood [122].

Sometimes we see the Zealots in action. Shortly after the incident related above, some Jews travelling from Galilee to Jerusalem were murdered in a Samaritan village. Cumanus, bribed by the Samaritans, closed his eyes. Then a band of Zealots appeared who laid the surroundings waste and killed all the inhabitants [123].

e. Felix after the Zealots

After Cumanus came Felix (c.52-c.60), a freedman and a favourite of Claudius. Under his harsh rule things went from bad to worse. "Practising every kind of cruelty and lust, he wielded royal power with the instincts of a slave", says Tacitus contemptuously [124]. He was constantly behind the

Zealots who, in his eyes, just as in those of Josephus, were no more than 'bandits'; however, the people sympathized with them. Treason enabled him to lay his hands on Eleazar, one of the Zealot leaders, and to send him to Rome, together with many others. "It is impossible to calculate the number of bandits whom he crucified and of the citizens whom he tracked down and punished as their accomplishes" [125]. The only result was that lawlessness steadily increased [126].

f. The Sicarii in action

It was now the turn of the 'Sicarii', the 'dagger-people' (from 'sica', dagger [127]), murderous people who suddenly struck, preferably in the middle of a crowd. They belonged to the most radically anti-Roman, anti-pagan sections of the population; in their hatred against the occupying power they thought everything permissible, even assassination. Their targets were all those who collaborated with the Romans or who were, rightly or wrongly, suspected of doing so. A great many people might fear that they would be done away in this abrupt and savage way. Their principal victim was nobody less than a former High Priest, Jonathan ben Anan [128]. This man was far from being pro-Roman; he had been instrumental in the deposition of the cruel governor Cumanus [129]. His successor Felix was not a hair better, and Jonathan had rebuked him for his behaviour. The governor, who took this very ill, hired Sicarii who struck at Jonathan when he ascended to the Temple [130].

g. Growing anarchy

There was frenzy afoot. People resorted massively to the desert there to await the downfall of the Romans and the coming of the Kingdom of God [131]. An anonymous Egyptian, calling himself a prophet, succeeded in assembling a large band of followers with whom he planned to ascend the Mount of Olives; from there, like a second Joshua, he would order the walls of Jerusalem to come down, so that he and his followers could freely enter the city. Felix set his legionaries upon him; they dispersed the group, killing some four hundred of them and making two hundred prisoners. The prophet himself came away unscathed [132].

Felix's hard hand did not help the Romans at all. Judaea was gliding off into a state of anarchy. Political agitators and self-appointed prophets "incited many to revolt, exhorting them to assert their independence, and threatening to kill anyone who submitted willingly to Roman domination and to suppress all those who would willingly accept servitude". Deploying in gangs throughout the country, they looted houses and set villages on fire so that all Judaea "felt the effect of their frenzy" [133]. The method they used for reaching their objectives was that employed by all terrorist gangs in history : destabilizing society.

Felix was recalled at some moment between 58 and 60 and replaced by Porcius Festus, a moderate man. But the harm done was already irreparable. The new governor proved unable to quell the anarchy. When he died in 62, he was succeeded first by Albinus (62-64) and then by Gessius Florus (64-66), two pronounced scoundrels, Roman magistrates of the worst kind; both plundered the country, its cities, and their inhabitants to their hearts' desire. It is as though Rome reserved the worst scum she had among her magistrates for ruling over Judaea. She bore a heavy responsibility for the outbreak of the revolt. But the other side was not without blame either. Part of the Jewish population reacted to the Roman brutalities and extortions with indiscriminate murder. Who would be surprised that the powder-keg finally exploded? It was the governor himself who put the spark to the tinder.

h. The outbreak of the revolt

Florus, who was obviously not rich enough yet, in April or May 66 planned to requisition seventeen talents from the Temple treasury, claiming it was for the service of the Emperor (Nero at that time) [134]. He took a detachment of soldiers with him to the Temple; probably he expected resistance. A riotous crowd, railing loudly at Florus, assembled in front of the Temple; a basket went around to collect money for this apparently poor, destitute man [135]. Taking this as an insult, the procurator marched on the city with cavalry and infantry and took up his abode in the royal palace. As Josephus writes, "the Jews passed the night in fear and humiliation" [136].

The next morning Florus summoned the chief priests and the notables, made them stand at the foot of the dais on which he was seated, and insisted on apologies. The answer was that he should not take notice of a few irresponsible hotheads who, anyway, were not be found. This retort made the procurator still more furious; he ordered his men to attack the market square and massacre everybody they found there. The soldiers went far beyond this noble duty; they penetrated into the houses killing left and right. Peaceful and harmless citizens were arrested and crucified. The total number of victims is given as thirty-six hundred [137]. When Berenice, the sister of King Agrippa II [138], attempted to intervene, she was threatened by the soldiery so that she had to barricade herself in the palace [139].

Agrippa, who was in Alexandria in the time of the disturbances, hastened to Jerusalem; on June 3, haranguing the crowd from the roof of his palace, he exhorted them to be obedient to the Roman authorities. The people declared they were ready to obey the Emperor. But when he asked them to be subservient to Florus too, their patience snapped. They became so furious that he hastily left the city [140].

5. The First Jewish War, A.D. 66-70

a. Fighting in Jerusalem

There was open rebellion now. A party of extremists surprised the fortress of Masada, near the south-western shore of the Dead Sea, massacred its Roman garrison, and encamped a Jewish one in it [141]. Meanwhile, Eleazar, the son of the High Priest Ananias, decided to interrupt the daily sacrifice for the well-being of the Emperor [142]; it was a Zealot idea that the most holy place in the world should not be defiled by sacrifices offered on behalf of a pagan ruler who thought himself to be a god [143]. According to Schürer, this "was tantamount to an open declaration of revolt against the Romans" [144]. The more moderate leaders tried in vain to make the Zealots desist from this measure [145]. At the request of these moderates, Agrippa sent three thousand horsemen to help them; their squadrons drove the rebels from the upper city but were unable to conquer the lower city and the Temple [146].

There was now not only a anti-Roman revolt on but also a civil war. Heavy fighting went on in the city for seven days, with the rebels gaining the upper hand. They reconquered the upper city and set the palaces of the High Priest and the Herodian family and the public archives on fire. Ananias himself was murdered. Later even the Roman fortress in town, the Antonia, next to the Temple square, was captured and set on fire. The Roman cohorts took their refuge in three fortified towers of the Herodian palace in the upper city. Finally, these soldiers had to surrender their arms, and, in spite of a guarantee of free withdrawal, were butchered to the last man [147].

b. Zealot and Roman ferocity

Thus the rebels began to conduct what became known as 'the Jewish War' in a radically dualistic way : everything and everybody in Judaea that was Roman had to be wiped out, and preferably also that whole heathen Empire, if possible. Where they could, the Romans paid back in kind. In Caesarea, according to Josephus, in one hour's time twenty thousand Jews were massacred; those who succeeded in escaping were caught and brought in chains to the navy arsenal [148]. By way of reaction Jewish bands fell upon villages in Syria and in the south, burning and killing as they went [149].

As a reprisal, the Syrians began to slaughter the Jews living in their midst; their possessions were plundered. The one who had killed the most Jews, writes Josephus, was considered the most glorious [150]. In Ascalon twenty-five hundred Jews were murdered, in Ptolemais two thousand, in Tyre numerous others [151]. Even in Alexandria, with its strong Jewish element, incidents between Jews and Greeks took place. Finally, Tiberius Alexander, the prefect, sent the troop into the Jewish quarters; they were allowed to stab and plunder freely. The victims were innumerable [152].

c. A failed Roman attack on Jerusalem

Of course, the Romans had to react. During the summer of A.D. 66 Cestius Gallus, the governor of Syria, assembled a considerable force of one legion, two thousand battle-hardened men from other legions, and six cohorts of cavalry, while many auxiliary troops were provided by vassal-kings. Agrippa was present in person [153]. In September this force began to move, scorching the earth where it went; finally, it encamped near Jerusalem [154].

Starting from Mount Scopus, at three miles from the walls, Cestius began attacking the city, storming it for five days on end. On the sixth day a Roman shock-battallion, supported by archers, reached the Temple Mount and prepared to set the gate on fire, but finally failed in its attempt. It should be noted that during this siege the moderates were ready to open the gates for Cestius [155]. But the governor lost nerve and withdrew.

When the retreating Romans were marching through a narrow gorge, they were surprised by the Jews. In the ensuing fight a great number of legionaries fell, among them several high officers, while the Romans had to abandon almost all of their train. With a small part of his army Cestius himself escaped to Antioch. The Roman losses amounted to five thousand three hundred infantry and four hundred and eighty cavalry. With the captured siege-machines the victors triumphantly returned to Jerusalem [156].

d. Palestine liberated

We are now in October 66. The result of their victory was that the Jews had liberated their country, from Judaea in the south to Galilee in the north. The moderate part remained opposed to the rebellion which they considered a foolhardy adventure. Their leaders now left the city and joined Cestius in Antioch [157]. Amongst those who also left Jerusalem were the Christians - the whole Christian community, says Eusebius; they migrated to Pella, a city east of the Jordan in Peraea [158]. From this time the early Christian Church ceased to be a Jerusalem-based community.

Probably somewhat confounded by their unexpected but complete success, the Jews, in view of the unavoidable Roman counter-attack, began to organize their defence; commanders were appointed for the Holy City, Judaea, Idumaea, and Galilee; in this last country Flavius Josephus, the (future) historian of this war, was put in charge [159]. Since this northern province would bear the brunt of the Roman onslaught, he had an important but also difficult task, for the Galilean population was untrained for war. In his history of the war he boasts that he put an army of a hundred thousand young men on foot which he trained in the Roman manner [160].

But he was not generally trusted. He "knew the Romans too well to believe in a real and final success of the rebellion. From the outset his heart was not wholly in the cause he represented and at times he somewhat incautiously permitted this to be seen" [161]. As a consequence, he barely escaped being deposed by the high command in Jerusalem [162].

e. Vespasian in command

"When Nero heard of the reverses that had occurred in Judaea, he was seized, as will go without saying, by a secret sentiment of bewilderment and alarm, but publicly he showed only arrogance and anger" [163]. The man he needed was Vespasian, the future emperor, an experienced and trusted military commander. In the winter of 66/67 Vespasian travelled to Syria to collect troops there, while his son Titus, yet another future emperor, was sent to Alexandria with orders to bring Legio XV from there [164]. The forces that father and son marshalled between them amounted to some sixty thousand men, three legions in full strength, twenty-three cohorts of auxiliaries, six battalions of cavalry, and finally the contingents brought by the vassal-kings wich, once again, included Agrippa [165].

f. The reduction of Galilee

The beginning of the Roman campaign in April or May 67 constituted a pathetic anti-climax for the Jews. As soon as the legions, 'burning for combat', were crossing the frontier of Galilee, Josephus' raw conscripts began to deplore their defection and dispersed in all directions, "not only before any fight had taken place but even before they had sighted the enemy". Without a sword being drawn, the whole country-side fell into the hands of the Romans. With what was left of his forces Josephus fled to Tiberias. Only the Galilean fortresses remained under the control of the Jews [166].

Capturing the fortress-towns proved not such an easy task as Vespasian may have expected. True enough, Gabara was conquered in the first assault; not one inhabitant survived it. The surrounding villages were devastated, and their population sold into slavery [167]. Then came the turn of Jotapata. Josephus left Tiberias in order to defend the town, although, as he confesses himself, he did not believe in the success of the insurgence, but "he had rather die a thousand deaths than betray his fatherland" [168]. Situated on the top of a mountain, Jotapata was strong enough to withstand a siege for some time. The first Roman assaults ended in failure. At one occasion Vespasian himself was wounded in his foot by a javelin.

On the fourty-seventh day of the siege a deserter notified the Roman commander that the besieged were so exhausted that even the sentries on the walls could not keep their eyes open. On the strength of this communication Titus scaled the wall with a handful of men, killed the sleeping sentries, and without making any noise, penetrated into the city, helped by a thick mist. They opened the gates and let the legionaries in. A horrible carnage followed; the choice was between being killed and being enslaved. The town with its fortifications was razed to the ground. The day was July 7, 67 [169]. After the capture of the town, Josephus was found hiding in a cave; he was arrested and brought before Vespasian who spared his life [170].

During the siege of Jotapata, Vespasian dispatched a task-force to capture the town of Japha [171], not far from the beleaguered city. Two thousand fugitives were stranded there between the Roman lines and the walls of the town; these were all massacred. When the town itself was stormed and captured, all the males were killed - to the number of fifteen thousand, says Josephus -, while the women were destined for slavery [172]. According to Josephus, who speaks contemptuously of them, the Samaritans too were considering rebellion. In order to forestall this, Vespasian sent another taskforce which found them assembled on their holy mountain, the Garizim. Invited to surrender, the Samaritans refused after which the mountain was scaled; eleven thousand six hundred persons in all lost their lives [173]. The war had evidently assumed a genocidal character.

g. The reduction of Agrippa's townships

The campaign of 67 seemed to be at an end and the troops were already in their winter-quarters, when news came that Tiberias and Taricheai had revolted. Ironically enough, both towns formed part of the kingdom of Agrippa II who was such a staunch friend of Vespasian. The revolt was not generally supported in the towns, as it was nowhere in the Jewish lands; the loyal leaders of Tiberias fled to Vespasian imploring him to spare the town. The instigator of the revolt, Jesus ben Saphat, an old enemy of Josephus, had to fall back on Taricheai [174]. Without meeting resistance the Romans took Tiberias and did not molest its inhabitants; they then proceeded to Taricheai. The forces of Jesus ben Saphat were defeated by the legionaries - of whom 'a supernatural frenzy' had taken possession - in the plain just north of the town. Riding through the water of the lake, the Romans under the command of Titus entered the town from the unwalled lake-side and made a great slaughter there until Titus stopped it.

Vespasian came in person to sit in judgment over the town. He divided the indigenous population from the rest because it had disapproved of the revolt. He obviously had some scruples against killing the rebels, but his friends overcame them by assuring him that "against Jews there could be no question of impiety" [175]. This revealing judgment shows how deeply, how dualistically anti-Jewish the Roman attitude was [176]. Vespasian permitted the immigrants who, in his eyes, were the real rebels, to leave the town along the road to Tiberias. On their way thither the legionaries killed the twelve hundred persons who were considered useless; six thousand robust men were dispatched to Greece to work there at the construction of a canal through the

Isthmus of Corinth. The last four hundred Vespasian presented to Agrippa who sold them into slavery [177].

h. John of Gischala

As always after a military or political failure, the question arose who was to blame for the loss of Galilee. For the Zealots this was not a difficult question : the fault lay entirely with the leadership in Jerusalem whose conduct of the war was found not energetic enough. The man who brought this leadership down was John of Gischala, 'an impostor with a very subtle spirit', wrote Josephus [178]. Gischala was a small town in northern Galilee, the modern Al-Jish. It was the last town in Galilee to be subjected by the Romans. Although the mood of its inhabitants was not warlike, John succeeded in organizing the resistance; then Vespasian sent Titus thither with cavalry [179]. Titus, reports Josephus, did not wish to take the town by storming it since he feared that his horsemen would massacre the population, "and he was already satiated with carnage" [180].

During the ensuing negotations with the Romans, John escaped in the night from the town with his infantry, mainly consisting of Zealots, and took the road to Jerusalem. Many citizens, with their women and children, accompanied him, glad to be out of the reach of the horsemen. But John, who was a pitiless man, felt encumbered by this lamenting crowd, and abandoned them to their fate, continuing his southbound march [181]. When on the next day Titus had entered the town without encountering resistance, he sent his squadrons after John who had already reached Jerusalem. Not finding the Zealots, the horsemen threw themselves on the non-combatants, killed some six thousand fugitives, and brought nearly three thousand women and children back. With this event the last resistance in Galilee ended.

j. Civil war in Jerusalem

It was November 67 when John and his party entered the Holy City. The Romans were weak, he told the inhabitants; they would never be able to scale the walls of the city. The young men rallied eagerly to him, and from all Judaea armed bands - 'nothing but robbers', says Josephus contemptuously - came to join him [182].

The first target of the fanatical hatred of the Zealots was the priestly aristocracy whom they suspected of wishing to deliver the town into the hands of the enemy [183]. A number of aristocrats, some of them members of the Herodian family, were thrown into prison where, somewhat later, they were murdered [184]. Wanting to have a High Priest of their own choice, the Zealots designated one by lot, a simple citizen, utterly unknown, called Phannias (also spelled as Phanni or Pinchas). The simple soul had not the slightest idea of what a High Priest had to do but they hoisted them into the sacred vestments and summarily briefed him on how to act [185].

Having had enough now, those of the old leaders who were still free in their movements, began to recruit men in order to fight the Zealots. With those whom they had assembled they drove the Zealots - who were in the minority - into the inner court of the Temple [186]. This is, of course, plain civil war, and one with the same dualistic character as the Jewish-Roman war and intimately connected with it. For the Zealots it was : who is not for us is against us, and since the moderate party was not supporting them, it was considered pro-Roman. Which meant that the moderates had to be destroyed.

Having been reduced to such straits, the Zealots resolved to call the Idumaeans to their assistance; they were not ashamed to ask the help of the hereditary enemies of Israel [187]. The Idumaeans, or Edomites [188], were only too quick to respond to this invitation and with twenty thousand men marched on Jerusalem. But the old leadership was still in command of the city and did not let them in [189]. On the night of their arrival a violent thunderstorm broke over the city; torrential rains fell and thunder-clap followed thunder-clap. The shivering Idumaeans stood beneath the walls, protecting themselves against the downpour with their shields above their heads. In this ordeal some daring Zealots groped their way to the gate near their allies, sawed it open, and allowed them in [190].

Hardly were the Idumaeans in than they began to kill left and right and to plunder to their hearts' content. The inhabitants were hacked down in masses. No quarter was given; people were slaughtered 'like a herd of impure animals'. Josephus estimates the number of those killed at twelve thousand [191]. Having fulfilled their noble task, the Idumaeans returned home [192]. But now the Zealots themselves took over and made many new victims. With John of Gischala in command, there was only one punishment : the capital one. Jerusalem was in the grip of a reign of terror [193].

k. Vespasian leaves the scene

Gleefully observing this spectacle, Vespasian's officers exhorted him to take his chance and, profiting from the confusion, capture Jerusalem. But the commander-in-chief feared that in case of an attack the two parties would unite again; he would rather let them weaken themselves. In the meantime he could rest his army [194]. In the spring of 68 he made his first incursion into Judaea. He was able to instal his Legio V in a fortified camp at Emmaus within walking distance of the capital [195]. Somewhat later, on June 20, Jericho was occupied where all the inhabitants still in town were killed [196]. Everything was now ready for an all-out attack on Jerusalem. But then something unexpected happened.

On June 9, 68, the Emperor Nero was murdered. This news reached Vespasian when he was at Caesarea [197]. He immediately suspended the operations in order to see what turn the events at Rome would take; then he heard that Galba had become emperor. He sent Titus to Rome to receive the new ruler's orders with regard to the Jewish war, but his son had not yet reached the imperial capital when, on January 15, 69, Galba in his turn was assassinated [198]. He was succeeded by Otho.

The troubles in Rome gave the Jews a year of respite, but in June 69, with Jerusalem in a state of complete anarchy, Vespasian reopened the offensive. Now almost all of Judaea was occupied which left the capital in an isolated position [199]. But it was not Vespasian who would lead his legions in the final assault on the Jewish capital. Vitellius, a successful general, contested Otho for the emperorship; after Otho's suicide on April 17, 69, he became the sole ruler. Or so he thought, for now Vespasian entered the fray.

Leaving Palestine behind him, he was proclaimed emperor in Alexandria on July 1, 69. Later, when Vitellius had been murdered on December 20, 69, he crossed to Italy and ascended the throne in the summer of 70. He left the task he had not completed in the hands of his son Titus.

1. Jerusalem besieged

For the siege of Jerusalem Titus had four regular legions at his disposal, plus a great number of auxiliaries from Syria to which force the contingents of the vassal-kings must be added [200]. Legio X, while pitching camp on the Mount of Olives, was so fiercely attacked by Jewish detachments that it was almost driven off; it was only Titus's great personal bravery that enabled it to keep the position [201]. But although an enormous danger threatened the Holy City, party strife within its walls continued as though no enemy were near. In the spring of 69 a Zealot band under the command of Simon bar-Giora had found its way into Jerusalem. Fed up as it was with the despotism of John, the people welcomed him, but discovered soon enough that they now had two equally despotic masters [202]. The two Zealot factions were now fighting each other to which somewhat later a third, under Eleazar, a son of Simon, was added; John and Eleazar were each in possession of part of the Temple precincts - all this with the enemy before the gates [203]!

Titus started his approach of the city from the north. Here he began battering the outer wall with his siege-machines. It was only then, when the wall was crumbling, that the factions in town joined hands for a common defence [204]. They fought bravely and almost frustrated the Roman designs. After fourteen days a breach was made in the wall; a little later the attackers were masters of the whole outer defense [205]. They broke down a long stretch of it on May 25, 70. A few days later Titus moved his machinery to the inner northern wall; nine days after the capture of the outer northern wall he was in possession of it [206].

Titus next began to build ramparts in front of the northern wall of the upper city in the west and of the Antonia in the east; his four legions were massed between the second and third walls [207]. Food had by now become so scarce in the city that many poor people took the risk of venturing outside the wall in search of food. Many were caught by the enemy and crucified in sight of the defenders; Josephus, who was present in the Roman camp, says that there were not enough crosses for so many victims [208]. Finally, the food situation became so critical that John distributed the oil and the wine which were used in the sacrificial cult to the people. Josephus writes with great indignation of this [209]. He obviously thought nothing of the fact that he, in this crucial hour, was on the side of the enemy.

In the dark night of July 24 the Romans attacked the Antonia; twenty legionaries got in through a breach, killed the sleeping sentries, and let their comrades in; the defenders were driven back into the adjoining Temple precincts after desperate fighting in the dark. The captured Antonia was razed to the ground [210]. It was on that same day that the daily offerings of the morning and evening sacrifices ended, never to be resumed [211].

m. The end of everything

After the fall of the Antonia, Titus concentrated his efforts on the Temple area. It would be no easy task to conquer it since the large complex was surrounded by high walls. He prepared the assault very carefully by erecting four ramparts against the outer wall of the complex [212]. With these works steadily progressing, John, the Jewish commander, assured his men that the city would never be taken, since it belonged to God [213]. On August 27 the Roman battering-rams were brought into action, but to no avail because the walls were too high and too thick [214]. Titus then ordered his men to set the gates on fire. The flames quickly did their work; turning inwards, the conflagration began to consume the porticoes along the inner side of the wall [215]. When the fire was extinguished, the outer Temple court lay practically open for the Romans.

At this stage Titus called a council of war to discuss what to do with the Temple. Some pleaded for destroying it since it was the great rallying-point of those rebellious Jews; others were prepared to spare it if only the defenders would evacuate it, but to burn it down in case of resistance being offered. If we may believe Josephus, the supreme commander himself would not hear of destroying such a beautiful building; orders were given to the troops to spare it [216]. However, there is a real chance that the Jewish historiographer wanted to exonerate Titus.

On August 29, the Romans, now in possession of the outer court, opened the assault on the inner court. According to tradition, the Temple had been set on fire by the Babylonian King Nebuchadnessar II in that self-same night of 568 B.C. [217]. During a fierce Jewish counter-attack, a Roman legionary, 'pushed on by a superhuman impulse', says Josephus, but contrary to the orders given, threw a brand through a window of one of the chambers that were built around the Temple itself. On hearing this fateful news, still according to Josephus' version of the events (we have no other), Titus came rushing in and ordered the soldiers to extinguish the flames. But the confusion was so great that his voice was not heard. Instead, his men, wild with fury, threw ever more firebrands into the building. All around the defenders fell in heaps [218].

The flames having not yet reached the interior of the Temple, Titus was able to enter the Holy and the Holy of Holies, looking around in amazement at the treasures he saw there. Still hoping to save the Temple, he gave orders to that effect [219]. But the soldiers were carried away by their fury, by their lust for booty, and also by their hatred of the Jews. When the fire reached the interior, Titus and his officers left; impeded by nobody, the flames did their work.

With the Temple still burning, the slaughter went on relentlessly; the legionaries massacred everyone they saw without regard for sex or age [220]. By command of Titus, the priests who surrendered were killed [221]. All the buildings around the Temple, including the Archives, and a great part of the lower city were equally put on fire on the orders of Titus [222]. The triumphant Romans planted their ensigns in the inner court (which was forbidden to pagans) and sacrificed to their gods there [223].

The last defenders retreated to the upper city. Methodically as ever, Titus prepared the attack on it. Ramparts were erected, battering-rams brought up. On September 25 a breach was made into the wall. Exhausted as the defenders were, there was little resistance. Whole families were found dead in their rooms; those still living were massacred. Soon this part of the town too was ablaze [224]. John of Gischala emerged from the subterranean tunnels, dying from hunger; he was imprisoned for life. His co-commander Simon was killed [225]. What remained of the town was demolished [226].

n. The last stand

Considering his task accomplished, Titus left the mopping up operations to his subordinates. In the country some fortresses were still holding out; they were captured the one after the other in the months following the fall of Jerusalem. The hardest nut to crack was Masada, a mountain fortress made famous by the excavations of Yadin. It stood on an almost inaccessible rock near the Dead Sea and was defended by the last Zealots under the command of Eleazar ben Yair. The Romans experienced the greatest difficulties in reducing this position. When finally the besiegers stood ready to storm it, the defenders first killed their families and then themselves. On their entering the fortress, the Romans were met by a profound silence [227]. With this event, which occurred in April 74, all resistance in Palestine was over.

6. Why was the Temple destroyed?

Let us pause for a moment and stare at the smouldering ruins of the Temple. Why did the Romans do what they did? They had not only beaten down a rebellion, as they had done so often and would do again in all parts of their Empire, they had also ripped out the heart of a religion - of the only religion that was fundamentally different from all religions they knew. The attitude of the Romans with regard to Jews and Judaism was at best one of arrogant tolerance, at worst one of a destructive dualism of which the burning Temple eloquently testified. For whether or not Titus gave the order to destroy it - we shall have to come back to this -, it was in any case not an accident but a deliberate act on the part of the furiously anti-Jewish legionaries.

Since the days of Augustus, the first Emperor, it was the god-given task of the Roman Empire to establish and safeguard the Pax Romana; all the nations of the Empire must enjoy the blessings of the general peace. The guarantee of this peace was the ruler; for this reason he was entitled to religious veneration by his subjects [228]. The protective deity of the Empire and its Pax Romana was Jupiter Capitolinus, so called because he had his earthly abode on the Capitoline hill in Rome which was also the political centre of Roman rule. It was he who gave Rome her victories; it was he who guaranteed the eternity of Roman dominion. And he was the personal protector of the Emperor who, in his turn, was an image of this divinity. According to the official imperial ideology, all peoples and nations might believe what they wanted and venerate all the godheads of their choice, if only they were prepared to sacrifice to the great imperial god [229].

But at the back of the Roman mind there lurked the dumb fear that the Empire might go the way of all the realms of Antiquity. The Romans were not really afraid of the western tribes and nations, but they were mightily apprehensive of the attitude of the Orientals. It was in the East that all the great Empires that had preceded the Roman one had held their sway. The Romans knew that they were not really accepted in the East, that they were seen there as parvenus and barbarians. Oracles and prophesies were rife that an oriental king would rise up and drive away the oppressors. In utterances and expressions such as these the East was pitted against the West along the old dualistic dividing line. The Jewish Sybilline books spoke of a fundamental conflict between Rome and Asia : Rome is a wench who will be chased away by her mistress [230].

Josephus mentions a prophecy which, according to him. had incited the Jews to go to war against the Romans, namely, that "in that time (sc. of the rebellion) a man of their country would become the master of the inhabited world; the Jews believed that this prediction referred to them" [231]. The Romans too were acquainted with this prophecy [232]. Roman fears that the Jewish revolt would spread over the whole Orient were not very real but they existed [233]. Schwier states that, after the end of the war and the destruction of the Temple, Rome became the ultimate enemy in Jewish apocalyptic books [234]. The political propaganda of the Flavians served to allay the dark fears the Romans had of the East [235].

For the Flavian dynasty the victory over the Jews was of paramount importance. On December 19, 69, the temple of Jupiter on the Capitol went up in flames during the fighting for the throne between the adherents of Vitellius and those of Vespasian. The Flavians were considered guilty of this deed which robbed the imperial god of his home. This meant that the emperorship of Vespasian began under bad auspices. The new dynasty was, therefore, in dire need of legitimation, the more so because they were widely seen as upstarts who did not come from a great noble family [236]. Imperial propaganda made the most of the victory in the Jewish War [237]. Schwier puts forward the hypothesis that there is a direct connection between the destruction of the Jupiter temple in Rome and that of Jahve in Jerusalem (there are only eight months between these two events) [238]. There is no direct evidence for this supposition but, anyhow, the Romans were not in the habit of destroying great cult centres; they rather incorporated them into their own politic-religious system.

In connection with this hypothesis Schwier supposes that the plans for the wholesale destruction on the Holy City and, in consequence, of the Temple were premeditated [239]. At least two ancient authors, Sulpicius Severus [240] and Orosius [241], impute the responsibility for it directly to Titus himself. Titus reproached the Jews for being continually rebellious since the day that Pompey brought them into the orbit of Rome, and now they had even resorted to open warfare [242]. Menacingly he said that he came to their city with severe orders which his father had given him to his regret [243]. Do these 'severe orders' leave much room for speculation? Add to this that an inscription on Titus's triumphal arch in Rome expressly states that he acted in accordance with the precepts and counsels of his father [244].

The commander-in-chief mentioned 'nation, town, and Temple' in one breath [245]. "Your people are dead, your Temple destroyed; and is not your town in my power?" [246]. His prediction that there would be no salvation for them, now that the Temple lay in ruins, make it clear that he, and probably his father too, saw the Temple as the symbol and centre of Jewish resistance

[247]. The elimination of this centre of an alien cult that was fundamentally inimical to Rome - Sulpicius thought that in the later Emperor's view the Jewish religion was illicit [248] - served to prove the supremacy of Jupiter Capitolinus [249].

Of course, Titus got his triumph once he had returned to the imperial city in June 71. A group of stoutly built Jewish POW's walked in the procession. But what will have struck the eyes of the onlookers more was that, among other utensils and valuables from the Temple, two sacred objects were carried through the streets of Rome, the Table of the Shewbread and the Seven-branched Candlestick; there was also a copy of the Torah to be seen [250]. In this way it was impressed upon the Romans, not only that the Flavian dynasty was legitimate, but still more, that their Jupiter, the Capitolinus, had triumphed over his competitor; the Jewish God was put into the custody of the Roman one [251]. The claim of Judaism that their religion was universal and their God the ruler of the whole world had been invalidated [252].

The modern visitor of Rome can still see the Arch of Titus standing on the Forum. On the inside of the gateway, reliefs show images of the triumphal procession; the Table of the Shewbread and the Candlestick are clearly discernible. No self-respecting Jew ever passes under this Arch. And in my opinion no Christian should do so either.

7. Between the two wars

a. The heavy hand of Rome

After the end of the war the heavy hand of Rome still rested on the Jews, not only those of Palestine but on the Diaspora Jews too. The humiliating temple tax, henceforward destined for Jupiter Capitolinus, was exacted with great severity under Domitian (81-96). Suetonius relates how Jews who tried to evade its payment by denying that they were Jewish were denounced to the authorities. He himself was present when a ninety-year-old man had to show in a law-court whether or not he was circumcized [253]. Domitian was particularly hostile to Judaism : the making of converts was heavily penalized and apostasy encouraged [254]. Under Nerva (96-98) the situation became somewhat more relaxed; this ruler would not make use of informers, but all the same the tax had to be paid [255].

b. New Jewish rebellions

After Masada had fallen, there were minor disturbances among the Jews of Alexandria and Cyrene; the Palestinian Jews, however, were sufficiently intimidated to keep a very low profile for the next half century. It was only at the end of Trajan's reign that the Jews, exasperated by the repression, became assertive again. Pent-up emotions, caused by oppression and humiliation, began to seek an outlet. If the Romans considered the Jews their enemies, the Jews were ready to pay back in kind; there was still a score to be paid off.

In Egypt and Cyrene, where the Jews were very numerous, a revolt broke out in 115. They fell on the Gentiles there, "as if possessed by a wild spirit of mutiny" [256]; Appian even speaks of a 'war' [257] which, indeed, caused him to take to his heels [258]. In the following weeks the sedition spread over the whole of Egypt; the Roman garrisons had the greatest difficulties in coping with it and did not always come off best. But finally they got the upper hand; in Alexandria a great number of Jews were put to death [259]. Much Jewish property was confiscated; a festival was instituted to commemorate the Roman victory [260].

In Cyrenaica the Jewish insurgents even had a 'king'. Some pagan temples were destroyed by them, but what is worse : they also massacred a great number of their non-Jewish compatriots; Dio even speaks of 220.000 victims. This same author has hair-raising things to say about atrocities committed by the insurgents [261]. In this he may have been inspired by hatred against the Jews, but we may take it for granted that they did not behave in the most gentle of ways. Trajan had to send an experienced commander to quell the revolt. It ended in the usual way : thousands and thousands of Cyrenaican and Egyptian Jews were executed [262].

Next it was the turn of Cyprus where, if we may believe Dio, 240.000 pagans were killed by Jews; they turned Salamis, the capital, upside down. The numbers are doubtless exaggerated but that there were many victims has to be accepted. Once the revolt was over, Jews were forbidden to live on the island; if a ship were stranded on its coast, Jews who managed to get ashore, were to be executed [263].

When the ageing Trajan was campaigning against Parthia, the Jews of Mesopotamia (in his rear, that is) began to rise. The Emperor sent a general against them with the express command 'to sweep them out of the country'. Once again countless Jews lost their lives [264].

The short period 115-117 was one of ferocious warfare between Romans and Jews. Little love was lost on either side which shows how dualistic the situation had got.

8. The Second Jewish War, A.D. 132-135

a. The causes of the rebellion

In this same period Palestine too did not remain wholly tranquil, for there minor disturbances occurred [265]. But a really great revolt, which became the Second Jewish War, broke out in that country in 132, during the reign of Hadrian. Of Hadrian's religious policy it can be said that he promoted the official Roman religion with great zeal but that he held all the alien ones in contempt [266]. It is hard to state what exactly was the cause of this rebellion. Two different causes are worth consideration.

The same ancient author who reports it writes that this Emperor forbade circumcision, and that this triggered off the Jewish revolt [267]. But the Jews were by no account the only nation to practise circumcision; a law of this kind would have hit many others. In fact, the decree did not speak of circumcision but of 'mutilating the genitals', and by this castration is meant. This was seen as equivalent to murder. It seems, however, that Hadrian did not distinguish between castration and circumcision. In his eyes circumcision was a barbaric custom. But probably it was not his intention to attack the

Jews exclusively. However, the Jews, for whom circumcision meant reception into the Covenant, saw it as a venomous measure directed against them [268].

A second incitement to revolt is to be found in Hadrian's plans for Jerusalem. As has been related, a Roman garrison had established itself in the ruins of the city. Since this garrison needed servants, a number of Jews had trickled back there since A.D. 70. Hadrian, who was a great traveller, everywhere combining sight-seeing and work, toured the East in the years 128-132. His voyages brought him also to Jerusalem, probably in 130. He found the town in a pitiable state, still half in ruins; the stumps of the great buildings testified to the glory that had passed away [269]. He made plans to rebuild it, but not as a Jewish city. It had to become a pagan town with the fateful name of Ælia Capitolina (his own name was Ælius Hadrianus). Ælia Capitolina would have a temple too, one dedicated to Jupiter, the Capitolinus, to be erected on the site where the Temple of Jahve once stood [270]. It is a matter of dispute when exactly the reconstruction began [271] but it will be understood that the plans alone were sufficient to make the Jews furious. This is yet another specimen of the callousness the Romans so often displayed with regard to the feelings of other nations. Hadrian is much praised in modern times as a model ruler; as such he is glorified in Marguérite Yourcenar's novel 'Mémoires d'Hadrien' (1951), but this measure must be stigmatized as less than tactful.

b. The revolt of Bar Kochba

A charismatic leader came forward to lead the revolt; his name was Simon Bar Kochba [272]. His enemies nicknamed him 'Koziba' = Son of the Lie, whereas his admirers called him 'Bar (or Ben) Kokhba' = Son of the Star. Very probably this name was given to him by Rabbi Akiba, a famous Jewish sage of that period, who applied to him the biblical text : "A star shall go forth from Jacob" [273]. When Akiba saw Simon, he greeted him with these words : "This is King Messiah" [274]. His official title was 'Prince of Israel'; once again, the Messianic prophecies seemed near fulfilment, at least in the eyes of the common people [275].

We do not know exactly when the revolt broke out; the usual date is A.D. 132 [276], but it may also have been the autumn of 131 [277]. Nor is there much information about where and how it started. Anyhow, once it had begun, the rebellion spread like wildfire. The first phase of the revolt consisted of guerilla warfare. The whole country was turned upside down by the insurgents, and woe to those who did not adhere to them [278]! It may be assumed that Jerusalem fell into their hands, which was no great feat of arms since the town hardly existed [279]. The moral impact of the occupation of the Holy City must have been great; a new calendar came into use which dated with the years of the 'Liberation of Israel'. A central government was installed which is described by Schürer as 'strong and authoritarian' [280]; the districts had their own leaders.

The military operations are difficult to follow; so much is certain that at a given moment Palestine was cleansed of Roman troops. As always after the first setback, the Roman authorities began to react vigorously. Troops were assembled from far away provinces; Hadrian entrusted the command to an experienced general, Julius Severus, who had to travel from Britain, where he was stationed, to Palestine. It is not even impossible that the Emperor too made his appearance on the spot [281].

The suppression of the revolt lasted several years. Since nothing could be gained by open warfare, the Romans resorted to the wearisome tactics of tracing down the insurgents wherever they hid in the wilderness. The most effective means was blocking the caves where they hid and then starve them out. In this way they were all 'annihilated, exterminated, and eradicated', as Dio writes in dualistic terms [282]. Some strongholds held out very long. The last Jewish detachments, with Bar Kokhba among them, succumbed at Bettir [283]. They were finally overwhelmed in A.D. 135; Bar Kokhba, 'the author of this madness', writes Eusebius, was executed [284].

c. The aftermath

Hadrian and Julius Severus left a desert behind them when they triumphantly returned to Rome. Hundreds and hundreds of villages were destroyed; "many wolves and hyenas entered their cities (of the Jews) and howled" [285]. The country which had hardly recovered from the damage done in the First Jewish War was again severely depopulated. A considerable part of the population was sold into slavery so that many slave markets became overcrowded and prices fell. Many Jews died during the transports [286]. Those who settled in Jerusalem after A.D. 70 were chased away and replaced by Gentiles [287].

The city was to be entirely pagan henceforward; Jews were forbidden to enter it under pain of death [288]. On the site where the Temple had stood a temple dedicated to Jupiter Capitolinus arose, that same temple that had been the cause of the revolt [289]. There were more new buildings. One of these was the southern gate, on the road to Bethlehem; it is said that on it was the image of a pig - which, needless to say, was a deliberate insult to the Jews for whom the pig was an unclean animal. "The total paganisation of Jerusalem", writes Schürer, "was the fulfilment of a scheme long before attempted by Antiochus Epiphanes" [290].

The Jews of Judaea were not the only ones affected. The decree forbidding circumcision remained in force. To quote Schürer once again, this was, "to the Jewish mind, tantamount to a ban on Judaism itself" [291]. This ushered in the most dualistic phase in Roman-Jewish relations. Of course, the Jews remained restive under this yoke. "Here the Roman administration were faced with the choice of either tolerating the religious rites or totally destroying the people" [292]. But Hadrian's successor Antoninus Pius was no Hitler; confronted with Jewish unruliness, he decided on relaxation of the anti-Jewish legislation. Circumcision was permitted again.

9. The later phases

a. Judaism turned in upon itself?

Official Roman policy reverted more or less to the policy of tolerance inaugurated in the days of Julius Caesar. But the propagation of the Jewish faith remained prohibited. Conversions from paganism to Judaism became an exception. The two great revolts left deep scars, not only in this sense that Palestinian Jewry needed a very long time to recover from the wounds inflicted on it. What is more important is this. Before the First Jewish War Judaism and the Jews had been quite a presence in the Empire, lively and vital, and although not always loved, yet influential. Now this was over. Certainly not all the ties between Jewry and the secular Graeco-Roman world were severed, but Judaism showed a marked tendency to turn in it upon itself, to keep itself more aloof from that world than it had done in former days.

Speaking of the new situation of Jewry in the Empire, we can start from a judgment by Schürer : "The division between them (the Jews) and the rest of the world became more pronounced ... The Jews thus tended to become more and more strangers in the Gentile world, despite the many bonds linking them to it" [293]. In my opinion, this statement by this distinguished scholar is not entirely wrong. However, two other scholars, both of them of great repute, Geza Vermes and Fergus Millar, the editors of the English translation of Schürer's History, added a cautionary note qualifying to some extent what that author had to say about the position of Jewry after A.D. 135.

Vermes and Millar mention above all Hellenistic influences on Jewish life, to be found in rabbinic writings, in Greek inscriptions on Jewish tombs, or in the architecture and decoration of synagogues. Although this certainly indicates a measure of osmosis, it does not really invalidate Schürer's opinion. These two scholars also point to the survival of proselytism [294]. This would certainly be more convincing. But this survival of proselytism is a moot point to which I shall have to return later [295]. I for one do not believe that there was much proselytizing after the Second Jewish War. Although Antoninus Pius exempted the Jews from the ban on circumcision, it remained intact for every other Roman. "If anyone performs it on those not of the same religion (i.e. by birth), he is punished under the code of castration" [296].

b. The situation of the Jews from Cyrenaica to Asia Minor

The real problem with Schürer's statement is that it is too global. In Egypt and Cyrenaica the Roman backlash after the events of 115-117 had been so severe that the Jewish community never fully recovered from it (in Cyprus all Jewish life had come to an end). "The evidence from the papyri of the presence of a large, cohesive community in Egypt, found rather abundantly before 70 C.E., diminishes, until after the year 200 C.E. it becomes almost negligible" [297].

Regarding Palestine, the Jewish homeland, it was the standard policy of Rome to prevent the foundation of a Jewish kingdom there. Just as there was no longer a High Priest, there must not be a King of Israel either. But, as Juster says, in the course of time the Romans recognized 'a chief sui generis, a sovereign without territorial power, a, in some ways, spiritual chief of all the Jews of the Empire, ... even of those in Palestine'. This chief was called the Patriarch. We do not know when this office was instituted, but there is evidence for it from the end of the second century. He was the head of the Jewish sacerdotal hierarchy and appointed the religious functionaries of the communities. At the same time he was the highest juridical authority in religious matters. The fact that the Patriarch was nominated by the Emperor points to an official relationship between the Empire and Jewry [298]; Wilken even speaks of 'cordial relations' [299].

For a time the ravaged Jewish communities of Palestine kept a very low profile, but during the third century they began to recover. In Caesarea at this time there was a flourishing Jewish community. Evidence that runs counter to Schürer's statement comes mainly from Asia Minor. In Sardis where the largest Jewish synagogue of Antiquity stood Jews were members of the city council; in the fourth century we find Jewish officials in public life, although mainly on its lowest levels [300]. In many cities Jewish boys were educated in the gymnasia.

c. Should we speak of dualism?

The great problem is how we, keeping in mind our overall theme, should define the Roman-Jewish relationship as it existed in the decades and centuries after the two Jewish Wars. Was it or was it not dualistic? And if it was dualistic, was it radically or relatively dualistic? Starting from my original definition of dualism as I presented it in the Preface of Volume I, and which I never altered or amended, there have to be two poles which are opposed to each other and which stand apart from each other. There was surely not much love lost between the Empire and Judaism. This was never the case but in the first and second centuries A.D. the existing animosity, which is discernible on both sides, grew into bitter enmity. In the third and fourth centuries the situation became somewhat more relaxed.

A second important element in my definition is that there should be no middle term, if the word 'dualism' is to be applied. Since the beginning of the third century there was a Jewish Patriarch. Are we allowed to see him as a 'middle term', a link between the Empire and Jewry? The fact that he was nominated by the Emperor does not make him a Roman official; he did not fit into the imperial fabric as consuls and praetors and governors did. It was the Jewish ethnos where he belonged; his function served to chararacterize this ethnos as Jewish rather than Roman. The Christians too had a 'patriarch', in the person of the bishop of Rome, but the Empire never acknowledged this highest ecclesiastic as such. This too stresses the situation of the Jews as a 'status aparte'.

Then there was the granting of Jewish citizenship to all Jews a few decades later. Of course, this eased their situation somewhat. But we should not forget that Caracalla did not take this measure in order to gratify the Jews. That they became 'cives romani' was simply a side-effect of the fact that all the inhabitants of the Empire acquired the citizenschip in a body. Caracalla could hardly have exempted the Jews - a measure that would have created more problems than it solved.

It is also stated in my definition that one of the poles should be considered inferior to the other; it will be despised, denigrated, and thwarted, and perhaps there will be attempts to eradicate it. Beginning with this last point, we should not assume that the Empire followed a genocidal policy regarding the Jews. However, by the same token, at times it showed very little regard for Jewish lives; the number of victims of the revolts in Egypt, Cyprus, and Palestine was astronomically high, although there was no intention of destroying the whole Jewish nation. In Part IV of this chapter we shall have ample occasion to see how many, many Graeco-Roman authors wrote in denigrating, even insulting terms about the Jews and their religion; most of them did nothing at all to remedy their gross ignorance of all things Jewish.

It must be admitted that, as time passed, a certain measure of osmosis can be detected between the state and the Jewish ethnos, exemplified by the fact that Jews served on city councils and occupied (minor) official functions. But as far as I can see, this was only at the local level and by no means everywhere, for instance not in Egypt and Cyrenaica and, still less, in Rome herself. There never were Jewish consuls, praetors, censors, senators, or governors of provinces. There was also never a Jewish Emperor, although there have been Arian and Roman-Catholic rulers.

It is true that the Jews of the Empire, in contrast to Christians, suffered no persecutions because of their faith. This does not mean that the pagan state entertained a high opinion of their creed. If one Emperor or other favoured the Jewish religion - Julian the Apostate (361-363) is a case in point -, they did so to isolate the better the Christian creed which they hated. Julian, for instance, did his best to explain away the differences between Judaism and the beliefs of other nations. As David Rokeah writes, his "attitude towards the Jews was generally defined by the needs of his polemics against the Christians" [301]. So we must not conclude too hastily that there was a fundamental change in Roman policy.

On the whole, Roman officialdom was not favourably disposed towards Judaism; it rather feared than admired it. Its monotheism, with the accompanying refusal to do homage to the divine Emperor, remained a thorn in the Roman side. The Jewish religion was a privileged one in the respect that the Jews were officially permitted to practise it. But they had to pay a price for this favour! There was the 'fiscus judaicus', the Jewish tax, collected from every Jew, proselytes included. This tax was officially destined for Jupiter Capitolinus; in this way the Jews were forced to pay homage, by a detour, to the imperial high godhead. A second humiliating restriction was the ban on circumcision for converts.

d. Conclusion

It is time to draw a conclusion. In my opinion the situation of Judaism in the second century A.D. was one of radical dualism. In that time the Empire and Judaism were poles apart; the state had not yet overcome its fear of the 'eternally rebellious Jews'; the Jews still smarted under the effect of their disastrous defeats. This situation in the third century changed into one of relative dualism. The state resumed its policy of toleration; Judaism was once again a privileged religion. But, when all is said and done, Judaism was not more than tolerated; the Jews were considered a 'Fremdkörper' within the fabric of the Empire. The authorities hardly knew how to handle them [302]. The Jews on their side, on the ground of their religion, considered themselves as separate, with their own non-Roman, non-Hellenistic way of life.

This situation of relative dualism, of tolerance with restrictions, is specifically exemplified in the prohibition against Jews entering Jerusalem. The Holy City itself, the centre of their religion and cult and history, was out of bounds for them. It had to remain a purely pagan city. It was only two centuries later, after Constantine the Great had ascended the throne, that this hateful measure was somewhat relaxed. Now once a year, on the anniversary of the destruction of the Temple, Jews were allowed in. Saint Jerome, who lived in Palestine, describes how they had to bribe the sentries in order to gain entrance. Weeping they stood on the site of the Temple, lamenting to the sound of the shofars, the ram's horns [303].

PART IV GREEK AND ROMAN AUTHORS ON JEWS AND JUDAISM

1. Greek authors

We begin with some big strides, for from Homer to Aristotle not one author mentions them. Even the much-travelled Herodotus passes them over in silence. Were these authors totally unacquainted with the existence of Jews? Or were they simply not interested? Who can say?

We have to wait until the end of the fourth century B.C. to find the first evidence of Jews in Greek literature. Emilio Gabba thinks that "this new awareness was one of the direct results of the eastern world being thrown open to the enquiring spirit of the Greeks, in the wake of Alexander's victorious expedition". He adds that at that time "the information is still uncertain and sometimes mistaken" [304]. It irritated later Jewish authors like Josephus that Greek authors were so slow in taking cognizance of Judaism; they argued that their own civizilization was so much older than the Hellenic one [305].

a. Theophrastus

The very first author to speak of Jews was Theophrastus, who succeeded Aristotle as head of the Academy in 322 B.C. According to him, the Jews formed part of the Syrian nation; he calls them 'philosophers', high praise in the mouth of a Greek. "They converse with each other about the deity." What he finds repellent in their religion is that they "sacrifice live victims" which is 'a terrible thing'. "If one ordered us to sacrifice in the same way we would have recoiled from the entire business." Here we see the sophisticated Greek viewing the sacrificial rite with turned up nose [306].

b. Hecataeus

More ample information comes from Hecataeus, the famous Greek geographer who lived about 300 B.C.. He showed himself sympathetic toward the Jewish religion and is even reported to have written a book on the Jews which is lost [307]. Hecataeus was so positive about Judaism that we may call him a philosemite. He knows about the emigration of the tribe from Egypt, owing to a pestilence arising there, he says, and presents unwarranted information that part of it landed in Greece. The main part, however, reached Judaea under the leadership of Moses, who was 'outstanding both for his courage and his wisdom'. It was he who founded Jerusalem and built the Temple; he gave the people their laws and divided it into twelve tribes. He also founded the priesthood, putting a High Priest at its head. Furthermore, Moses was a warrior who, with his army, annexed much territory. Later the Jewish nation came under foreign rule [308]. Although this information is partly incorrect and anachronistic, Stern thinks that its author relied on a Jewish spokesman. If this is correct, it would be the first instance of contact between Jews and Greeks [309].

c. The Jews as 'philosophers'

It became a favourite topic among Greek authors that the Jews were 'philosophers'. Two contemporaries of Hecataeus, Megasthenes [310] and Clearchus [311], refer to them with this term. A cautionary remark should be made here : the Greek word 'philosophia' is a wide net; it contains much which it no longer contains today, for instance religion. The Greeks had no separate word for 'religion'. The authors I quoted do not use the word as a term of abuse; quite the contrary! In their opinion the Jews were a people devoted to religion. But the term would have confounded the prophets.

About 200 B.C. Hermippus of Smyrna even went so far as to state that Pythagoras owed his doctrine to the Jews and "introduced many points of Jewish law into his philosophy" [312]. It is evident that with 'philosophy' the Pythagorean way of life is meant. The Jewish philosopher Aristobulus of Paneas, who was active in the second century B.C., contended that not only Pythagoras, but Socrates and Plato too, had their philosophy from Moses; poets like Homer and Hesiod owed a great deal to the Jewish language [313].

This philosopher was attempting to do the same as Philo did later : trying to mediate between the pagan Hellenistic world and biblical theology.

d. A harsh word

The first harsh word is to be found in a Hellenistic historian of the second century B.C., Agatharchides of Cnidus, who called the Jewish religion an 'untimely superstition' [314]. This term would be repeated over and over again by later Greek and above all by Roman authors. There are, of course, more authors, most of them of minor importance, who briefly refer to events in Jewish history, without showing what they think of Jews. The first author who seems to be acquainted with the Old Testament is Ocellus Lucanus in the second century B.C.; he is clearly alluding to Gen. 1 [315].

e. The tone changes

So far the tone of Greek scholarship had been neutral or vaguely benevolent. But this began to change. A great number of Jews lived outside Palestine in the Diaspora, the Dispersion; important concentrations of Jews existed here and there, the greatest in Alexandria. The Diaspora Jews, often grouping together in the towns of the Hellenistic East and of the Roman Empire, stuck to their faith and remained true to their ancestral customs. As I wrote above, they were unable to take upon themselves all the obligations of polis life, in particular its religious duties. This constituted a constant source of friction because the Greeks neither understood nor appreciated this attitude of aloofness from what was considered most important in polis life [316].

As Tcherikover has expounded, there was more to it than the religious antagonism alone. There was also the political factor of the Jews wishing to live in their autonomous ethnic units, and the social factor of their adhering to customs which the Greeks (and later the Romans too) found strange and even repellent, for instance circumcision. Tcherikover sums up the problem in these words that "the Jews did not resemble the other nations"; in other words, they did not conform to the pattern. And they were too numerous to overlook them [317]. This serves to explain why the tone of Greek authors grew more and more hostile.

It is improbable that the educated Hellenistic public was either well-informed about Judaism or even mildly interested in it. A communication by Agatharchides says vaguely that "there is a nation called Jews, who have a great and strong city called Jerusalem" [318], followed by words of Polybius to the effect that the Jews "live near the Temple of Jerusalem" [319].

f. Posidonius

In the beginning of the last century B.C. Posidonius became the ancestor of diverse genres of anti-Semitic propaganda. The Jews are no longer 'philosophers'; they are "sorcerers who pretend to use incantations" [320], in other words, they are dangerous people. Anything goes in this kind of propaganda, however nonsensical and absurd. It may be patently wrong but this does not matter. Posidonius relates how Antiochus IV Epiphanes, on entering the Jerusalem Temple in 168 B.C., found a man there, a Greek, who was obviously being fattened; kidnapped by the Jews as he was, he was destined to be killed after a year of copious diet, after which the Jews would consume his flesh, while swearing an oath of hostility to the Greeks. As far as I know, this is the very first mention of the ritual murder attributed to the Jews. Josephus, who reports this story, has it from his adversary Apion who read it in some work by Posidonius. Apion added that the Jews worshipped an ass's head, a fact that was also discovered by Antiochus during his visit to the Temple [321]. Gabba attributes this story to the inability of the Greeks to imagine a god of whom there was no statue or image [322].

Stern, in his collection, leaves aside another story, this time reported by Diodorus Siculus, because he thinks it highly dubious whether it should be ascribed to Posidonius [323]. But others, Reinach among them, think that Posidonius was its original source. But from whomsoever it may have come to us, it is a highly important communication because we find in it the first indication of genocide to be practised against the Jews. Having triumphed over them, King Antiochus VII Sidetes of Syria, entered Jerusalem in 132 B.C.

His friends advised him to make an end of the whole Jewish nation; they said that the Jews were hated by all humanity, and they, on their part, considered all others as their enemies. The king, however, refused to follow this advice for which Diodorus praises him.

However, Diodorus too presents the story of the ass, relating how the king saw in the Holy of Holies the statue of a bearded man with a book in his hand and seated on an ass; he thought that this statue represented Moses. Antiochus defiled the Temple by offering a pagan sacrifice there [324]. Historically false as this report may be, it, nevertheless, vividly illustrates the fiercely anti-Semitic attitude of the last Seleucid rulers.

g. Apollonius Molon

The attacks on Judaism gathered more force in the hands of Apollonius Molon who wrote between 100 and 75 B.C. He was a man with great influence since Caesar and Cicero came to attend his lessons at Rhodes; Radin calls him 'one of the most considerable figures of his day' [325]. Josephus asserts that he did not write a special treatise against the Jews but that his accusations are dispersed throughout his whole oeuvre (of which very little remains) [326].

h. Alexander Polyhistor

In this same period Alexander Polyhistor, a Greek from Miletus, wrote a book 'On the Jews' of which only fragments have been preserved by Eusebius and Clement of Alexandria. In these fragments he shows himself acquainted with the Old Testament; he is, however, wide off the mark when stating that a woman called Moses gave the Jews their Law [327].

j. Diodorus Siculus

The 'Bibliotheca historica' of Diodorus Siculus, the Sicilian, written towards the end of the first century B.C., is generally seen as a derivative work, largely dependent on previous authors. His own benign attitude towards Judaism probably reflects that of his source. He mentions Moses as a great lawgiver, on a par with other celebrities like Lycurgus of Sparta and Zoroaster whose name is rendered by him as 'Zarathraustes'. Moses received his law from a god with the name of 'Iao' [328]. "Here, for the first time in Greek literature", writes Stern, "the name Iao designates the Jewish God". This name is never used by orthodox Jews and occurs only rarely in Greek and Latin authors, but frequently in magical papyri and amulets [329], to which should be added its occurence in Gnostic texts. Diodorus' passages referring to Jewish history show no animosity against the Jews [330].

k. Nicolaus of Damascus

It is often assumed that pagan authors were generally hostile to Judaism, and that "early Christian attitudes towards Judaism were influenced negatively by the pagan environment" [331]. By no means all Greek authors spoke denigratingly of Judaism; Diodorus is a case in point. Another is Nicolaus of Damascus who lived in the last decades of the first century B.C. His 'Histories' are lost, apart from fragments preserved by Josephus. Since 14 B.C. he was the adviser and personal friend of King Herod the Great; as such he came into contact with things Jewish (he was not a Jew himself nor was he a proselyte).

"Clearly he possessed a thorough knowledge of Jewish history and of Jewish religious practices. The surviving fragments are devoid of the errors and distortions that characterize the works of his Alexandrian and Roman contemporaries" [332]. He is reported to have spoken with great respect of the Jewish customs in wich, he said, there was 'nothing inhuman' - which was the opinion of so many other authors; these customs, he asserted, and particularly the Sabbath, are 'the gist of life' [333].

l. Pompeius Trogus

Somewhat less complimentary is a contemporary of Nicolaus, Pompeius Trogus, whose voluminous work 'Historiae philippicae' has come to us only in an Epitome by Justinus, composed around A.D. 300. Pompeius devoted his thirty-sixth book to Judaism. On the whole he is friendly to the Jews, stating that "by their justice combined with religion, it is almost incredible how powerful they became" [334]. But there are also the usual distortions, making, Moses, for instance, a son of Joseph [335]. We go somewhat further downhill with the statement that the Jews were expelled from Egypt because they were suffering from scabies and leprosy [336].

m. Strabo

Another contemporary is Strabo whose famous 'Geography' has come to us in full; in his sixteenth book he has quite a lot to say about Jews, their history and religion. Although he too is prone to making errors, he is on the whole reasonably well-informed. "Completely absent is the element of anti-Semitic propaganda" [337]. Moses and his successors are described as 'truly pious'. He left Egypt because the Egyptians venerated beasts and cattle (while "the Greeks are also wrong in modelling gods in human form"); instead, he founded a religion of the one God who is 'the creator of heaven and earth'. No images may be made of him [338].

n. Lysimachus

We now come to Lysimachus whom Stern calls "the Graeco-Egyptian writer who displayed the most marked anti-Semitic tendencies. It seems that he lived before Apion, perhaps in the second or first century B.C.E." [339]. He wrote a book with the title 'Ægyptiaca' in which he speaks from time to time of Judaism; the fragments of this work are preserved in Josephus' book against Apion. First of all, he comes up with the story that the Jews, living a mendicant existence in Egypt and seeking refuge in the temples, were afflicted with leprosy, scurvy, and other maladies. On the orders of Pharaoh the victims of leprosy and scurvy were packed into sheets of lead and sunk into the ocean. The rest were led away into the desert to perish there. We are very near the idea of genocide here! But led by 'a certain Moses', they managed to reach Judaea [340]. This Moses was 'a charlatan and an impostor' [341].

o. Apion

We are fairly well-informed about another Graeco-Egyptian scholar, Apion, who flourished somewhat later than Lysimachus, between 100 and 50 B.C. He too wrote a book on Egyptian history called 'Ægyptiaca'. Clement of Alexandria wrote that Apion's hatred of Jewry was so great that he wrote a book 'against the Jews'. It is not clear whether this work formed a part of the Ægyptiaca or wether it was a separate work. Josephus took him to task in his 'Contra Apionem'; he would not have taken the trouble to refute him if he had not found him an authoritative person. Stern thinks that Apion was 'a rather popular writer' [342]; in fact, Aulus Gellius tells us that "his books were not without fame" [343]. Now we know that a considerable part of the Alexandrian population was Jewish; we also know that there was often friction there between the Graeco-Egyptians and the Jews, and that they sometimes came to blows. We may safely assume, with Stern, that there was much animosity in the town against the Jews; what authors like Lysimachus and Apion have to say of them in all probability mirrors the feelings of the educated Hellenistic classes of that great harbour-town [344].

Here again we find the story that the Jews who were expelled from Egypt were lepers, blind and lame [345]. Very probably this communication forms part of the stock-in-trade of the polemic against the Alexandrian Jews of this time. Long ago the sorry lot had been driven out and now they had returned! "They came from Syria", Apion writes, "and settled by the sea without a harbour", that is, on the outskirts of Alexandria [346]. Such people are no true Alexandrians [347].

In his references to Judaism Apion did not shrink from the grossest distortions. The story that the Jews venerated an ass's head in their Temple is found in this author too [348], just as that of the man who was fattened in the Temple [349]. With regard to this tale, says Josephus, Apion was the spokesman of others. Another nonsensical anecdote is that about the origin of the Sabbath. This word is derived from the Egyptian word 'sabbatosis', which means 'disease of the groin'. During their march through the desert the

Jews developed tumors in the groin; after reaching Judaea, "they rested on the seventh day, and called that day 'sabbaton'" [350].

The laws of the Jews are unjust and their religious ceremonies erroneous [351]; their sacrificing of animals, their not eating pork, and their practice of circumcision are subjects only fit for derision [352]. At the back of all this is the charge that Jews do not worship the same gods as other people [353]. He shows himself angered by Jewish 'apartheid' and alleges that the Jews "swear by the God who made heaven and earth and sea to show no goodwill to a single alien, above all to Greeks" [354]. The accusation that the Jews are the enemies of mankind would be repeated over and over again throughout history.

In the period under consideration, says Gabba, "the Greek and Roman view of Judaism continued essentially to pass through the filter of Egyptian history, that is to say, through a hostile tradition" [355]. This tradition must have remained influential, or else Josephus, who wrote a century or more later, would not have deemed it necessary to refute it.

p. 'On the sublime'

The first half of the first century of the Christian era saw the appearance of an anonymous treatise called 'On the sublime'; its author is usually referred to as Pseudo-Longinus. This author is "one of the very few Greek authors to quote the Bible before the spread of Christianity in the realm of the Roman Empire" [356]. He called Moses 'no mean genius' who understood the nature of the divine so well that he could write : "God said, 'Let there be light, and there it was'" [357]. These laudatory words are so exceptional that it is sometimes thought the author was a hellenized Jew, but on the strength of certain other passages in this work we are not forced to accept this supposition [358].

q. Plutarch

We shall close our survey of pagan Greek authors on Jews and Judaism with what Plutarch, a famous and widely read historian and scholar, around A.D. 100 had to say of these subjects. This writer who was, among other things, also a historian of religion, showed some interest in Judaism. We can agree with Gager that he combined 'sound information, misconceptions, and free speculation'. Although he does not seem to have consulted the Old Testament, his pieces of information on ritual practices, holidays, and historical events are accurate. "These fragments of sound information set Plutarch apart from most pagan authors" [359].

On the other hand, he remains in line with his contemporaries by stating that the Jews honour the ass (who led them in the desert to a spring of water); he does not say, however, that they venerate this animal as divine [360]. When all is said and done, Plutarch found the Jews a superstitious (and barbarous) nation, for instance because they observed the Sabbath [361]; on the whole, says Gager, there is 'no hint of sympathy or admiration'. When Plutarch's friends engage in a discussion on the identity of the Jewish godhead, they are indulging in 'free-wheeling speculations' culminating in the speculation that this god is 'none other than Dionysus' [362].

r. Conclusion

Taking all together, the attitude of pagan Greek authors, in so far as they are not totally unconcerned, with a few notable exceptions, varies from coolly distant through critical to downright hostile. Direct knowledge of Holy Scripture is rare, although with the Septuagint a translation was available. Obviously these authors did not often take the trouble to consult Jews on their religion and habits. The result is a tangle of misconceptions; the manner in which Jews and Judaism are depicted is, on the whole, not favourable.

2. Roman authors

a. Cicero

It was centuries after the first Greek authors mentioned Jews and Judaism that a Roman writer showed himself aware of the existence of this nation. He was nobody less than the famous rhetor and scholar Cicero, in the last century B.C. His disparaging remarks set the tone for many others, though not for all Latin authors. Cicero did not immerse himself deeply in things Jewish; his treatise on the nature of the gods, 'De natura deorum', does not mention Jewish religious tenets at all. With Stern, " we must conclude that the Jews were not within the orbit of his immediate interests' [363]. Learned though he was, he did not possess a more than superficial knowledge of Judaism.

The Jews he found a people 'born to be slaves' [364] and their religion a 'barbara superstitio' [365] - a religion from which a true Roman should keep as far distant as possible -, for "the practice of their sacred rites was at variance with the glory of our Empire, the dignity of our name, the customs of our ancestors". The gulf between Roman and Jews was clearly unbridgeable; the gods themselves support the Romans in this, for, says Cicero with heavy irony, "how dear it (Jewry) was to the immortal gods is shown by the fact that it has been conquered, let out for taxes, made a slave" [366].

b. Varro

The appropriative habit of ancient authors of equating Jahve with Graeco-Roman divinities becomes apparent in Varro (first century B.C.) who wrote that the god of the Jews was the same as Jupiter, "thinking that it makes no difference by which name he is called, so long as the same thing is understood" [367]. Varro also believed that Jahve is called 'Iao' 'in Chaldean mysteries' [368].

c. Other authors

Seneca, the philosopher and the mentor of Nero, is not well-disposed towards the Jews either. Theirs is 'an accursed race'; their religion is superstitious. The practice of the Sabbath is inexpedient since it makes people idle away a seventh of their lives [369].

For Petronius, a comic poet of the first century A.D., the main characteristic of Jews was that they are circumcized, a custom that he repeatedly derides [370]; he also knows that they worship a pig-god [371].

Quintilianus, the Spanish grammarian of the second half of the first century A.D., saw in Moses 'the founder of the Jewish superstition'; this nation is 'a curse to others' [372]. His compatriot and contemporary Martial believed that the Sabbath was a day of fasting [373] and that circumcision meant lechery [374]; the custom of circumcision invoked his derision [375].

d. Tacitus

We now come to Tacitus, the outstanding historian, who lived from A.D. ca. 56 to 120. In his Historiae he has much to say of Jews. His "is the most detailed account of the history and religion of the Jewish people in classical Latin literature ... (His account) reflects the feelings of influential circles of Roman society in the age following the destruction of the Temple ... Its subsequent influence, especially after the revival of interest in Tacitus in the sixteenth century, may be considered out of all proportions to its inherent merits" - this is the judgment of Menahem Stern [376].

What this distinguished author had to tell about Jews and Judaism was, in fact, no more than a banal anti-Semitic outburst. He is vague about the origin of the Jewish nation. Did the Jews come from Crete? Or from Ethiopia? Or were they Assyrian refugees, 'a landless people' [377]? He is more explicit about the reasons for the departure of the tribe from Egypt : they were expelled because of a plague. A certain Moses led them away; after a seven days' march they reached Palestine and founded a city with a temple [378]. This is all he has to relate of Jewish history before Pompey came to Judaea.

Moses, this author wrote, in order "to establish his influence over this people for all time" - the Romans were always thinking in terms of power -, "introduced new religious practices, quite opposed to those of all other nations. The Jews regard as profane all that we hold sacred; on the other hand, they permit all that we abhor". He speaks scornfully of their sacrifices, their fasting, and their Sabbath [379]. All their "customs are base and abominable and owe their persistence to their depravity ... Jews are extremely loyal toward one another, and always ready to show compassion, but toward every other people they feel only hate and enmity". They eat apart and sleep apart and keep aloof from foreign women. This does not mean that they practice chastity, for "among themselves nothing is unlawful". Those whom they convert to their religion are taught "to despise the gods, to disown their country (i.e. the Roman Empire), and to regard their parents, children, and brothers (i.e. who are still pagans) as of no account ... The ways of the Jews are preposterous and mean" [380].

Gager discusses the reasons for this fierce attack. Tacitus may have wanted to explain to his readers that the Jews, a despicable race, had a rebellious nature. He also "appears to have advanced his history as a rationale for the anti-Semitism of conservative senatorial groups in Rome". Furthermore, our historian, who was an official of the Roman public religion, may have been troubled by the fact that not a few of his compatriots showed themselves attracted to Judaism. His "treatment of Judaism is thoroughly in tune with the times and reflects a widespread view of Judaism in traditional anti-Jewish circles of the late first century" [381].

e. Juvenal

A decade or two later the poet Juvenal referred more than once to Jews in his satirical poems, and without exception in an unpleasant tone. They flout the laws of Rome and revere only the Jewish law that was handed down to them by Moses in a secret volume which remained forbidden to the non-circumcized [382]. Gager calls this judgment a 'semi-official anti-Semitic charter' [383]. To authors like Tacitus and Juvenal, Judaism was something profoundly un- and anti-Roman. In order to combat it, they could not afford to be too fastidious.

PART V PUBLIC OPINION

1. Sympathy for Judaism

Is it possible to gauge the sentiments of the mass of Roman citizens regarding their Jewish compatriots? We can consult quite a number of official, scholarly, and literary documents in which Jews and Judaism are mentioned, but evidence of what artisans, shopkeepers, and peasants thought of their Jewish neighbours is deplorably scarce : they were the people who did not commit their ideas to paper. Were the Jews universally hated? Were they despised because of their religion, their 'apartheid'? Not by everybody. In our days novelty is the great thing, but in the times we are speaking of, it was antiquity. Judaism commanded a certain measure of respect because it was so ancient; in this respect it compared favourably with Christianity which was new, too new. Graeco-Roman authors would not have inveighed so vehemently against Judaism if they had not felt that it exerted a certain attraction on their compatriots. Their sharpest weapon was ridicule.

Not a few Romans, even members of the senatorial class, showed sympathy for the Jewish religion. Pagan sympathizers often preferred to see this religion as a philosophy, as a school of thought that did not differ so much from schools they were acquainted with, the Stoa for instance. Philo used to present his Jewish religion as philosophy, even as the true philosophy [384]; to many pagans it must have seemed a 'cult of wisdom' rather than a sacrificial or ritual cult. But, as Gager remarks, sympathy not often led to actual adherence. "Many Gentiles adopted one or another practice from Judaism, without embracing the whole system. The understanding of Judaism was not always profound" [385]. And there was also the ban on circumcision. But while some people saw Judaism as a 'philosophy', to others it was a superstition and a barbarous one at that.

2. Friction between Jews and Gentiles

We know almost nothing of how Jews and Gentiles went about with one another at, say, street-level. I am thinking here of neighbours, of artisans and shopkeepers of the same trade, and of clerks in the same office. Was their intercourse friendly? It probably was, at least superficially so. We do not know how much of the anti-Judaistic attitude of so many Graeco-Roman authors filtered down to the lower strata of the population. True enough, many people were illiterate and could not read Greek or Latin. But on the other hand, it is improbable that these opinions would remain confined to the educated classes.

I have already described the events of 115-117 in Egypt. They show that, at least in that country, and in particular in Alexandria with its large Jewish population, there was considerable tension between Jews and Gentiles - a tension that discharged itself in reciprocal slaughter. Greeks, Egyptians, and Romans joined hands against the Jews. Decades later the victory over the Jews was still celebrated by the Gentile part of the population.

But already in the first century A.D., in the year 38, there had been outburst of irritation against the Jews. The initiative this time lay with the 'Greeks' of Egypt, the Hellenized Egyptians. They had been the privileged class under Ptolemaean rule, but since the Romans had taken over, their status was subject to deflation. They now were the equals of the Jews they despised. This led to considerable friction. With the tacit permission of Flaccus, the Roman governor, the Greeks attacked the Jewish quarters of Alexandria, made a great many victims, desecrated the synagogues, and humiliated the Jewish elders in public. There even arose a plan to set up a statue of the Roman Emperor, Caligula, in the synagogues. When Claudius, who had a more favourable opinion of Jews, had succeeded Caligula as emperor, the Jews of Alexandria wrought their revenge on the Gentiles in town. The new Emperor reinstated the Jews in their old rights, and this led to the restoration of order [386].

3. The causes of anti-Jewish attitudes

The Dutch scholar Sevenster carefully canvassed the causes of anti-Judaistic (he himself uses the term 'anti-Semitic') attitudes in Antiquity. We should refuse, he says, to speak of 'racism'. Both racism and nationalism are notions which were unknown to the ancients. Sevenster concludes a chapter entitled 'Race' with these words : "Not a single indication is to be found in ancient literature that anti-Semitism in the ancient world used the theory of race as a weapon of attack" [387].

The alleged wealth of the Jews in Antiquity belongs to the stock-in-trade of the anti-Semitic propaganda of modern times. This wealth, with the corresponding social status, is thought by several writers to have aroused the jealousy and even the hatred of their non-Jewish fellow-citizens. If we might believe such authors, finance and commerce were largely in the hands of Jews who, because of this, were able to exert an inordinate influence on political affairs. But there is little or nothing to corroborate this point of view. Banking and commerce in the Empire were not specifically Jewish. Of course, there were some wealthy Jews, but the great mass of Jewry was poor. And they were despised for their poverty by the more affluent classes of society. Sevenster concludes that "the information available clearly demonstrates, in any case, that the economic status of the Jews was diversified and that there was no special reason for hating them for their wealth or their economic power" [388].

There is more substance in the accusation levelled at the Jewish population that they were privileged. The Jewish ethnos lived according to very particular and uncommon rules; it was unable to sustain this mode of live 'without the benefit of certain privileges' [389]. On the whole the Roman authorities were fairly tolerant of Judaism. The result of this tolerance was that the situation of the Jews in some respects was considerably different from that of other groups; they were, for instance, not obliged to take part either in the emperor cult or in that of the polis divinities.

As I wrote earlier, this certainly caused friction, also because the Jews, in their turn, "were not prepared to recognise the other forms of cult and life as equal to their own ... Criticism of the policy of tolerance found expression in the lower echelons of officials and among pagan fellow-citizens in a particularly antagonistic attitude towards the Jews" [390]. Jews were found to be strange, ill-adapted, difficult. Sevenster believes that this strangeness was 'the most fundamental reason for pagan anti-Semitism' [391]. The pagans vaguely understood why the Jews kept themselves so apart : it was because of their God. Because the Jews did not participate in either the imperial or local cults, they were charged with 'asebeia' = impiety. This does not mean that they were thought to venerate no God at all, but that they did not acknowledge the imperial and local divinities. Therefore, they were described as 'irreverent' and 'unholy'.

4. Jewish apartheid

How difficult it is to come to a conclusion with regard to this Jewish apartheid is shown by the somewhat contradictory utterances of Robert Wilken. "There is little evidence", he writes, "that Judaism entered on a period of isolation or that it set up 'hedges' to protect Jews from the inroads of a larger culture. The Jews continued to be as much a part of the social and cultural world of late antiquity as they had been prior to the loss of the Temple and the city of Jerusalem". But then this author goes on to say that "the openness of the Jews to the society in which they lived did not mean that Jews were absorbed by the higher culture. Jews who were receptive to Greco-Roman culture did not cease being Jews" [392]. We may well ask how great a part of the Jewish ethnos was really 'receptive' to Hellenistic culture; the great mass consisted of artisans, shopkeepers, labourers, and peasants who did not come into contact with its more refined products.

Two pages further on, where he is speaking of the Antiochene Jews, Wilken writes that they had been sharing the city's fortunes for over six hundred years. "Yet, while sharing in the city's culture and its way of life, the Jews stood apart" [393]. I feel that what he is saying of the Jews of Antioch may be applied to those of the whole Empire. It has long been the idea, first advanced by Harnack in his 'Das Wesen des Christentums' (1900), that after

16. Esth. 3:11.
17. Esth. 4:14.
18. Esth. 3:7.
19. Esth. 9:20-32.
20. Esth. 13:14.
21. Esth. 3:8.
22. Esth. 13:5-7.
23. Esth. 9:16.
24. 'Esther' is one of the few books that are never mentioned in the New Testament, Wildeboer, Buch Esther 176.
25. Vol. IV, Ch. II.15f.
26. From 'L'amusante ménagerie' by an anonymous author, Paris, 1837.
27. See for this passage Tcherikover, Hell.civ. 277-279.
28. Tcherikover, Hell.civ. 301/302.
29. Radin, Jews 165.
30. Tcherikover, Hell.civ. 331.
31. Tcherikover, Hell.civ. 322.
32. Schürer. Hist. III.1, 127.
33. Juster, Les Juifs II, 1, says that "par rapport uux cités grecques ils (the Jews) sont des étrangers de nationalité juive". He adds, however (p.2) : "Les nombres des Juifs qui jouissaient des droits politiques locaux dut être beaucoup plus grand que l'on le croit". But for this last statement Juster relies entirely on Josephus.
34. Livy 5.21.3-5.
35. See for this passage Radin, Jews 44-45.
36. Macrobius, Sat. 3.9.7-8.
37. Jos., Ant. 14.225-264.
38. Juster, Les Juifs I, 218 and note 3.
39. Jos., Ant. 14.242-245.
40. Jos., Ant. 14.193. See Vol. X, Ch. V.4b.
41. Smallwood, Jews 135-137.
42. Smallwood, Jews 147.
43. Smallwood, Jews 148.

NOTES TO CHAPTER V

1. Poliakov, Hist.Antisem. I,21, says that the mean of the often very widely diverging estimates by Harnack, Juster, et alii, is one million in Palestine and three or four million in the Diaspora = 7 ā 8 % of the total population of the Empire.

2. A recent essay on the extension of the Diaspora is that by Tessa Rajak, The Jewish community and its boundaries (1992) (see Bibliography).

3. Bar-Hebraeus, Historia, p. 73. This author is a late source, for he lived 1226-1284.

4. Jos., Ant. 1.133 and 15.39.

5. I guess that Feldman means that it was easier to become a Christian than a Jew; (male) Jews had to be circumcized, Christians only baptized. Jews had to fulfil the endless number of stipulations of the Law; Christians were far easier off.

6. Feldman, Anti-Sem. 37.

7. Juster, Les Juifs I, 180-209.

8. Juster's list is, so to speak, elaborated by Schürer, History III.1, 3-86. Additional information is given by Smallwood, Jews 122, note 13. I refer the reader to the list of pilgrims to Jerusalem at the first Pentecost, the foundation day of the Christian Church, given by Luke in Acts 2:9-11; he mentions people coming from as far as Parthia. Another list is given by Philo, Legatio 281-282.

9. Vol. VII, Ch. VI.1b.

10. See for this passage Juster, Les Juifs I, 209-212. with the notes.

11. Jos., Ant. 14.115.

12. Cic., Pro Flacco 28.67-68.

13. Feldman, Anti-Sem. 37.

14. Jos., Contra Apion 2.5.49. But what to think of two communications by Josephus, the first being that in 145 B.C. Ptolemy VII Physcon delivered all the Jews of Alexandria, bound and naked, to be trampled down by drunken elephants (the victims were miraculously saved), Jos., Contra Apion 2.5.53-54., and the second that Ptolemy Lathyrus in 88 B.C. during an invasion of Judaea ordered his soldiers to cut women and children to pieces, boil them, and even taste them, Jos., Ant. 13.345? Insofar as such atrocities are really historical, they should not be seen as anti-Semitic outbursts but rather as incidents in the often recurring struggles for the throne; both Ptolemies who are mentioned were pretenders. See Isaac, Genèse 74-75.

15. See Vol. VI, Ch. II.11.

But would it not be sensible to listen what the Jews themselves had to say of their apartheid? I am thinking here of two open-minded and Hellenized scholars who, in spite of their being steeped in Greek culture, had not repudiated their Jewish faith - I refer to Josephus and Philo. The first asked himself why pagan authors knew and understood so little of Judaism and the Jewish way of life. "We do not live", he wrote, "in a maritime country, we do not devote ourselves to commerce, we do not receive foreigners which is the ordinary result of commercial activities. Our cities are built far from the sea, and since we live in a fertile country, we cultivate it arduously, our main care being to nourish our schildren." Of course, he is speaking here of Palestine. But then he adds something that can be applied to the Diaspora Jews too. "For us observing our laws and pious practices which have been transmitted to us in agreement with these laws, is the most necessary work of our lives. Add to these reasons the peculiarity of our way of life" [400].

In his life of Moses, Philo quotes the blessing of Balam over the people of Israel [401] citing the words of this prophet that Israel is destined to live alone and not be 'reckoned among other nations'. But he adds something that is not to be found in Numbers, namely that Israel shall live alone "not because their dwelling-place is set apart from others and their land severed from others, but because in virtue of their peculiar customs they do not mix with others in order not to depart from the ways of their fathers" [402]. This quotations prove that both authors were convinced that the Jewish apartheid was something fundamental.

To return now to Sevenster, and this must also be the last word of this chapter on Judaism in the Roman Empire. "Fundamentally", he writes, "what really annoyed them (the Romans) was that 'sovereign self-sufficiency' of Judaism which occupied a special position in the ancient world, which was the only religion that remained 'foreign', aloof, in the Roman Empire ... In this seldom disowned strangeness, emanating from the way of life and thought prescribed by the Torah, lies the profoundest cause for the anti-Semitism of the ancient world" [403].

----

the catastrophes Judaism isolated itself from the outside world, concentrating on the Torah and perfectly content with its own peculiar way of life. Soon enough protests against this point of view became loud; Jewish scholars pointed to the great biblical concept of universalism. There originated a 'dialectical antithesis between two attitudes, the one of retrospective seclusion and the other of extroverted accessibility' [394] - two opinions that cannot both be correct. Would the truth lie somewhere in the middle?

In a voluminous study [395] Martin Hengel actually steered a middle course. Study of the Talmud proves that the sages were well acquainted with things Greek. Hengel came to the conclusion that Palestinian Judaism of the first centuries A.D. was so thoroughly hellenized that one should speak of 'Hellenized Judaism'. This did, however, not prevent him from stating that there was not only an encounter but also a conflict between Judaism and Hellenism, and that this Hellenism was received and repudiated at the same time. This leads inevitably to the conclusion that, whereas some Jews felt attracted by Hellenism, others rejected it out of hand. There is nothing to surprise us in this. Conservative Romans like Cato were also averse to Greek influences; for orthodox Jews there was the additional factor - which also came to play a role for Christians - that Greek culture was pagan.

Urbach's solution for the dilemma is that the Judaism of the first three centuries A.D. was not hermetically sealed off against the surrounding world. But, "nevertheless, their (the Jews') consciousness of the distinction between Israel and the nations is emphatic" [396]. The gulf separating Jewry from 'the others' is graphically expressed by the 'blessings of distinction' to be pronounced at the end of the Sabbath and at the close of festivals. These speak of the distinction between 'sacred and profane, between light and darkness, between Israel and the Gentiles, between the Sabbath and the six working-days' [397]. This indicates where Judaism situated itself : apart and separate. Let us pay attention to what Dio wrote, an author who was certainly not anti-Judaistic. The Jews, he said, "are distinguished from the rest of mankind in practically every detail of their way of life" [398]. Compare this to what the Letter to Diognetus states about the difference between Christians and other men which "is neither in country nor language nor customs" [399].

44. Jos., Ant. 14.195-196.
45. Jos., Ant. 14.200.
46. Jos., Ant. 14.204 and 195.
47. Jos., Ant. 14.219-222.
48. Jos., Ant. 16.160-173. We do not know exactly why the cities tried to prevent this ending of monies, but it is a fair guess that they had economic reasons : probably they did not want to see their precious metal exported, see Firpo, Giudei 355.
49. Jos., Ant. 16.31-57.
50. Juster, Les Juifs I,219, note 4.
51. Juster, les Juifs I, 219-220.
52. Sevenster, Roots 145.
53. Sevenster, Roots 145.
54. Leon, Jews of Rome 16.
55. Philo, Ad Gaium 24.159-160.
56. Philo, In Flaccum 1.1 (517).
57. He was either Gaius Sentius Saturninus or his brother Lucius Sentius Saturninus, see Leon, Jews 17, note 2.
58. Jos., Ant. 18.81-84.
59. Firpo, Giudei 538.
60. Tac., Ann. 2.85. This remark reminds me of one made during the ill-famed 'Wannsee Konferenz' in January 1942 in Berlin where lower German officials were briefed about the assembling of the Jews and their transport to the east; the gathered officials were told that, if during this operation a good many succumbed, this was not a thing to be deplored.
61. Suet., Tib. 36.
62. Dio 57.18.5.
63. Radin, Jews 307. When Tacitus is writing of four thousand freedman 'tainted with superstition', these words "are meaning less unless they refer to non-Jewish proselytes", Radin, Jews 308. See further the extensive treatment of this incident in Radin, Jews 306-313.
64. Philo, Legatio 160-161.
65. Dio 60.6.6.
66. Firpo, Guidei 538.
67. Philo, Legatio 45.358-367.

68. According to Philo, Legatio 35.265, it was not his statue but one of Zeus.
69. Philo, Legatio 34.256.
70. 2Macc.11:15-37.
71. 1Macc.8.
72. See Vol. VI, Ch. II.11.
73. 1Macc.14:27-46.
74. Jos., Ant. 13.255-256.
75. Jos., Ant. 13.257-258.
76. According to Jos., War 1.64-65, Hyrcanus entrusted this task to his sons with their Greek names, Aristobulus and Antigonus.
77. Jos., Ant. 13.275-281.
78. Jos., Ant. 13.395-397.
79. Schürer, Hist. II, 14.
80. Quoted by Schulim Ochser s.v. 'Peraea', Jew.Enc. IX, 595 (1905).
81. See Vol. X, Ch. IV.24e.
82. Jos., Ant. 14.75; War 1.156.
83. Ginsburg, Rome 80.
84. Mary Smallwood speaks of the 'the Hasmonaean client prince'; see her extensive treatment of his episode in her 'The Jews under Roman Rule', pp. 21-30.
85. The relation Syria-Palestine is succinctly described by Baumann, Rom und die Juden, 2-3.
86. Jos., Ant. 14.331-332 and 379.
87. Jos., Ant. 14.370-385. See Baumann, Rom und die Juden 88-96, Die Neuordnung Palästinas durch Caesar.
88. Jos., Ant. 4.469-491.
89. Bevan, The Jews, CAH IX (1932), 406. See for the family connections of the Herodians the chart in Smallwood, The Jews XX.
90. 'The Idumaean client king', says Mary Smallwood who presents a detailed report of his reign in her 'The Jews under Roman Rule' 60-104.
91. Jos., Ant. 17.299-303.
92. Jos., Ant. 17.317-323; War 2.93-100.

93. Jos., War 2.111. The Emperor banished the ethnarch to Vienna (Vienne) on the Rhône.
94. It is sometimes erroneously stated that Judaea became an integral part of the province of Syria, but, as Momigliano, Ricerche 6, says, this theory "non ha più bisogno di confutazione".
95. Jos., War 2.117.
96. Smallwood, The Jews 146 : "This city was more convenient than Jerusalem for sea communication with Rome, while at the same time within easy reach of the capital (=Jerusalem), and, being furnished with Greco-Roman cultural amenities, it had an atmosphere more congenial to Roman officials than Jerusalem".
97. Millar, Roman Near East 43-44.
98. See Vol. IV, Ch. II.15g.
99. Jos., Ant. 14.403.
100. Jos., Ant. 17.43.
101. For this reason we should not be too quick to dismiss the Gospel story of the Massacre of the Innocents at Bethlehem, Mt. 2:13-18 as 'legend'.
102. Schürer, Hist. II, 84.
103. Could this be the oldest expression of the idea of the 'translatio imperii'? I find no mention of it in Werner Goez's book 'Translatio imperii' (see Bibliography), although he refers once (p. 118) to Josephus, but in another context.
104. Jos., War 5.364, 366-368, 378.
105. See for this passage Prause, Herodes 211-228.
106. Jos., War 2.56.
107. Jos., War 2.57-59; Tac., Hist. 5.9.
108. Jos., War 2.60-65.
109. Firpo, Giudei 544.
110. Smallwood, Jews 106.
111. Jos., War 2.41-54, Ant. 17.254-268.
112. See Vol. X, Ch. VI.15e.
113. Jos., War 2.66-75, Ant. 17.286-298.
114. Smallwood, Jews 113.
115. Not be confused with the Judas of Sepphoris.
116. Jos., War 2.117-118.

117. Jos., War 2.118.
118. Hengel, Untersuchung 308-315.
119. Firpo, Guidei 545.
120. Schürer, Hist. I, 455.
121. Jos., War 12.224, Ant. 20.108.
122. Jos., War 2.224-227, Ant. 20.109-112.
123. Jos., War 2.232-235, Ant. 20.118-120. Later, on the complaints of the Jews, Claudius deposed and banished Cumanus, Jos., War 2.245, Ant. 20.136. According to Tac., Ann. 12.54, it was not Cumanus but Felix who was then in charge.
124. Tac., Hist. 5.9.
125. Jos., War 2.253, Ant. 20.160.
126. Tac., Ann. 12.54.
127. Jos., Ant. 20.186.
128. Jonathan ben Anan had been High Priest in A.D. 36/37.
129. Jos., War 2.245-246.
130. Jos., Ant. 20.162-164.
131. Jos., War 2.259, used quite another term, namely to prepare for insurrection, which may be true since, as Schürer remarks, "retreat into the desert as a prelude to military action is characteristic of Jewish resistance groups from the Maccabean times onwards", Schürer, Hist. I,464.
132. Jos., War 2.161-163, Ant. 20.169-72; see also Acts 21:38.
133. Jos., War 2.164-165.
134. Jos., War 2.293. Perhaps the Jews were in arrears with paying their tribute to Rome.
135. Jos., War 2.294.
136. Jos., War 2.296-301.
137. Jos., War 2.305-308.
138. Herod Agrippa II, 54-92, is the last king of the Herodian family; he was not the king of Judaea, but of a vassal-kingdom in the north of Palestine that comprised parts of Galilee (with Tiberias) and Peraea. During the Jewish War he remained staunchly on the Roman side.
139. Jos., War 2.310-311.
140. Jos., War 2.343-407, with the long speech of Agrippa.

214. Jos., War 6.220-222.
215. Jos., War 6.228 and 232-235.
216. Jos., War 6.236-243.
217. Jos., War 6.250.
218. Jos., War 6.254-259.
219. Is Josephus again attempting to exonorate the Roman commander-in-chief?
220. Jos., War 6.271.
221. Jos., War 6.321-322.
222. Jos., War 6.354-355.
223. Jos., War 6.316.223.
224. Jos., War 392-408.
225. Jos., War 6.433-434.
226. Jos., War 6.434 and 7.1-4.
227. Jos., War 7.389-406.
228. For a more extensive treatment see Schwier, Tempel. 2.2.1.a, Ideale Konzeption : Die Pax Romana als Bestandteil der Prinzipatsideologie, 202-218.
229. See Schwier, Tempel, 2.2.1.b : Positive Erwartung : Jupiter als Garant der römischen Herrschaft, 218-231.
230. Schwier, Tempel 239.
231. Jos., War 6.312-313; he added that the oracle in reality referred to Vespasian "who was proclaimed emperor during his stay in Judaea".
232. See Tac., Hist. 5.13 and Suet., Vesp. 4.5.
233. Jos., War 1.4 and 3.3.
234. Schwier, Temple 245.
235. Schwier, Tempel 2.2.1.c : Negative Befürchtung : Der Untergang der römischen Herrschaft und das Erstarken des Orients, 231-250.
236. Schwier, Temple 283.
237. Schwier, Tempel 287-292.
238. Schwier, Tempel 330-331.
239. Schwier, Tempel 284.
240. Sulp.Sev., Chron. 2.30.6-7.
241. Orosius 7.9.5-6.

182. Jos., War 4.128 and 135-138.
183. Jos., War 4.146.
184. Jos., War 4.140-141 and 145.
185. Jos., War 4.155-157.
186. Jos., War 4.196-205.
187. Jos., War 4.228-232.
188. See Vol. IV, Ch. II.15g.
189. Jos., War 4.235-236.
190. Jos., War 4.286-300.
191. Jos., War 4.305-333.
192. Jos., War 4.354.
193. Jos., War 4.355-365.
194. Jos., War 4.366-373.
195. Jos., War 4.444-445.
196. Jos., War 4.450-451.
197. Jos., War 4.491.
198. Jos., War 4.497-502.
199. Jos., War 4.550-555.
200. Jos., War 5.41-42.
201. Jos., War 5.71-97.
202. Jos., War 4.573-577.
203. Jos., War 5.2-38.
204. Jos., War 5.278-279.
205. Jos., War 5.291-302.
206. Jos., War 5.331-347.
207. Jos., War 5.356-358.
208. Jos., War 5.447-451.
209. Jos., War 5.562-566.209.
210. Jos., War 5.680-693.
211. Jos., War 6.94.
212. Jos., War 6.149-151.
213. Jos., War 6.98.

170. This is not exactly the most reputable episode in Josephus's tortuous life. When the invaders and defenders were still fighting in the streets, Josephus, the commander of the garrison, 'aided by some divine providence' ('daimonooi tini'), succeeded in reaching, via a deep pit, a cave where he found forty others hiding with a quantity of food sufficient for a long time. He remained there for two days. On the third day he was betrayed to the Romans by a captive. Vespasian sent two tribunes to fetch him considering "that the outcome of the war depended largely on his capture". In spite of long parleying with the tribunes, Josephus refused to come out. When he heard that the legionaries were threatening to put his hiding-place on fire, he was on the brink of giving in. But his comrades in the cave pointed their swords on him to kill him if he surrendered himself to the Romans. They asked him to commit suicide. Finally, they decided to kill themselves; each stabbed his neighbour. But when the turn came to Josephus, he spared himself and the life of his neighbour. He was brought to the Roman camp where, according to his own version of the events, the Romans were much impressed with his personality. Having appeared before Vespasian, he prophesied that he would become emperor, just as his son Titus. He remained two years in custody but was treated with consideration; Vespasian even presented him with a Jewish girl, a captive, whom he married, in spite of the fact that he was already married to a woman whom he had left behind in Jerusalem. Once he was set free, he assumed the Roman clan name of 'Flavius' and henceforward remained in the service of Vespasian and Titus, Jos., War 3,340-408. This whole story, with its improbabilities, serves to explain why the author of the book, Flavius Josephus, a Roman by adoption, became a traitor to the Jewish cause. When the news of his defection became known, there was a general outcry against him in Jerusalem. Jos., War 3.438-442.

171. The modern town of Yafa, two miles south-west of Nazareth.

172. Jos., War 3.289-306.

173. Jos., War 3.307-315.

174. This seems to be the modern Chirbet el-Kerak at the south-western corner of Lake Tiberias, where the Jordan flows out of it.

175. Jos., War 3.536.

176. Schwier, Tempel 13.

177. Jos., War 462-542.

178. Jos., War 4.85.

179. Jos., War 4.84-87.

180. Jos., War 4.92.

181. Jos., War 4.106-111.

141. Jos., War 2.408.
142. Jos., War 2.409.
143. Prigent, Fin 17.
144. Schürer, Hist. I, 486.
145. Jos., War 2.410.
146. Jos., War 2.417-422.
147. Jos., War 2.426-454.
148. Jos., War 2.457.
149. Jos., War 2.458-460.
150. Jos., War 2.461-465.
151. Jos., War 2.477-478.
152. Jos., War 2.487-498.
153. Jos., War 2.499-501.
154. Jos., War 2.502-528.
155. Jos., War 2.528-539.
156. Jos., War 2.540-555.
157. Jos., War 2.556-558.
158. Eus., HE 3.5.2; Epiph., Adv.haer. 29.7, and De mens. et pond. 15. Schürer, Hist. I, 498, thinks that this exodus took place somewhat later, namely when the Zealots got in total command of the city. The question is extensively treated by Brandon, Fall of Jer., Ch. IX.
159. Jos., War 2.562-584.
160. Jos., War 2.569-584.
161. Schürer, Hist. I, 490.
162. Jos., War 2.585-646.
163. Jos., War 3.1.
164. Jos., War 3.3-8.
165. Jos., War 3.64-69.
166. Jos., War 3.127-131.166.22.
167. Jos., War 3.132-134.
168. Jos., War 3.136-137.
169. Jos., War 3.135-339.

242. Jos., War 6.329.

243. Jos., War 6.344.

244. CIL 6.944. In Jewish sources Titus is always the great villain, whereas Vespasian comes off slightly better (friendly communication by my daughter Dr. Th.A.M. Smidt van Gelder-Fontaine).

245. Jos., War 6.328.245.

246. Jos., War 6.349.

247. Jos., War 6.346; Schwier, Tempel 286.

248. In fact this author spoke of the Jewish **and** the Christian religion as both being illicit. The addition of the Christian religion may have been an anachronism on Sulpicius' part; it is not very probable that already in A.D. 70 Christianity played a great part in either Vespasian's or Titus's thought. However, Sulpicius has an interesting idea to add, namely that, still according to Titus, the Christian religion had originated from the Jewish one; "once the root had been eradicated, the stem would perish easily enough". To me it seems probable that this idea was at the back of Hitler's mind. Anyhow, Sulpicius saw clearly how closely related Judaism and Christianity were; deadly damage to the one would mean deadly damage to the other. See for the stance taken by Jos. Schürer I, 506, note 115.

249. Schwier, Tempel 332.

250. Jos., War 7.148-150. Vespasian had these objects deposited in the Pax temple. The original Torah scroll of the Temple and its purple curtain found a place in his palace, Jos., War 7.158-162. According to Schürer, Hist. I, 510, "it is not known what happened to them afterwards. They were probably taken to Africa by Geiseric when the Vandals sacked Rome in A.D. 455, and from there transferred to Constantinople by Belisarius, when he destroyed the Vandal Empire in A.D. 534". What happened later to the cult objects is not clear; in any case, they have disappeared without a trace. It does not seem probable to me that Crusaders took them with them, when they thoroughly plundered the Byzantine capital in 1204, for they would have mentioned it, and the objects would have emerged somewhere in the West. A real possibility is that they vanished when the Turks captured the city in 154. See Gregorovius, Gesch.Stadt Rom I, 210-211.

251. Schürer, Hist. I, 332.

252. Schwier, Tempel 337 : "Die metaphysische Bedrohung durch den kultisch nicht integrierbaren und schliesslich bekämpften jüdischen Gott war jedoch nun in römischen Augen abgewendet. Jawhe befand sich (symbolisch) in Rom unter der Ägide der römisch-flavischen Pax, seine Steuern kamen Jupiter zugute, und in Jerusalem war eine

römische Legion stationiert, so dass dort statt eines Tempels ein Fahnenheiligtum existierte".

253. Suet., Dom. 12.2.

254. Dio 67.14.2.

255. Dio 68.1.2. On the authority of Hegesippus Eusebius relates that the Emperors Vespasian (HE 3.12), Domitian (HE 3.19-20), and Trajan (HE 3.32.3-4) had all Jews of Davidic descent executed "in order to extirpate the royal line on which the Jews had set their hopes". Schürer, Hist. I, 528, says that "there is no way of checking the historical truth of this story".

256. Eus., HE 4.2.2.

257. Appian, Rom.hist., Civ.Wars 2.90.

258. Appian, fr. 19.

259. Eus., HE 4.2 and Chron. sub 115, pp. 553/554; Orosius 7.12.

260. From papyri quoted by Schürer, Hist. I, 531.

261. Dio 68.22.

262. Eus., HE 4.2.

263. Dio 68.32; Eus., Chron., pp. 556.

264. Eus., HE 14.2; Orosius 7.12.7; Dio 68.32.

265. Schürer, Hist. I, 533/534.

266. Spartianus, Vita Hadriani. Hist.Aug. 22.10.

267. Spartianus, Vita Hadriani, Hist.Aug. 14.2.

268. Schürer, Hist. I, 540.268.

269. Epiphanius, De mes. et pond. 13.

270. Dio 69.12.

271. Dio 69.12 says : before the revolt, Eus., HE 4,64, says 'after the war'.

272. There are several spellings of his name : Koziba, Kosiba (in Hebrew sources), Choosiba (in the Greek transliteration), and in more recent texts Kokheba. Kochba, Kokhba. etc.; the name Simon is found on coins of the period, see Schürer, Hist. I, 543.

273. Num. 24:17.

274. Schürer, Hist. I, 543, note 130.

275. Schürer, Hist. I, 544. Eus., HE 4.6.2, holds a very low opinion of the man; he says he was bloodthirsty and mercenary, and that, with that name 'star', he tried to befool the people into thinking that he had fallen as a star from heaven. The strongly Messianic character of the

movement prevented Jewish Christians in Palestine from taking part in it. Jus., 1Ap. 31.6, says that Bar Kokhba molested them if they did not repudiate and blaspheme Jesus the Messiah, while Eus., Chron. sub 132, writes that he afflicted Christians with several vexations.

276. Given by Eus., Chron. sub 132.
277. Prigent, Fin 139.
278. Dio 69.12.3.
279. The sources do not refer to an occupation but see the arguments for it given by Schürer, Hist, I, 545. It is possible that a restoration of the Temple was planned, Schürer, Hist. I, 545/546.
280. Schürer, Hist. I, 545/546.
281. See Schürer, Hist. I, 549/550.
282. Dio 69.13.3.
283. Probably not far from Jerusalem, Eus., HE 4.6.13.
284. Eus., HE 4.6.3.
285. Dio 69.14.3.
286. Schürer, Hist. I,553.
287. Dio 69,12,2; Eus., HE 4.6.4.
288. Just., 1Ap. 47.6.
289. Dio 12,1.
290. Schürer, Hist. I, 553/554.
291. Schürer, Hist. I, 555.
292. Schürer, Hist. I, 555.
293. Schürer, Hist. I, 556.
294. Schürer, Hist. I, 556, note 192.
295. Vol. XI, Ch. I.
296. Justinianus, Digest 48.8.11, quoted by Gager, Anti-Sem. 92. On p. 62 this author makes the astonishing statement that the ban "had the effect of promoting proselytism once again". If this is correct, he should have had to explain it. On p. 92 he writes that the fact that the ban had to be renewed is "but further evidence of the policy's failure". In this he is followed by Wilken, John Chrysost. 51/52, who says that "the laws on proselytism are the most significant for determining the status of the Jews in the Empire, because they restrict Jewish activity ... Later legislation reiterated some of these laws, and this may mean that the laws had little effect or were not enforced. As is always the case in using laws as historical sources, one must place them within

the framework of what is known from other sources. They must be set against the backdrop of the archaeological and literary evidence". Now the great problem is that there exists precious little evidence concerning Jewish proselytism.

297. Evasio de Marcellis s.v. 'Egypt from the End of the Second Temple Period to the Moslim Conquest', Enc.Jud. 6 (1971), 490.

298. Juster, Juifs I, 392-399.

299. Wilken, John Chryst. 46.

300. Wilken, John Chryst. 48-49.

301. David Rokeah s.v. 'Julian the Apostate', Enc.Jud. 10 (1971), 468.

302. There exists a book that probably contains more with regard to this subject, M. Schuhl, Les préventions de Rome contre la nation juive. Paris, 1892. I was unable to lay my hands on it.

303. Hier., In Soph. 1 to Soph. 15:6.

304. Gabba, Growth 614.

305. Gabba, Growth 616.

306. Where would we be, for informations like this, without Stern's seminal work, Greek and Latin authors (see Bibliography)? This passage comes from a lost treatise by Theophrastus, De pietate, quoted by Porphyrius, De abstinentia 2.26, Stern I, 10. A somewhat older collection is that by Reinach, Textes (see Bibliography).

307. It is mentioned by Jos., Contra Ap. 1.183, and by Origen, Contra Cels. 1.15. A book on Abraham, allegedly written by Theophrastus and mentioned by Clement of Alexandria and Eusebius, may be assumed to be, according to Stern I, 22, 'a product of Jewish propaganda'.

308. Quoted by Diod.Sic. 40.3 from a book (lost) called 'Ægyptiaca', Stern I, 26-29.

309. Stern I, 21. Jos., Contra Ap. 1.183-204, also gives long excerpts from Hec.'s book on the Jews. Many authors feel that these are not authentic, because they are so panegyric about them, with arguments which Stern seeks to rebut. Gabba, Growth 625, supposes that Hec. got his information directly from the strong Jewish element in Alexandria.

310. In his 'Indica', quoted by Clem.Al., Strom. 1.15.72.5, Stern I, 46.

311. In 'De somno', quoted by Jos., Contra Ap. I, 176-183, Stern I, 49-50.

312. From his 'De Pythagora', quoted by Jos., Contra Ap. 1.162-165, and from his 'De legationibus', quoted by Origen, Contra Cels. 1.15.134, Stern I, 95-96.

313. Quoted by Eus., Praep.Ev. 7.10.5, and Clem.Al., Strom. 5.14.97. See Schürer, Hist. III.1, 582, and Gabba, Growth 638.313.
314. Quoted by Jos., Contra Ap. 12.5-6, Stern I, 108.
315. In his 'De universi natura', Stern I, 133.
316. Gabba, Growth 636.
317. Tcherikover, Hell.Civ. 369-372.
318. Quoted by Jos., Ant. 12.5-6, Stern I, 108.
319. Polybius, Historiae, quoted by Jos., Ant. 12.135-136, Stern I, 113.
320. Quoted by Strabo, Geogr. 16.2.43, Stern I, 147.
321. Quoted by Jos., Contra Ap. 2.91-96 and 79, Stern I, 146-147.
322. Gabba, Growth 643.
323. Stern I, 143.
324. Diod.Sic. 34, fr. 1, in Reinach 56-59.
325. Radin, Jews 198.
326. Jos., Contra Ap. 2.14.148.
327. Stern I, 159-164.
328. Diod.Sic. 1.94.12.
329. Stern I, 172.329.22.
330. Gager, Anti-Sem. 68/69.
331. Gager, Anti-Sem. 36; this author combats this view.
332. Gager, Anti-Sem. 70.
333. Jos., Ant. 16.42.43.
334. Just., Epit. 2.16.
335. Just., Epit. 1.11.
336. Just., Epit. 1.12.
337. Gager, Anti-Sem. 73.
338. Strabo, Geogr. 16.35.
339. Stern I, 382.
340. Jos., Contra Apionem 1.305-310.
341. Jos., Contra Apionem 2.145.
342. Stern I, 390.
343. Aul.Gell., Noct.Att. 5.4.5.

344. Stern I, 390.
345. Jos., Contra Apionem 2.15.
346. Jos., Contra Apionem 2.33.
347. Jos., Contra Apionem 2.38.
348. Jos., Contra Apionem 2.80.
349. Jos., Contra Apionem 2.91-96.
350. Jos., Contra Apionem 2.21.
351. Jos., Contra Apionem 2.125.
352. Jos., Contra Apionem 2.137.
353. Jos., Contra Apionem 2.79.
354. Jos., Contra Apionem 2.121.
355. Gabba, Growth 653.
356. Stern I, 361; the others are Diodorus Siculus and Ocellus Lucanus.
357. On the subl. 9.9, Stern I, 364.
358. Stern I, 362.
359. Gager, Anti-Sem. 78/79.
360. Quæstiones conviviales 5.2, Stern I, 556.
361. De superstitione 3, Stern I, 549.
362. Quæst.conv. 6.2, Stern I, 557-558; Gager, Anti-Sem. 79.
363. Stern I, 193.
364. De provinciis consularibus 5.10, Stern I, 203.
365. Pro Flacco 28.67, Stern I, 197.
366. Pro Flacco 28.69, Stern I, 198.
367. Quoted by Augustine, De consensu evangelistarum 1.22.30 and 31.27.42, Stern I, 210.
368. Quoted by Lydus, De mensibus 4.53, Stern I, 212.
369. De superstitione, quoted by Augustine, De civitate Dei 6.11, Stern I, 431.
370. Satyricon 68.8, 102.14, fr. 37, Stern I, 447-448.
371. Fr. 37, Stern I, 444.
372. Institutio oratoria 3.37.21.
373. Epigrammata 14..4, Stern I, 524.

374. Epigrammata 7.30, Stern I, 525.
375. Epigrammata 7.82 and 9.94, Stern I, 526-528.
376. Stern II, 1.
377. Tac., Hist. 5.1.1-2.
378. Tac., Hist. 5.3.1-2.
379. Tac., Hist. 5.4.1-3.
380. Tac., Hist. 5.5.1-5.
381. Gager, Anti-Sem. 64.
382. Juvenal, Satura 14.96-106, Stern II, 102/103.
383. Gager, Anti-Sem. 65.
384. Gager, Anti-Sem. 84/85; see my Vol. VIII, Ch. I, especially sections 7 and 8.
385. Gager, Anti-Sem. 86.
386. See Vol. VIII, Ch. I.1.
387. Sevenster, Roots 56.
388. Sevenster, Roots 88.
389. Sevenster, Roots 145.
390. Sevenster, Roots 145/146.
391. Sevenster, Roots 89.
392. Wilken, John Chrysost. 63.
393. Wilken, John Chrysost. 65.
394. Urbach, Self-Isolation 271.
395. Martin Hengel, Judentum und Hellenismus, 1969.
396. Urbach, Self-Isolation 298.
397. Pesahim 10.1.103b.
398. Dio 37.17.
399. Diogn. 5.1.
400. Jos., Contra Apionem 1.60-61.
401. Num. 23:9.
402. Philo, Vita Moysi 1.278.
403. Sevenster, Roots 143/144.

CHAPTER VI

ROMANS AND GREEKS, GREEKS AND ROMANS

1. The non-Greek origin of Rome

The Romans were convinced that their city had a non-Greek origin. The ancestor of the Roman royal house, Aeneas, one of the defenders of Troy, escaped from this city after it had been set on fire by the Greeks. Having wandered about for a long time, he finally arrived in Latium at the mouth of the Tiber. His son Ascanius - a pure Trojan, since his mother Creusa was born in Troy - became the founder of Alba Longa. From him the twelve Albanian kings descended. King Numitor, the last but one, was the father of Rhea Silvia; on her the god Mars fathered the twins Romulus and Remus, the founders of Rome. This ancestry gave the Romans an origin that was not only divine but also Trojan [1].

There is a touch of antagonism to the Greeks in this. These histories, found in Virgil's 'Aeneid' and in the first book of Livy's 'Roman history', are legends rather than historical accounts, of course. But the point is that there is also a strong element of competition with the Hellenes in them. If the Greeks had a long and prestigious history, the siege and sack of Troy being its oldest event, the Romans refused to take second place to them on the assumption that their historical lineage too began in Troy. It is interesting to note that Greek historiography for a long time knew nothing of a connection between Aeneas and the origin of Rome, although it was known that the Trojan hero had sailed westward [2].

This anti-Greek sentiment, reflected in the myth of Trojan origin, remained always discernible in Roman politics. The Emperor Claudius (41-54) granted the city of Ilion (Troy) a perpetual exemption from tax, on the ground that the Trojans were the ancestors of the Roman people; it was then alleged that, already earlier, the Senate had only been ready to conclude a treaty with the Seleucid (Greek) King Seleucus (IV) on the condition that he gave the citizens of Ilion, the 'kinsfolk' (consanguinei) of the Romans, freedom of taxes [3].

2. The first contacts

According to Roman tradition, the relationship between Greeks and Trojans began already before 500 B.C., when the first Greek ever to enter Rome, a woman from Cumae, said to be the Sibylle, a prophetess, came to King Tarquinius Superbus and offered him nine books of divine oracles. However, she asked such an exorbitant price for them that the king thought she was out of her mind. She then burned three books, and when the king again refused to pay, yet another three. Finally Tarquinius bought the remainder for the same price she had first asked. The woman disappeared never to be seen again [4].

Whether or not this story is historical, and whether the Sibylline Books were Greek or Etruscan or came from Asia Minor, it was, so would Roman tradition have it, a prophetess from Greek Cumae who introduced the Romans to these oracles, which fortified them in their idea that their history was fated from above. The Sibylline Books were considered an irreplaceable treasure. They were kept for centuries in the vaults under the temple of Jupiter Capitolinus and, since Augustus, in the Apollo temple on the Palatine; a special priestly college had the guardianship over them [5]. Whenever Rome was in great danger, the Senate ordered the priests to consult the oracles. Stilicho, the Vandal who ruled the Empire around A.D. 400, had them burned - a clear sign that Rome's end was drawing near [6].

Equally intriguing is the story of a Roman embassy to Athens in 451/450 B.C., with the object of inquiring after the codification of Athenian law by Solon [7]. This story may be a later invention, but it proves that the

Romans were not ashamed to acknowledge their debt to the Greeks in a field in which they considered themselves experts. However, by and large, in the sixth and fifth centuries the Roman and Greek worlds were not deeply interested in each other [8].

Until 300 B.C. Rome had hardly any Greeks under her aegis, while for the Greeks Latium was virtually an unknown country on the fringes of the civilized world [9]. They did not even understand that Latins and Etruscans were different peoples; it was only as a result of the conquest of Veii by Rome in 396 [10] that the Greeks began to realize this. The first event in Rome's history that caught the attention of the Hellenes was the capture of the city by the Celts in 387 B.C. [11]. In 334 B.C. King Alexander I of Epirus concluded a treaty with Rome, when he was campaigning in South Italy; this was the very first political contact. The first Greek city with which Rome had a special relationship, starting around 300 B.C., was not Athens but Massillia (Marseille) [12].

3. The Greeks brought under Roman control

For the Romans it was impossible to behave as if no Greeks existed, since they had them next-door. Not far to the south, in Campania, important Greek cities were to be found, Cumae, for instance, the oldest Greek settlement in Italy, and Naples. In all southern Italy Greek colonies abounded, in such numbers that the region was called 'Magna Graecia'.

Rome began to penetrate into the Hellenic world with her successful campaign against the city of Naples in 328/327 B.C.; after Rome's victory a 'foedus', a treaty of friendship with the Neapolitans, was concluded [13]. In this context Livy makes the depreciatory remark that the Greeks are 'more valiant in words than in deeds' [14]. In the decades after 350 B.C. Rome, in an often laborious process, gradually conquered Magna Graecia and brought the Hellenes living there under her dominion [15]. Later also Greece itself and the Greek cities of Asia Minor came under Roman rule [16]. Around 100 B.C. Rome had gathered almost all Greeks under her wings. After three centuries of warfare she had not only the autochthonous Hellenes but also the Hellenistic kingdoms under her control, with Egypt as the last acquisition. What must occupy us now is the cultural and ideological relationship between the Greeks and Romans [17].

4. The Romans as barbarians

The tendency among the Hellenes was to consider the Romans barbarians. What the geographer Eratosthenes around 235 B.C. wrote of them is rather comic. Although he rejected the usual division of mankind into Hellenes and barbarians, he called the Romans (and the Carthaginians) barbarians, with the qualification that they were 'refined' ones, since they had such excellent political constitutions [18]. In 239 B.C. a Roman embassy came to Aetolia - the very first intervention of Rome in the affairs of mainland Greece - in order to tell the Aetolians to stop their aggression against Acarnania. The retort of the Aetolians was : who do you think you are? Stay out of Greece! You weren't even able to chase the Celts from Italy, whereas we defeated them (they did, indeed, in 279 B.C.). You are no more than shepherds, your city has been founded on murder, you live on territory you have stolen [19].

Unambiguous language this! The Aetolians never got over their resentment against Rome. But sentiments like this must have smouldered in the Hellenic mind generally. As Albrecht Dihle wrote, it was only in the days of the Emperors that the Greeks were prepared to concede the Romans the status of a civilized people. But we should not overlook the fact that cultured Romans wrote and spoke Greek then; this made them sufficiently hellenized to become Greeks by adoption [20].

There is no denying that for centuries Rome had a bad press with many Greek authors. "To educated Greeks, Romans never appeared anything but a race of upstarts" [21]. The Romans had no Homer; their language was crude and not fit for great literary works. Roman high society was found vulgar and immoral. It was considered a bad habit that Roman matronae, in contrast to their Greek sisters, moved freely about in society and went to dinner-parties [22].

Cicero reports an incident that highlights the distance between Roman and Greek conceptions of decent behaviour. A certain Rubrius arranged a dinner-party at which a Greek, Philodamus, was also present. When the bumpers had gone around for some time, the host invited his Greek guest to send for his daughter - a request that was received 'with astonished silence'. "It was not the Greek custom", the father explained, "for women to be present at a men's dinner-party." When one of the other guests insisted that the girl should be sent for, the party ended in a fight between Rubrius's slaves and those of Philodamus; there was even a fatal victim in this Roman-Greek mini-war [23].

Just as modern Europeans use to think that Americans are people with thoroughly bad taste in aesthetic matters, so the Greeks found the Romans only a little short of being vandals. With regard to art, the Romans had to sail by the Hellenic compass. Not that they respected the Hellenes for their expertise in this sphere. By no means! They found it childish. 'This decorative stuff', as Cicero dubbed it, might afford pleasure to Greeks, but Romans felt it consisted of 'negligible trifles' [24]. "It is indeed quite astonishing what delight a Greek will take in things of which a Roman thinks so little" [25]. The Romans had the manly task of governing the world. There was not much original art in Rome, and what there was, in public and private, was stolen in Greek towns, as Cicero readily admitted. "No community anywhere in Asia or in Greece has of its own free will sold any statue, or any picture, or any civic work of art whatever to anyone on any occasion ... Nothing is causing, or has caused, more distress to the Greeks than such plundering of temples and towns" [26].

Cicero, who saw himself as a paragon of Roman scholarship, voluntarily paraded himself as a philistine. Speaking of a marble Cupid by Praxiteles, he unblushingly stated that he had only learned the name of the sculptor in the course of his investigations as a prosecutor [27]. It is as though a modern counsel for the prosecution, referring to a stolen Rodin, would say : "Never heard of the guy, looked him up in an encylopedia". There were, of course, cultured Romans but, as Balsdon, on whom I am heavily leaning for this paragraph, writes : "It was evident to the Greeks that there was a

323

considerable affectation in the pretentiously cultured Roman and that the average Greek was born with a 'spiritual' quality which most Romans lacked" [28].

Lucianus wrote contemptuously of those Roman aristocrats who must needs have a Greek scholar in their house. "If you have a long beard, present a distinguished appearance, are neatly dressed in a Greek mantle, and everybody knows you for a grammarian or a rhetorician or a philosopher, it seems to him (a rich Roman) the proper thing to have a man of that sort among those who go before him and form his escort; it will make people think him a devoted student of Greek learning and in general a person of taste in literary matters. (But) the chances are ... that, instead of your marvellous lectures, it is your beard and your mantle that you have let for hire ... The purpose for which he engaged you, saying that he wanted knowledge, matters little to him; for as the proverb says, 'what has an ass to do with a lyre?'" [29].

5. The Romans unbeloved

The fact that the Romans had overrun the Hellenic world did not make them beloved. They were reproached for their desire for booty, for the corruption of their officials and tax-collectors, for the insensibility and callousness of their policy, for their arrogance and their demonstration of superiority. Balsdon states that in Diodorus' account of the slave rising of 133 B.C. in Sicily, the words 'arrogant' and 'arrogance' occur twelve times [30]. Fronto wrote that "in reality no one in Rome has any warm affection". In all his life he had never met a Roman whom he might call 'affectionate' [31].

6. Some positive views

To redress the balance somewhat, it is necessary to note that there were also Greek authors who had a more positive idea of Rome : I mention Aristides, Arrian, Appian, Cassius Dio, Polybius, Posidonius, Dionysius of Halicarnassus, Diodorus Siculus, Plutarch. Balsdon calls some of them 'mongrels', 'Greeks who were at the same time Romans, men with significant careers in Roman administration' [32]. Hardly anyone of them was blind to the negative side of the Roman character and of Roman politics. What they admired was the Roman Empire rather than the Romans. In their eyes the Empire was a world-historical achievement. Probably they all agreed with what Dionysius wrote, namely that "by a universal law of nature, which time cannot destroy, it is ordained that superiors shall ever govern their inferiors" [33]. If the Romans lorded it over the Greeks, then this was simply fated, and one had better accomodate oneself to it. What these authors had to praise in Rome was mainly that she had created stable conditions in the eastern world. The centuries of internecine warfare between the poleis, followed by two centuries of bloody struggles between the succesor-states, were over now. All the same, it was Plutarch's aim in the parallel lives to demonstrate that Greece had just as many great politicians and generals as Rome.

On the whole, we can distinguish two periods in the reactions of the Greeks to Roman rule. The first, running from the first contacts until the middle of the last century B.C., is one of active resistance to subjugation [34]. The second, the centuries of the Emperors, is characterized by Bette Forte as 'Greeks reconciliated' and 'Greeks as Partners in Roman Rule and Educators of Roman Rulers' [35]. In the last century of the Empire the centre of gravity of imperialism shifted back from the West to the East, when Constantinople became the second capital and finally the real one. When the western Empire collapsed, it was the eastern Empire that subsisted.

7. The Romans and the Greek language

There is, of course, yet another side to the coin : what did Romans feel about and write about the Greeks? Some imprecision clung to the term 'Greek' (Graecus). Sometimes it denoted the inhabitants of mainland Greece, those of the Greek poleis along the coast of Asia Minor, the Greek populations of Magna Graecia and Sicily, and the citizens of the Greek colonies along the shores of the Mediterranean and the Black Sea. But the term could also be applied to the hellenized population groups in Asia Minor and Egypt, that is, to people that were not ethnic Greeks. In the last case the Romans often had a problem in distinguishing hellenized Asiatics and Egyptians from other Asiatics and Egyptians, with the consequence that, in their eyes, the hellenized shared the inferior qualities attributed to the non-hellenized [36].

In his comprehensive study of Roman-Greek relations Nicholas Petrocheilos states that the spread of the Greek language to Rome was a highly important factor in these relations. "It was in the first place through their knowledge of Greek that the Romans were exposed to the pressure of superior Greek achievement in the intellectual and other fields; in the second place, the influence on the Greek language on their own in itself called forth varying attitudes of acceptance and reactions" [37]. There was not only a cultural necessity to know Greek but also a political and social one. The Roman Empire comprised millions and millions of native Greek speakers, whole regions where nothing but Greek was spoken. In order to communicate with their subjects in the East, Roman officials had to know Greek.

Add to this that, for a long time, Latin remained a provincial language (and in Greek eyes a barbaric one), whereas Greek was the lingua franca of the oecumene. "Greek literature is read in nearly every nation under the heaven, while the vogue of Latin is confined to its own boundaries, and they are, we must grant, narrow", wrote Cicero [38]. It must not be thought, however, that in the course of time Rome too became a Greek-speaking city. Knowledge of Greek remained restricted to the leading circles; the mass of the population went on speaking Latin and knew no Greek or only very little.

The predominance of the Greek language must have given the Romans a sense of inferiority. There were, as goes without saying, reactions to this. For instance, Greek might be a language fit for philosophy but not for the treatment of serious subjects - such serious subjects being those of a political and juridical nature [39]. There was resistance against the use of Greek in Roman society. Cicero was even reprimanded because he had addressed the Syracusan city council in Greek; "to have talked to a Greek audience in its own language was, it would appear, something quite intolerable" [40]. Romans should, obviously, speak Latin on all occasions.

8. Characteristics of the Greeks according to the Romans

In his systematic study of Roman attitudes towards the Greeks Petrocheilos sums up the characteristics the Greeks had according to the Romans [41]. The first is Greek volubility, contrasted with the more sober and concise Latin tongue. Having listened to the speech of a Greek orator, the younger Pliny remarked that such men "mistake volubility for content, and thus overwhelm you with an endless torrent of cold and unaffecting periods" [42]. Greek affluence of speech - Greeks talked too rapidly, it was found - often irritated the Romans; "it is often represented by Roman writers in the form of an antithesis between verba and res" [43]. In the days of Old Cato some Greek philosophers came to Rome, and young Romans flocked to the lecture room to hear them. But Cato did not share this enthusiasm because the Greeks' reputation was 'based on mere words more than one achieved by martial deeds'. He would propose that "these men may return to their schools and lecture to the sons of Greece, while the youth of Rome give ear to their laws and magistrates, as heretofore" [44].

The Romans found Greek speakers inept. They liked to expatiate even on subjects with which they were unacqainted. Not without relish Cicero relates how a Greek philosopher, called Phormio, had held forth to Hannibal, whom he had met in Ephesus, 'for several hours upon the functions of a commander-in-chief and military matters in general". Asked for a reaction, the battle-hardened general replied that "he had seen many old madmen but never one madder than Phormio" [45]. The man was, in any case, mad enough to lecture to the greatest general of his days on the art of war.

This leads to the related reproach that the Greeks were arrogant and impudent (we saw already that the Greeks, from their side, found the Romans arrogant and haughty). Roman authors also accused the Greeks of levity, in contrast to their own 'gravitas'. Levity means instability, rashness, irresponsibility, untrustworthiness, excitability [46]. Cicero, who was just as voluble as any Greek, was ready to grant them literature, knowledge of many arts, charm of speech, keenness of intellect, richness of diction. "But truth and honour in giving testimony that nation has never cherished" [47]. In other words, Greeks were unreliable.

This brings us along the shortest road to the next negative notion, that of deceit. We find this in Virgil's much quoted line : "I fear the Greeks, even when bringing presents" (Timeo Danaos et dona ferentes) [48], and also : "Do you think any gifts of the Greeks are free from treachery?" [49]. Another well-known saying, namely 'ex uno disce omnes', has its origin here too : "Hear now the treachery of the Greeks and from one learn the wickedness of all" [50].

Romans thought Greeks showed a tendency to luxuriousness whereas they themselves were proud of their own frugality. They used the verb 'graecare' which means 'playing the Greek', with the connotaion of leading a life of dissipation. A character in Plautus's 'Mostellaria' exhorts his guests with these words : "Drink, live like Greeks (pergraecamini), eat, gorge yourself, kill the fatted calf!" [51].

This inevitably leads to the Roman idea that Hellenes showed a lack of manliness. Listen to the author of the Letter to Caesar who is believed to be Sallust : "Among that people (the Greeks) manliness, vigilance, and industry are wholly lacking" [52]. Or to Horace who sneered that "Roman army-exercises are fatiguing to one used to Greek ways" [53]. If Livy, referring to a special occasion, says that "the Greeks were poltroons and refused to risk an engagement" [54], Petrocheilos thinks that this is 'applicable to the Greeks in general' [55].

In the context of the Graeco-Roman relationship, the Latin term 'Graeculus' = Greeklet plays a significant role. It may have an affectionate connotation but it can also be used to express contempt. Petrocheilos says that "it reflects the quality of the relationship of Roman and Greek; by virtue of being a diminutive it can express a variety of attitudes from the mildly patronising to the openly contemptuous". He adds that it "thus becomes a handy instrument, especially for the orator, in arousing and exploiting anti-Greek sentiment" [56].

I conclude with a quip by Juvenal which perfectly expresses the mixture of admiration and irritation the Romans felt with regard to the Greeks : "Men of Rome, it is our Rome turned Greek that I cannot stomach ...

Conceive him (the Greek), if you can. A many-sided person he has brought up in himself : schoolmaster, professor, mathematician, painter, masseur, diviner, tight-rope dancer, doctor, wizard, your hungry little Greek knows all things alike : tell him to ascend to heaven, and he will do it" [57].

9. A dualistic relationship?

On the whole the Roman attitude towards the Greeks, their culture, and their way of life was ambiguous. They certainly found much to admire in it; they knew that their own culture was inferior to the Hellenic civilization [58]. They were even ready to learn from the Greeks : Greeks were much in vogue in Rome as paedagogues, teachers, administrators, bookkeepers, and what not. As Gruen writes, "Hellenism had great advantage for the Romans. It served both to enrich their heritage and to highlight the special merits of their (the Roman) nation" [59]. There occurred, doubtless, a certain hellenization of Roman life, what with those high-society Romans who could speak Greek and willingly did so. On the other hand, the Romans thought themselves far superior in those fields which they themselves found most important : political management, the art of warfare, legislation, and matters of jurisdiction and jurisprudence.

The decisive question is whether this relationship must be dubbed dualistic. On the surface it was certainly not so. The whole Hellenistic world became an integral part of the Roman Empire, neatly divided into provinces. And whereas the imperial government had to contend with rebellion after rebellion in the West and North Africa, the Hellenistic East kept its peace. The centuries of the Emperors are characterized by Bette Forte as 'Greek conciliation' and 'Greek partners in Roman rule and educators of Roman rulers' [60]. The orientals obviously had accomodated themselves to the new situation. Greeks found their way into the imperial administration and often fulfilled important functions in it. Their language was recognized and in use as the second tongue of the Empire. The big exception was formed exactly by a non-hellenized population group, the Jews, who rose in rebellion several times.

It had not always been so. During the Republic there had been a sometimes outspoken and often dumb resistance against Roman rule in the Greek world [61]. In the time of the Emperors the educated and intellectual classes among the Greeks showed themselves better satisfied with Roman rule. This need not surprise us since they were coddled by the Romans and their Emperors. It should, however, be kept in mind that, as Palm remarks, "almost all authors of this period came from Asia; at the best their origin was Greek, not their fatherland". And then, as this same scholar writes, we detect in these writers a certain tendency to 'deromanize' the Empire, to make it less authentically Roman. The trend was to view it almost as an abstract entity, as a non-nation world empire, which means taking it away from the ethnic Romans. Behind this there was the urge "to consider the monarchical Empire philosophically, to see it as the realization of the Greek ideas of the world state". To such authors the Empire consisted of two equal parts : politically it was Roman, culturally it was Greek; in this way it became a Greek-Roman concern" [62].

So far so good. But on a deeper and more basic level things looked different. Several times in earlier volumes I spoke of an East-West diaphragm, a chasm between the occidental and and oriental halves of it, between the Latin and the Greek worlds. As I have often argued, it was (and still is) as though an invisible frontier was drawn from south to north through the Adriatic partitioning the oecumene into two halves, an eastern and a western one, two worlds different from each other and viewing each other with distrust and incomprehension. The romanized and hellenized populations eyed each other with a sometimes hardly disguised contempt. They felt uncomfortable with being part of the same body politic. The westerners always were uneasy with their eastern co-citizens; the easterners never fully accepted the dominion of the West. The East showed a permanent tendency to go its own way. Ambitious men, like Caesar and Mark Antony, counted, for their political purposes, on the East, which was more congenial to them, rather than on the West - so much so that one is allowed to speak of an abortive Empire of the East, a grand design which made the political circles of Rome feel very uncomfortable [63].

The mastery of these large territories with their highly civilized and sophisticated populations always constituted a source of uneasiness for Rome. The Roman Empire was the last remaining, all-comprising imperium of Antiquity. But it was a western-based empire, whereas the cradle of all imperialisms was Mesopotamia. The heir of all oriental imperialisms was Alexander the Great whose successors opposed the Romans, when they began to penetrate into the eastern world. Rome, as a western power, was a newcomer to that world and as such basically foreign to its ethos, its civilization, and its aspirations. Rome always feared the resurgence of the old imperialistic tendencies of the East. A man like Mithridates VI of Pontus considered himself a new Alexander and as such the inveterate opponent of Rome's imperialistic ambitions [64].

At the end of the fourth century the parting of the ways became constitutional. For the first time East and West became separated in 293, when each halve would have its own ruler. It was a sign of the times that the senior Emperor, Diocletian, was to govern the eastern half of the Empire. A significant step was taken in 330 when Constantinople was dedicated. It was not just another town, it was a new capital, second after Rome but steadily growing in importance. From the start it was a Christian city, without pagan temples, whereas Rome remained the main centre of the pagan cult. The centre of gravity of imperialism was seen shifting back from the West to the East. In 395 the split between east and West became definitive, when the Empire became a confederation of the Western and Eastern Empires, each with its own ruler, but henceforward without a common one. When the Western Empire collapsed, it was the Eastern Empire that subsisted for another thousand years.

Was the relationship dualistic? I think it was. There never was a moment when the occidental and oriental halves merged into an organic unity. There always remained a distance, a distance that was never bridged. The chasm even grew wider as time progressed. It was a curious sort of dualism since in this case each party considered the other inferior. Although there were conflicts between the two halves and their rulers, they did not seek to destroy each other. For this reason we should not speak of radical dualism. But without doubt the relationship was relatively dualistic.

NOTES TO CHAPTER VII

1. See Vol. X, Ch.II.2d-e.
2. Bayer, Rom und die Westgr. 307 and 310.
3. Suet., Claudius 25.3.
4. Aulus Gellius, Noct.Att. 1.19; Dion.Hal. 4.62.1-3.
5. Dion.Hal. 4.67.5.
6. Rutilius Num., De reditu.
7. Dion.Hal. 10.52.4 and 54.3; Livy 3.33.5.
8. Bayer, Rom und die Westgr. 328/329.
9. We find the first reports on Rome and Romans in Greek authors in Schmidt, Rom und die griech. Welt 9-15.
10. See Ch. II.5b.
11. Bayer, Rom und die Westgr. 330. See Ch. II.5c.
12. Bayer, Rom und die Westgr. 332/333.
13. Livy 8.22.5-8 and 25-26.
14. Livy 8.22.5.
15. See Vol. X, Ch. II.12-13.
16. This the subject of Vol. X, Ch. IV.
17. Only recently Flinterman described the Greek attitude, in particular that of intellectuals, in his Power, Paideia, pp. 117-127 Greek self-awareness and Roman rule.
18. Strabo, Geogr. 1.4.9.
19. Justinus, Epit. 28.2.
20. Dihle, Griechen 52.
21. Balsdon, Romans 160.
22. Nepos, Proeemium 6-7; see Ch. IV, Part IV.5.
23. Cic., In Verr. 2.1.66-67.
24. Cic., In Verr. 2.13.132.
25. Cic., In Verr. 2.4.134.

26. Cic., In Verr. 2.4.132-133.
27. Cic., In Verr. 2.4.4.
28. Balsdon, Romans 178.
29. Lucianus, De mercede 25.
30. Balsdon, Romans, 286, note 56; Diod.Sic. 34/35, 33 sqq.
31. Fronto, Letter to Lucius Verus 6.
32. Balsdon, Romans 193.
33. Dion.Hal. 1.5.2.
34. This process is amply documented by Deininger, Widerstand (see Bibliography).
35. Forte, Rome (see Bibliography).
36. See Petrocheilos, Rom, Att. 17-21.
37. Petrocheilos, Rom.Att. 23.
38. Cic., Pro Archia 23.
39. Petrocheilos, Rom.Att. 27.
40. Cic., In Verr. 2.4.147.
41. See for this subject also Wardman, Rome's Debt, Ch. I, The Greek Character.
42. Pliny, Ep. 5.20.4.
43. Petrocheilos, Rom.Att. 37.
44. Plut., Cato maior 22.4-5. See Vol. VI, Ch.III.7a. See for an extensive treatment of Cato's attitude Gruen, Culture, Ch. 2, Cato and Hellenism. Cato, says Gruen, was the 'arch-critic of Hellas and Hellenism ... He became an emblem of resistance to the alien intrusion" (p. 52). Nonetheless, he was fairly familiar with Greek culture.
45. Cic., De oratore 2.28.75.
46. Petricheilos, Rom.Att. 40/41.
47. Cic., Pro Flacco 4.9.
48. Virg., Aeneid 2.49.
49. Virg., Aeneid 2.43/44.
50. Virg., Aeneid 2.65.
51. Plautus, Mostellaria 54/65.
52. Letter to Caesar 9.3.

53. Horace, Satire 2.2.9.
54. Livy 7.26.11.
55. Petrocheilos, Rom.Att. 47.
56. Petrocheilos, Rom.Att. 53.
57. Juven., Sat. 3.60-78.
58. Wilkinson, Roman Experience, Ch. 3 The Impact of Greece describes the influence Greece had on Rome in several fields. Whereas this scholar speaks of an 'impact', Wardman, Rome's Debt to Greece (see Bibliography) speaks of a 'debt'.
59. Gruen, Culture 271.
60. Forte, Rome (see Bibliography).
61. Fuchs, Widerstand 5.
62. Palm, Rom 130-133.
63. This is the subject of Vol. X, Ch. V.
64. See Vol. X. Ch. IV.15-24.

BIBLIOGRAPHY

I ORIGINAL SOURCES

A COLLECTIONS

DER BABYLONISCHE TALMUD II. Herausgeber Lazarus Goldschmidt. Berlin, 1901.

CODEX INSCRIPTIONUM LATINARUM. Berlin, 1863-1936. (Quoted as CIL).

CORPUS CIVILE. I IUSTINIANI INSTITUTIONES. Ed. Paul Krueger. Berlin, 1882.

CORPUS SCRIPTORUM ECCLESIASTICORUM LATINORUM. Vienna.

THE CORRESPONDENCE OF MARCUS TULLIUS CICERO. Vol. VI. Eds. Robert Yelverton and Louis Claude Purser. Dublin, 1933².

EXCERPTA HISTORICA. Ed. Carolus de Boor. Vol. I. Berlin, 1903.

HISTORIA AUGUSTA. HISTOIRE AUGUSTE. Ed. J.-P. Callu. Paris, 1992.

INSCRIPTIONES LATINAE SELECTAE. Ed. Hermannus Dessau I. Berlin, 1892.

MONUMENTUM ANCYRANUM. RES GESTAE DIVI AUGUSTI. Herausgeber Hans Volkmann. Berlin, 1964.

ORATORUM ROMANORUM FRAGMENTA. Ed. Henrica Malcovati. Turin, 1976 4 (1930 1) (quoted as ORF).

THE OXYRHYNCHUS PAPERS XIV. Eds. Bernard P. Grenfell and Arthur S. Hunt. London, 1920.

PANEGYRICI LATINI. Panégyriques latins. Texte établi et traduit par Édouard Galletier. Collection Budé. Paris, 1949.

PATROLOGIA GRAECA. Paris. (Quoted as PG).

PATROLOGIA LATINA. Paris. (Quoted as PL).

RES GESTAE DIVI AUGUSTI. Ed. Jean Cagé. Paris, 1966 (1935[1]).

REINACH, Théodore, Textes d'auteurs grecs et romains relatifs au Judaïsme. Hildesheim, 1963.

SCHMIDT, Hatto H., Rom und die griechische Welt : von der Freiheit bis 133 v.Chr. Antike Quellen in Übersetzung. München, 1992.

SCRIPTORES HISTORIAE AUGUSTAE. Translated by David Magie. Loeb Classical Library 263. Cambridge (Ms.)/London, 1954 (1932[1]) (quoted as HA).

B INDIVIDUAL AUTHORS

AMMIANUS MARCELLINUS
  Historiae. Translated by J.C. Rolfe. Loeb Classical Library 300, 315, 331. Cambridge (Ms.)/London.

APPIANUS
  Appian. Roman History. Translated by Horace White. Loeb Classical Library 2-5. Cambridge (Ms.)/London.

ASCONIUS, Quintus
  Q. Asconii Pediani Commentarii. Ed. Caesar Giarratano. Amsterdam, 1967.

ATHENAEUS
  The Deipnosophists (cited as Ath.). Translated by Charlez Burton Gulick. Loeb Classical Library, seven volumes. Cambridge (Ms.)/London.

AULUS GELLIUS
  Noctes atticae. Attic Nights. Translated by John C. Rolfe. Loeb Classical Library. Cambridge (Ms.)/London, 1927.

AURELIUS, Marcus -- Antoninus
  The communings with himself of --. Translated by C.R. Haines. Loeb Classical Library 58. Cambridge (Ms.)/London, 1961 (1916[1]).

BAR-HEBRAEUS
  Historia compendiosa dynastiniarum. Ed. Edward Pocock. Oxford, 1963.

CAESAR, Gaius Julius
  1. Bellum civile. Civil Wars. Translated by A.G. Peskett. Loeb Classical Library 39. Cambridge (Ms.)/London, 1914.
  2. De bello gallico. Gallic War. Translated by H.J. Edwards. Loeb Classical Library 72. Cambridge (Ms.)/London, 1917[15].

CICERO, Marcus Tullius
1. Pro Archia poeta. Translated by N.H. Watts. Loeb Classical Library 159. Cambridge (Ms.)/London, 1923.
2. Pro Balbo. Translated by J.H. Freese. Loeb Classical Library 447. Cambridge (Ms.)/London, 1958.
3. Brutus. Translated by G.L. Hendrickson. Loeb Classical Library 342. Cambridge (Ms.)/London, 1939[5].
4. In Catilinam. Translated by C. Macdonald. Loeb Classical Library 324. Cambridge (Ms.)/London, 1977.
5. Epistolae ad Atticum. Letters to Atticus. 3 volumes. Translated by E.O. Winstedt. Loeb Classical Library. Cambridge (Ms.)/London.
6. Epistolae ad Famulares. Letters to his Friends. 4 volumes. Translated by E.O. Winstedt. Loeb Classical Library. Cambridge (Ms.)/London.
7. De imperatore.
8. Pro Marcello. Translated by N.H. Watts. Loeb Classical Library 252. Cambridge (Ms.)/London, 1931.
9. De officiis. Translated by Walter Miller. Loeb Classical Library 30. Cambridge (Ms.)/London, 1913.
10. De oratore. Translated by H. Rackham. Loeb Classical Library 349. Cambridge (Ms.)/London, 1942.
11. Philippica. Philippics. Translated by Walter C.A. Kerr. Loeb Classical Library 1926. Cambridge (Ms.)/London, 1926.
12. Pro Flacco. Translated by C. Macdonald. Loeb Classical Library 324. Cambridge (Ms.)/London, 1977.
13. Pro Rabirio perduellionis reo. Translated by H. Grose Hodge. Loeb Classical Library 198. Cambridge (Ms.)/London, 1927.
14. Pro Sestio. Translated by J.H. Freese, revised by R. Gardner. Loeb Classical Library 309. Cambridge (Ms.)/London, 1958.
15. Pro Sexto Roscio Amerino. Translated by J.H. Freese. Loeb Classical Library 240. Cambridge (Ms.)/London, 1930.
16. Tusculanae disputationes. Translated by J.E. King. Loeb Classical Library 268. Cambridge (Ms.)/London, 1945.
17. In Verrem. The Verrine Orations II. Translated by L.H.G. Greenwood. Loeb Classical Library 293. Cambridge (Ms.)/London, 1935.

(CICERO)
Rhetorica ad Herennium. Translated by Harry Caplan. Loeb Classical library 403. Cambridge (Ms.)/London, 1954.

CLAUDIANUS, Claudius
Panegyricus dictus Honorio Augusto sextum consuli. Claudii Claudiani Carmina. Ed. John Barrie Hall. Bibliotheca Teubneriana. Leipzig, 1985.

CLEMENS
Clement of Alexandria
1. Paidagogos. PG 8. (1857).
2. Stromateis. Les Stromates. Texte et traduction de Marcel Cassier et autres. Series : Sources chrétiennes 38, 278, 279. Paris, 1954-1981.

DIO CASSIUS
Roman History. 9 volumes. Translated by Earnest Cary. Loeb Classical Library. Cambridge (Ms.)/London.

DIODORUS SICULUS
Library of History. 12 volumes. Loeb Classical Library. Cambridge (Ms.)/London.

DIONYSIUS HALICARNASSENSIS
Roman Antiquities. 7 volumes. Translated by Earnest Cary. Loeb Classical Library. Cambridge (Ms.)/London.

DONATUS, Aelius
Commentum Terenti. Rec. Paulus Wessner. Leipzig, 1905.

EPIPHANIUS
1. De mensuribus et ponderibus. PG 41. Paris, 1867.
2. Panarion haeresium. Die griechischen Schriftsteller der ersten drei Jahrhunderte. Epiphanius I. Herausg. Karl Holl. Leipzig, 1915.

EURIPIDES
Phoenissae. Phoenician Maidens. Translated by Arthur S. Way. Loeb Classical Library 11. Cambridge (Ms.)/London, 1979.

EUSEBIUS
1. Chronicorum libri duo. PG 19. Paris, 1857.
2. De martyribus Palestinae. PG 20. Paris, 1857.
3. Praeparatio evangelica. PG 21. Paris, 1857.
4. De vita Constantini. PG 20. Paris, 1857.

EUTROPIUS
Breviarium ab urbe condita. Ed. Carolus Santini. Bibliotheca Teubneriana. Leipzig, 1979.

FESTUS, Rufus
Rufi Festi Breviarium rerum gestarum populi romani. Rec. Wendelinus Foerster. Wien, 1884.

FLORUS, Lucius Annaeus
Epitome of all the wars of the Roman people. Translated by E.S. Forster. Loeb Classical Library 231. Cambridge (Ms.)/London, 1929.

FRONTINUS
Frontinus. The Stratagems. Edited and translated by Ch.E. Bennett. London/New York, 1925.

FRONTO, Marcus Cornelius
Letter to the Emperor Lucius Verus Ao. 163. The Correspondence of Marcus Cornelius Fronto. Translated by C.R. Haines. Loeb Classical Library 113. Cambridge (Ms.)/London, 1920.

GAIUS
Gaii Institutiones. Gaius, Institutes. Ed. Julien Reinach. Collection Budé. Paris, 1950.

GALENUS
De differentia pulsuum. Claudii Galeni Opera Omnia VIII. Ed. C.G. Kühn. Hildesheim, 1965 (photostatic reprint of the edition Leipzig, 1824).

HORATIUS
1. Carmen saeculare. Horace. The Odes and Epodes. Translation by C.E. Bennett. Loeb Classical Library 33. Cambridge (Ms.)/London, 1968 (1914 1).
2. Epistolae. Horace, Satires, Epistles and Ars Poetica. Translated by H. Rushton Fairclough. Loeb Classical Library 194. Cambridge (Ms.)/London, 1978 (1926[1]).

IULIUS CAPITOLINUS
De vita Gordiani tertii. HA.

JOSEPHUS, Flavius
1. Antiquitates judaicae. Antiquities. Loeb Classical Library. 8 vols. Cambridge (Ms.)/London.
2. Bellum Judaicum. The Jewish War. Translated by H.St.J. Thackeray. Loeb Classical Library 203 and 210. Cambridge (Ms.)/London, 1927 and 1928[5].
3. Contra Apionem. Against Apion. Translated by H.St.J. Thackeray. Loeb Classical Library 186. Cambridge (Ms.)/London, 1926 5.
4. Vita. The Life. Translated by H.St.J. Thackeray. Loeb Classical Library 186. Cambridge (Ms.)/London, 1926[5].

JUSTINUS
Justini Epitoma historiarum Philippicarum Pompei Trogi. Ed. F. Ruehl, Bibliotheca Teubneriana. Leipzig, 1886.

JUVENALIS
Saturae. S.G. Owen (ed.), Thirteen satires of Juvenal. London, (1924, 1903[1]).

LAMFRIDIUS, Aelius
De vita Alexandri Severi. HA II.

LICINIANUS
Grani Liciniani Reliquae. Ed. Nicola Criniti. Leipzig, 1981.

LUCIANUS
De mercede conductis potentiam familiaribus. Translated by A.M. Harmon. On Salaried Posts in Great Houses. Loeb Classical Library 130. Cambridge (Ms.)/London, 1960 (1921[1]).

LIVIUS, Titus
Livy, Roman History. 14 volumes. Loeb Classical Library. Cambridge (Ms.)/London.

MACROBIUS
Macrobii Ambrosii Theodosii Saturnaliorum Convivia. A cura di Nino Marinone. Torino, 19722 (1967[1]).

MINUCIUS FELIX
Octavius. Translated by G.H. Rendall. Loeb Classical Library 250. Cambridge (Ms.)/London, 1931.

NEPOS, Cornelius
Prooemium. Oeuvres. Ed. Anne-Marie Guillemin. Collection Budé. Paris, 1970.

OROSIUS
Orose. Histoires. Texte établi et traduit par Marie-Pierre Arnaud-Lindet. Paris, 1991.

OVIDIUS, Publius -- Naso
Tristia. Translated by Arthur Leslie Wheeler. Loeb Classical Library 151. Cambridge (Ms.)/London, 1988[1] (revised by C.P. Gould).

PATRICIUS, Petrus
Historia. Exc.hist. I, Excerpta de legationibus Pars I.

PHILO
1. In Flaccum. Against Flaccus. Translated by F.H. Colson. Loeb Classical Library 363. Cambridge (Ms.)/London, 1941 4.
2. Legatio ad Gaium. On the Embassy to Gaius. Translated by F.H. Colson. Loeb Classical Library 379. Cambridge (Ms.)/London, 1962 2.
3. Vita Moysis. Life of Moses. Translated by F.H. Colson. Loeb Classical Library 289. Cambridge (Ms.)/London, 1950 (1935 1).

PLAUTUS, Titus Maccius
Bacchides. T. Macci Plauti Comoediae I. Ed. W.M. Lindsay. Oxford (1968) (1904[1].

PLINIUS, Gaius -- Secundus
Historia Naturalis. Pliny the Elder. Natural History. 10 volumes. Cambridge (Ms.)/London, 1938-1962.

PLINIUS, Gaius -- Caecilius Secundus
Epistulae. Pliny the Younger. Letters translated by Betty Radice. Loeb Classical Library 55. Cambridge (Ms.)/London, 1969.

PLUTARCH
1. Gaius Marius. Translated by B. Perrin. Loeb Classical Library 101. Cambridge (Ms.)/London, 1920.
2. Caesar. Translated by B. Perrin. Loeb Classical Library 99. Cambridge (Ms.)/London, 1919.
3. Cato Maior. Translated by B. Perrin. Loeb Classical Library 46. Cambridge (Ms.)/London, 1914.
4. Crassus. Translated by B. Perrin. Loeb Classical Library 65. Cambridge (Ms.)/London, 1916[6.]
5. Galba. Translated by B. Perrin. Loeb Classical Library 103. Cambridge (Ms.)/London, 19265.
6. Pompey. Translated by B. Perrin. Loeb Classical Library 87. Cambridge (Ms.)/London, 1916.
7. Sertorius. Translated by B. Perrin. Loeb Classical Library 100. Cambridge (Ms.)/London, 1919.
8. Sulla. Translated by B. Perrin. Loeb Classical Library 80. Cambridge (Ms.)/London, 1916.
9. Tiberius and Gaius Gracchus. Translated by B. Perrin. Loeb Classical Library 102. Cambridge (Ms.)/London, 1921.

RUTILIUS
Claudius Rutilius Numantinus, De Reditu. Ed. Emanuele Castorina. Firenze (1967).

SALLUSTIUS, Gaius -- Crispus
1. Bellum Iugurthinum. Translated by J.C. Rolfe. Loeb Classical Library 116. Cambridge (Ms.)/London, 1921.
2. Historiae reliquae. Ed. Bert. Maurenbrecher. Berlin, 1891.
3. Oratio Lepidi. In 2.
4. Oratio Philippi. In 2.

SENECA, Lucius Annaeus
1. De clementia. L. Annaeus Seneca, Philosophische Schriften 5. Darmstadt, 1989.
2. De consolatione ad Marciam. Translated by John W. Basore. Loeb Classical Library 254. Cambridge (Ms.)/London, 1932.
3. Ad Lucilium Epistulae Morales. Translated by Richard M. Gummere. Loeb Classical Library 310. Cambridge (Ms.)/London, 1970-1979.
4. De providentia. Translated by John W. Basore. Loeb Classical Library 214. Cambridge (Ms.)/London, 1928.

SPARTIANUS, Aelius
1. De Vita Hadriani. HA.
2. De Vita Severi. HA.

STRABO
Geography. 8 volumes. Translated by Horace L. Jones. Loeb Classical Library. Cambridge (Ms.)/London.

SUETONIUS, Gaius -- Tranquillius
1. De grammaticis et rhetoribus. Suétone, Grammaires et rhéteurs. Ed. Marie-Claude Vacher. Paris, 1993.
2. The Lives of the Caesars I (Julius Caesar, Augustus, Tiberius). Translated by J.C. Rolfe. Loeb Classical Library 31. Cambridge (Ms.)/London, 1914. II (Claudius, Nero, Vespasianus, Domitianus). Idem, vol. 38.

SULPICIUS SEVERUS
Chronica. CSEL 1. Vienna, 1866.

TACITUS, Cornelius
1. Annales. Annals. Translated by John Jackson. Loeb Classical Library 249, 312 and 322. Cambridge (Ms.)/London.
2. Dialogus de oratoribus. Translated by W. Peterson, revised by M. Winterbottom. Loeb Classical Library 35. Cambridge (Ms.)/London, 1970.
3. Germania. Translated by M. Hutton, revised by E.H. Warmington. Loeb Classical Library 35. Cambridge (Ms.)/London, 1914[1], revised edition 1970[2].
4. Historiae. Histories. Translated by Clifford H. Moore. Loeb Classical Library 35, 111, 249. Cambridge (Mass.)/London.

THEMISTIUS
Themistii orationes quae supersunt I. Eds. H. Schenkl and G. Downey. Leipzig, 1965.

THEODORETUS
Haereticarum fabularum compendium. PG 83. Paris, 1864.

VALERIUS MAXIMUS
Valerii Maximi factorum et dictorum memorabilium libri novem. Rec. Carolus Kampf. Leipzig, 1888.

VARRO, Marcus Terentius
M. Terenti Varronis Saturarum Menippearum Reliquiae. Ed. Alexander Riese. Leipzig, 1865.

VELLEIUS PATERCULUS
Roman History. Translated by F.W. Shipley. Loeb Classical Library 152. Cambridge (Ms.)/London, 1924.

VICTOR, C. Iulius
C. Iulii Victoris Ars Rhetorica. Eds. Remo Giomini and Silvana Celentano. Bibliotheca Teubneriana. Leipzig, 1980.

VIRGILIUS, Publius -- Maro
Aeneide. Virgil, The Aeneid. Translated by H.R. Fairclough. Loeb Classical Library 63/64. Cambridge (Ms.)/London, 1935/1934.

VOPISCUS, Flavius -- Syracusanus
De vita Carini. The Scriptores Historiae Augustae. Translated by David Magie. Loeb Classical Library 263. Cambridge (Ms.)/London, 1954 (1932[1]).

ZONARAS
Ioannes Zonaras, Epitome historiarum.
1. Forms part of the Loeb Classical Library edition of Cassius Dio (see above).
2. Rec. Ludovicus Dindorf(ius). Leipzig, 1868-1875.

ZOSIMUS
Historia nea. Zosime, Histoire nouvelle. Texte établi et traduit par François Pachoud. Paris, 1971.

A WORKS OF REFERENCE

Dictionnaire des antiquités grecques et romaines. Eds. Ch. Daremberg et Edm. Saglio. Paris, 1877.

Encyclopaedia judaica. Jerusalem.

The Jewish Encyclopedia. New York/London.

Paulys Real-Encyclopädie der Classischen Altertumswissenschaft. Neue Bearbeitung herausgegeben von Georg Wissowa. Stuttgart (PW).

Der kleine Pauly. München.

B COLLECTIONS

Aufstieg und Niedergang der römischen Welt I, 1972, II.3, 1975, XXIII.2, 1980. Berlin/New York, 1975.

Cambridge Ancient History (quoted as CAH).

The Cambridge History of the Jews.

Dictionnaire de Théologie catholique. Paris.

Kurzer Hand-Commentar zum Alten Testament. Herausgeb. Karl Marti. Abt. XVII Die fünf Megillot. Freiburg i.B./Leipzig/Tübingen, 1898.

STERN, Menahem, Greek and Latin authors on Jews and Judaism. Edited with Introductions, Translations and Commentary by --. I From Herodotus to Plutarch. Jerusalem, 1974.

Storia di Roma 4. Caratteri e morfologie. Torino, 1989.

Studies in Ancient Society. Eds. Josine Blok & Peter Mason. Amsterdam, 1987.

C MONOGRAPHS

ADCOCK, F.E., Caesar's Dictatorship. CAH IX (1932).

ALFÖLDI, A.,
1. The crisis of the Empire (A.D. 249-270). CAH XII (1939).
2. The invasions of peoples from the Rhine to the Black Sea. CAH XII (1939).

ANDERSON, J.C.,
1. The Eastern Frontiers under Augustus. CAH X (1934).
2. The Eastern Frontiers from Tiberius to Nero. CAH X (1934).

ATHANASSIDI, Polymnia, Julian. An intellectual Biography. London/New York (1992, first published Oxford, 1981, as 'Julian and Hellenism').

BABELON, Jean, Impératrices syriennes. Paris, 1957.

BALSDON, J.P.V.D., Roman Women. Their history and habits. London (1962).

BAMBERGER, Bernard J., Proselytism in the Talmud Period. Cincinnati, 1939.

BAUMANN, Uwe, Rom und die Juden. Die römisch-jüdischen Beziehungen von Pompeius bis zum Tode des Herodes (63 V.Chr.-4 v.Chr.). Reihe : Studia philosophica et historica, Band 4. Zweite, unveränderte Auflage. Frankfurt am Main, 1983.

BAYER, Erich, Rom und die Westgriechen bis 280 v.Chr. In : Aufstieg und Niedergang I.

BELLEN, Heinz, Grundzüge der römischen Geschichte. Darmstadt, 1994 (1966[1]).

BENGTSON, Hermann, Marcus Antonius. Triumvir und Herrscher des Orients. München (1977).

BERNSTEIN, Alvin H., Tiberius Sempronius Gracchus. Tradition and Apostasy. Ithaca and London (1978).

BEVAN, E.R., The Jews. CAH IX (1932).

BLEICKEN, Jochen, Rom und Italien. Propyläen Weltgeschichte. 4. Band. Berlin/Frankfurt/Wien (1963).

BRADLEY, Keith .R.,
1. Slavery and Rebellion in the Roman World, 140 B.C.-70 B.C. Bloomington and Indianapolis/London (1989).
2. Slaves and Masters in the Roman Empire. A Study in Social Control. Collection Latomus, Vol. 185. Bruxelles, 1984.

BRANDON, S.G.F., The Fall of Jerusalem and the Christian Church. A Study of the Effects of the Jewish Overthrow of A.D. 70 on Christianity. London, 1951.

BRAUN, René, Julien et le Christianisme. L'Empereur Julien.

BROWN, Peter
1. The Body and Society. Men, Women and Sexual Renunciation in Early Christianity. New York (1988).
2. The Making of Late Antiquity. Cambridge (Mass.)/London, 1978.

CANTARELLA, Eva, La vita delle donne. Storia di Roma 4.

CARCOPINO, Jerôme
1. Autour des Gracches. Études critiques. Paris, 1928.
2. Sylla ou la monarchie manquée. Paris, 1931.

CARY, M., The First Triumvirate. CAH IX (1932).

CHARLESWORTH, M.P., The Avenging of Caesar. CAH X (1936).

COURTOIS, Christian, Les Vandales et l'Afrique. Paris, 1955.

DEININGER, Jürgen, Der politische Widerstand gegen Rom in Griechenland, 217-86 v.Chr. Berlin/New York, 1971.

DIHLE, Albrecht, Die Griechen und die Fremden. München (1994).

DOBLHOFER, Georg, Die Popularen der Jahre 111-99 vor Christus. Eine Studie zur Geschichte der späten römischen Republik. Wien/Kölm, 1990.

DYSON, Stephen L., Native Revolt Patterns in the Roman Republic. Aufstieg II.3.

ENSSLIN, W.,
1. The End of the Principate. CAH XII (1939).
2. Sassanid Persia. CAH XII (1939).

FELDMAN, Louis H., Anti-Semitism in the Ancient World. In : History and Hate.

FERENCZY, Endre, From the patrician state to the patricio-plebeian state. Budapest, 1976.

FIRPO, Giulio, I Giudei. Storia di Roma II.

FLINTERMAN, Jaap-Jan, Power, *Paideia* & Pythagoreanism. Greek Identity, Conceptions of the Relationship between Philosophers and Monarchs and Political Ideas in Philostratus' Life of Apollonius. Dutch Monographs on Ancient History and Archaeology, Vol. XIII. Amsterdam, 1995.

FORTE, Bette, Rome and the Romans as the Greeks saw them. Rome, 1972.

FUCHS, Harald, Der geistige Widerstand gegen Rom in der antiken Welt. Berlin, 1964.

GABBA, Emilio, The Growth of Anti-Judaism or the Greek Attitude to the Jews. The Cambridge History of the Jews. II. Cambridge, 614.

GAGER, John G., The Origins of Anti-Semitism. Attitudes towards Judaism in Pagan and Christian Antiquity. Oxford University Press. Oxford/New York (1983).

GARDNER, Jane F., Women in Roman Law & Society. London/Sydney (1986).

GARDNER, R., The Enfranchisement of Italy. CAH IX (1932).

GESCHE, Helga, Caesar. Erträge der Forschung 51. Darmstadt, 1976.

GINSBURG, Michel S., Rome et la Judée. Contribution à l'histoire de leurs relations politiques. Paris, 1928,

GOEZ, Werner, Translatio Imperii : ein Beitrag zur Geschichte des Geschichtsdenkens und der politischen Theorien im Mittelalter und in der frühen Neuzeit. Tübingen, 1958.

GRANT, Michael
1. History of Rome. London (1978).
2. Nero. London (1970).

GREENHALGH, Peter
1. Pompey. The Republican Prince. London, 1981.
2. Pompey. The Roman Alexander. London, 1980.

GREGOROVIUS, Ferdinand, Geschichte der Stadt Rom im Mittelalter I. Stuttgart, 1859.

GRUEN, Erich S., Culture and National Identity in Republican Rome. Ithaca (NY), (1992).

GUEY, Julien, Essai sur la Guerre Parthique de Trajan (114-117). Bibliothèque d"Istros'. Bucarest, 1937.

GÜNTHER, Rigobert, Der Aufstand des Spartacus. Die grossen sozialen Bewegungen der Sklaven und Freien am Ende der römischen Republik. Köln, 1980.

HASEBROEK, Johannes, Untersuchungen zur Geschichte des Kaisers Septimius Severus. Heidelberg, 1921.

HEMELRIJK, Emily, Women's Demonstrations in Republican Rome. Studies in Ancient Society.

HENGEL, Martin, Untersuchungen zur jüdischen Freiheitsbewegung in der Zeit von Herodes I. bis 70 n.Chr. Arbeiten zur Geschichte des antiken Judentums und des Urchristentums. Band I. Leiden/Köln, 1976.

HEUSS, Alfred, Römische Geschichte. Braunschweig, 1964.

HORST, Dieter and GüNTHER, Rigobert, Römische Geschichte bis 476. Berlin, 1979.

ISAAC, Jules, Genèse de l'antisémitisme. Essai historique. Paris (1956).

JONES, Henry Stuart, The Princeps. CAH X (1939).

JUSTER, Jean, Les Juifs dans l'Empire romain. Leur condition juridique, économique et sociale. New York (reprint van 1914[1]).

KEAVENEY, Arthur, Sulla. The Last Republican. London/Sydney/Dover (NH), (1982).

LAST, Hugh,
1. The Enfranchisement of Italy. CAH IX (1932).
2. Gaius Gracchus. CAH IX (1932).
3. The Principate and the Administration. CAH XI (1936).
4. Tiberius Gracchus. CAH IX (1932).
5. The Wars of the Age of Marius. CAH IX (1932).

LEON, Harry J., The Jews of Ancient Rome. Philadelphia, 1960.

LEPPER, F.A., Trajan's Parthian War. Oxford Classical & Philosophical Monographs. London, 1948.

LONGDEN, R.P., The Wars of Trajan. CAH XI (1936).

MEYER, Eduard, Caesars Monarchie und das Principat des Pompeius von 66 bis 44 v.Chr. Stuttgart/Berlin, 1918.

MILLAR, Fergus, The Roman Near East 31 BC-AD 337. Cambridge (Ms.)/London, 1993.

MITCHELL, Richard E., Patricians and Plebeians. The origin of the Roman state. Ithaca (NY)/London (1990).

MOMIGLIANO, Arnaldo, Ricerche sull'organizzazione della Giudea sotto il dominio romano (63 a.C.-70 d.C.). Amsterdam, 1967.

MOMMSEN, Theodor
1. Römische Geschichte II. Berlin, 1933[14], 1852[1]).
2. Römisches Staatsrecht, II.1. Handbuch der römischen Alterthümer. Leipzig, 1874.

NOCK, A.D., Religious Developments from the Close of the Republic to the Death of Nero. CAH X (1939).

OOTEGHEM, J. van,
1. Caius Marius. Namur, 1964.
2. Pompée le Grand. Bâtisseur d'Empire. Bruxelles, 1954.

PALM, Jonas, Rom, Römertum und Imperium in der griechischen Literatur der Kaiserzeit. Skrifter utgivna av Kungl. Humanistiska Vetenskapssamfundet i Lund. Lund, 1959.

PERELLI, Luciano, I populares dai Gracchi alla fine della Reppublica. Torino (w.d.).

PETROCHEILOS, Nikalaos, Roman attitudes to the Greeks. Athens, 1974.

POLIAKOV, Léon, Histoire de l'antisémitisme. I Du Christ aux Juifs de cour. Paris (1955).

POMEROY, Sarah B., Goddesses, Whores, Wives and Slaves. Women in Classical Antiquity. New York, 1975.

PRAUSE, Gerhard, Herodes der Grosse. Hamburg, 1977.

PRIGENT, Pierre, La fin de Jérusalem. Neuchatel (CH), (1969).

RADIN, Max, The Jews among the Greeks and Romans. Philadelphia, 1915.

RAJAK, Tessa, The Jewish community and its boundaries. The Jews among Pagans and Christians.

349

ROBINSON, Frederick Walter, Marius, Saturninus und Glaucia. Beiträge zur Geschichte der Jahre 106-100 v.Chr. Jenaer Historische Arbeite, Heft 3. Bonn, 1912.

SADDINGTON, D.B., Race Relations in the Early Roman Empire. Aufstieg II.3.

SHOCHAT, Yanir, Recruitment and the Programme of Tiberius Gracchus. Collection Latomus, Vol. 169. Bruxelles, 1980.

SCHÜRER, Emil, The History of the Jewish People in the Age of Jesus Christ. Revised English version by Geza Vermes, Fergus Millar and Matthew Black. Edinburgh, 1979 (first German edition 1885-1924.

SCHWIER, Helmut, Tempel und Tempelzerstörung. Untersuchungen zu den theologischen und ideologischen Faktoren im ersten jüdisch-römischen Krieg (66-74 n.Chr.). Reihe : Novum Testamentum et orbis antiquus 11. Göttingen, 1989.

SCULLARD, H.H.
1. From the Gracchi to Nero. A history of Rome from 133 B.C. to A.D. 68. London, 1976[4] (1959[1]).
2. A History of the Roman World 753-146 B.C. London/New York (19804, 1935[1]).

SEVENSTER J.N., The Roots of Pagan Anti-Semitism in the Ancient World. Supplements to Novum Testamentum Vol. XLI. Leiden, 1975.

SMALLWOOD, E. Mary, The Jews under Roman Rule. From Pompey to Diocletian. Studies in Judaism in Late Antiquity Vol. 20. Leiden, 1976.

SPANN, Philip O., Quintus Sertorius and the Legacy of Sulla. Fayetteville, 1987.

STAMPACCHIA, Giulia, La tradizione della guerra di Spartaco da Sallustio a Orosio. Biblioteca degli studi classici e orientali 6. Pisa, 1976.

STOCKTON, David, The Gracchi. Oxford, 1979.

TARN, W.W., The War of the East against the West. CAH X (1936).

TCHERIKOVER, Victor, Hellenistic Civilization and the Jews. Translated from the Hebrew manuscript by S. Applebaum. Philadelphia, 1959.

VAGANAY, L., s.v. Porphyre. Dict.Théol.cath. 12.2. Paris, 1935.

VEYNE, Paul, Humanitas : De Romeinen en de anderen (The Romans and the others). In : De wereld van de Romeinen (The world of the Romans, translation of L'uomo romano, a cura di Andrea Giardina. Roma/Bari. 1989). Amsterdam, 1992.

VOGT, Josef,
1. Ancient Slavery and the Ideal of Man. Translated by Thomas Wiedemann. Oxford (1974).
2. Kulturwelt und Barbaren. Zum Menschheitsbild der spätantiken Gesellschaft. Akademie der Wissenschaften und Kultur. Abhandlungen der geistes- und sozialwissenschaftlichen Klasse. Jhrg. 1967, nr. 1. Wiesbaden, 1967.
3. Die römische Republik. München, 1973^6 (1932^1).

WALLON, H., Histoire de l'esclavage dans l'Antiquité II. 1879^2.

WARDMAN, Alan, Rome's Debt to Greece. London, 1976.

WILDEBOER, D.G., Das Buch Esther. In : Kurzer Hand-Commentar, Abt. XVII.

WILKINSON, L.P., The Roman experience. London (1975).

ZINSERLING, Verena, Women in Greece and Rome. New York (1973) (Leipzig, $1971^{1)}$.

GENERAL INDEX

Abraham, 314
Acarnania, 321
Achaemenid(s), 115, 165, 234
Adcock, F.E., 101, 134
Adriatic Sea, 57, 89, 92, 108, 111, 329
Aegean Sea, 93, 161
Aelia Capitolina (Roman name for Jerusalem), 274
Aemilius Paullus (Roman commander), 12, 201
Aeneas, 151, 318
Aetolia(n)(s), 321
Africa, 328
Agatharchides of Cnidus, 284, 285
Ager publicus, 19, 22, 35
Agrigentum (Agrigento) (town in Sicily), 206
Agrippa, Marcus Vipsanius (friend of Augustus), 118, 148-149
Agrippa II, Herod (King of the Jews, Tetrarch of Galilee), 256, 257, 258, 259, 261, 262, 306
Ahasuerus (Artaxerxes) (the Persian Emperor in the Book of Esther), 232-233, 234
Akiba (Jewish Rabbi), 274
Alans (German tribe), 175
Alaric (King of the Visigoths), 176, 188
Alba Longa, Albanian, 318
Albania, 90
Albinus, 255
Alemanni, 174, 175, 176
Alexander I, king of Epirus, 320
Alexander the Great, 79, 100, 154, 159-160, 169, 238, 282, 329, 330

Alexander Jannaeus (Jewish High Priest), 246
Alexander Polyhistor, 286
Alexandria(n)(s), 94, 95, 120, 121, 229, 230, 244, 256, 257, 259, 265, 272, 284, 289, 296, 301, 314
Alexandrian War, 240
Alföldi, A., 182, 184
Algeria see Numidia
Alps, 35, 109, 173, 174, 194, 195, 212, 213
American(s), 322
Amida, 168 (Diyarbakir), 167
Ammianus Marcellinus, 167, 168, 171, 182, 183
Ammonius (Egyptian Roman), 186
Ananias (Jewish High Priest), 256, 257
Ancona, 86
Anderson, J.C., 179, 180
Anglosaxon, 176
Anio (river), 64
Annius, Caius (governor of Spain), 73
Antigenes (Sicilian slave owner), 205, 206
Antigonus (Jewish High Priest), 247, 304
Antonia (Roman fortress in Jerusalem), 248, 257, 265-266, 266
Antoninus Pius (Roman Emperor), 143, 149, 276, 277
Antioch(ene), 148, 158, 159, 162, 163, 164, 168, 169, 181, 229, 237, 258, 298
Antiochus IV Epiphanes (Seleucid King), 231, 237, 276, 285

Antiochus V (Seleucid king), 244
Antiochus VII Sidetes (Seleucid King), 115, 285, 286
Antonius, Lucius (brother of Marcus Antonius), 114
Antonius, Marcus, 85, 92, 95, 103, 104-121, 135, 145, 151
Antyll(i)us (sergeant of the consul Opimius), 27
Apamea (town in Syria), 205
Apennines, 212
Apion, 285, 288, 289-290
Apollonia (Poian, town), 92
Apollonius Molon, 286
Appianus, 14, 15, 17, 18, 22, 24, 25, 36, 39, 41, 44, 45, 46, 47, 48, 49, 50, 54, 56, 61, 62, 67, 83, 91, 109, 122, 123, 124, 125, 126, 127, 128, 129, 130, 131, 132, 133, 134, 135, 136, 137, 138, 139, 180, 212, 225, 226, 272, 312
Appius Claudius, 13, 19, 43
Apulia, Apulians, 38, 60, 87, 205, 212
Aquileia (Venice), 173
Arabia, 160, 229
Aramaic, 230
Arausio (Orange), 72
Arcadius (Roman Emperor), 152
Arch of Titus in Rome, 271
Archelaus (Herodian king of Judaea), 248, 252
Ardashir I, Persian King, 161-162
Arian, 280
Ariminium (Rimini), 86, 108
Aristides, 323
Aristobulus (son of Hyrcanus II), 304
Aristobulus of Paneas, 283
Aristotle, 282
Arles, 229
Armenia(n), 78, 95, 116, 119-120, 146, 153-159, 161, 162, 163, 164, 165, 166, 167, 169, 170, 171, 216, 229
Arpinum (Arpino), 30
Arretium (Arezzo), 86
Arrian, 323
Arsaces, King of Armenia, 154
Arsacid dynasty, 156, 157, 158, 160, 161, 180
Arsinoe (Queen of Egypt), 96
Artabanus V, King of Parthia, 153-154, 161
Artaxata (Armenian town), 155
Ascalis, King of Mauretania, 74
Ascalon (town in Syria), 257
Ascanius, 318
Ascona (town), 59
Asculum (Ascoli Piceno), 38, 39
Ashkenazim, 230
Asia Minor, 37, 38, 39, 51, 52, 53, 54, 55, 58, 64, 78, 80, 82, 83, 93, 94, 95, 116, 144, 148, 151, 153, 157, 158, 159, 162, 164, 165, 168, 174, 196, 206, 219, 229, 236, 240, 241, 248, 278, 320, 322, 324, 329
Asiatic(s), 120, 140, 325
Assyria(n), 146, 160, 229, 293
Atargatis (Syrian goddess), 206
Athanassidi, Polymnia, 183
Athenaeus, 223
Athenian(s), 50, 216, 219, 319
Athenion (a Cilician slave, leader of a slave revolt, later 'king' of the slaves in Sicily), 209-210
Athens, 158, 186, 229, 319, 320
Athongaeus (Jewish rebel leader), 251
Atlantic Ocean, 100
Attaleia (Antalya), 93
Attalus III, King of Pergamum, 19, 20
Attica, 207
Atticus, Titus Pomponius (pen-friend of Cicero), 109
Augur, 7
Augustinus, Aurelius, 316
Augustus, 8, 29, 104-105, 106-114, 116-121, 135, 136, 140-142, 145, 146, 149, 153, 172, 190, 217, 228, 241, 242, 248, 250, 269, 319
Aulus Gellius, 289, 315
Aurelianus (Roman Emperor), 164
Austria, 229
Auvergne, 174
Aventine hill, 4, 6, 27

Babelon, Jean, 178

Babylon, 159, 160
Babylonia(n), 159, 160, 228, 229, 230, 267
Babylonian captivity, 231
Bacchics, 19
Bactria, 115
Balam, 300
Balkans, 89, 100, 105, 112, 148, 150, 151, 162, 172, 191, 212, 214
Balsdon, 218, 227, 322, 323, 331, 332
Baltic Sea, 173
Band-e-Kaisar, 163
Bar-Hebraeus, 228, 301
Barbarian(s), 73, 86, 186, 187, 188, 193, 321-323
Bataafse Petroleum Maatschappij, 221
Batavia (the Betuwe NL), 192, 196
Batavia (Dutch name of the Indonesian capital), 192
Batavia Castra (Passau), 192
Batavian(s), 191-196, 221
Batavian Legion, 192
Batavian Republic, 192
Batavier Line (Dutch steamship company), 221
Batavus (Dutch bicycle mark), 221
Battle of Actium, 121
Battle of Adrianople, 175, 176
Battle of Betriacum, 193
Battle of Carrhae, 83, 116, 119, 129, 153, 165, 169
Battle of Issus (A.D. 194), 148
Battle of Munda, 97
Battle of Petelia, 214
Battle of Pharsalus, 92-93, 95
Battle of Philippi, 113, 114
Battle of Polentia, 188
Battle of Pydna, 12
Battle of Thapsus, 95
Battle of Zela, 95
Baumann, Uwe, 304
Bayer, Erich, 331
Belgian, Belgium, 176
Belisarius (Roman comes), 311
Bellen, Heinz, 23, 46, 49, 104, 134, 135, 138
Beloch, Julius, 228

Bengtson, Hermann, 136, 137
Berenice (sister of King Agrippa II), 256
Bernstein, H., 21, 44, 45
Bethlehem, 276, 305
Bettir (Palestinian town), 275
Betuwe (NL) see Batavia
Bevan, E.R., 304
Bezabde (town), 168
Bible, 290
Bibulus, Marcus Calpurnius (consul), 81
Bithynia, 78, 95, 208
Black Sea, 151, 161, 324
Blake, William, 102
Bleicken, Jochen, 43
Boccus, King of Mauretania, 51
Bohemia, 173
Bologna, 111, 229
Bonn, 229
Book of Esther, 232, 232-236
Book of Numbers, 300
Book of Ruth, 234
Bordeaux, 229
Bradley, Keith R., 200, 223, 225, 226
Brabant, 176
Brandon, S.G.F., 307
Brinno (Cannenefate commander), 193
Britain, 146, 175, 191, 229, 275
Brown, Peter, 219, 226
Bructeri (Germanic tribe), 194
Brundisium (Brindisi), 59, 79, 87, 90, 92, 108, 117, 158, 214
Bruttium, 176, 213, 214
Brutus, Decimus (senator, murderer of Caesar), 108, 109, 110
Brutus, Lucius Iunius (forefather of the next), 103
Brutus, Marcus, 109, 136
Brutus, Quintus Servilius Caepio (murderer of Caesar), 103, 105, 111, 113, 136
Bulgaria, 175
Burgundy, 176
Busento, 176
Byzantine, 143
Byzantine (Empire), 152, 171, 311

Byzantium, 151, 174

Caesar, Julius, 8, 29, 46, 66, 77, 80-103, 104, 105, 106, 107, 108, 116, 119, 120, 121, 124, 130, 131, 132, 133, 134, 135, 140, 145, 151, 153, 191, 221, 240, 241, 243, 247, 276, 286, 329
Caesarea (residence of the procurators of Judaea), 248, 257, 264, 278
Caesarion (son of Caesar and Cleopatra), 120
Caius Billius, 21
Calabria, 214
Caligula, 244, 296
Calpurnia (third wife of Caesar), 104
Camillus, Marcus Furius, 238
Campania, 53, 67, 107, 108, 214, 320
Campus Martius, 62, 70, 96
Canary Islands, 74
Cannenefates (Germanic tribe), 193
Cantabri (Iberian tribe), 190
Cantarella, Eva, 217, 218, 227
Capitol, 15, 60, 203-204
Capitoline hill, 20, 27, 28, 36, 51, 60, 100, 269, 270
Cappadocia, 95, 156, 158, 163, 164
Capri, 153
Capua, 55, 57, 60, 87, 210, 211, 215
Caracalla, Marcus Aurelius Antoninus, 197, 222, 279
Carbo, Cn. Papirius (consul), 59, 62, 73
Carcopino, Jerôme, 45, 69, 125, 126
Carrhae, 164, 165
Carinus (historian), 179
Carthage, Carthaginian(s), 12, 22, 26, 101, 177, 204, 205, 238-239, 321
Carthago nova (Cartagena), 73
Cary, M., 128
Caspian Sea, 100
Cassius, Gaius -- Longinus (murderer of Caesar), 111, 113, 213
Castelfranco (town), 109
Castra Vetera (Xanten), 194, 195

Catilina, Lucius Sergius, 86
Cato Marcus Porcius -- Censorinus (the Elder), 10, 217, 326, 332
Cato Uticensis, Marcus Porcius (senator), 85, 88, 94, 96, 103, 299
Catulus (consul), 70-71
Caucasus Mountains, 78, 100
Caudine Forks, 156
Celt(s), Celtic, 6, 35, 40, 41, 54, 110, 189, 194, 195, 211, 212, 215, 222, 320, 321
Celtiberian, 73, 74, 75, 76
Censor(s), 98, 280
Cerialis, Petilius (Roman general), 195-196
Cestius Gallus (governor of Syria), 258
Chaldaean, 292
Charlemagne, 151
Charlesworth, P., 112, 137
Chatti (Germanic tribe), 192
Chicago, 10
China, 175
Chinese Wall, 175
Christian(s), 19, 215, 231, 239, 258, 271, 279, 280, 287, 290, 299, 301, 311, 313, 330
Christianity, 168, 217, 229, 290, 295, 311
Ciaceri, E., 84, 129
Cicero, Marcus Tullius, 10, 12, 23, 24, 28, 41, 43, 45, 46, 47, 48, 49, 50, 59, 71, 84, 88, 90, 102, 104, 107, 109, 110, 112, 122, 123, 124, 125, 127, 128, 129, 130, 134, 135, 136, 185, 186, 189, 205, 220, 224, 230, 286, 292, 301, 322, 325, 326, 331, 332
Cilicia(n), 51, 78, 168, 206, 209
Cimbri, 32, 51, 58, 72, 172, 173, 210, 213
Cinna, Lucius Cornelius, 55, 56-59, 73, 80
Circus maximus, 100, 106
Civilis, Julius, 191-196, 221
Civilis, Paulus (brother of Julius), 193
Claudia (daughter of Appius Claudius, wife of Tiberius

Gracchus), 43
Claudianus, 188, 220
Claudius, Caius -- Gaber (Roman general), 212
Claudius, Tiberius -- Nero Germanicus (Roman emperor), 217, 228, 248, 253, 296, 306, 319
Clearchus, 283
Clemens Alexandrinus, 215, 226, 286, 289, 314, 315
Cleon (leader of a slave revolt in Sicily), 206-207
Cleopatra IX, Pharaoh of Egypt, 95, 99, 113, 115, 120, 121
Coen, Jan Pieterszoon (first governor of the Dutch East Indies), 192
Col de Pertus (Pyrenees), 76
Cologne, 229
Comitia centuriata, 3, 41, 50, 131
Comitia plebis tributa, 50
Comitia populi tributa, 50
Commodus (Roman Emperor), 143, 149
Communist Party of Germany, 211
Concilium plebis, 19, 22, 34, 41, 53, 55, 66
Concordia Augustorum, 150
Consentia (Cosenza), 176
Constans (Roman Emperor), 151, 152
Constantine I the Great, 8, 150, 151, 166, 183, 188, 220, 281
Constantine II, 151, 152
Constantinople, 151, 152, 171, 311, 324, 330
Constantius I Chlorus, 150
Constantius II, 151, 152, 166-168, 168
Constitutio Antoniana, 197
Consul(s), consulate, 7, 57, 58, 67, 71, 98, 131, 135, 280
Corbulo, Domitius (Roman general), 154-156
Cordoba, 97, 229
Corfinium (Italica), 38
Corinth(ian), 101, 202, 229
Cornelia (mother of the Gracchi), 12
Cornelia (daughter of Cinna and first wife of Caesar), 66, 80

Cornelia (daughter-in-law of Crassus and second wife of Pompey), 83, 93, 94, 129
Corsica, 111, 117, 176, 189
Courtois, Christian, 177, 184
Crassus, M. Licinius, 76-77, 81-83, 95, 116, 129, 153, 213-214
Creusa, 318
Crete, 229, 293
Crimea, 229
Crixus (subcommander of Spartacus), 211, 212, 213, 225
Croatia, 229
Crusaders, 311
Ctesiphon, 115, 154, 159, 161, 164, 169, 229
Cumae, 67, 319, 320
Cumanus, Ventidius (procurator of Judaea), 253, 254, 306
Cyprus, 94, 229, 273, 278, 280
Cyrenaica, 241, 272, 278, 280
Cyrene, 272
Cyrus I, King of Persia, 154, 231

Dacia, 146, 152, 157, 172, 174
Dahn, Felix (German novelist), 176
Dalmatia, 229
Danube, 152, 158, 172, 173, 174, 175, 191, 192
Darius, Parthian prince, 154
David (king), 235, 249
Dead Sea, 246, 256, 268
Delos, 201, 207
Delphi, 229
Demetrius I (Seleucid king), 245
Democracy, democratic, 5
Demophilus (Sicilian slave owner), 206
Dessau, Hermannus, 178
Diaspora (Dispersion), 228, 229-238, 239, 241, 244, 253, 261, 284, 300, 301
Dictator, 26, 62, 63, 67, 69, 83, 88, 90, 95, 97, 102, 104, 105
Dihle, Albrecht, 321, 331
Dio Cassius, 64, 90, 91, 106, 124, 125, 128, 129, 130, 131, 132, 133, 134, 135, 136, 137, 138, 140, 141, 178, 179, 180, 181, 190, 191, 197,

208, 221, 223, 224, 226, 243, 272, 273, 299, 303, 312, 313, 317, 323
Diocletianus, Gaius Aurelius Valerius, 143, 149-150, 165-166, 174, 200, 330
Diodorus Siculus, 17, 18, 44, 48, 49, 205, 207, 223, 224, 225, 285, 286, 286-287, 287, 314, 315, 316, 323, 332
Diognetus (Christian author), 299, 317
Dionysius Halicarnensis, 42, 204, 224, 323, 324, 331, 332
Dionysos, 120, 291
Diophanes (teacher of Tiberius Gracchus), 21
Doblhofer, Georg, 47
Domitianus, 149, 271, 312
Drumann-Groebe, 68
Drusus, Nero Claudius, 145, 192
Dualism, dualistic, 1, 2, 4, 5, 8, 15-16, 22, 39, 58, 68, 69, 75, 91, 100-101, 102, 107, 120, 121, 144, 145, 145-147, 152-153, 171, 186, 187, 188, 191, 202, 215, 218, 220, 234, 235, 250, 250-251, 252, 257, 263, 273, 279-281, 281, 328-331
Dutch, 176, 191, 192, 220, 235, 268
Dyrrhachium (Durazzo, Dürres), 90, 92, 143
Dyson, Stephen L., 189, 190, 191, 196, 220, 222

Ecclesiastes, 234
Edessa (Urfa), 159, 163
Edom(ite), 245, 247, 249, 263-264
Egypt(ian), 94, 96, 99, 113, 120, 121, 142, 144, 151, 158, 161, 164, 186, 196, 229, 230, 231, 236, 243, 248, 254, 272, 278, 280, 283, 288, 289, 290, 293, 296, 320, 325
Elbe, 145
Eleazar ben Yair (Zealot leader), 254, 265, 268
Eleazar (son of the High Priest Ananias), 256
Elegeia (Ilidsha), 158
Emesa (Homs), 143
Emmaus (town in Judaea), 264

English, 141
Ensslin, W., 142, 178, 181, 182
Ephesus, 113, 158, 174, 326
Epiphanius (Christian author), 307, 312
Epirus, 92, 201, 320
Equestrian class, order, 11, 25, 29, 30, 37
Equites (knights), 11, 24-25, 35, 40, 66, 67, 76, 84
Eratosthenes, 321
Esquiline Forum, 54
Esther (the female main character in the Book of Esther), 232-233, 233, 234
Ethiopia, 229, 293
Etruria(n), Etruscan, 13, 39, 57, 63, 70, 205, 238, 319, 320
Eunus (a Syrian slave, later 'king' of the slaves in Sicily), 205-207
Euphrates, 115, 116, 145, 152, 153, 154, 156, 157, 159, 160, 161, 162, 163, 164, 165, 167, 168, 169, 171
Euric (King of the Visigoths), 176
Euripides, 102, 134
Europe(an), 5, 38, 144, 146, 151, 159, 160, 322
Eusebius (Christian author), 258, 275, 286, 307, 312, 313, 314, 315
Eutropius, 131, 179, 182, 226

Faesulae (Fiesole) (town in Etruria), 70
Fannius, Caius (consul), 26
Fascist Party of Italy, 135
Feldman, Louis, 229, 301
Felix (procurator of Judaea), 252-253, 254-255, 306
Ferenczy, Endre, 8, 43
Festus, Porcius, 255
Firpo, Giulio, 243, 303, 305, 306
Fiscus judaicus, 280-281
Flavian dynasty, 149, 157
Florus (historian), 25, 37, 38, 39, 46, 48, 49, 56, 64, 70, 123, 124, 125, 126, 214, 224, 225, 226
Florus, Gessius (procurator of Judaea), 255-256
Flaccus, Fulvius (tribune), 26, 27,

28, 29, 47
Flaccus (client of Cicero), 230
Flaccus (governor of Egypt), 296
Flavian dynasty, 269, 271
Flinterman, Jaap-Jan, 332
Formiae (Italian town), 200
Forte, Bette, 324, 328, 333
Forum Gallorum (town), 109
Forum Romanum, 4, 6, 15, 29, 56, 58, 64, 66, 77, 105, 106, 112, 140
France, 73, 76, 176, 229
Frank(s), 152, 174, 176, 177, 192
Franke, Alfred, 222
Fregellae, 47
French, 177, 190, 192
Frontinus, Sextus Iulius, 124, 136, 180, 214
Fronto, Marcus Cornelius, 332
Fuchs, Harald, 333
Fulvia (first wife of Mark Antony), 114, 117
Fulvia (Roman matrona, proselyte), 242-243

Gabara (Galilean town), 260
Gabba, Emilio, 282, 285, 290, 314, 315, 316
Gaetulians (North African tribe), 190
Gager, John G., 291, 294, 295, 313, 315, 316, 317
Gaius (jurist), 223
Galba, Servius Sulpicius (Roman Emperor), 136, 193, 264
Galerius (Roman Emperor), 150
Galilee, 246, 247, 248, 249, 251, 252, 253, 258, 259, 259-261, 262, 306
Gallia Cisalpina Cispadana, 40, 72
Gallia Cisalpina, 81, 107, 108, 110, 189, 213
Gallia Transalpina, 81
Gallia Narbonensis, 72, 111
Gallienus (Roman Emperor), 174
Gardner, Jane F., 49, 227
Gardner, R., 122
Gaul, 35, 64, 81, 82, 84, 85, 88, 89, 90, 96, 111, 121, 151, 152, 169, 174, 175, 176, 191, 212
Gauls(s) see Celts

Geiseric (King of the Vandals), 177
Gellius, Aulus, 331
Genseric (Geiseric) (Vandal king), 191, 311
German(s), Germanic, 32, 33, 72, 152, 165, 171-174, 188, 192, 194, 195, 212, 222
Germany, 100, 145, 146, 172, 194, 211, 229
Gesche, Helga, 106, 135
Ginsburg, Michel S., 304
Gischala (Al-Jish, Galilean town), 262
Glaucia, Cn. Servilius, 33, 34, 36, 66
Gnosis, Gnostic, 229, 287
Gödel, Kurt, 144-145, 147
Golden Horn, 151
Gordianus III (Roman Emperor), 162, 181
Gothic, Goths, 173, 174, 175
Gracchi, 52, 67, 101
Gracchus, Gaius, 12, 19, 23-29
Gracchus, Sempronia (sister of the Gracchi), 12
Gracchus Tiberius (father of the Gacchi), 12
Gracchus, Tiberius, 12-21, 21, 22, 23, 43, 44, 68
Grant, Michael, 6, 25, 42, 43
Great Britain, 98
Greece, 51, 59, 113, 174, 176, 186, 196, 198, 199, 211, 223, 229, 233, 283, Ch. VI passim
Greek(s), 12, 20, 41, 93, 94, 115, 120, 121, 151, 186, 187, 188, 197, 218, 229, 230, 234, 236, 238, 244, 257, 261, 277, 282-291, 292, 296, 299, 300, 312, Ch. VI passim
Greenhalgh, Peter, 126, 127
Gregorius XIII (Pope), 101
Gregorovius, Ferdinand, 311
Gruen, Erich S., 328, 332, 333
Guadalquivir (river), 74
Günther, Rigobert, 43, 225
Guey, Julien, 158, 180, 181

Hadrianus, 143, 149, 160, 191, 273-274, 275, 276

Halicyae (town in Sicily), 208
Haman (character in the Book of Esther), 232-233, 234
Hannibal, 61, 62, 63, 75, 193, 213, 326
Harnack, Adolf von, 228, 298, 301
Hasebroek, Johannes, 178
Hasmonaean, 231, 245, 246, 247, 304
Hebrew, 233, 235
Hecataeus, 282-283, 283, 314
Hegesippus (Christian author), 312
Hellenic, Hellenes see Greek
Hellenism, Hellenistic, 231, 236, 237, 284, 285, 289, 299, 328, 332
Hemelrijk, Emily, 227
Hengel, Martin, 299, 306, 317
Henna (Enna) (town in Sicily), 205, 206, 207
Heracles, 79
Herdonius, Appius (leader of a slave revolt), 204
Hermippus of Smyrna, 283
Herod I the Great, 247-248, 249, 250, 251, 287
Herod Antipas (son of Herod the Great, tetrarch of Galilee), 248
Herodianus, 181
Hesiod, 283
Heuss, Alfred, 43, 189, 220
High Priest(s) of the Jews, 241, 245, 247, 257, 263, 278, 283, 306
Hispania Citerior, 73
Hitler, Adolf, 40, 68, 69, 126, 276, 311
Homer, 45, 93, 282, 283, 321
Homines novi, homo novus, 10, 11, 29, 30, 31, 72
Honorius (Roman Emperor), 152, 177
Horatius, Quintus -- Flaccus, 147, 179, 220, 223, 327, 333
Horst, Dieter, 43
Hortensius, Quintus (senator), 77
Humbert, G, 220
Hungary, 175, 229
Huns, 175
Hyrcanus II (Jewish High Priest), 247, 304

Iberian, 76, 89, 90, 111, 175, 190
Ibiza, 74
Idumaea(n), 245, 247, 249, 259, 263-264
Ilion (Troy), 151, 319
Illyria, 59
Imperator, 98, 109
Imperialism, imperialistic, 15, 16, 100-101, 102, 144, 146, 162, 186, 189, 329, 330
India, 159
Indo-European, 115
Indonesia, 221
Indus, 115
Interrex, 62, 70
Ionia, 241
Iranian, 115
Isaac, Jules, 301
Isis, 120, 243
Islands of the Blest, 74
Israel (nation, people), 235, 250, 252, 299, 300
Israeli, 44
Istanbul, 152
Isthmus of Corinth, 262
Italian(s), 23, 25, 29, 36, 37, 38, 39, 41, 51, 61, 63, 102, 110, 178, 189, 199
Italian Republic, 41
Italica see Corfinium
Italy, 9, 14, 16, 19, 22, 26, 32, 35, 38, 40, 41, 52, 59, 60, 61, 63, 85, 86, 88, 90, 95, 103, 106, 111, 113, 114, 117, 118, 140, 148, 151, 152, 174, 175, 176, 177, 189, 193, 194, 195, 202, 205, 212, 219, 229, 265, 320, 321
Iulian dynasty, 149
Iulius Capitolinus, 181
Ius Latii, 25

Jacatra (now Jakarta), 192, 221
Janiculus hill, 57, 58
Japha (Galilean town), 260
Java (Yafa), 192
Jericho, 251, 264
Jerome (Father of the Church), 281, 314

Jerusalem, 79, 241, 244, 247, 248, 254, 256, 258, 259, 262, 263-264, 265-268, 274, 275, 276, 281, 283, 285, 298, 301, 305, 308, 311, 313
Jesus Christ, 246, 247, 313
Jesus ben Saphat (Jewish rebel leader), 261
Jew(s), Jewry, 185, Ch. V passim, 328
Jewish, Ch. V passim
Johannes Hyrcanus (Jewish High Priest), 245-246
John of Gischala (Jewish rebel leader), 262, 264, 265, 266, 268
Jonathan ben Anan (Jewish High Priest), 254, 306
Jones, Henry Stuart, 179
Jordan, 246, 258, 308
Joseph (Jewish patriarch), 288
Josephus, Flavius, 230, 237, 240, 241, 242-243, 247, 250, 251, 252, 254, 256, 257, 259, 259-261, 262, 263, 264, 266, 267, 269, 282, 285, 286, 287, 288, 300, 301, 302, 303, 304, 305, 306, 307, 308, 309, 310, 311, 314, 315, 316, 317
Jotapata (Galilean town), 260
Joshua, 254
Jovianus (Roman Emperor), 171
Jovinianus (Roman Emperor), 152
Judaea, 79, 237, 241, 244, 244-271 passim, 283, 288, 290, 293, 301, 306, 310
Judaism, 229, 231, 243, 249, 252, 268, 271, 272, 276, 276-277, 279, 280, 281, 282, 283, 285, 286, 287, 288, 289, 291, 292, 293, 294, 295, 297, 299, 300, 305, 311
Judas the Maccabee, 244, 245
Judas (Galilean rebel leader), 251, 305
Judas (founder of the Zealot sect), 252
Jugurtha, 30, 31, 32, 51
Jugurthine War, 51
Julia (aunt of Julius Caesar, wife of Marius), 30
Julia (daughter of Caesar, first wife of Pompey), 81, 82

Julia Domna (wife of Septimius Severus), 143
Julian the Apostate, 152, 168-171, 182, 183, 280
Julian Calendar, 101
Junius Pennus, M. (tribune), 22-23
Juno (goddess), 238-239
Junonia (proposed Roman colony), 26
Jupiter (Capitolinus), 5, 143, 239, 240, 269, 270, 271, 274, 281, 292, 311
Juster, Jean, 228, 229, 241, 278, 301, 302, 303, 314
Justinus (Christian author), 313
Justinus (historian), 223, 287, 315
Juvenalis, Decimus Iunius, 294-295, 317, 327, 331, 333

Keaveney, Arthur, 53, 122, 125
Kennedy, John F., 168
Khorasan (Iranian province), 115
Knights see Equites

Laelius Sapiens, C. (senator), 23
Lake Tiberias, 308
Lake Trasimene, 125
Lamentations of Jeremiah, 234
Lampridius, 181
Larcius Marcedo (Roman senator), 200
Larissa (Greek town), 93
Last, Hugh, 43, 46, 47, 179
Latifundia, 10
Latin(s), 25, 26, 38, 63, 73, 182, 186, 287, 291, 293, 296, 319, 325, 329
Latinitas, 187
Latium, 57, 318, 320
Lavinius (Lavino, river), 111
Lentulus Batiatus (owner of a school, for gladiators at Capua), 211, 225
Leo I (Pope), 177
Leon, Harry J., 303
Lepidus, M. Aemilius, 69-70, 74, 89, 90, 110, 111-114, 117, 118, 118-119, 126
Lepper, F.A., 180

Leptis Magna, 142
Lex agraria (of Saturninus), 34-35, 37
Lex frumentaria, 24
Lex Hortensia, 68
Lex iudiciaria, 24-25
Lex Sempronia agraria, 13-19, 22
Lex de sociis et nomine latino, 25-27
Lex Varia, 39-40, 52
Libanius (orator), 166, 169, 182, 183
Liburnia (town in Illyria), 59
Libya, 229
Licinianus, Granus, 124, 126
Licinius (co-emperor of Constantine the Great), 150
Licinius, Publius -- Nerva (governor of Sicily), 208, 209
Lictor(es), 96
Lilybaeum (Marsala) (town in Sicily), 208
Liri (river), 30
Livius Drusus, M. (tribune), 26, 37, 40, 49, 302
Livius, Titus, 1, 4, 5, 42, 43, 46, 47, 122, 123, 125, 128, 136, 137, 204, 224, 318, 320, 327, 331, 333
Longden, R.P., 181
Lucania, Lucanians, 38, 60, 61, 63, 214
Lucianus, 323, 332
Lucas (Gospel author), 301
Lucca, 82
Lucullus, Lucius Licinius, 214
Ludi saeculares, 146-147
Lupercalia, 103
Lusitanians, 74, 190
Luxemburg, 176
Lycurgus, 287
Lyons, 229
Lysimachus (Greek author), 288, 289

Maccabean, 306
Maccabees, Wars of the, 231, 245
Macedonia(n), 9, 10, 59, 90, 107, 108, 113, 167, 191, 214, 229, 238
Macedonian Empire, 154
Macrobius, Ambrosius Theodosius, 223, 302
Madeira, 74
Magister equitum, 95
Magna Graecia, 320, 324
Magnentius (Roman general), 152
Main, 174, 176
Mainz (see also Novaesium), 175, 195
Manchester, 10
Manes (spirits of the dead), 39
Manilius, C. (tribune), 78
Manumissio, 215
Mao Zedong, 68, 125
Marcellis, Evasio de, 314
Marcomanni, 173
Marcus Antonius, 247, 329
Marcus Aurelius, 143, 149, 173, 191
Marcus Octavius, 17, 18, 19
Marius, C., 29, 30-37, 51-58, 66, 72, 73, 80, 86, 88, 122, 127, 145, 172
Marius, C. (son of the former), 60, 61, 63-64, 73
Mars, 147, 318
Marsi, 38
Martialis, Marcus Valerius, 293
Marx, Karl, 210, 225
Masada (fortress near the Dead Sea), 256, 268, 272
Massilia (Marseille), 89, 229, 320
Mauretania(n)(s), 73, 74, 190, 191, 229
Mauretanian War, 191
Maximinianus (co-emperor of Diocletian), 143, 150, 165
Maximinus Thrax (Roman Emperor), 162
Media, 115, 160, 228, 231
Mediterranean Sea, 73, 102, 151, 153, 324
Megallis (wife of the slave owner Demophilus), 206
Megara quarter in Carthage, 13
Megasthenes, 283
Melitene (Malatya), 158
Memmius (prospective consul), 36
Mesopotamia, 115, 146, 159, 160, 161, 162, 163, 164, 165, 166, 167, 168, 169, 171, 228, 231, 273, 330

Messiah, 249-250, 252, 274, 313
Messina, 229
Metellus clan, 72
Metellus Numidicus, Quintus Caecilius, 30, 33-35, 37, 64-65
Metellus Pius, Quintus Caecilius (son of the former), 76
Metellus Pius Scipio, Quintus Caecilius (consul, adoptive son of the former, father-in-law of Pompey), 83, 85, 124, 129
Meyer, Eduard, 135, 228
Michelet, Jules, 68
Milan, 174, 229
Milete, 118, 286
Millar, Fergus, 248, 277, 305
Mitchell, Richard E., 2, 42, 43
Mithridates I, King of Parthia, 115
Mithridates II, King of Parthia, 116
Mithridates VI, King of Pontus, 33, 39, 48, 51, 59, 64, 66, 78, 95, 116, 329
Mithridatic War, 59
Moguntiacum (Mainz), 194
Momigliano, Arnaldo, 305
Mommsen, Theodor, 5, 35, 42, 43, 48, 211, 225
Mongolian, 175
Mons Sacer (Holy Mountain), 4, 8
Montilla (Spanish town), 97
Mopsukrene (Mopsuestia) (town), 168
Mordecai (uncle and guardian of Esther), 232-233, 233, 234
Morgantina (town in Sicily), 207, 209
Morocco see Mauretania
Moselle, 195
Moses, 283, 286, 287, 288, 293, 294, 300
Mount Garganus (Monte Sant' Angelo), 213
Mount Garizim, 245, 261
Mount of Olives, 254, 265
Mussolini, Benito, 135
Mutina (Modena), 108-109, 110, 213
Mytilene, 93, 148

Nabalia (unidentified river in the Netherlands), 196, 221, 222, 225
Naissus (Nisj) (town), 168
Naples, 84, 157, 229, 320
Nasica (pontifex maximus), 20
Nazareth, 308
Nebuchadnessar II, 267
Neoplatonism, 217
Neapolitans, 320
Nepos, Cornelius, 331
Nero, 154-156, 158, 172, 193, 255, 259, 264, 293
Nerva (Roman Emperor), 143, 149, 272
Netherlands, 99, 176, 192
Neuss see Novaesium
New Testament, 302
Nicholas of Damascus, 241, 287
Nilsson, M.P., 179
Nisibis, (town), 162, 164, 166, 167, 171, 229
Nobilitas, 9
Nock, A.D., 179
Nola (town in Campania), 53
Nonnius (Roman nobleman), 34
Norba (town in Latium), 63
North Africa, 9, 26, 30, 31, 33, 61, 64, 74, 88, 90, 94, 96, 111, 117, 118, 121, 142, 144, 151, 175, 176, 177, 190, 191, 248, 311
Novaesium (Neuss), 194, 195
Numantia, Numantines, 13, 21, 22, 190
Numidia(n), 33, 55, 191, 203, 216, 229
Numitor, king of Alba Longa, 318

Ocellus Lucanus, 284, 316
Ochser, Schulim, 304
Octavia (sister of Augustus, second wife of Mark Antony), 117
Octavius, Cneius (consul), 56-57
Octavianus see Augustus
Octavius Gaius see Augustus
Odaenathus, Septimius (Roman general), 163-164
Odoacer (King of the Germans in Italy), 9, 1777-178
Old Testament, 230, 231, 235, 284, 286, 291

Ooteghem, J. van, 52, 84, 85, 122, 126, 129, 130
Opimius L. (consul), 27, 28
Optimates, 22, 29, 33, 34, 37, 40, 56, 66, 69, 76, 80, 84, 91, 112
Orestes (father of Romulus Augustulus), 177
Origenes, 314
Orontes (Syrian river), 205
Orosius, Paulus, 36, 47, 48, 125, 127, 144, 182, 183, 214, 226, 270, 310, 312
Orphic, 217
Osca (Huesca), 75
Osroes, King of Armenia, 161
Osroes, King of Parthia, 157, 159
Ostrogoths, 175, 188
Otho, Marcius Salvius (Roman emperor), 193, 264
Ovidius, Publius -- Naso, 186, 220

Pact of Brundisium, 117
Paestum, 214
Paetus, Caecennius, 156
Palatine hill, 37, 319
Palestine, Palestinian, 158, 228, 229, 230, 231, 241, 245, 246, 247, 248, 252, 253, 258, 265, 268, 271, 273, 275, 276, 278, 281, 284, 293, 299, 300, 301, 304, 306, 313
Palm, Jonas, 238, 329, 333
Palmyra, 163-164
Pannonia (Hungary), 148, 191
Parthia(n)(s), 51, 83, 100, 103, 115-116, 119-120, 138, 146, 152, 153-171, 173, 180, 186, 247, 273
Parthamasiris, King of Armenia, 158
Particularism, 186
Passau, 192
Passover festival, 248, 253
Patras (Greek town), 59
Patres, 8
Patres conscripti, 8
Patriarch (Jewish), 278, 279
Patrician(s), 1-9, 9, 22, 29, 43, 144, 202
Patricius, 9
Patricius (historian), 182
Pax Romana, 188, 196, 250, 269

Pella (town in Peraea), 258
Pelusium (Egyptian town), 94
Pentecost feast, 251, 301
Peraea, 246, 251, 258, 306
Perelli, Luciano, 32, 48, 123
Pergamum, Pergamenes, 19, 20
Perperna (second-in-command of Sertorius), 76
Pertinax (Roman Emperor), 148
Perugia, 114
Persian(s), 143, 146, 167, 168, 182, 231, 232, 233, 234
Persian Empire, 115, 152, 154, 161-171, 232, 233, 235
Persian Gulf, 158, 159, 160
Pescennius Niger, Caius, 148
Petrocheilos, Nicholas, 325, 326, 327, 332, 333
Petronius, 293
Phannias (Pnani, Pinchas, Jewish High Piest), 263
Pharaoh(s), 144, 231, 288
Pharisees, 249, 250
Pharnaces (son of Mithridates VI), 95
Philippus (freedman of Pompey), 94
Philippus Arabs (Roman Emperor), 162
Philo (Jewish author), 242, 244, 284, 295, 300, 303, 304, 317
Philodamus (Greek visitor to Rome), 322
Phormio (Greek philosopher), 326
Picenum, Picenians, 38, 213
Pistoclerus (character in a play by Plautus), 199
Plato, 217, 283
Plautus, Titus Marcius, 199, 223, 327, 332
Plebeian(s), 2-9, 9, 22, 25, 27, 29, 43, 144
Plebiscita, 5
Plebs, 2, 3, 4, 77, 101
Plinius, Gaius -- Secundus (Pliny the Elder), 79, 105, 127, 135, 332
Plinius, Gaius -- Caecilius Secundus (Pliny the Younger), 200, 221, 223, 325
Plutarchus, 12, 13, 18, 21, 26, 27,

31, 34, 43, 44, 45, 46, 47, 48, 49, 51, 52, 61, 82, 83, 88, 92, 122, 123, 124, 125, 126, 127, 128, 129, 130, 131, 132, 133, 135, 137, 139, 214, 225, 226, 291, 323, 324, 332
Po, 40, 189
Poitiers, 229
Poliakov, Léon, 301
Polybius, 285, 315, 323
Pomeroy, Sarah, 217, 226, 227
Pompeia (granddaughter of Sulla, second wife of Caesar), 80
Pompeii, 229
Pompeiopolis see Soloi
Pompeius Strabo, Cn. (father of Pompey the Great), 39, 53, 57, 71
Pompeius, Gnaeus (Pompey the Great), 57, 71, 75-94, 95, 97, 107, 116, 117, 129, 202, 214, 239, 246, 270, 293
Pompeius, Gnaeus (son of the former), 97
Pompeius, Sextus (brother to the former), 114, 117-118
Pompeius Trogus, 287-288
Pons Sublicius, 28
Pontifex (maximus), 7, 20, 98
Pontius Telesinus (Samnite commander), 61
Pontus, 96, 138
Populares, 29, 33, 47, 52, 58, 91, 144
Porta Collina in Rome, 61, 62
Porphyrius, 314
Posidonius, 285-286, 323
Praeneste (Palestrina), 62, 204
Praetor(s), 7, 30, 34, 38, 40, 53-54, 63, 280
Prause, Gerhard, 305
Praxiteles, 322
Prigent, Pierre, 307, 313
Proletarii, 2, 15, 22, 101, 114
Propontis (Sea of Marmara), 151
Proscription lists, 65, 66, 73
Proselyte(s), proselytism, proselytizing, 229, 243, 277, 281, 287
Provence, 176
Pseudo-Longinus, 290

Ptolemaean(s), 231, 242, 296, 301
Ptolemais (town in Syria), 257
Ptolemy VII Physcon, 301
Ptolemy XIII, Pharao of Egypt, 94
Ptolemy Lathyrus, 301
Publius (son of Crassus and first husband of Cornelia), 129, 189
Punic War, Second, 10, 11
Purim feast, 233
Puteoli (town), 107
Pyrenees, 73, 76, 175
Pythagoras, 283
Pythagorean(s), 217, 283

Quadi (German tribe), 173
Quaestor(s), 7, 30, 31, 50, 64
Quintilianus, Marcus Fabius, 293
Quintus Memmius (Roman legate), 244

Rabbis, 250
Radin, Max, 237, 243, 286, 302, 303, 315
Rajak, Tessa, 301
Ravenna, 85, 177, 229
Reinach, Théodore, 285, 314, 315
Rembrandt, 192
Remus, 318
Republic of the United Netherlands, 192
Reusch, Wilhelm, 179
Rhea Silvia, 318
Rhegium (Reggio di Calabria), 213
Rhine (frontier), 145, 146, 152, 165, 172, 174, 175, 176, 192, 194, 195, 221
Rhodes, 35, 80, 94, 229, 286
Rhône, 72
Robinson, Frederick Walter, 48
Rodin, Auguste, 32
Rokeah, David, 280, 314
Roman-Catholic (Church), 258, 280, 301
Roman Empire, 11, 20, 62, 73, 81, 95, 100, 101, 103, 108, 109, 111, 120, 125, Ch. III passim, 185, 187, 188, 189, 190, 191, 196, 203, 207, 216, 228, 229, 239, 241, 245, 250, 252, 257, 268-269, 277, 278, 279,

280, 281, 284, 290, 292, 294, 297, 298, 300, 301, 313, 323, 324, 325, 328, 330
Romania, 146
Romanization, 191, 196
Rome (city), 1, 9, 10, 11, 13, 17, 19, 21, 22, 23, 25, 26, 30, 31, 32, 35, 38, 40, 42, 53, 54, 55, 56, 57, 58, 59, 60, 62, 63, 65, 70, 71, 72, 75, 76, 79, 81, 82, 84, 86, 87, 88, 90, 91, 95, 96, 97, 100, 105, 106, 110, 111, 112, 117, 119, 121, 127, 140, 141, 142, 147, 148, 151, 154, 156, 158, 160, 164, 173, 176, 177, 186, 189, 193, 195, 202, 204, 205, 207, 210, 214, 215, 218, 222, 230, 238, 239, 242, 243, 244, 245, 254, 264, 275, 280, 294, 311, 318, 330
Romulus, 1, 2, 77, 101, 147, 318
Romulus Augustulus (Roman Emperor), 177
Royal Dutch Shell, 221
Rubicon (river), 86
Rubrius (Roman gentleman), 322
Rufus Festus, 182
Rupilius, Publius (Roman general), 207
Rutilius, Claudius -- Numantinus, 331

Sabbath, 240, 287, 289, 291, 293, 294, 299
Sabine(s), 72, 204
Sabinus (procurator of Judaea), 251-252, 253
Saddington, D.B., 220
Salamis (capital of Cyprus), 273
Salles, Cathérine, 225
Sallustius Gaius -- Crispus, 31, 47, 70, 71, 126, 327
Sallustius (governor of Gaul), 169
Salvius (a Sicilian slave, later 'king' of the slaves in Sicily), 209-210
Samaria (country), 245, 246
Samaria (town), 246
Samaritan(s), 245, 253, 260-261
Samnite(s), 38, 57, 61, 62, 63
Samnium, 63
Sardes (town in Asia Minor), 278
Sardinia, 23, 70, 74, 89, 111, 117, 121, 176, 189, 229, 243
Sasanian dynasty, 146, 161, 169
Saturnalia, 197-198
Saturninus, L. Apuleius, 33-36, 48
Saturninus, either Gaius Sentius or Lucius Sentius (friend of Tiberius, husband of Fulvia), 242-243, 303
Saturnus, 197
Satyrus (leader of a slave revolt in Sicily), 210
Schmidt, Hatto H., 331
Schochat, Yanir, 44
Schürer, Emil, 238, 246, 250, 256, 275, 276, 277, 278, 301, 302, 305, 306, 307, 311, 312, 313, 315
Schuhl, M., 314
Scipio, Lucius Cornelius (consul), 60, 64
Scipio, Lucius (son of the former), 60
Scipio Aemilianus Africanus Numantinus, Publius Cornelius, 12, 19, 21, 22, 23, 26, 45, 238
Scipio Africanus Maior, Publius Cornelius, 12
Scipio, Publius Cornelius -- Nasica see Metellus Pius, Quintus Caecilius
Scullard, H.H., 42, 48, 49, 50, 70, 126
Schwier, Helmut, 269, 270, 308, 310, 311
Scyth(s), 188
Sea of Marmara (Propontis), 151
Segovia, 76
Sejanus, Lucius Aelius, 242, 243
Seleucid (Empire), 79, 115, 116, 231, 233, 242, 245, 246, 286, 319
Seleucus IV, 319
Seleukeia, 115
Selinus (town), 160
Sempronii (Roman clan), 12, 43
Sephardim, 230
Sepphoris (Galilean town), 251, 252
Septimius Severus (Roman Emperor), 142-144, 148
Septuagint, 291
Senate, 1, 2, 4, 5, 7, 8, 10, 13, 17, 18, 19, 20, 21, 23, 24, 25, 26, 27,

28, 29, 33, 36, 37, 39-40, 53, 55, 57, 58, 59, 62, 65, 67, 70, 71, 75, 80, 81, 83, 84, 85, 87, 90, 91, 94, 98, 100, 102, 103, 104, 105, 106, 107, 109, 110, 112, 117, 119, 131, 140, 141, 150, 154, 159, 185, 208, 212, 213, 241, 243, 247, 248, 319
Senate House, 27, 28, 36, 105
Senator(s), 1, 3, 5, 7, 17, 18, 20, 23, 25, 27, 33, 34, 35, 39, 41, 52, 53, 58, 62, 66, 67, 72, 81, 88, 90, 104, 140, 245, 280
Senatorial class, 11, 33, 37, 39, 56, 80
Senatusconsultum, 27, 36, 70, 85, 140
Seneca, Lucius Annaeus, 68, 124, 125, 126, 200, 203, 223, 224, 293
Serbia, 168
Sertorius, Quintus, 71, 72-76, 190, 193
Servilius, C. (praetor), 38
Servilius fountain in Rome, 6
Setia(ns) (town near Rome), 204
Seven-branched Candlestick, 271
Sevenster, J.N., 297-298, 300, 303, 317
Severus Alexander (Roman Emperor), 161
Severus, Julius (Roman general), 275
Shakespeare, William, 68, 105, 126
Shapur I, King of Persia, 162-164
Shapur II, King of Persia, 166-171
Shapur III, King of Persia, 171
Shoshtar (town), 163
Sibylle, 319
Sibylline Books, 319
Sicarii, 254
Sichem (town in Samaria), 245
Sicily, Sicilian, 61, 62, 88, 89, 111, 117, 118, 119, 121, 176, 189, 205-210, 213, 229, 286, 323
Simon the Maccabee, 245
Simon (Peraean rebel leader), 251
Simon bar-Giora (Zealot commander), 265, 268
Simon bar-Kochba, 274-275, 312, 313

Sirmium (town), 167
Smallwood, Mary, 301, 302, 304, 305
Smidt van Gelder-Fontaine, Th.A.M., 311
Social War, 51, 59, 71, 189
Socrates (historian), 183
Socrates (the philosopher), 283
Soloi, town in Cilicia, rebaptized Pompeiopolis, 78
Solon, 319
Song of Songs, 234
Spain, Spanish, 9, 10, 13, 19, 21, 22, 23, 30, 61, 72-76, 81, 82, 89, 97, 105, 117, 121, 151, 152, 174, 175, 176, 190, 192, 229, 293
Spann, Philip O., 72, 75, 126, 127
Sparta, 220
Spartacists, 213
Spartacus, 210-215
Spartacus, Communist Party -- (NL), 225
Spartakusbund (German communist organization), 211
Spartianus, 181, 312
Stalin, Joseph, 68
Stampacchia, Giulia, 225, 226
Stern, Menahem, 283, 285, 287, 288, 289, 291, 293, 314, 315, 316, 317
Stilicho, 188, 319
Stockt, 295on, David, 19, 44, 45
Stoa, Stoic, 215
Strabo, 124, 128, 178, 201, 223, 230, 288, 315, 331
Straits of Gibraltar, 74
Straits of Messina, 214
Suetonius, Tranquillius Gaius, 103, 124, 125, 128, 129, 130, 133, 134, 135, 136, 178, 226, 243, 271, 303
Sulla, Lucius Cornelius, 31, 39, 51-69, 69, 70, 71, 72, 73, 74, 75, 76, 78, 80, 86, 87, 88, 90, 112, 145, 312, 331
Sulpicius, Publius -- Rufus (tribune), 52-55, 56, 122, 310
Sulpicius Severus (author), 270, 271, 311
Susa, 232

Sybilline books, 103, 269
Syracuse, Syracusan, 229, 235
Syria(n), 79, 91, 94, 116, 120, 121, 143, 156, 158, 162, 163, 164, 167, 205, 206, 229, 237, 245, 246, 247, 248, 251, 257, 258, 259, 265, 282, 285, 289, 304, 305

Table of the Shewbread, 271
Tacitus, Cornelius, 141, 172, 178, 179, 180, 184, 192, 193, 194, 196, 221, 222, 227, 243, 253, 293-294, 303, 306, 317
Talmud, 230, 299
Tarento, 229
Taricheai (Palestinian town, Chirbet el-Kerak), 261, 308
Tarn, W.W., 120, 139
Tarquinius Superbus, 3, 319
Tauromenium (town in Sicily, Taormina), 118, 207
Tcherikover, Victor, 236, 237, 238, 284, 302, 315
Teano (Teanum) (town), 60
Temple of Apollo in Rome, 319
Temple of Bellona in Rome, 62
Temple of Castor and Pollux in Rome, 28
Temple of Concordia in Rome, 29
Temple of Diana in Rome, 27
Temple of Divus Iulius in Rome, 140
Temple of Janus in Rome, 162
Temple of Jahve in Jerusalem, 235, 239, 240, 241, 242, 244, 247, 248, 251, 253, 254, 255, 257, 258, 263, 265, 266-267, 268-271, 274, 276, 281, 283, 285, 286, 289, 293, 298, 311, 313
Temple of Jupiter Capitolinus in Jerusalem, 276
Temple of Jupiter in Rome, 60, 270, 319
Temple of Minerva in Rome, 28
Temple of Pax in Rome, 311
Temple of Quirinus in Rome, 100
Temple of Saturnus in Rome, 18
Temple of Venus Genitrix in Rome, 99
Tencteri (Germanic tribe), 194

Terentius, Publius -- Afer, 203, 224
Tetrarchy, 150, 151
Teutoburgerwald, 251
Teutons, 32, 51, 72, 172, 173
Themistius (orator), 188, 220
Theodoric, 9
Theodosius I, 152, 171
Theodotus (Egyptian politician), 94
Theophrastus, 282, 314
Thessalonica (Saloniki), 90-91, 131
Thessaly, 92
Thrace, Thracian(s), 112, 191, 211, 229
Timesitheus (Roman general), 162, 181
Thucydides, 45
Thurii, 213
Tiber, 21, 28, 29, 60, 64, 202, 204, 318
Tiberias (town in Palestine), 260, 261, 306
Tiberius, 145, 149, 153, 242, 243
Tiberius Alexander (prefect of Egypt), 257
Tigranes II, King of Armenia, 116
Tigranocerta (Armenian town), 155
Tigris, 115, 155, 159, 166, 167, 168, 169, 171
Tiridates, King of Armenia, 156-157, 158, 180
Titus Flavius Vespasianus, 259, 260, 261, 264, 265, 265-268, 271, 308, 311
Titus Manius (Roman legate), 244
Toga pretexta, 98
Toga purpurea, 98
Toledo, 229
Torah, 237, 271, 299, 300, 311
Toxandria, 176
Trajanus, 143, 149, 157-160, 272, 273, 312
Tralles (town in Asia Minor), 240
Treaty of Misenum, 117
Trèves, 195
Tribuni plebis, tribunate, 4-5, 8, 17, 18, 20, 22, 24, 25, 26, 33, 34, 36, 37, 39, 40, 42, 50, 56, 68, 73, 77, 78
Tribunicia potestas, 70, 77, 148

Triocala (Caltabellota? town in Sicily), 209, 210
Trojan, 318, 319
Troy (Ilion), 151, 318
Tunisia, 95
Turks, 311
Twelve Tables (of Roman law), 6, 42
Tyre, 257

Urbach, Ephraim E., 299, 317
Universalism, 186
Utica (town), 96

Vale of Tempe, 93
Valens (Roman emperor), 152, 171, 175
Valentinianus I, 152, 175
Valerianus (Roman Emperor), 163, 164
Valerius Maximus, 45, 47, 63, 124, 125, 133
Vandal(s), 175, 176, 177, 191, 311, 319
Varinius, Publius (Roman general), 212
Varius Hybrida, Q. (tribune), 39, 40
Varius (leader of a band of slaves in Sicily), 208
Varro, Marcus Terentius, 292
Varus, Publius Quinctilius, 146, 172, 252
Veii (Etrurian town), 238, 320
Velleius Paterculus, 45, 49, 61, 122, 123, 124, 125, 130, 137
Veluwe (NL), 221
Venamaus (subcommander of Spartacus), 211, 225
Venus, 99, 106
Vergilius, Publius -- Maro, 117
Vermes, Geza, 277
Verres, Gaius, 189
Verus, Lucius (socius of Marcus Aurelius), 149
Vespasianus, Titus Flavius, 193, 194, 195, 222, 259-264, 270, 308, 310, 311, 312
Vesuvius, 211
Veyne, Paul, 185, 220
Via Appia, 60, 215

Via Egnatia, 90
Via Latina, 60
Victor, Aurelius, 46, 48
Vienna (Vienne) (town on the Rhône), 305
Virgilius, Publius -- Naso, 146, 179, 318, 327, 332
Visigoths, 175, 176, 177
Vitellius, Aulus (Roman general and emperor), 193, 194, 264-265, 270
Vogt, Joseph, 12, 43, 187, 199, 220, 223
Volaterrae (Volterra), 63
Volkmann, Hans, 43
Volsci (Italian tribe), 204
Vologases, King of Parthia, 155-157, 180
Volundum (Armenian town), 155

Waal, 192
Wahram (Bahram) III, King of Persia, 165
Wallon, H., 204
Wannsee Konferenz, 303
War of Varus, 252
Wardman, Alan, 332, 333
Weynand, 47
Wildeboer, D.G., 235, 302
Wilken, Robert, 278, 298, 313, 314, 317
Wilkinson, L.P., 333

Yadin, Yigal (Israeli general and archaeologist), 268
Yorkshire, 216
Yourcenar, Marguérite, 274

Zealot(s), 248, 249, 252, 253-254, 256, 262-265, 307
Zenobia, Queen of Palmyra, 164
Zeus, 304
Zinserling, Verena, 216, 226
Zonaras (historian), 163, 181, 182
Zoroaster, 287
Zosimus (historian), 163, 179, 181, 182, 183